D0380073

The Wild Flowers
of California

MARY ELIZABETH PARSONS

The Wild Flowers of California

Their Names, Haunts, and Habits

Illustrations by
MARGARET WARRINER BUCK

With a New Table of Changes
in Nomenclature Prepared by

ROXANA S. FERRIS
Department of Biological Sciences
Division of Systematic Biology
Stanford University

Dover Publications, Inc., New York

Published in Canada by General Publishing Company, Ltd., 30 Lesmill Road, Don Mills, Toronto, Ontario.

Published in the United Kingdom by Constable and Company, Ltd., 10 Orange Street, London W. C. 2.

This Dover edition, first published in 1966, is an unabridged and unaltered republication of the third edition of the work, revised and corrected, as published by Cunningham, Curtiss & Welch in 1907. The Dover edition contains a new table of changes in nomenclature prepared by Mrs. Roxana S. Ferris, Department of Biological Sciences, Division of Systematic Biology, Stanford University.

International Standard Book Number: 0-486-21678-0
Library of Congress Catalog Card Number: 66-21182
Manufactured in the United States of America
Dover Publications, Inc.
180 Varick Street
New York, N. Y. 10014

TABLE OF CONTENTS

" Were I, O God, in churchless lands remaining,
Far from all voice of teachers or divines,
My soul would find in flowers of thy ordaining
Priests, sermons, shrines !"

PREFACE TO THE THIRD EDITION

On the 18th of April, 1906, the book-plates of "THE WILD FLOWERS OF CALIFORNIA" were in the press-rooms for the printing of a new edition, and in consequence suffered the fate shared by thousands of other books in our city upon that and the two or three succeeding days of disaster.

It has therefore been necessary to have entirely new plates made.

While this has caused much extra labor and inconvenience, it has at the same time proved an excellent opportunity for the making of some desirable improvements.

A number of new flowers have been added, the nomenclature has been brought up to date, and, for the sake of those who wish to study plants in a somewhat more scientific manner and to become acquainted with their botanical relationships, an artificial key has been added, together with scientific and popular descriptions of all the plant families represented in this work.

The Linnæan key, which groups plants by the number of their stamens, has been used because it is simple and easily understood and traces plants to their genera without a separate key for each of the large plant families.

The book has also been given a new dress in which to start upon its new life—new, yet not so dissimilar as to be unrecognizable by old friends.

In the present edition a limited number of copies have been printed upon deckle-edge water-color paper, with wider margins and gilt top, and bound handsomely in ooze-leather. This *edition de luxe* may be had from the publishers or the author in two styles,—one in which the illustrations are printed as in the ordinary edition, the other in which they have been printed lightly for those who desire to color them.

With these few words of explanation we send forth this new edition of "THE WILD FLOWERS OF CALIFORNIA," with the hope that it may prove helpful in the future as in the past.

KENTFIELD, CALIFORNIA, November, 1906.

PREFACE TO THE FIRST EDITION

To THE thoughtless a flower is often a trivial thing,—beautiful perhaps, and worthy of a passing glance,—but that is all. But to the mind open to the great truths of the universe, it takes on a deeper significance. Such a mind sees in its often humble beginnings the genesis of things far-reaching and mighty. Two thousand years ago one grain of the shower of pollen wafted upon the wind and falling upon a minute undeveloped cone, quickened a seed there into life, and this dropping into the soil pushed up a tiny thread of green, which, after the quiet process of the ages, you now behold in the giant Sequoia which tosses its branches aloft, swept by the four winds of heaven.

Whether manifesting itself in the inconspicuous flower upon the tree or in the equally unassuming inflorescence of the vegetable, or unfurling petals of satin or gauze of brilliant hue and marvelous beauty, the blossom is the origin of most that is useful or beautiful in the organic world about us. Strip the world of its blossoms, and the higher forms of life must come to a speedy termination. Thus we see the flower playing a wonderfully important part in the cosmos around us. It becomes henceforth not only a thing of beauty for the gratification of the æsthetic sense, but the instrument by which Nature brings about the fullness of her perfection in her own good season.

There is perhaps no nature-study that can yield the same amount of pure and unalloyed pleasure with so little outlay as the study of the wild flowers. When one is interested in them, every walk into the fields is transformed from an aimless ramble into a joyous, eager quest, and every journey upon stage or railroad becomes a rare opportunity for making new plant-acquaintances—a season of exhilarating excitement.

Mr. Burroughs, that devout lover of nature, says:—"Most young people find botany a dull study. So it is, as taught from the text-books in the schools; but study it yourself in the fields and woods, and you will find it a source of perennial delight. Find your flower, and then name it by the aid of the botany. There is so much in a name. To find out what a thing is called is a great help. It is the beginning of knowledge; it is the first step. When we see a new person who interests us, we wish to know his or her name. A bird, a flower, a place—the first thing we wish to know about it is its name. Its name helps us to classify it; it gives us a handle to grasp it by; it sheds a ray of light where all before was darkness. As soon as we know the name of a thing, we seem to have established some sort of relation with it."

Having learned the name of a flower or plant, or having been formally introduced to it, as it were, our acquaintance has but just begun. Instead of being our end and aim, as it was with students of botany in the olden times, this is but the beginning. If this were our ultimate aim, all our pleasure would be at an end as soon as we had learned the names of all the plants within our reach. But the point of view has changed and broadened. The plant is now recognized as a *living organism*, not a dead, unchanging thing. It is *vital;* it grows; it is amenable to the great laws of the universe; and we see it daily complying with those laws, adapting itself to its surroundings—or perishing. It becomes a thing of absorbing interest when we trace the steps by which it has come to be what it is; when we note its relationship to other closely allied forms, and locate its place in the great world of plants.

A thoughtful observation of the structure of plants alone will fill the mind with amazement at the beauty of their minutest parts, the exquisite perfection of every organ. Then it is most interesting to notice the various kinds of places where the same plants grow; how they flourish in different soils and climates; how they parry the difficulties of new and unaccustomed surroundings, by some change of structure or habit to meet the altered conditions—as clothing themselves with wool, to prevent the undue escape of moisture, or twisting their leaves to a vertical position for the same purpose, or sending their roots deep into the earth to seek perennial sources of moisture, which enables them to flourish in our driest times. It is wonderful to note, too, the methods employed to secure the distribution of the seed—how it is sometimes imbedded in a delicious edible fruit; again furnished with hooks or bristles that catch in the hair of passing animals, or springs that throw it to a distance, or silken sails that waft it away upon the wings of the wind. Then the insects that visit plants. It is marvelous to note how plants spread their attractions in bright colors and perfumes and offerings of honey to bees, butterflies, and moths that can carry their pollen abroad, and how they even place hindrances in the way of such as are undesirable, like ants.

Studied in this way, botany is no longer the dry science it used to be, but becomes a most fascinating pursuit; and we know of no richer field in which to carry on the study of flowers than that afforded in California.

There has been a long-felt need of a popular work upon the wild flowers of California. Though celebrated throughout the world for their wealth and beauty, and though many of them have found their way across the waters and endeared themselves to plant-lovers in many a foreign garden, the story of their home life has never yet been told.

It has been the delightful task of the author and the illustrator of the present work to seek them out in their native haunts —on seashore and mesa, in deep, cool cañon, on dry and open hill-slope, on mountain-top, in glacier meadow, by stream and lake, in marsh and woodland, and to listen to the ofttimes marvelous tales they have had to unfold. If they shall have succeeded in making better known these children of Mother Nature to her lovers and appreciators, and in arousing an interest in them among those who have hitherto found the technical difficulties of scientific botany insurmountable, they will feel amply rewarded for their labors.

The present work does not claim by any means to be a complete flora of the region treated. Our State is so new, and many parts of it have as yet been so imperfectly explored, that a comprehensive and exhaustive flora of it must be the work of a future time, and will doubtless be undertaken by some one when all the data have been procured. Such an attempt, however, were it possible, is without the scope of the present work.

California, with her wonderfully varied climate and topography, has a flora correspondingly rich and varied, probably not surpassed by any region of like area in the Northern Hemisphere. Thus the author finds herself confronted with an embarrassment of riches rather than with any lack of material; and it has often been exceedingly difficult to exclude some beautiful flower that seemed to have strong claims to representation. She therefore craves beforehand the indulgence of the reader, should he find some favorite missing.

In making a choice, she has been guided by the following general principles, and selected, *first*—the flowers most general in their distribution; *second*—those remarkable for their beauty of form or color, their interesting structure, history, or economic uses; *third*—those which are characteristically Californian. At the same time, those which are too insignificant in appearance to attract attention and those too difficult of determination by the non-botanist have been omitted. Flowering plants only have been included.

Many of our species extend northward into Oregon and Washington. Thus, while this work is called "THE WILD

FLOWERS OF CALIFORNIA," it will in a certain measure apply equally well to Oregon and Washington.

It has been the aim of the author to picture for the most part the flowers peculiarly Californian, leaving Mrs. Dana's charming book, "How to Know the Wild Flowers," to illustrate those we possess in common with the Atlantic Slope, thus making the works the complements one of the other.

Mrs. Dana has kindly permitted the author to use her plan of arrangement—*i. e.* of grouping all the white flowers in one section, the yellow in another, the pink in a third, and so on, which, in the absence of a key, greatly facilitates the finding of any given flower. The flowers of each section have been arranged as nearly as possible according to their natural succession in the seasons, with a few exceptions.

Such confusion is rife in the nomenclature of Californian plants, and the same plant is so often furnished with several names,—and several plants sometimes with the same name,— that the authority is in every instance quoted, in order to make it perfectly clear what plant is meant by the name given. Wherever allusion is made to the Spanish-Californians, the Spanish-*speaking* Californians are meant, very few of whom are Castilians at the present day, most of whom are of an admixture of races.

The flower-cuts are all from pen-and-ink drawings by the illustrator; and all but four are from her own original studies from nature. These four, which it was impossible for her to procure, have been adapted by her from other drawings, by the aid of herbarium specimens. They include *Aphyllon fasciculatum, Fremontia Californica, Hosackia gracilis,* and *Brodiæa volubilis.* It has been impossible upon so small a page to maintain a uniform relative size in the drawings, for which reason the plant-descriptions in fine print should be consulted for the size.

The author and the illustrator desire to make grateful acknowledgments to many kind friends throughout the State who have rendered them assistance in numerous ways. Their gratitude is due in particular to Miss Alice Eastwood, of the California Academy of Sciences, who, by her unfailing kindness and encouragement, as well as by her personal assistance, has rendered them invaluable aid. Also, to Mr. Carl Purdy, of Ukiah, who, from his wide experience as a grower of our native liliaceous plants, has a knowledge of them shared by few or none, and who has generously placed at their disposal the results of his observations. They also tender their thanks to the Southern Pacific and the North Pacific railways, who, by the generous granting of reduced rates and passes, have made possible a wider personal acquaintance with the flowers than could have otherwise been enjoyed.

San Rafael, Cal., October 15, 1897.

TABLE OF PLATES

xiii

TABLE OF PLATES

xiv

TABLE OF PLATES

HOW TO USE THE BOOK

WHEN gathering flowers with a view to ascertaining their names with the help of the botany, the whole plant—root, stem, leaves, flowers, buds, and fruit—should be secured, if possible. This will avoid much uncertainty in the work.

The anthers are best seen in the unopened buds, and the ovary in old flowers or those gone to seed. A cross-section of the ovary will show the number of its cells.

The flowers should be sorted into colors, and each in turn looked for in its own color-section. In arranging the flowers according to color, some difficulty has been experienced, because the pink blends so gradually into the purple, and the purple into white, etc., that it has been impossible sometimes to say accurately to which section a flower rightly belongs. In such a case search must be made in the other probable section. Sometimes the same flower occurs in several colors, in which case it is usually put into the section in whose color it most frequently occurs. In some cases it has been more convenient to place a flower with another of the same genus but of a different color, in order to save repetition of technical description. In the Red Section have been included flowers of a scarlet hue, not those of crimson or magenta hues, as these have a tendency to merge into pink or purple. Flowers of a greenish-white are usually put into the White Section, those of more decided green into the Miscellaneous.

It is an excellent plan for the student to write a careful description of his plant before beginning to look for it in the book; commencing with the root, passing on to stems, leaves, inflorescence, calyx, corolla, etc., taking the order of the technical descriptions in the book. This will serve to do away with that vacillating condition of mind which is often the result of reading a number of plant-descriptions before fixing firmly in mind the characters of the specimens under consideration.

A magnifying-glass,—or a small dissecting microscope and a good Zeiss lens, if more careful work is to be done,—a couple of dissecting needles, a pocket-knife, and a small three- or four-inch measure, having one of the inches divided into lines, will be required for examining specimens.

It is a good plan to make a note of the date and place of collection of all plants, as it is often of great interest to know these facts at some future time. It is also an excellent plan to keep a note-book and jot down any unusual or interesting facts observed about plants.

Plants are grouped into great orders, or families, which are made up of a number of genera, each genus consisting of a number of species. Species are composed of similar individuals which have the power of producing others of like kind. Every plant has two Latin names; the first a generic name, answering to the last name of a person; the second a specific name, answering to a person's given name. The latter is usually descriptive of some quality or character of the plant, the name of the place where found, or of its discoverer, or of some person in whose honor it is named. This dual name serves to clearly distinguish the species from all others, especially when the name of the person by whom the specific name was bestowed is added.

Each plant-family bears an English title, which is usually the name of its best-known genus. Thus the order *Leguminosæ* is known as the "Pea Family" because *Lathyrus,* or the pea, is its best-known genus. In many instances the English names borne by orders in the Eastern States have no significance with us, as the type genus is not found in our flora. In most such cases we have given the name of the genus best known among us, to which we have added the other; thus, "Baby-eyes or Waterleaf Family."

Most of our plants have common English names, and the same plant is often known by one name in one locality and by another in another. Hence, while these names are often pretty and apt, they cannot serve for the accurate identification of the plant. For this we must consult its Latin name, by which it is known all over the world.

If the scientific description of any plant seem insufficient, further information may be gained about it if reference be made to the descriptions under "Plant Families or Orders" (p. lv) and "A Few of Our Largest and Most Important Genera" (p. lxxxvi). Thus, if the plant under consideration be *Pentstemon cordifolius* (p. 356), turn back to the description of the Figwort family, and afterward to that of the genus *Pentstemon* (p. xci), which applies to all the plants of this particular genus, and will aid in the more certain identification of the specimen in hand.

Wherever the terms used are not understood, reference should be made to the "Explanation of Terms" or to the Glossary.

For the identification of species not found in the present work, other books should be consulted. The two large volumes of the botany of the Geological Survey of California are the most complete of anything thus far published. In addition to these, "The Synoptical Flora of North America," as far as published (the *Gamopetalæ*, the *Compositæ*, and some orders of the *Polypetalæ*), furnishes valuable aid. Professor E. L. Greene's works, "The Botany of the Bay Region," "Pittonia," and "Flora Franciscana," furnish excellent plant-descriptions for the more advanced botanist, and Professor Willis L. Jepson's "Flora of Western Middle California" will prove helpful. The author's technical descriptions have in every instance been verified by comparison with one or more of the above works.

Miss Eastwood's little volume, published as Part Second of "Bergen's Elements of Botany," (and also issued in separate form,) is recommended for use in connection with the present work, as it embodies in a compact form a general view of the method of classification of plants, showing their places in the plant-world and their relations to one another. It also contains very clear descriptions of plant-families. To the student who becomes interested in knowing more about the structure of plants, Gray's "Structural Botany" will prove useful; and "The Natural History of Plants," by Kerner, (translated from the German by Oliver,) will prove a fascinating book.

EXPLANATION OF TERMS

[The following simple definitions of the more common terms used have been mostly taken or adapted from the works of Asa Gray and others, and will prove useful to those unacquainted with botany, or to those whose memories require refreshing. For further explanation of terms, see Glossary, p.421.]

ROOTS

The **root** is that portion of the plant which grows downward, fixing it to the soil, and absorbing nourishment from the latter. True roots produce nothing but root-branches or rootlets.

Simple or unbranched roots are named according to their shapes—

> *conical,* when like the carrot;
> *napiform,* when like the turnip;
> *fusiform,* when like the long radish.

Multiple, or branched, roots may be—

> *fascicled,* or bunched, as in the dahlia;
> *tubercular,* when furnished with small tubers;
> *fibrous,* when threadlike.

STEMS

The **stem** is the ascending axis of the plant, which usually bears the leaves, flowers, and fruit. The points on the stem to which the leaves are fastened are called the **nodes;** and the portions of stem between the nodes are called the **internodes.** The angle formed by the upper side of the leaf and the stem is called the **axil.**

Stems aboveground are classed as—

> *erect,* when growing upright;
> *procumbent,* when lying on the ground without rooting;

>*decumbent,* when lying on the ground with the tip ascending;
>
>*diffuse,* when loosely spreading;
>
>*creeping,* when growing on the ground and rooting.

Stems underground are classed as **rhizomes** (or **root-stocks**), **tubers, corms,** and **bulbs,** the forms passing into one another by gradations.

>A **rhizome,** or **rootstock,** is a horizontal underground stem. It is sometimes thick, fleshy, or woody, as in the iris;
>
>a **tuber,** is a short, much thickened rootstock, having eyes or buds—of which the potato is an example;
>
>a **corm** is a depressed and rounded, solid rootstock; it may be called a solid bulb; the garden cyclamen is an example;
>
>a **bulb** is a leaf-bud, commonly underground, with fleshy scales or coats; the lily is an example.

LEAVES

Leaves are the green expansions borne by the stem, outspread in the air and light, in which assimilation is carried on. They may be said to be the stomachs of the plant. A typical leaf consists of three parts—the **blade,** the **foot-stalk** (or **petiole**), and a pair of **stipules.** Yet any one of these parts may be absent.

>The **blade** is the expanded portion of the leaf and the part to which the word *leaf,* in its commonest sense, is applied;
>
>the **stipules** are small, usually leaflike bodies borne at the base of the petiole, usually one on either side;
>
>the **petiole** is the stalk of the leaf.

Leaves are **simple,** when having but one blade; **compound,** when having more than one, when each blade is called a **leaflet.**

Compound leaves are said to be—

> *pinnate,* when the leaflets are arranged along the sides of a petiole, or rather of its prolongation, the rachis;
>
> *abruptly pinnate,* with an even number of leaflets;
>
> *odd-pinnate,* with an odd leaflet at the end;
>
> *palmate,* or *digitate,* when the leaflets all diverge from the summit of the petiole, like the fingers of a hand.

VENATION

The venation, or veining, of leaves relates to the mode in which the woody tissue, in the form of ribs, veins, etc., is distributed in the cellular tissue.

There are two principle modes—

> the *parallel-veined,* of which the iris is an example;
>
> the *reticulated-veined,* or *netted-veined,* of which the elm is an example.

Small veins are called **veinlets.**

FORM

As to general form, or outline, leaves are:—

Those broadest in the middle—

> *peltate,* or shield-shaped, when rounded, with the stem attached to the center, or near it—as in the garden nasturtium;
>
> *orbicular,* when circular in outline, or nearly so;
>
> *oval,* when having a flowing outline, with the breadth considerably more than half the length, and both ends alike;
>
> *elliptical,* when twice or thrice as long as broad, and having a flowing outline, and both ends alike;
>
> *oblong,* when nearly twice or thrice as long as broad;
>
> *linear,* when narrow, several times longer than wide, and of about the same width throughout;
>
> *acerose,* when needle-shaped—like the pine.

Those broadest at the base—

> *deltoid,* when having the triangular shape of the Greek letter *delta* (Δ);
>
> *ovate,* when having an outline like the section of a hen's-egg, the broader end downward;
>
> *lanceolate,* or lance-shaped, when several times longer than broad, and tapering upward, or both upward and downward;
>
> *subulate,* when shaped like an awl;
>
> *cordate,* when ovate, with a heart-shaped base;
>
> *reniform,* when like the last, only rounder and broader than long;
>
> *auriculate,* when having a pair of small blunt projections, or ears, at the base;
>
> *sagittate,* or arrow-shaped, when those ears are acute and turned downward, the body of the leaf tapering upward;
>
> *hastate,* or halberd-shaped, when the ears or lobes point outward.

Those broadest at the apex—

> *obovate,* when inversely ovate;
>
> *oblanceolate,* when inversely lanceolate;
>
> *spatulate,* when rounded above, and long and narrow below, like a druggist's spatula;
>
> *cuneate,* or wedge-shaped, when broad above, tapering by straight lines to an acute base;
>
> *obcordate,* when inversely cordate.

Sometimes no one of the above terms will describe a leaf, and it becomes necessary to combine two of them; as, *linear-spatulate, ovate-lanceolate,* etc.

THE APEX

Leaves are classified according to their apices; as—

> *emarginate,* when having a decided terminal notch;
>
> *truncate,* when abruptly cut off;

obtuse, when ending in a blunt or roundish extremity;

acute, when ending in an acute angle, without special tapering;

acuminate, when tapering into a narrow, more or less prolonged end;

mucronate, when abruptly tipped with a small, short point.

THE MARGIN

Leaves are classified according to their margins; as—

entire, when the margin is completely filled out to an even line;

repand, or *undulate,* when the margin is a wavy line;

dentate, or *toothed,* when the teeth point outward;

crenate, or *scalloped,* when dentate, with the teeth rounded;

serrate, when having small sharp teeth directed forward;

incised, when cut by sharp and irregular incisions more or less deeply;

lobed, when cut not more than half-way to the midrib, and the divisions or their angles are rounded;

cleft, when cut half-way down or more, and the lobes or sinuses are narrow or acute;

parted, when the cutting reaches almost but not quite to the midrib;

divided, when the blade is cut into distinct parts, thus making the leaf compound.

All these terms may be modified by the words *pinnate* or *palmate;* thus—*pinnately parted, pinnately divided, palmately parted, palmately divided,* etc.; also by the adjectives *once, twice, thrice,* etc.

As sepals and petals are but modified leaves, *i. e.* leaves that have undergone a morphological change to fit them for new duties, all that has been said about the form, the apex, and the margins of leaves is equally applicable to them.

TEXTURE

Leaves vary as to texture, and may be—

coriaceous, or leathery;   *fleshy,* or thick;
succulent, or juicy;   *herbaceous,* or thin.
scarious, or dry and thin;

ARRANGEMENT

According to their arrangement on the stem, leaves are—

alternate, when distributed singly at different heights on
the stem;

opposite, when two stand opposite each other at the
nodes;

whorled, when more than two are borne at a node,
equidistant in a circle around the stem.

INFLORESCENCE

Inflorescence is a term commonly applied to the mode of
flowering—*i. e.* to the arrangement of blossoms on the stem
and their relative positions to one another.

A **peduncle** is the stem of a solitary flower, or the
main stem of a flower-cluster;

a **scape** is a peduncle growing from the ground;

a **pedicel** is the stem of each flower in a cluster;

a **bract** is a small floral leaf;

an **involucre** is a collection of bracts around a flower-
cluster or around a single flower.

Flowers may be solitary or clustered.

Solitary flowers or flower-clusters are—

terminal, when borne at the summit of the stem;

axillary, when borne in the axils of the leaves.

A flower-cluster is called—

a **raceme,** when the flowers are arranged along the
axis upon pedicels nearly equal in length;

a **corymb,** when the flowers are arranged as in the raceme, with the lower pedicels elongated, making the cluster flat-topped;

an **umbel,** when the pedicels arise from the same point, like the rays of an umbrella, and the cluster is flat-topped;

a **panicle,** when compound, irregularly made up of a number of racemes;

a **thyrse,** when it is a contracted panicle, or a mixed inflorescence, whose main axis is indeterminate, but whose secondary or ultimate clusters are cymose;

a **spike,** when like a raceme, the flowers being without pedicels;

a **spadix,** when it is a fleshy spike, generally enveloped by a large bract, called a **spathe,** as in the calla-lily;

an **ament,** or **catkin,** when it is a pendent spike, with scaly bracts, like the willow;

a **head,** when it is a shortened spike, with a globular form;

a **cyme,** when it is branched and flat-topped, usually compound, with the older flowers in the center of each simple cluster.

THE INDIVIDUAL FLOWER

Flowers have four kinds of organs—**sepals, petals, stamens,** and **pistils**—symmetrically arranged around a central axis. All these organs may be present, or one or more may be absent. When all are present the flower is said to be a **complete** flower.

The **calyx** is the outer floral envelop, which is more often green, though it is sometimes colored. It may consist of a number of separate parts, called **sepals,** or these may be more or less united.

The **corolla** is the inner floral envelop. It is usually colored, and forms the most beautiful feature of the flower, and plays an important part in attracting insects to it, which may carry on the work of fertilization. It may consist of a number of separate parts, called **petals,** or these may be more or less united, in which case the corolla is said to be *gamopetalous.* When the calyx and corolla are much alike, and seem like one floral circle, this is referred to as a **perianth.**

The **stamens** and **pistils** are called the **essential organs** of a flower, because they are necessary to the maturing of the fruit.

Perfect flowers have both sets of essential organs.

Imperfect flowers have but one set of essential organs.

Staminate (or male) *flowers* have only stamens.
Pistillate (or female) *flowers* have only pistils.
Neutral flowers have neither.

Regular flowers are those in which the organs of the same kind are similar.

Symmetrical flowers are those which have the same number in each set of organs, or an even multiple of that number.

THE STAMEN

The **stamen** consists of two parts—the **filament** and the **anther.** The filament is the stalk of the stamen. The anther is the little case holding the **pollen,** or powdery substance, which, falling upon the stigma, is conducted downward into the ovary, where it quickens the ovules into life. The anther normally consists of two cells, which more often open lengthwise for the discharge of the pollen, though they sometimes open by terminal pores or chinks, or by uplifting lids.

An anther is said to be—

basifixed, when attached to the filament by its base;

versatile, when attached at some part only of its back or front, to the tip of the filament on which it swings freely;

adnate, when its cells are placed on either side of the top of the filament, which shows as a connective between them;

extrorse, when it faces outward;

introrse, when it faces inward.

Stamens sometimes undergo a morphological change, taking the form of scales or other bodies (as is the case in many of our *Brodiæas*), when they are called **staminodia.**

THE PISTIL

The **pistil** is the organ occupying the center of the flower. It consists of three parts—the **ovary,** or the enlarged part below, consisting of one or more cells or cavities, and containing the ovules, or unfertilized seed; the **style,** or the stem which upholds the stigma; the **stigma,** or the roughened portion which receives the pollen.

The pistil is *simple,* when it has but one ovary, style, stigma, etc.; *compound,* if any one of these is duplicated. The simple pistil, or an element of a compound pistil, is often called a **carpel.**

THE FRUIT

The **fruit** is the ripened ovary. After the ovules have been fertilized, the ovary is called a **pericarp.** Fruits may be either *fleshy* or *dry.*

The following are some of the principal kinds of dry fruits :—

A **capsule** is a dry, dehiscent (splitting) fruit, composed of more than one carpel or division;

an **akene** is a small, dry, hard, one-celled, one-seeded indehiscent fruit;

a **follicle** is a pod formed from a single pistil, dehiscing along the ventral suture only;

a **legume** is a simple pericarp, opening by both seams;

a **samara** is a dry, indehiscent fruit, having a wing;

a **nut** is a hard, one-celled, one-seeded, indehiscent fruit, like an akene, but larger.

The following are some of the principal kinds of fleshy fruits :—

The **pome** is a fruit like an apple or pear;

the **pepo,** or **gourd,** is a fruit like that of the melon, squash, etc.;

the **drupe** is like that of the cherry, plum, and peach;

the **berry** is like that of the grape, currant, and tomato.

Aggregate fruits are those in which a cluster of carpels, all of one flower, are crowded upon the receptacle into one mass; as in the raspberry and blackberry.

SYNOPSIS OF KEY TO FLOWERING PLANTS

KEY TO THE FLOWERING PLANTS
CONTAINED IN THIS WORK

STAMEN ONE

Has no representative.
(See "Stamens Borne on the Pistil," at end of key.)

STAMENS TWO

Leafless marsh herbs with coral-like branching stems and no conspicuous flowers. **Salicornia,** in **Chenopodiaceæ.**
Plants with ordinary herbage, opposite leaves, and irregular flowers.
Ovary entire, not divided exteriorly; two-celled; calyx four-parted.
Veronica, in **Scrophulariaceæ.**
Ovary divided into four lobes exteriorly.
Filaments with a lateral branch. **Salvia,** in **Labiatæ.**
Filaments without a lateral branch.
Audibertia, in **Labiatæ.**

STAMENS THREE

Flowers contained in involucres. **Chorizanthe,** in **Polygalaceæ.**
Flowers not contained in involucres.
Calyx and corolla both present.
Calyx of two sepals.
Style two-cleft. **Spraguea,** in **Portulacaceæ.**
Style three-cleft. **Montia,** in **Portulacaceæ.**
Calyx-limb deciduous, of numerous plumose bristles.
Valeriana, in **Valerianaceæ.**
Calyx apparently absent because of its obsolete limb; corolla rotate; white; tendril-bearing vines. **Echinocystis,** in **Cucurbitaceæ.**
Calyx petaloid; corolla absent; coarse trailing vines with yellow flowers and gourd fruit. **Cucurbita,** in **Cucurbitaceæ.**

STAMENS THREE—*Continued.*

Perianth petaloid, of six separate segments, or gamopetalous and six-lobed.

Borne on the ovary.

Segments similar, spreading. **Sisyrinchium,** in **Iridaceæ.**

Outer segments recurved, inner erect.

Iris, in **Iridaceæ.**

Borne on the receptacle.

Alternate segments reflexed. **Scoliopus,** in **Liliaceæ.**

Alternate segments not reflexed.

Brodiæa, in **Liliaceæ.**

STAMENS FOUR

Ovary one-celled.

Corolla gamopetalous.

Irregular; bilabiate; plants with no green herbage.

Aphyllon, in **Ericaceæ.**

Regular; plants with green herbage.

Calyx-tube adnate to the ovary.

Dipsacus, in **Dipsaceæ.**

Calyx-tube free from the ovary.

Gentiana, in **Gentianaceæ.**

Corolla polypetalous; shrubs or trees.

Rhus, in **Anacardiaceæ.**

Corolla wanting; diœcious shrubs, with flowers in aments.

Garrya, in **Cornaceæ.**

Ovary two-celled.

Corolla polypetalous; petals four; shrubs or trees.

Cornus, in **Cornaceæ.**

Corolla gamopetalous.

Regular.

Swamp herbs, with large banana-like leaves; flowers on a spadix surrounded by a spathe. **Lysichiton,** in **Araceæ.**

Twining parasites, without chlorophyll.

Cuscuta, in **Convolvulaceæ.**

Herbs or woody plants; square-stemmed; with whorled leaves.

Galium, in **Rubiaceæ.**

Irregular.

Corolla spurred; leaves alternate.

Linaria, in **Scrophulariaceæ.**

Corolla only saccate or gibbous at base; leaves mostly alternate.

Antirrhinum, in **Scrophulariaceæ.**

Stamens Four—*Continued.*

Corolla erect; ventricose; short; lobes five, short, one reflexed; a small scale in the throat in lieu of the fifth stamen.

Scrophularia, in **Scrophulariaceæ.**

Corolla declined; middle lobe of lower lip inclosing the stamens and style. **Collinsia,** in **Scrophulariaceæ.**

Corolla tubular; open; sterile filament of the fifth stamen long and conspicuous. **Pentstemon,** in **Scrophulariaceæ.**

Corolla funnel-form with spreading bilabiate border; stigma dilated, two-lipped.

Herbs. **Mimulus,** in **Scrophulariaceæ.**

Shrubs or woody plants.

Diplacus, in **Scrophulariaceæ.**

Corolla narrow; lower lip very small in proportion to the upper; floral bracts colored conspicuously; calyx cleft before and behind. **Castilleia,** in **Scrophulariaceæ.**

Corolla with lower lip large in proportion to the upper.

Orthocarpus, in **Scrophulariaceæ.**

Corolla laterally compressed; upper lip long, arched, sometimes beaked; lower, of three small lobes; calyx five-toothed.

Pedicularis, in **Scrophulariaceæ.**

Ovary two- to four-celled.

Shrubs or trees; with two-seeded drupes; style three- or four-cleft.

Rhamnus, in **Rhamnaceæ.**

Shrubs with minute flowers in a head; with style entire and much exserted. **Cephalanthus,** in **Rubiaceæ.**

Ovary four-celled.

Herbs; calyx-tube prolonged beyond the ovary; petals four, with claws. **Clarkia,** in **Onagraceæ.**

Shrubs with white berries. **Symphoricarpus,** in **Caprifoliaceæ.**

Ovary four-lobed, becoming four seedlike nutlets.

Corolla with border not conspicuously bilabiate, hairy-ringed at base within; woody plants, with veiny leaves.

Sphacele, in **Labiatæ.**

Corolla with bilabiate border.

Upper lip never hooded or galeate.

Flowers in heads. **Monardella,** in **Labiatæ.**

Flowers solitary; axillary; small; white; fragrant trailing vines.

Micromeria, in **Labiatæ.**

Upper lip hooded or galeate.

Calyx bonnet-like. **Scutellaria,** in **Labiatæ.**

STAMENS FOUR—*Continued.*

Calyx bilabiate; filaments two-forked, one fork bearing the anther.
Brunella, in **Labiatæ.**
Calyx ten-toothed. **Marrubium,** in **Labiatæ.**
Calyx almost equally five-toothed.
Stachys, in **Labiatæ.**
Calyx five-cleft; stamens spirally coiled in bud and long-exserted
in flower. **Trichostema,** in **Labiatæ.**

STAMENS FIVE

Pistil one.
Corolla gamopetalous; borne on the receptacle.
Fruit, four nutlets.
Ovary with four sutures, finally separating into four nutlets.
Corolla funnel-form; throat naked.
Heliotropium, in **Boraginaceæ.**
Ovary four-parted; nutlets ventrally adherent to the persistent
style, three-cornered, with barbed prickles on their edges
or all over their backs.
Racemes mostly bracteate. **Lappula,** in **Boraginaceæ.**
Racemes mostly bractless. **Cynoglossum,** in **Boraginaceæ.**
Ovary deeply four-parted; nutlets inserted by their ventral side
above their base on a pyramidal disk.
Flowers yellow. **Amsinckia,** in **Boraginaceæ.**
Flowers violet or blue. **Mertensia,** in **Boraginaceæ.**
Ovary deeply four-parted; nutlets attached near the middle of
their ventral face to a columnar prominence rising from a
flat disk. **Plagiobothrys,** in **Boraginaceæ.**
Fruit a one-celled capsule with a free central placenta.
Corolla-lobes reflexed. **Dodecatheon,** in **Primulaceæ.**
Corolla rotate with spreading lobes.
Anagallis, in **Primulaceæ.**
Corolla salver-form. **Primula,** in **Primulaceæ.**
Fruit a one-celled capsule with two parietal placentæ, which some-
times meet, making it two-celled.
Calyx with an extra reflexed lobe at each sinus.
Nemophila, in **Hydrophyllaceæ.**
Calyx without extra reflexed lobes.
Style single, undivided. **Romanzoffia,** in **Hydrophyllaceæ.**
Style two-cleft; corolla without appendages.
Ellisia, in **Hydrophyllaceæ.**

STAMENS FIVE—*Continued.*

Style from two-cleft to two-parted; corolla appendaged within at base by ten vertical scales; herbs.

Corolla deciduous; blue, white, or purple.

Phacelia, in **Hydrophyllaceæ.**

Corolla withering persistent; yellow.

Emmenanthe, in **Hydrophyllaceæ.**

Styles two, with capitate stigmas; woody herbs or shrubs.

Eriodictyon, in **Hydrophyllaceæ.**

Styles none or very short; stigmas two, thin, flat; funnel-form corolla, with plaited and toothed folds in the sinuses.

Gentiana, in **Gentianaceæ.**

Fruit two- to many-celled.

Corolla four- to five-lobed; leafless parasites, with no green herbage. **Cuscuta,** in **Convolvulaceæ,**

Corolla funnel-form to salver-form; flowers pink; anthers finally spirally twisted. **Erythræa,** in **Gentianaceæ.**

Corolla funnel-form; stigmas two.

Gentiana, in **Gentianaceæ.**

Corolla rotate; stigmas three; filaments hairy at base, somewhat declined. **Polemonium,** in **Polemoniaceæ.**

Corolla rotate; style and stigma one; filaments woolly.

Verbascum, in **Scrophulariaceæ.**

Corolla rotate to funnel-form or salver-form; stigmas three; filaments not declined. **Gilia,** in **Polemoniaceæ.**

Corolla salver-form; stamens unequally inserted in its throat.

Phlox, in **Polemoniaceæ.**

Corolla funnel-form; plicate; five-angled.

Capsule smooth.

Climbing and twining herbs.

Convolvulus, in **Convolvulaceæ.**

Herbs, not climbing and twining.

Nicotiana, in **Solaneæ.**

Capsule prickly. **Datura,** in **Solaneæ.**

Corolla campanulate; anthers opening by terminal pores; shrubs.

Rhododendron, in **Ericaceæ.**

Corolla funnel-form, irregular; stamens of unequal length, one of them sterile. **Pentstemon,** in **Scrophulariaceæ.**

Fruit a berry.

Corolla rotate; anthers opening by terminal pores or chinks.

Solanum, in **Solaneæ.**

xxxix

STAMENS FIVE—*Continued.*

Corolla gamopetalous; borne on the ovary.
  Fruit a capsule.
    Corolla regular, five-lobed; stamens distinct.

Campanula,	in **Campanulaceæ.**

Corolla irregular, bilabiate; stamens united into a tube.

Bolelia (Downingia),	in **Lobeliaceæ.**

  Fruit a berry.
    Corolla regular; berry white.

Symphoricarpus,	in **Caprifoliaceæ.**

    Corolla regular; berries in flat clusters, blue; trees.

Sambucus,	in **Caprifoliaceæ.**

    Corolla irregular; shrubs or woody climbers; berries red or black.

Lonicera,	in **Caprifoliaceæ.**

Corolla polypetalous; borne on the receptacle.
  Flowers regular.
    Fruit a capsule.
      Ovary one-celled.
        Style one, three-cleft; sepals two.

Flowers mostly red.	**Calandrinia,**	in **Portulacaceæ.**
Flowers mostly white.	**Montia,**	in **Portulacaceæ.**

        Styles two. Calyx five-toothed.

Heuchera,	in **Saxifragaceæ.**

      Ovary two-celled; styles two.

Boykinia,	in **Saxifragaceæ.**

      Ovary three-celled. Style single, three-cleft.

Ceanothus,	in **Rhamnaceæ.**

      Ovary five-celled; styles five.

Linum,	in **Linaceæ.**

    Fruit consisting of five, tailed carpels, separating away from a central axis at maturity.

Erodium,	in **Geraniaceæ.**

    Fruit a drupe or drupelike; trees or shrubs.
      Ovary one-celled; styles three.

Rhus,	in **Anacardiaceæ.**

      Ovary two- to four-celled. Style single, short, three- or four-cleft.

Rhamnus,	in **Rhamnaceæ.**

  Flowers irregular.
    Lower petal spurred; capsule one-celled; herbs.

Viola,	in **Violaceæ.**

Stamens Five—*Continued.*

Petals not spurred; fruit a large nut in a leathery pod; trees.

Æsculus, in **Sapindaceæ.**

Corolla polypetalous; borne on the ovary.

Flowers in racemes; leaves lobed. **Ribes,** in **Saxifragaceæ.**

Flowers in umbels; leaves compound.

Aralia, in **Araliaceæ.**

Corolla absent; calyx petaloid and gamopetalous.

Flowers numerous in a head subtended by several separate bracts.

Abronia, in **Nyctaginaceæ.**

Flowers one to several, contained in a campanulate calyx-like involucre. **Mirabilis,** in **Nyctaginaceæ.**

Pistils two.

Ovaries distinct at base, but united by their stigmas; corolla gamopetalous; herbs with milky juice; pollen in powdery grains.

Apocynum, in **Apocynaceæ.**

STAMENS SIX

Exogenous plants; with net-veined leaves and parts of the flowers not in threes.

Ovary one-celled.

Sepals and petals four; pod necklace-like.

Raphanus, in **Cruciferæ.**

Sepals and petals six, in front of one another; fruit a berry.

Flowers yellow; shrubs. **Berberis,** in **Berberidaceæ.**

Flowers white; herbs. **Vancouveria,** in **Berberidaceæ.**

Sepals and petals four to nine; fruit dry drupes; shrubs or trees.

Rhus, in **Anacardiaceæ.**

Calyx and corolla seven-parted—sometimes six- to nine-parted; small herbs with simple stems, bearing at summit a whorl of leaves; flowers pink. **Trientalis,** in **Primulaceæ.**

Calyx four-cleft; petals four; ovary stalked; shrubs with yellow flowers and bladdery pods. **Isomeris,** in **Capparidaceæ.**

Sepals two; petals four, irregular. **Dicentra,** in **Fumariaceæ.**

Sepals six; petals wanting; stigmas three; flowers without involucres. **Rumex,** in **Polygonaceæ.**

Calyx six-cleft or parted; petaloid; corolla wanting; flowers contained in small involucres, one to three in each.

Chorizanthe, in **Polygonaceæ.**

S<small>TAMENS</small> S<small>IX</small>—*Continued.*

Calyx and corolla both wanting; flowers minute, sunk in the axis of a conical spike, which is surrounded by five to eight large white petal-like bracts. **Anemopsis,** in **Piperaceæ.**

Ovary two-celled; fruit a pod.

Pod long, cylindrical, long-beaked; flowers large, yellow. **Brassica,** in **Cruciferæ.**

Pod compressed; flowers purple or white. **Arabis,** in **Cruciferæ.**

Pod four-sided or flattened; flowers large, pale yellow or orange. **Erysimum,** in **Cruciferæ.**

Pod compressed, pointed; roots tuberiferous; flowers large, white. **Dentaria,** in **Cruciferæ.**

Pod obcordate; small; many-seeded; flowers very small, white. **Capsella,** in **Cruciferæ.**

Pod small, roundish; cells one- to two-seeded. **Lepidium.** in **Cruciferæ.**

Pod oblong-cylindrical; seeds in two rows; plants growing in water; leaves pungent, pinnatifid; flowers small, white. **Nasturtium,** in **Cruciferæ.**

Pod constricted into divisions, necklace-like; divisions filled with corky pith; flowers large, white, yellowish, or purplish. **Raphanus,** in **Cruciferæ.**

Endogenous plants; with parallel-veined leaves (except *Trillium*), and the flower-parts in threes.

Fruit a capsule.

Plants with scaly bulbs; stems tall; leaves mostly whorled.

Flowers campanulate, nodding, not over two inches long; style three-cleft; nectary round. **Fritillaria,** in **Liliaceæ.**

Flowers campanulate or spreading, large and showy; style undivided; nectary a long groove. **Lilium,** in **Liliaceæ.**

Plants with corms; leaves radical, with a few stem-leaves in some.

Flowers solitary or racemose, without bracts on a scape-like stem; leaves two, broad. **Erythronium,** in **Liliaceæ.**

Flowers solitary on a simple stem or terminal on the branches, or in umbel-like clusters; without bracts; outer perianth segments smaller, inner larger and showy, usually bearing a gland at base within; leaves linear. **Calochortus,** in **Liliaceæ.**

Flowers in umbels, with bracts.

Perianth segments distinct, or nearly so.

STAMENS SIX—*Continued.*

Filaments with a cup-shaped appendage surrounding the base. **Bloomeria,** in **Liliaceæ.**

Filaments not appendaged; leaves semi-terete. **Muilla,** in **Liliaceæ.**

Perianth segments united into a tube below; filaments sometimes winged or appendaged; sometimes three of the stamens replaced by three staminodia. **Brodiæa,** in **Liliaceæ.**

Plants with coated bulbs; perianth segments distinct; leaves all radical.

Flowers on scapes in bractless racemes, blue: **Camassia,** in **Liliaceæ.**

Flowers on a scape in a bractate raceme, white. **Zygadenus,** in **Liliaceæ.**

Flowers in a large, very loosely and widely branching panicle, with small scarious bracts. **Chlorogalum,** in **Liliaceæ.**

Plants with a short thick rootstock.

Stems tall; leaves large, boat-shaped. **Veratrum,** in **Liliaceæ.**

Stemless plants; leaves all radical, linear, very numerous, long and flexible. **Xerophyllum,** in **Liliaceæ.**

Stems simple, bearing at summit a whorl of three broad, net-veined leaves and a single flower. **Trillium,** in **Liliaceæ.**

Fruit a berry; plants with rootstocks.

Apparently stemless, the broad leaves arising from the ground; flowers crimson, on a peduncle a foot or so high; berries blue. **Clintonia,** in **Liliaceæ.**

Stem simple, leafy; flowers small, in a raceme or panicle. **Smilacina,** in **Liliaceæ.**

Stem forked; flowers at the ends of the leafy branches under the leaves. **Disporum,** in **Liliaceæ.**

Fruit capsular.

Stemless plants; leaves serrate, swordlike, in a bristling hemisphere; flower panicle tall and large, of many white waxen bells. **Hesperoyucca,** in **Liliaceæ.**

Fruit pulpy.

Caudex short and covered with refracted dead leaves, or none; leaves long, swordlike, thread-bearing on the margin; panicles very large, of many waxen white bells. **Yucca,** in **Liliaceæ.**

Stamens Six—*Continued.*

Trees, gaunt and straggling; leaves rigid, crowded, sessile, linear; panicles ovate, comparatively small.

Cleistoyucca, in Liliaceæ.

STAMENS SEVEN

Calyx seven-cleft; corolla seven-parted.

Trientalis, in **Primulaceæ.**

Calyx five-toothed; petals four or five; unequal; with claws.

Æsculus, in **Sapindaceæ.**

Calyx of two sepals; corolla on the receptacle.

Calandrinia, in **Portulacaceæ.**

Sepals and petals four to nine; shrubs.

Rhus, in **Anacardiaceæ.**

STAMENS EIGHT

Corolla polypetalous.

Ovary one-celled; shrubs or trees. **Rhus,** in **Anacardiaceæ.**

Ovary four-celled.

Seeds with a hairy crown.

Calyx-tube prolonged considerably beyond the ovary; its limb petaloid, deciduous. **Zauschneria, in Onagraceæ.**

Calyx-tube not greatly prolonged.

Epilobium, in **Onagraceæ.**

Seeds without a hairy crown; naked.

Calyx-tube prolonged beyond the ovary; lobes of its limb reflexed.

Anthers versatile; flowers yellow or white, fading to rose.

Œnothera, in **Onagraceæ.**

Anthers basifixed; flowers never yellow, usually pink, sometimes white.

Petals with claws. **Clarkia,** in **Onagraceæ.**

Petals without claws. **Godetia,** in **Onagraceæ.**

Corolla gamopetalous.

Borne near the summit of the ovary; anthers opening by terminal pores; fruit a berry; shrubs. **Vaccinium,** in **Ericaceæ.**

Corolla and calyx wanting; flowers sunk in the axis of a conical spike, surrounded by large petal-like white bracts.

Anemopsis, in **Piperaceæ.**

xliv

STAMENS NINE

Flowers small, contained in involucres.
 Involucres campanulate, many-flowered.
         Eriogonum, in **Polygonaceæ.**
 Involucres tubular; one- to three-flowered.
         Chorizanthe, in **Polygonaceæ.**
Flowers not in involucres.
 Anthers four-celled, with uplifting valves; fruit a large greenish
  or purple drupe; trees with aromatic leaves.
         Umbellularia, in **Lauraceæ.**
 Anthers two-celled, opening lengthwise; fruit small drupes; leaves
  not aromatic; trees or shrubs. **Rhus,**   in **Anacardiaceæ.**

STAMENS TEN

Anthers opening by terminal pores.
 Corolla polypetalous.
  Herbs.
   Flowers on a leafy stem; petals spreading widely; style short.
        Chimaphila, in **Ericaceæ.**
   Flowers on a scape; petals concave, not spreading widely; style
    long.   **Pyrola,** in **Ericaceæ.**
   Shrubs with white flowers. **Ledum,** in **Ericaceæ.**
 Corolla gamopetalous.
  Fruit a berry; flowers comparatively small.
   Berry red, with granular coat. **Arbutus,** in **Ericaceæ.**
   Berry smooth, mostly dry and bony.
        Arctostaphylos, in **Ericaceæ.**
   Berry black-purple, aromatic, edible; shrubs; leaves broad, ovate.
        Gaultheria, in **Ericaceæ.**
   Berry black when ripe; shrubs; leaves lanceolate, set obliquely to
    the stems.   **Vaccinium,** in **Ericaceæ.**
  Fruit a capsule.
   Shrubs; leaves broad; flowers large.
        Rhododendron, in **Ericaceæ.**
   Heathlike undershrubs.
    Flowers clustered.   **Bryanthus,** in **Ericaceæ.**
    Flowers solitary on long filiform stems.
        Cassiope, in **Ericaceæ.**

STAMENS TEN--*Continued.*

Glandular-viscid, leafless herbs.

Pterospora, in **Ericaceæ.**

Fleshy, leafless plants, with brilliant crimson flowers in a scaly-bracted raceme. **Sarcodes,** in **Ericaceæ.**

Anthers opening lengthwise.

Fruit a pod; stamens distinct; flowers papilionaceous.

Trees with simple rounded leaves.

Cercis, in **Leguminosæ.**

Shrubs with spiny branchlets; flowers magenta-colored.

Xylothermia, in **Leguminosæ.**

Herbs with conspicuous stipules; flowers yellow.

Thermopsis, in **Leguminosæ.**

Fruit consisting of five carpels, separating at maturity from a central axis.

Style one; strong-scented shrubs with small two-foliolate leaves and distinct stipules. **Larrea,** in **Zygophyllaceæ.**

Styles five.

Tails of carpels bearded. **Erodium,** in **Geraniaceæ.**

Tails of carpels not bearded.

Flowers pink, white, or purple; not yellow.

Geranium, in **Geraniaceæ.**

Flowers yellow or white, or both.

Flœrkea, in **Geraniaceæ.**

Fruit consisting of five carpels, united and forming a five-celled capsule.

Herbs with three foliolate leaves.

Oxalis, in **Geraniaceæ.**

Fruit a dried calyx-tube, containing one to three akenes.

Heathlike shrubs, with feathery panicles of small white flowers.

Adenostoma, in **Rosaceæ.**

Fruit a capsule.

Ovary two-celled; cells tending to separate into two carpels at maturity.

Leaves peltate. **Peltyphyllum,** in **Saxifragaceæ.**

Leaves not peltate. **Saxifraga,** in **Saxifragaceæ.**

Ovary and capsule one-celled.

Flowers fringed, rose-colored; styles two.

Tellima, in **Saxifragaceæ.**

Stamens Ten—*Continued.*

Flowers with petals cleft; styles three.
  Joints swollen; leaves opposite.

      Silene,   in **Caryophyllaceæ.**
  Joints not swollen; leaves alternate.

      Lithophragma, in **Saxifragaceæ.**
Flowers with entire petals; sepals two.

      Calandrinia,   in **Portulacaceæ.**
Ovary three- to five-celled.
  Small straggling woody plants; leaves opposite, three-ribbed;
    flowers small, white.   **Whipplea,**   in **Saxifragaceæ.**
Fruit consisting of several distinct carpels.
  Herbs with fleshy leaves.
    Corolla gamopetalous.
      Leaves flat, in a rosette. **Dudleya,**   in **Crassulaceæ.**
      Leaves cylindrical, in tufts.

      Stylophyllum, in **Crassulaceæ.**
    Corolla polypetalous.   **Sedum,**   in **Crassulaceæ.**
Fruit a small dry drupe or a berry.
  Shrubs or small trees.   **Rhus,**   in **Anacardiaceæ.**

STAMENS TWELVE

Perianth three-cleft; on the ovary. **Asarum,**   in **Aristolochiaceæ.**
Petals five; sepals two.   **Calandrinia,**   in **Portulacaceæ.**
Petals five; calyx tubular, ten-ribbed.

      Adenostoma, in **Rosaceæ.**
Petals five; bog plants with tubular pitchers for leaves.

      Darlingtonia, in **Sarraceniaceæ.**
Petals none; calyx-tube cylindric; fruit an akene with long feathery
  tail.   **Cercocarpus,** in **Rosaceæ.**

STAMENS MANY

Trees, shrubs, or woody plants.
  Fruit a drupe.
    Style one; stamens indefinite. **Prunus,**   in **Rosaceæ.**
    Styles five; stamens fifteen. **Nuttallia,**   in **Rosaceæ.**
  Fruit a berry.
    Evergreen shrubs; berries scarlet, smooth-coated, in large clusters.

      Heteromeles, in **Rosaceæ.**

STAMENS MANY—*Continued*

Deciduous shrubs; berries dark purple.

Amelanchier, in **Rosaceæ.**

Prickly shrubs; fruit aggregate. **Rubus,** in **Rosaceæ.**

Fruit a dry capsule.

Flowers white.

Minute, in large feathery panicles.

Ovary one; one-celled; heathlike shrubs with short, needle-like leaves. **Adenostoma,** in **Rosaceæ.**

Pistils five, separate; shrubs with ordinary leaves.

Holodiscus (Spiræa), in **Rosaceæ.**

Small, in hemispherical heads. **Neillia,** in **Rosaceæ.**

Medium (*i. e.* an inch or less across); leaves much dissected; fragrant. **Chamæbatia,** in **Rosaceæ.**

Large (over an inch across), clustered; leaves opposite.

Philadelphus, in **Saxifragaceæ.**

Very large; solitary; plants woody, with glaucous, slashed leaves.

Romneya, in **Papaveraceæ.**

Flowers yellow, poppy-like. **Dendromecon,** in **Papaveraceæ.**

Flowers red, chrysanthemum-like.

Calycanthus, in **Calycanthaceæ.**

Fruit a hip; prickly shrubs, with alternate pinnate leaves.

Rosa, in **Rosaceæ.**

Fruit solitary or clustered akenes with plumed tails.

Akenes solitary; trees. **Cercocarpus,** in **Rosaceæ.**

Akenes in a head; woody climbers.

Clematis, in **Ranunculaceæ.**

Cactaceous, leafless plants, covered with spines and minute prickles.

Shrubby, with cylindrical or flattened joints.

Opuntia, in **Cactaceæ.**

Low, horrent globes.

Plants large, ribbed; fruit green. **Echinocactus,** in **Cactaceæ.**

Plants small; fruit scarlet. **Mamillaria,** in **Cactaceæ.**

Bog plants; leaves tubular pitchers. **Darlingtonia,** in **Sarraceniaceæ.**

Water-plants with large rounded leaves, usually floating on the water; flowers yellow. **Nuphar,** in **Nymphaceæ.**

Terrestrial herbs.

Ovary and capsule one; one-celled.

Prickly; leaves lobed or divided.

Argemone, in **Papaveraceæ.**

Stamens Many—*Continued.*

    Bristly; leaves lobed or divided.

                    Romneya,   in Papaveraceæ.

    Smooth.

        Sepals united in a cap, falling in bud.

                    Eschscholtzia,   in Papaveraceæ.

        Stepals two.

            Stigma several-lobed.

                Juice yellowish.   **Meconopsis,**   in Papaveraceæ.

                Juice milky.   **Papaver,**   in Papaveraceæ.

                Style three-cleft.   **Calandrinia,**   in Portulacaceæ.

        Sepals four to eight; leaves radical.

                    Lewisia,   in Portulacaceæ.

        Sepals five; leaves opposite; styles two to five.

                    Hypericum,   in Hypericaceæ.

        Calyx-limb five-lobed; style three-cleft.

                    Mentzelia,   in Loasaceæ.

    Ovaries several in a ring, splitting into separate capsules at maturity.

                    Platystemon,   in Papaveraceæ.

    Ovary four- to twenty-celled; fleshy herbs with opposite-angled leaves and edible fruit.   **Mesembryanthemum,** in Ficoidæ.

    Ovaries several or very numerous.

        Calyx five-lobed.

            Fruit a scarlet berry; flowers white.

                    Fragaria,   in Rosaceæ.

            Fruit dry akenes; flowers yellow.

                    Potentilla,   in Rosaceæ.

        Calyx of separate sepals.

            Flowers regular.

                Sepals and petals both present.

                    Sepals green or greenish.

                      Akenes numerous, dry.

                    Ranunculus,   in Ranunculaceæ.

                  Carpels few, large, leathery in fruit.

                    Pæonia,   in Ranunculaceæ.

                Sepals petaloid.

                  Petals five, all spurred.

                    Aquilegia,   in Ranunculaceæ.

Stamens Many—*Continued.*

Sepals only present; corolla wanting.

Colored, petaloid.   **Anemone,**   in **Ranunculaceæ.**

Flowers irregular.

Sepals and petals both present, the former colored and petaloid.

Upper sepal prolonged into a long spur.

    Delphinium,   in **Ranunculaceæ.**

Upper sepal arched into a helmet.

    Aconitum,   in **Ranunculaceæ.**

STAMENS UNITED BY THEIR FILAMENTS INTO ONE OR MORE SETS

United into one set.

Stamens three.   **Sisyrinchium,**   in **Iridaceæ.**

Stamens five.

Corolla polypetalous.   **Erodium,**   in **Geraniaceæ.**

Corolla gamopetalous; irregular.

    Bolelia,   in **Lobeliaceæ.**

Stamens eight.   **Polygala,**   in **Polygalaceæ.**

Stamens ten.

Corolla regular.

Anthers two-celled.

Ovary five-celled.

Herbs; flowers perfect, pink.

    Oxalis,   in **Geraniaceæ.**

Shrubs; petals none; calyx petaloid, yellow.

    Fremontodendron, in **Sterculiaceæ.**

Carpels five, around a central axis, splitting away from it at maturity.

Stamens all fertile.   **Geranium,**   in **Geraniaceæ.**

Alternate stamens sterile.

    Erodium,   in **Geraniaceæ.**

Anthers one-celled.

Calyx furnished with bractlets.

Stigmas linear; shrubs.

    Lavatera,   in **Malvaceæ.**

Stigmas capitate; shrubs.

    Malvastrum,   in **Malvaceæ.**

Calyx without bractlets, stigmas linear; herbs.

    Sidalcea,   in **Malvaceæ.**

1

Stamens United by Their Filaments, etc.—*Continued.*

  Corolla irregular.

    Petals five; papilionaceous; herbs; anthers of two forms, alternately oblong and rounded.   **Lupinus,**   in **Leguminosæ.**

    Petal only one! Shrub or tree.   **Amorpha,**   in **Leguminosæ.**

United into two sets.

  Stamens six; ovary one-celled; flowers two-spurred.

          Dicentra,   in **Fumariaceæ.**

  Stamens eight; ovary two-celled; flowers irregular.

          Polygala,   in **Polygalaceæ.**

  Stamens ten.

    Trees or shrubs; flowers with only one petal.

          Amorpha,   in **Leguminosæ.**

    Herbs.

      Anthers of two forms.   **Lupinus,**   in **Leguminosæ.**

      Anthers uniform.

        Pod spirally coiled.   **Medicago,**   in **Leguminosæ.**

        Pod not spirally coiled.

          Small, globular; leaflets three.   **Melilotus,**   in **Leguminosæ.**

          Bladdery-inflated; leaves odd-pinnate.

            Astragalus, in **Leguminosæ.**

          Linear, several-seeded.

            Leaves odd-pinnate, without tendrils; flowers yellow, or white, or pink, never blue.

            Hosackia,   in **Leguminosæ.**

            Leaves abruptly pinnate, ending in a tendril or bristle.

              Stamen-tube oblique at top; style hairy around and below the apex.   **Vicia,**   in **Leguminosæ.**

              Stamen-tube straight at top; style hairy only on its inner side.   **Lathyrus,** in **Leguminosæ.**

United into many sets.

  Sepals five, distinct; styles two to five.

          Hypericum, in **Hypericaceæ.**

  Calyx-limb five-lobed; style three-cleft.

          Mentzelia,   in **Loasaceæ.**

STAMENS UNITED BY THEIR ANTHERS

Flowers composite, *i. e.* borne in heads on a receptacle and surrounded by an involucre of bracts.

Yellow, or mainly yellow.

Heads composed of both ray- and disk-flowers.

Leaves radical.

Large, hastate, or sagittate, woolly; flower-heads large.

Balsamorrhiza, in **Compositæ**.

Leaves opposite.

Linear; heads small, one inch across.

Baeria,   in **Compositæ**.

Leaves all alternate.

Heads large and solitary.

Leaves large, cordate, on long slender petioles.

Venegasia,   in **Compositæ**.

Leaves large, oval, about a foot long; short-petioled.

Wyethia,   in **Compositæ**.

Leaves smaller, ovate-lanceolate; plants woody at base; disk-flowers black-purple.   **Encelia**,   in **Compositæ**.

Leaves oblong or cuneate-oblong, sessile; plants woody at at base; flower-buds covered with milk-white gum.

Grindelia,   in **Compositæ**.

Leaves linear; rays narrow and very numerous.

Pentachæta,   in **Compositæ**.

Leaves divided into linear divisions; rays yellow, blending into white at top; disk all yellow.

Leptosyne,   in **Compositæ**.

Leaves pinnatifid; rays yellow, changing sharply into white at tip; stamens of disk-flowers black.

Layia,   in **Compositæ**.

Heads small, in flat-topped clusters.

Eriophyllum confertiflorum,
in **Compositæ**.

Heads small, in panicles.   **Solidago**,   in **Compositæ**.

Lower leaves sometimes opposite, the rest mainly alternate.

Plants glandular and viscid.

Heads large; ray-flowers usually with some dark brown at base.   **Madia**,   in **Compositæ**.

Heads medium, or small; flowers all yellow or white.

Hemizonia,   in **Compositæ**.

Stamens United by Their Anthers—*Continued.*

Plants not glandular-viscid.
Very tall; heads large, with brown centers or disk-flowers.
Helianthus, in **Compositæ.**
Not very tall; heads an inch or so across; all yellow; leaves white-woolly. **Eriophyllum arachnoideum,**
in **Compositæ.**
Heads composed of ray-flowers only; large.
Leaves lanceolate, laciniate-pinnatifid; flowers succeeded by a globe of down. **Troximon,** in **Compositæ.**
Leaves divided into linear divisions.
Malacothrix Californica,
in **Compositæ.**
Heads composed of tubular disk-flowers only; small.
Stems low, creeping, and rooting; heads smooth, like a brass button. **Cotula,** in **Compositæ.**
Stems low, much branched, spreading; marginal corollas conspicuously enlarged into the semblance of ray-flowers.
Lessingia Germanorum,
Flowers white. in **Compositæ.**
Ray- and disk-flowers both present.
Heads large, solitary. **Erigeron,** in **Compositæ.**
Heads medium, solitary; foliage strong-scented.
Anthemis, in **Compositæ.**
Heads small, in flat-topped clusters.
Achillea, in **Compositæ.**
Ray-flowers only present. **Malacothrix saxatilis,**
in **Compositæ.**
Disk-flowers only present, these filiform; but the scales of the involucre resembling ray-flowers.
Flowers yellowish-white, with fragrance resembling slippery-elm.
Gnaphalium, in **Compositæ.**
Flowers pure white, with dark centers or disk-flowers.
Anaphalis, in **Compositæ.**
Flowers diœcious; fertile flowers with copious silken down at maturity. **Baccharis,** in **Compositæ.**
Flowers blue.
Stems tall; juice milky; no disk-flowers, only strap-shaped ray-flowers. **Cichorium,** in **Compositæ.**
Flowers pink, lavender, or purple.
Ray- and disk-flowers both present.

STAMENS UNITED BY THEIR ANTHERS—*Continued.*

Rays extremely numerous. **Erigeron,** in **Compositæ.**
Rays less numerous. **Aster,** in **Compositæ.**
Disk-flowers only present.
Stems erect, slender; branchlets filiform.
 Lessingia, in **Compositæ.**
Flowers greenish, inconspicuous.
Disk-flowers only, present; herbs or undershrubs with bitter-fragrant foliage. **Artemisia,** in **Compositæ.**
Flowers not composite.
Low plants; flowers irregular, blue.
 Bolelia, in **Lobeliaceæ.**
Tall plants; flowers irregular; brilliant cardinal-red.
 Lobelia, in **Lobeliaceæ.**

STAMENS BORNE ON THE PISTIL

Anther one.
Lip of the perianth saccate; small plants, with one leaf and one pink flower. **Calypso,** in **Orchidaceæ.**
Lip saccate; leaves radical, white-veined; spikes many-flowered; flowers white. **Goodyera,** in **Orchidaceæ.**
Lip flat, furnished with a spur. **Habenaria,** in **Orchidaceæ.**
Lip not spurred; entire plant white and colorless!
 Cephalanthera, in **Orchidaceæ.**
Lip not spurred, but bent abruptly upon itself.
 Epipactis, in **Orchidaceæ.**
Lip not spurred or bent abruptly, adnate to the column; leafless herbs, without chlorophyll. **Coralorrhiza,** in **Orchidaceæ.**
Lip embracing the column with its base, perianth oblique; flowers in a spirally twisted spike. **Spiranthes,** in **Orchidaceæ.**
Anthers two.
Lip a pouch or pocket. **Cypripedium,** in **Orchidaceæ.**
Anthers five.
Herbs with milky juice; ovaries two; pollen in waxy masses; a hooded appendage (nectary) behind each anther; seeds with silky down.
Appendages horned. **Asclepias,** in **Asclepiadaceæ.**
Appendages not horned. **Gomphocarpus,** in **Asclepiadaceæ.**
Anthers six.
Twining, woody plants, with curious pouched flowers; appearing before the large cordate leaves.
 Aristolochia, in **Aristolochiaceæ.**

PLANT FAMILIES OR ORDERS
REPRESENTED IN THIS WORK

ORDER I.

Ranunculaceæ. BUTTERCUP OR CROWFOOT FAMILY.

Herbaceous or somewhat shrubby plants. *Leaves.* — Various—no stipules. *Sepals, petals, stamens, and pistils.*—All distinct and free. *Sepals.*—Four or more; often colored, and petal-like. *Petals.*—Equaling the number of sepals and alternating with them when present. *Stamens.* —Numerous; on the receptacle at base of pistils. *Pistils.*—One to many. *Ovaries.*—Superior. *Fruit.*—Akenes, or follicles.

An order comprising over thirty genera, widely distributed over the world. Many are beautiful and are cultivated for ornament, and some are medicinal.

Of our thirteen genera, the most important are *Clematis, Ranunculus, Anemone, Aquilegia, Delphinium, Aconitum, Pæonia,* etc.

ORDER II.

Berberidaceæ. BARBERRY FAMILY.

Herbs or shrubs. *Leaves.* — Mostly alternate; compound; without stipules. *Flowers.*—Perfect, with organs distinct; remarkable for having the six sepals, petals, and stamens before each other, instead of alternating. *Sepals.*—Usually colored. *Anthers.*—Two; opening by uplifting valves. *Pistil.*—One; simple. *Ovary.*—One-celled; superior. *Style.* —Short, or none.

A small order of a dozen genera chiefly of temperate regions of the Northern Hemisphere.

Berberis, the barberry, is the only genus having many species. *Podophyllum,* a medicinal plant, of the Atlantic States belongs here.

We have three genera, the most important of which are *Berberis* and *Vancouveria.*

ORDER III.

Nymphaceæ. WATER-LILY FAMILY.

Aquatic perennial herbs, with horizontal rootstocks and sometimes tubers. *Leaves.*—Peltate or deeply cordate. *Flowers.*—Solitary on long peduncles. *Sepals, petals, and stamens.*—Indefinite, mostly numerous. *Pistils.*—Several, or one and many-celled and many-seeded. *Ovary or ovaries.*—Superior.

This order, which is of wide distribution, contains in eight genera the water-lilies and their relatives, the water-shields, and the Indian lotus.

There are no true water-lilies west of the Mississippi region, but we have here in California the so-called common yellow pond-lily, *Nuphar.*

We have but two genera in this order, of which *Nuphar* is the more important.

ORDER IV.

Sarraceniaceæ. PITCHER-PLANT FAMILY.

Bog plants, with pitcher-shaped or tubular and hooded leaves. *Flowers.*—Solitary on long peduncles. *Sepals and petlas.*—Five. *Stamens.*—Many. *Ovary.*—Superior; five-celled. *Style.*—Five-lobed.

A small order of only three genera, viz.:—*Sarracenia,* of the Atlantic States, containing several species; *Heliamphora,* a little-known genus of the mountains of Guiana; and *Darlingtonia,* with its one species—our wonderful California pitcher-plant.

ORDER V.

Papaveraceæ. POPPY FAMILY.

Herbaceous, or, in one or two cases, shrubby plants, usually with milky or yellow juice and narcotic or acrid properties. *Leaves.*—Mostly alternate; without stipules; entire or divided. *Flowers.*—Perfect; usually solitary and nodding in the bud. *Sepals.*—Two or three; caducous. *Petals.*—Twice as many. *Stamens.*—Indefinite; numerous. *Ovary.*—Superior; one-celled (except in *Romneya,* where it is several-celled). Stigmas one to several. *Fruit.*—A capsule.

An order of about seventeen genera and one hundred and thirty species mostly inhabiting the temperate and warm parts of the Northern Hemisphere. Many have very showy ornamental flowers. The opium of commerce is derived from the milky juice of the poppy.

Of our eight genera, the most important are *Platystemon, Romneya, Argemone, Meconopsis, Dendromecon,* and *Eschscholtzia.*

ORDER VI.

Fumariaceæ. BLEEDING-HEART OR FUMITORY FAMILY.

Tender perennial herbs. *Leaves.*—Alternate; dissected; compound. *Flowers.*—Irregular. *Sepals.*—Two. *Petals.*—Four, in dissimilar pairs. *Stamens.*—Six. *Ovary.*—Superior; one-celled; several- to many-seeded.

A small order of six genera, which by some botanists has been united to PAPAVERACEÆ.

Dicentra is the best known genus. *D. spectabilis,* of northern China, is the beautiful, showy bleeding-heart of our gardens. The more important of our two Californian genera is *Dicentra.*

ORDER VII.

Cruciferæ. MUSTARD FAMILY.

Herbs. *Leaves.*—Alternate; without stipules. *Flowers.*—Usually in racemes. *Sepals.*—Four. *Petals.*—Four; usually with spreading blade and narrowed base or claw; the blades spreading to form a cross. *Stamens.* — Six. *Ovary.* — Superior; two-celled (rarely one-celled). Style one, and simple; or none. Stigma entire or two-lobed. *Fruit.*— A capsule whose two cells split at maturity away from a central partition.

A large family, containing upwards of one hundred and seventy-five genera and between one and two thousand species; distributed all over the world. It contains a number of our common food plants, such as the cabbage, Brussels sprouts, turnip, radish, horseradish, mustard, etc.

We have about thirty genera, of which the most important are *Dentaria, Arabis, Erysimum, Brassica, Capsella, Raphanus,* and *Nasturtium.*

ORDER VIII.

Capparidaceæ. Caper Family.

Herbs or shrubs. *Leaves.*—Alternate; simple or palmately compound. *Flowers.*—Perfect. *Sepals or lobes of the calyx.*—Four. *Petals.*—Four; clawed. *Stamens.*—Six (or sometimes numerous). *Ovary.*—One- or two-celled, usually raised on a stalk.

An order of twenty-four genera of warm temperate or tropical regions, closely related to Cruciferæ. The caper plant is the best known representative of the order. We have in the West six genera, all belonging to the dry interior regions save one, *Isomeris,* which is found upon the Coast, and is also our best-known genus.

ORDER IX.

Violaceæ. Violet Family.

With us low herbs. *Leaves.*—Alternate or radical; stipulate; simple or lobed or parted. *Flowers.*—Irregular. *Sepals.*—Five. *Petals.*—Five; one of them spurred. *Stamens.*—Five. Anthers connivent over the pistil. *Ovary.*—Superior; one-celled. Style club-shaped. Stigma one-sided. *Fruit.*—A capsule.

An order of twenty-five genera, most of which are tropical shrubs. The best-known genus of the order, however, *Viola,* has a number of species, found in Europe, Siberia, and North America, and furnishes us with the delightful violet of the garden, lately brought to such perfection under cultivation, as well as many charming wild species.

Viola is our only genus.

ORDER X.

Polygalaceæ. Milkwort Family.

Herbs or shrubs. *Leaves.* — Alternate; simple; entire; without stipules. *Flowers.*—Apparently papilionaceous, but not truly so; very irregular. *Sepals.*—Five; the two lateral larger, petaloid, winglike. *Petals.*—Three or five. *Stamens.*—Six to eight, coherent in one or two sets and with the petals. Anthers one-celled, opening at top.

Ovary.—Superior; two-celled; two-seeded. *Fruit.*—A capsule, narrowly winged.

A peculiar order, whose flowers superficially resemble those of the pea. It comprises fifteen genera, scattered throughout temperate and warm climates.

The type genus, *Polygala,* is the only one in our country well known.

ORDER XI.

Caryophyllaceæ. PINK FAMILY.

Herbs, usually with swollen joints. *Leaves.*—Opposite. *Flowers.*—Perfect; regular. *Sepals.*—Distinct, and four or five; or united, and four- or five-lobed. *Petals.*—Distinct; four or five; sometimes wanting. *Stamens.*—Ten or fewer. *Ovary.*—Superior; one-celled. Styles two to five. *Fruit.*—A capsule.

A large order of thirty-five or more genera, containing upward of a thousand species, distributed all over the world, but more abundantly in temperate and cold regions. Many are very beautiful, and are cultivated in our gardens, the most familiar being the pink. The order is more largely represented in western than in eastern North America. To it belong the chickweed, the sand-spurry, the sandwort, etc.

Our most important genus is *Silene,* of which we have nearly twenty species. We have eight other genera.

ORDER XII.

Portulacaceæ. PURSLANE FAMILY.

Herbs. *Leaves.* — Simple; entire; opposite, alternate, or radical. *Sepals.*—Two (except in *Lewisia*). *Petals.*—Two to five or more; sometimes united at base. *Stamens.*—Few or many. *Ovary.*—Superior; one-celled. Style two- to three-cleft. *Fruit.*—A capsule.

An order of fifteen genera, the greater part American, widely distributed over the world. The most familiar flower to most people is the common portulaca of the garden.

We have seven genera, most important of which are *Calandrinia, Montia, Spraguea,* and *Lewisia.*

ORDER XIII.

Hypericaceæ. St. John's-wort Family.

Herbs or shrubs. *Leaves.*—Opposite; entire; punctate with translucent or dark-colored, glandular dots. *Flowers.*—Yellow; in cymes. *Sepuls and petals.*—Four or five. *Stamens.*—Numerous, in three sets. *Ovary.*—Superior; three-celled. Styles three. *Fruit.*—A capsule.

A small order, widely dispersed, of which the largest genus is *Hypericum,* or St. John's-wort, our only Californian genus.

ORDER XIV.

Malvaceæ. Mallow Family.

Herbs or shrubs with mucilaginous juice. *Leaves.*—Alternate; with stipules; usually palmately ribbed. *Calyx.*—Five-parted; sometimes having an extra calyx or whorl of bractlets. *Petals.*—Five; persistent; their bases united with each other and with the column of stamens. *Stamens.*—Numerous; united in a column. Anthers one-celled. *Ovaries.*—Superior, and either a number of ovaries in a ring around a projection of the receptacle, from which they separate at maturity, or one single ovary, three- to ten-celled. Styles united into one, at least at base.

A rather large order, distributed widely over the world. From the root of *Althæa officinalis* is obtained a mucilaginous substance used in the manufacture of marsh-mallows. This order also furnishes the highly important cotton-plant of commerce, *Gossypium.*

Of our eight genera, the best known are *Lavatera, Malva, Sidalcea,* and *Malvastrum.*

ORDER XV.

Sterculiaceæ. Sterculia Family.

A tropical order of shrubs and trees, closely related to Malvaceæ, but chiefly distinguished by their two-celled anthers. Our only genus is *Fremontodendron,* formerly *Fremontia.*

ORDER XVI.

Linaceæ. FLAX FAMILY.

Herbs. *Leaves.*—Simple; entire; alternate or opposite. *Flowers.*—Regular. *Sepals, petals, and stamens.*—Five. *Petals.*—Rolled up in the bud. *Ovary.*—Superior; four- to ten-celled. Styles two to five.

A small order, whose only important representative in temperate regions is the common flax, *Linum.*

Linum is our only genus.

ORDER XVII.

Zygophyllaceæ. CREOSOTE-BUSH OR BEAN CAPER FAMILY.

Herbs, shrubs, or trees. *Leaves.*—Opposite; mostly compound; stipulate. *Flowers.*—Solitary; perfect; regular; with their parts in fives, or rarely fours. *Sepals.*—Distinct or nearly so. *Stamens.*—In ours twice as many as the petals and inserted with them in two sets. Filaments distinct or nearly so; often with a scale on the inner side. *Ovary.*—Superior; with two to five carpels; or sometimes with twice as many cells. Style one. Stigma five- to ten-lobed. *Fruit.*—Dry.

An order chiefly tropical, containing about eighteen genera. They are mostly shrubs, or herbs with a woody base, whose wood is remarkable for its hardness. Their divaricate branches are jointed at their nodes. The guaiacum-tree furnishes the lignum vitæ of commerce, also gum guaiacum.

"Some of the family are so abundant in the Egyptian desert as to constitute a characteristic feature of its vegetation."

We have three genera in California, only one of which, *Larrea,* is wide-spread or well known.

ORDER XVIII.

Geraniaceæ. GERANIUM FAMILY.

Herbaceous plants or shrubs (ours all herbs), usually with swollen joints. *Leaves.*—Often with stipules; toothed, lobed or compound. *Flowers.*—Perfect; on axillary peduncles; regular or irregular, but generally symmetrical; with their parts in fives. *Stamens.*—Mostly in two sets, those alternate with the petals sometimes sterile. Filaments often either dilated or united in one set at the base. *Ovary.*—Superior; three- to five-lobed and celled, with a central axis.

An order of four genera, but about five hundred species; of wide distribution. It is specially characterized by the arrangement of the carpels around a central axis with long beak. Many have showy and handsome flowers and are cultivated, such as the numerous geraniums and pelargoniums.

In California our only genera are *Genanium, Erodium, Flœrkea,* and *Oxalis.*

ORDER XIX.

Rhamnaceæ. BUCKTHORN FAMILY.

Shrubs or small trees. *Leaves.*—Simple with small often caducous stipules. *Flowers.*—Regular; small. *Calyx.*—Four- or five-lobed. *Petals.*—Four or five or sometimes wanting. *Stamens.*—Equaling the number of petals and opposite them. *Ovary.*—Two- to four-celled; either free or adnate to the base of the calyx. Style or stigma two- to four-lobed. *Fruit.*—Berry-like, or drupelike, or dry.

An order of between thirty and forty genera and four or five hundred species, widely distributed over the world. From certain of our species of *Rhamnus* is manufactured the famous cascara sagrada, and from a certain species of *Zizyphus* is obtained the basis of jujube paste.

Our most important genera are *Rhamnus* and *Ceanothus,* although we have three others.

ORDER XX.

Sapindaceæ. MAPLE FAMILY.

This order comprises plants of widely different characters arranged under several sub-orders,—SAPINDACEÆ proper, ACERINÆ, and STAPHYLACEÆ,—which by some authorities have been considered as separate orders. It is therefore difficult to describe it as a whole.

As, of our five genera, *Æsculus* is the only one given in this work, the sub-order to which it belongs will be described.

SAPINDACEÆ PROPER.

Leaves.—Alternate, sometimes opposite; without stipules; mostly compound. *Flowers.*—Polygamous,—*i. e.* having both perfect and unisexual flowers upon the same plant; irregular and unsymmetrical. *Sepals and petals.*—Four or five. *Stamens.*—Five to ten. *Ovary*—Superior; two- to three-celled, with one or two ovules in each cell. *Fruit.*—In *Æsculus* a leathery pod.

To the order, as a whole, belong the maple and the box-elder (under ACERINÆ), and the buckeye and horse-chestnut (under SAPINDACEÆ).

ORDER XXI.

Anacardiaceæ. POISON-OAK OR SUMACH FAMILY.

Shrubs or trees with a resinous and usually acrid juice. *Leaves.*—Alternate; simple or compound; without stipules. *Flowers.*—Small; regular, with their parts mostly in fives; commonly polygamous or diœcious. *Ovary.*—Superior; one-celled and one-ovuled. Styles often three. *Fruit.*—Drupaceous.

This is a large order of nearly fifty genera and four or five hundred species.

The pistachio-nut is the product of *Pistacia vera;* the cashew-nut, and the pepper-tree cultivated in the South— *Schinus Molle*—belong here; also various species of *Rhus,* from which the wonderful Japanese lacquers are made.

Our only genus is *Rhus.*

ORDER XXII.

Leguminosæ. PEA FAMILY.

The order LEGUMINOSÆ is divided into three well-marked sub-orders—the Pea family proper, the Brasiletto family, and the Mimosa family. But as all our genera, save *Cercis,* fall under the first, we shall describe that only.

PAPILIONACEÆ. PEA FAMILY PROPER.

Herbs, shrubs, or trees. *Leaves.*—Usually alternate; compound; with stipules; the latter sometimes transformed into thorns or tendrils. *Flowers.* — Seldom solitary; usually in spikes, racemes, or umbels. *Calyx.*—Five-toothed; often bilabiate. *Corolla.*—Irregular; of five petals; *papilionaceous—i. e.* the two lower petals more or less cohe-rent, forming the *keel;* the two lateral ones often adherent to the keel, called the *wings;* the upper petal called the *standard* or *banner.* Sta-mens and pistil inclosed in the keel. *Stamens.*—Ten; their filaments either coherent into a tube surrounding the pistil; or nine of them united into a sheath, open above, the tenth lying in front of the cleft; or rarely all distinct. *Ovary.*—Superior; one-celled. *Style.*—Simple and incurved. *Stigma.*—Simple. *Fruit.*—A two-valved pod, of which the garden pea is typical.

The Pea family, including its three sub-orders, is one of the most important plant-families known. It is distributed over almost the entire world, and furnishes some of the most valu-able products to man. The Judas-tree, the numerous acacias, and the sweet-pea, are well known in our gardens; while among our most valuable vegetables are the bean, the pea, and the lentil. The clover and alfalfa are extremely important forage plants.

The order furnishes several important timber-trees, in dif-ferent parts of the world, such as the rosewood, the laburnum, and the locust; and yields numerous products of economic importance, such as licorice, senna, gum Senegal, gum Arabic, gum tragacanth, balsam of copaiba, balsam of Tolu, indigo, logwood, red sandalwood, etc.

In California we have twenty-one genera, the most important of which are *Thermopsis, Xylothermia, Amorpha, Lupinus, Melilotus, Medicago, Hosackia (Lotus), Astragalus, Vicia, Lathyrus, Cercis,* etc.

ORDER XXIII.

Rosaceæ. ROSE FAMILY.

Herbs, shrubs, or trees. *Leaves.*—Alternate; usually with stipules; simple or compound. *Flowers.*—Regular; mostly with their parts in fives; red, white, or yellow, never blue. *Calyx.*—Sometimes coherent with the carpels. *Stamens.*—Usually numerous. *Pistils.*—One to many; distinct and separate; or one with an inferior, one- to several-celled ovary.

A large order, comprising over seventy genera and a thou-sand species. It is distributed over the temperate regions and

lxiv

extends into the tropics, but its chief home is the north temperate zone. It contains many of our best fruits, such as the apple, pear, peach, plum, cherry, apricot, strawberry, raspberry, and blackberry; also many of our commonest ornamental shrubs, chief among which is the garden rose, which has been brought to such a wondrous perfection through centuries of cultivation. The *Quillaia saponaria* of the tropics yields the soap-bark of commerce.

Of our twenty-eight genera, the chief are *Prunus, Nuttallia, Holodiscus* (or *Spiræa*), *Neillia, Rubus, Chamæbatia, Cercocarpus, Fragaria, Potentilla, Adenostoma, Rosa, Heteromeles, Amelanchier,* etc.

ORDER XXIV.

Calycanthaceæ. Sweet-shrub Family.

Aromatic shrubs. *Leaves.*—Opposite; entire; without stipules. *Sepals, petals, and stamens.*—Indefinite and passing into one another; all coalescent below into a cup bearing on its inner surface numerous simple pistils, becoming akenes in fruit.

An order of two genera only—our *Calycanthus,* comprising in North America three species, and the Japanese genus, *Chimonanthus,* having but one species.

ORDER XXV.

Saxifragaceæ. Saxifrage Family.

Herbs, shrubs, or sometimes small trees. *Leaves.*—Mostly alternate or radical; without stipules. *Flowers.*—With parts in fives. *Petals.*—Distinct. *Stamens.*—Usually definite, not more than twice the number of calyx-lobes. *Pistils.*—Two to five, mostly united into a compound ovary, mainly superior. Styles inclined to be distinct. *Fruit.*—A capsule.

A large order of eighty-seven or more genera, containing five or six hundred species. It is mainly of the cooler regions of the world, particularly in the Northern Hemisphere. Of this order are the currant and gooseberry, also many ornamental flowers of our gardens, such as the *Hydrangea, Deutzia, Philadelphus, Heuchera,* and *Saxifraga.*

We have thirteen genera, the most important of which are *Saxifraga, Boykinia, Lithophragma, Tellima, Heuchera, Philadelphus, Whipplea,* and *Ribes.*

ORDER XXVI.

Crassulaceæ. Stonecrop or Orpine Family.

Succulent or fleshy plants. *Flowers.*—Regular; with the sepals, petals, stamens, and pistils all distinct and of the same number, three to twelve (or the stamens twice as many). *Carpels.*—Becoming follicles in fruit.

An order of about a dozen genera and over four hundred species, mostly inhabitants of temperate regions, and growing in hot, dry, exposed places. The order is not of any special economic importance, but some of its species are cultivated for their showy flowers or for their ornamental foliage, which is valuable for bedding purposes. South Africa is specially rich in species, and our western coast of North America has quite a number.

Of our four genera, the most important are *Dudleya* and *Stylophyllum* (both formerly included in *Cotyledon*), and *Sedum.*

ORDER XXVII.

Onagraceæ. Evening-Primrose Family.

Herbs, or, in warmer regions, one or two genera of shrubs. *Leaves.* —Alternate or opposite; without stipules; usually simple, though sometimes lobed or divided. *Flowers.*—Perfect; regular; their parts mostly in fours. *Calyx-tube.*—Adnate to the ovary; its free border lobed and often colored. *Stamens.*—As many or twice as many as the petals. *Ovary.*—Inferior; having as many cells as there are petals. Style single. Stigma capitate, or with as many lobes as there are ovary-cells.

An order containing over three hundred species in about thirty genera, widely distributed over the temperate regions of the world, although North America is richer in them than any other region. Some of the species are cultivated for their beautiful flowers, the most familiar example being the garden fuchsia. Many *Œnotheras* open their flowers at night, and so are known as "evening primroses." We have many beautiful flowers in this order native to California.

We have fourteen genera, the most important of which are *Zauschneria, Epilobium, Œnothera, Godetia,* and *Clarkia.*

ORDER XXVIII.

Loasaceæ. BLAZING-STAR OR LOASA FAMILY.

Herbaceous plants with either stinging or jointed and rough-barbed hairs. *Leaves.*—Opposite or alternate; without stipules; more or less divided. *Flowers.*—Solitary, on axillary peduncles. *Calyx.*—Adherent to the inferior one-celled ovary; its border four- or five-parted. *Petals.* —Five or ten. *Stamens.*—Numerous. Style single.

An order chiefly American, comprising about a dozen genera with over a hundred species, some of which are cultivated for their ornamental flowers.

Our most important genus is *Mentzelia,* though we have two others.

ORDER XXIX.

Cucurbitaceæ. GOURD FAMILY.

Herbs, mostly tendril-bearing and climbing. *Leaves.*—Alternate; palmately veined or lobed; without stipules. *Flowers.*—Monœcious or diœcious. *Petals.*—Commonly merged with the calyx and united into a perianth which is several-lobed. *Sterile flowers.*—Having two two-celled anthers and one one-celled; the cells usually long and contorted. *Fertile flowers.*—Having the calyx-tube adnate to a one- to three-celled ovary. Stigma lobed or parted.

A large order of eighty genera and six hundred species; widely distributed over the world, mainly in warm regions. Familiar to every one are the melon, watermelon, cucumber, pumpkin, squash, and gourd. The roots of many species, as well as the fleshy fruits of some, are strong purgatives.

Of our three genera, the most important are *Cucurbita* and *Echinocystis (Megarrhiza).*

ORDER XXX.

Cactaceæ. Cactus Family.

Fleshy, leafless plants of peculiar aspect; globular or columnar; ribbed or jointed; usually armed with bundles of spines. *Flowers.*—Often showy and beautiful. *Sepals, petals, and stamens.*—Numerous; their cohering bases united with the walls of the inferior, one-celled ovary. Style one, with several stigmas. *Fruit.*—Pulpy, or rarely a dry berry.

An order exclusively American, having a great many species contained in fifteen or twenty genera. The species are inhabiters of hot, dry regions, where they are able to subsist because of the imperfect evaporating pores of their skin, which enables them to conserve their moisture. They are interesting plants, largely cultivated in gardens, and many of them have very beautiful flowers. Some of them furnish forage for animals in regions otherwise barren of vegetation.

ORDER XXXI.

Ficoideæ. Fig-Marigold Family.

Fleshy, succulent plants. *Leaves.*—Mostly opposite; without stipules. *Calyx.*—Five-lobed. *Petals.*—Numerous. *Stamens.*—Numerous. *Ovary.*—Inferior; two- to many-celled.

A small order, mainly tropical and sub-tropical, of the Old World. Its species are most abundant in the hot sandy plains of the Cape of Good Hope. The leaves and seeds of some species are used as food by the natives of the countries of their growth, and a few others have some slight economic uses. We have one or two insignificant native genera and one supposedly introduced. Two species of the latter, *Mesembryanthemum,* are found abundantly on our seashore.

ORDER XXXII.

Umbelliferæ. Parsley Family.

Herbs with usually hollow stems. *Leaves.*—Mainly alternate and compound; with the base of the petiole sheathing the stem. *Flowers.*—Small; in umbels (generally compound umbels). *Calyx.*—Adnate to the ovary. *Petals.* — Five. *Stamens.* — Five. *Ovary.* — Inferior; two-celled. Styles two. *Fruit.*—Splitting into a pair of dry carpels.

A large order of about two hundred genera and over a thousand species, distributed all over the world, but most abundant in warm or temperate regions. Many are poisonous, such as the hemlock and water-hemlock. Among useful garden vegetables are the parsnip, carrot, and celery. The pleasant-flavored dill, fennel, caraway, and anise also belong to this order.

As this is a very difficult order for the amateur botanist, it has seemed best to omit from this work the plants belonging to it, and the student is advised to consult the regular systematic botanies for them.

ORDER XXXIII.

Araliaceæ. GINSENG FAMILY.

Resembling UMBELLIFERÆ, but differing in having the stems often woody, the umbels not regularly compound, the styles and carpels more than two, and the fruit fleshy (berry-like or drupelike).

An order of twenty-one genera and one hundred species, inhabiters of tropical and sub-tropical regions. Many plants of the order are medicinal and yield various drugs, prominent among which is the famous ginseng, so highly prized by the Chinese. The common English ivy of our gardens belongs to this order.

We have in California but one genus, *Aralia* (spikenard), containing only one species.

ORDER XXXIV.

Cornaceæ. DOGWOOD FAMILY.

Trees or shrubs, rarely herbs. *Leaves.*—Simple; entire; mainly opposite; without stipules. *Flowers.*—Perfect and cymose; or diœcious and in aments or catkins; with parts in fours or fives. *Calyx.*—Adnate to the one- or two-celled, inferior ovary. *Petals.*—Distinct. *Stamens.*—Four. Style and stigma simple. *Fruit.*—A berry.

An order of a dozen or so genera and something less than a hundred species, mainly of the temperate regions of the world.   Many species are cultivated for ornament, and the bark of some has the properties of quinine.

Our only genera are *Cornus* and *Garrya*.

ORDER XXXV.

Caprifoliaceæ.   HONEYSUCKLE FAMILY.

Shrubs, rarely herbs. *Leaves.*—Opposite; without stipules. *Calyx.*—Four- to five-cleft. *Corolla.*—Gamopetalous; four- to five-cleft; sometimes irregular. *Stamens.*—Four or five; distinct. *Ovary.*—Inferior; two- to five-celled (sometimes one-celled). Style one. Stigmas three or five.

An order of about a dozen genera and two hundred species, mainly of the north temperate zone.   It is of small economic importance, but gives us the honeysuckles and some other plants for ornamental cultivation.

Our more important genera are *Sambucus, Symphoricarpus,* and *Lonicera*.

ORDER XXXVI.

Rubiaceæ.   MADDER FAMILY.

Herbs or shrubs (or in the tropics trees). *Leaves.*—Opposite, with stipules; or whorled, without stipules. *Flowers.*—Perfect. *Calyx and corolla.*—Four- to five-lobed or toothed; the limb of the calyx sometimes obsolete. *Stamens.*—As many as the corolla-lobes. *Ovary.*—Inferior; two- to five-celled. *Style.*—One; entire or cleft.

One of the largest orders of flowering plants, having upwards of four thousand five hundred species contained in three hundred and seventy-three genera.   Its representatives are mostly tropical, though a few are of the temperate zones. The order is of great economic importance, and yields many valuable products, largely medicinal, among them quinine.   Of it is the coffee-plant, also the madder-plant, which yields a number of rich dyes.   The *Gardenias* and *Bouvardias* of our gardens also belong here.

We have only three genera, the most important of which are *Cephalanthus* and *Galium*.

lxx

ORDER XXXVII.

Valerianaceæ. VALERIAN FAMILY.

Herbs. *Leaves.*—Opposite; without stipules. *Flowers.*—Perfect or diœcious. *Calyx-tube.*—Consolidated with the inferior ovary; its limb sometimes obsolete, sometimes composed of teeth, chaff, or bristles. *Corolla.*—Tubular or funnel-form; often irregular; its limb three- to five-cleft. *Ovary.*—Three-celled, with only one perfect cell. Style filiform. Stigmas one to three. *Fruit.*—A dry akene.

An order of nine genera and three hundred species, mainly of the temperate and frigid zones; of small economic importance. The drug valerian is the product of one species.

We have two genera, of which *Valeriana* is best known.

ORDER XXXVIII.

Dipsaceæ. TEASEL FAMILY.

Leaves.—Opposite, or whorled; without stipules. *Flowers.*—In dense heads surrounded by an involucre. Each flower inclosed in a special, scarious, small calyx-like involucel. *Calyx.*—With tube adherent to the ovary, and border pappus-like, of bristles. *Corolla.*—Inserted in the throat of the calyx; tubular, with somewhat irregular, four- to five-parted limb. *Stamens.*—Four; alternate with the corolla-lobes, distinct. *Ovary.*—Inferior; one-celled. Style one, simple. *Fruit.*—Dry; indehiscent.

An order of six genera and one hundred and fifty species, all natives of temperate regions of the Eastern Hemisphere, and of very small importance. The order is closely allied to COMPOSITÆ, from which it differs mainly in its distinct stamens. The scabiosa of our gardens and the common teasel are its best-known plants.

We have no native genera, our only representative being the introduced teasel (*Dipsacus*).

ORDER XXXIX.

Compositæ. COMPOSITE FAMILY.

Herbs, rarely shrubs. *Leaves.*—Usually alternate; without stipules. *Flowers.*—In a close head on a common *receptacle,* surrounded by an *involucre,* whose divisions are called *scales* or *bracts. Calyx-tube.*—Adnate to the one-celled ovary; its limb (called a *pappus*) crowning its summit in the form of bristles, awns, scales, teeth, etc.; or cup-shaped; or else entirely absent. *Corolla.*—Either strap-shaped or tubular; in the latter chiefly five-lobed. *Stamens.*—Five (rarely four); on the corolla; their anthers united in a tube. *Style.*—Two-cleft at the apex. *Ovary.*—Inferior; one-celled. *Fruit.*—An akene. Flowers with strap-shaped corollas are called *ray-flowers* or *rays*. The *tubular flowers* compose the disk.

The Composite family is the largest of all plant families, numbering twelve thousand species and upward, and is widely distributed over the world.

In the cooler regions the plants are mostly herbaceous, but toward the tropics they gradually become shrubs, and even trees. In North America they comprise about one-sixth of all the flowering plants.

For so large a family there are comparatively few useful plants found in it. Among the products of the order may be mentioned chicory, lettuce, the artichoke, the vegetable oyster, arnica, chamomile-flowers, wormwood, absinth, elecampane, coltsfoot, taraxacum, oil of tansy, etc. But our gardens owe to this family innumerable beautiful and showy plants—such as the China aster, chrysanthemum, cosmos, zinnia, dahlia, ageratum, gaillardia, coreopsis, sunflower, etc.

The plants of this family are quickly recognized by the flowers being always borne in a head and surrounded by an involucre, and presenting the appearance of a single flower. The heads are sometimes made up entirely of one kind of flower. The dandelion and the chicory are examples of a head made up entirely of ray-flowers, while in the thistle the head consists of tubular flowers only. The more common arrangement, however, is the mixed one, comprising both tubular disk-flowers and strap-shaped rays, as in the daisy. The seeds are usually furnished with silken down or a delicate parachute to waft them abroad.

The identification of the flowers of this order is a very difficult matter, even for experienced botanists.

Our most important genera are *Grindelia, Pentachæta, Les-*

singia, Solidago, Aster, Erigeron, Baccharis, Anaphalis, Gna-phalium, Balsamorrhiza, Wyethia, Encelia, Helianthus, Lep-tosyne, Madia, Hemizonia, Layia, Venegasia, Baeria, Achillea, Artemisia, Cotula, Malacothrix, and *Troximon.*

ORDER XL.

Lobeliaceæ. LOBELIA FAMILY.

Herbs. *Leaves.*—Alternate; simple. *Flowers.*—Scattered, or in racemes; perfect. *Calyx.*—With five-lobed limb. *Corolla.*—Irregular; five-lobed; apparently bilabiate. *Stamens.*—Five, with their filaments united into a tube and their anthers into a ring. *Ovary.*—One- or two-celled; inferior. Style entire. Stigma commonly two-lobed and ringed with hairs. *Fruit.*—A capsule.

An order of twenty-eight genera and five hundred and forty species, distributed over the world with the exception of the frigid zones. Many of the species contain active poisons, and are dangerous plants.

We have four genera, chief of which are *Bolelia* (*Dow-ningia*) and *Lobelia.*

ORDER XLI.

Campanulaceæ. HAREBELL OR CAMPANULA FAMILY.

Herbs with milky juice. *Leaves.*—Alternate; without stipules. *Flowers.*—Regular; parts in fives; usually blue, sometimes white. *Calyx.*—With tube adherent to the ovary and lobes free. *Corolla.*—Gamopetalous; campanulate or rotate. *Stamens.*—Five; alternate with the corolla-lobes. *Ovary.*—Two- to five-celled; inferior. Style single; hairy above. Stigma two- to five-cleft. *Fruit.*—A capsule.

A small order, chiefly of temperate regions, important only as furnishing some ornamental plants to the garden, chief of which is the Canterbury-bell, *Campanula medium.*

The chief genus of the order in California, as elsewhere, is *Campanula.* To this genus belong the beautiful "bluebells of Scotland" and the various charming bell-flowers of the Swiss Alps.

ORDER XLII.

Ericaceæ. HEATH FAMILY.

Woody plants or perennial herbs. *Leaves.*—Simple; usually alternate (though sometimes opposite or whorled or entirely wanting). *Flowers.* —Mostly regular, with parts in fours or fives. *Calyx.*—Gamosepalous. *Corolla.*—Mostly gamopetalous, though in some polypetalous. *Stamens.* —As many or twice as many as the corolla-lobes. Anthers two-celled; opening by terminal pores. *Ovary.*—Superior or mainly so; usually with as many cells as petals or corolla-lobes. Style single. *Fruit.*—A capsule or berry.

A large order containing seventy-three genera and thirteen hundred species, natives of temperate and cold regions.

It is divided into four sub-orders, which by some authorities are considered separate orders. They are:—VACCINIEÆ, American shrubs, characterized by their inferior ovary and berry-like fruit; ERICINEÆ, shrubs or trees, with superior ovary, gamopetalous corolla, and introrse anthers; PYROLEÆ, mostly herbs, with polypetalous corolla, extrorse anthers, and superior ovary; MONOTROPEÆ, herbaceous root parasites, without green herbage.

Two genera of VACCINIEÆ furnish the huckleberry, blueberry, and cranberry. The sub-order ERICINEÆ contains a number of very important genera, of which are *Erica* (heath), *Rhododendron* (rhododendron and azalea), *Gaultheria, Kalmia, Arbutus,* etc. Of the sub-order PYROLEÆ, the most important genera are *Pyrola* and *Chimaphila*. The sub-order MONOTROPEÆ contains *Monotropa* (the Indian-pipe) and *Sarcodes* (the snow-plant).

Of our twenty Californian genera, the most important are *Vaccinium, Arbutus, Arctostaphylos, Gaultheria, Cassiope, Bryanthus, Rhododendron, Ledum, Chimaphila, Pyrola, Pterospora,* and *Sarcodes.*

ORDER XLIII.

Primulaceæ. PRIMROSE FAMILY.

Herbs. *Leaves.*—Simple, mainly entire, without stipules. *Flowers.*— Regular; gamopetalous. *Calyx and corolla.*—Each four- to eight-cleft, mostly five-cleft. *Stamens.*—As many as the corolla-lobes and opposite them, on its tube. Anthers two-celled, opening lengthwise. *Ovary.*— One-celled. Style and stigma entire. *Fruit.*—A capsule.

An order of about twenty-five genera and over three hundred species, of temperate regions, mainly alpine. Many highly prized flowers of our gardens belong to this order, such as the primrose, cowslip, polyanthus, auricula, cyclamen, and soldinelle.

Of our eight Californian genera, the most important are *Dodecatheon, Primula, Trientalis,* and *Anagallis.*

ORDER XLIV.

Apocynaceæ. Dogbane Family.

Herbs, shrubs, or trees (ours herbs) with milky juice. *Leaves.*— Opposite; entire; without stipules. *Flowers.*—Regular, with their parts in fives. *Corolla.*—Gamopetalous. *Stamens.*—Five, on the corolla alternate with its lobes. Anthers disposed to cohere with the stigma. Pollen of distinct powdery grains. *Ovaries.*—Two; distinct; superior. Styles and stigmas two, more or less united. *Fruit.*—A pair of pods.

An order of a hundred genera and over five hundred species, largely tropical and closely allied to the milkweeds. The species have a milky acrid juice that is often poisonous. India-rubber is obtained from several different plants of the order; others furnish valuable woods to the cabinetmaker and wood-carver and various medicinal barks and edible fruits, as well as very useful textile fibers. The oleander (*Nerium*), periwinkle (*Vinca*), and Chile jasmine (*Mandevilla*), common in our gardens, belong to this order.

Of our two Californian genera, *Apocynum* is the more important.

ORDER XLV.

Asclepiadaceæ. Milkweed Family.

Herbs (at least in the temperate regions) with milky juice.

In structure this order closely resembles Apocynaceæ, from which it differs chiefly in having the pollen in each anther-cell in one solid waxy mass, instead of in powdery grains.

lxxv

The order contains upwards of one hundred and forty genera and over nine hundred species. It is distributed over temperate and tropical regions, and its species yield many medicinal products. It includes the wax-plant (*Hoya*) and some other handsome greenhouse plants, the carrion-flower (*Stapelia*), and the milkweed (*Asclepias*), which has some interesting peculiarities of structure.

Of our four Californian genera, *Asclepias* and *Gompho-carpus* are the most important.

ORDER XLVI.

Gentianaceæ. Gentian Family.

Herbs with colorless, bitter juice. *Leaves.*—Opposite; entire; sessile; without stipules. *Flowers.*—Regular; perfect; with parts in fours or fives. *Corolla.*—Gamopetalous. *Stamens.*—As many as the corolla-lobes and alternate with them. *Ovary.*—One-celled. Style single or none. Stigmas usually two.

An order of about fifty genera and five hundred species, widely distributed over the world. Bitterness in every part is a characteristic feature of the plants of this order, which furnish many valued remedies to the pharmacopœia, chiefly bitter tonics. The gentians are the best known plants of the order, and are found in temperate or alpine regions, though singularly lacking in the polar regions. *G. crinita* is the beautiful "fringed gentian" of eastern North America.

Of our five Californian genera, *Gentiana* and *Erythræa* are the most important.

ORDER XLVII.

Polemoniaceæ. Phlox or Polemonium Family.

Herbs with bland, colorless juice. *Leaves.*—Simple or divided; without stipules. *Flowers.*—Regular; with parts in fives. *Corolla.*—Gamopetalous. *Stamens.*—On the corolla, alternate with its lobes. Anthers introrse. *Ovary.*—Superior; three-celled. Style three-lobed. *Fruit.*—A capsule.

An order of few genera, but upward of one hundred and fifty species, mainly natives of the western parts of temperate

North and South America. It is of no special importance, except as furnishing a few bright and beautiful flowers for cultivation. *Phlox Drummondi,* of Texas, has long been familiar in our gardens, and *Cobeæ scandens,* a handsome climber of Mexico, is becoming almost equally well known.

Of our four Californian genera, the most important are *Phlox, Gilia,* and *Polemonium.*

ORDER XLVIII.

Hydrophyllaceæ. BABY-EYES OR WATERLEAF FAMILY.

Mostly herbs—a few shrubby. *Leaves.*—Mainly alternate, although sometimes opposite; no stipules. *Flowers.*—Sometimes solitary, but mostly in scorpioid or coiled racemes or spikes; perfect; regular; with parts in fives. *Calyx.*—Five-parted or of five separate sepals. *Corolla.*—Gamopetalous. *Stamens.*—On the corolla-tube, alternate with its lobes. *Ovary.*—Superior; one- to two-celled. Styles two, distinct or partially united (wholly so in *Romanzoffia*). *Fruit.*—A capsule.

An order of about sixteen genera and one hundred and fifty species, nearly all North American, and most abundant in Western North America. The order is of no economic importance, but several Californian species are commonly cultivated.

We have a dozen genera, the most important of which are *Nemophila, Ellisia, Phacelia, Emmenanthe, Romanzoffia,* and *Eriodictyon.*

ORDER XLIX.

Boraginaceæ. FORGET-ME-NOT OR BORAGE FAMILY.

Mostly rough, pubescent herbs. *Leaves.*—Alternate; entire; without stipules. *Flowers.*—In scorpioid spikes or racemes; perfect; regular; with their parts in fives. *Calyx.*—Five-cleft or five-parted. *Corolla.*—Gamopetalous. *Stamens.*—On the corolla throat, alternate with its lobes. *Ovary.*—Superior; four-lobed; separating at maturity into four seedlike nutlets. Style single.

A rather large order, having sixty or seventy genera and upwards of six hundred species. It is of wide distribution, but is best represented in the temperate regions of the Northern

Hemisphere. It is of slight importance, although the roots of several species contain a reddish brown dye and a few are medicinal. The heliotrope and forget-me-not of our gardens belong to this order. Of our eleven Californian genera, the most important are *Heliotropium, Amsinckia, Lappula, Cynoglossum,* and *Plagiobothrys.*

ORDER L.

Convolvulaceæ. MORNING-GLORY OR CONVOLVULUS FAMILY.

Herbs, commonly twining or trailing (or, in warm climates, shrubs). *Leaves.*—Alternate. *Flowers.*—Regular; perfect; usually large and showy; opening but once. *Calyx.*—Mostly of distinct sepals. *Corolla.* —Gamopetalous; with four or five lobes or angles. *Stamens.*—As many as the lobes of the corolla and alternate with them. *Ovary.*—Superior; two- to three-celled; the cells sometimes divided. Styles one or two.

An order of about thirty genera and six hundred and sixty species, very abundantly found in the tropics, but rare in cold regions. It is not of great economic importance. The roots of many and the seeds of some are used as purgatives. The morning-glory of our gardens and the common sweet potato (*Ipomœa Batatas*) belong to this order, also the bindweed and dodder, among common weeds.

We have three genera in this order, the most important of which are *Convolvulus* and *Cuscuta.*

ORDER LI.

Solanaceæ. NIGHTSHADE FAMILY.

Mostly herbs or shrubs. *Leaves.*—Alternate; without stipules. *Flowers.*—Regular with their parts in fives. *Calyx.*—Five-cleft. *Corolla.* —Gamopetalous; plicate or folded in bud. *Stamens.*—Five. *Ovary.*— Two-celled; superior. Style single. *Fruit.*—A many-seeded berry or capsule.

An order of wide distribution in the warmer parts of the world, and containing sixty genera and nine hundred species. The plants of this order are usually of rank odor, and most of them contain narcotic properties, among them the belladonna, tobacco, henbane, stramonium, and nightshade. A few furnish useful foods, such as the potato, the tomato, and the egg-plant, and one is a much used condiment—capsicum, or red pepper. Familiar in our gardens are the petunia, the salpiglossis, floriponda, and several ornamental species of nicotiana, or tobacco.

Of our ten native genera, the most important are *Solanum, Datura,* and *Nicotiana.*

ORDER LII.

Scrophulariaceæ. FIGWORT FAMILY.

Herbs, sometimes shrubs. *Leaves.*—Opposite, whorled, or alternate. *Flowers.*—Perfect; solitary and axillary, or in racemes. *Calyx.*—Of five or four distinct or variously united sepals. *Corolla.*—Gamopetalous; four- or five-lobed or cleft; usually bilabiate. *Stamens.*—On the corolla; four, in pairs; or only two—the fifth and upper and sometimes the two lateral absent or reduced to sterile filaments or mere rudiments; rarely (as in *Verbascum*) all five present and fertile. *Ovary.*—Superior; two-celled. Style single. Stigma entire or two-lobed.

A large order of over one hundred and fifty genera, distributed over all parts of the world. Some are medicinal, such as *Digitalis* (the foxglove), and many are well-known ornamental plants in our gardens or greenhouses, such as the snapdragon, collinsia, foxglove, pentstemon, mimulus, calceolaria, etc.

This order is generously represented in California, as we have nineteen genera, the most important of which are *Verbascum, Linaria, Antirrhinum, Scrophularia, Collinsia, Pentstemon, Mimulus, Veronica, Castilleia, Orthocarpus,* and *Pedicularis.*

ORDER LIII.

Orobanchaceæ. BROOM-RAPE FAMILY.

Root-parasitic herbs, destitute of chlorophyll and green leaves. *Stems.* —Having dry or fleshy scales in place of leaves. Distinguished from SCROPHULARIACEÆ by its one-celled ovary.

A small order of the north temperate zone, comprising about a dozen genera and one hundred and fifty species. Several genera furnish medicines, and one yields a black dye. The order is, however, of small importance.

Of our two Californian genera, *Aphyllon* is the more important.

ORDER LIV.

Labiatæ. MINT FAMILY.

Mostly aromatic herbs with square stems. *Leaves.*—Opposite; simple; without stipules. *Flowers.*—Perfect. *Calyx.*—Three- to five-cleft or bilabiate. *Corolla.*—Bilabiate; the upper lip usually two-lobed or entire and the lower three-cleft or -parted. *Stamens.*—On the tube of the corolla; four in pairs, or two. *Ovary.*—Superior; four-lobed. Style single.

A large order of one hundred and twenty-five genera and over two thousand species, most abundantly represented in warm temperate regions. All the plants of this order are harmless; some are used in medicine or for condiments, and others are cultivated for their beautiful flowers. The familiar sage, pennyroyal, marjoram, thyme, catmint, spearmint, peppermint, etc., belong to this order.

We have eighteen genera in California, the chief of which are *Monardella, Micromeria, Sphacele, Salvia, Audibertia, Brunella, Marrubium, Stachys,* and *Trichostema.*

ORDER LV.

Nyctaginaceæ. FOUR-O'CLOCK FAMILY.

Herbs (or rarely woody plants). *Stems.*—Slender; with swollen joints. *Leaves.*—Entire; without stipules; mostly opposite. *Flowers.*—Perfect; often with a calyx-like involucre. *Calyx.*—Corolla-like; tubular to campanulate; its base constricted over the ovary and in fruit becoming thick and hard, inclosing the akene. *Corolla*—Wanting. *Stamens.*—Few. Filaments slender. Anthers rounded. *Ovary.*—One-celled; apparently inferior. Style and stigma simple. *Fruit.*—An akene.

An order of about twenty genera and one hundred or more species, found chiefly in the tropics, although one or two genera extend into temperate regions. Most of the plants of the order are obscure weeds and the roots of almost all are purgative. The "four-o'clock," or "marvel of Peru," is familiar in old-fashioned gardens, and a few *Abronias* are ornamental.

In California we have five genera, the most important of which are *Mirabilis* and *Abronia*.

ORDER LVI.

Polygonaceæ. BUCKWHEAT FAMILY.

Herbs or woody plants with swollen joints. *Leaves.*—Alternate or whorled, or sometimes only radical; entire; usually with dilated and clasping base. *Flowers.*—Mostly perfect on jointed pedicels; often contained in involucres. *Calyx.*—Usually petaloid; of three to six more or less united segments. Corolla wanting. *Stamens.*—Four to nine. *Ovary.*—Superior; one-celled; one-seeded. Styles two to four. *Fruit.* —An angled akene.

An order of thirty genera and seven hundred species, mostly of north temperate regions. The genus *Rheum* furnishes the officinal rhubarb, also the rhubarb or pie-plant of the garden. *Fagopyrum* is the well-known buckwheat. Some of the plants of this order furnish dyes, others tanning agents, and still others medicines. To this order belong the common dock and sorrel.

Of our ten genera, the most prominent are *Rumex, Erio-gonum,* and *Chorizanthe*.

ORDER LVII.

Chenopodiaceæ. GOOSEFOOT FAMILY.

Herbs or shrubs, often succulent, sometimes fleshy and leafless. *Leaves.*—Alternate; simple; without stipules. *Flowers.*—Small; sessile; clustered; with or without bracts; perfect or unisexual. *Calyx.*—Of five or fewer usually herbaceous and persistent sepals, or sometimes wanting in fertile flowers; sometimes becoming winged or appendaged. *Corolla.*—Wanting. *Stamens.*—As many as the sepals and opposite them or fewer; distinct; with two-celled anthers. *Ovary.*—Superior; one-celled. Styles or stigmas one to four. *Fruit.*—Dry.

An order of sixty genera and four hundred species; of wide distribution in cool countries; largely peculiar to maritime and saline localities. It is extensively represented in the alkaline regions of western America, and furnishes a number of cosmopolitan weeds. Of this order are the beet, spinach, and mangel-wurzel of the garden. Many plants of the order possess aromatic or medicinal qualities, and others yield soda in large quantities.

Of the fourteen genera of our flora, the best known are *Salicornia* and *Chenopodium*.

ORDER LVIII.

Lauraceæ. LAUREL FAMILY.

Aromatic trees and shrubs. *Leaves.*—Alternate; simple; entire; without stipules; mostly marked with minute pellucid dots. *Flowers.*—Either perfect or diœcious; in cymes or clusters; small; usually white or yellowish. *Calyx.*—Of four or six sepals. *Corolla.*—Wanting. *Stamens.*—Definite or somewhat indefinite; in three or four series; the inner often with two glands at base. Anthers opening by uplifting valves. *Ovary.*—Superior; one-celled. Style and stigma one. *Fruit.*—A berry or drupe.

A large order of fifty genera and nine hundred species, found mostly in cool parts of the tropics of Asia and America. It yields a number of valuable timbers, and many medicinal and other products, among which are cinnamon, camphor, cassia, sassafras, etc. To this order also belongs the alligator-pear, frequently brought to us from the tropics and much esteemed.

Our only genus is *Umbellularia*.

ORDER LIX.

Piperaceæ. YERBA MANSA OR PEPPER FAMILY.

Perennial acrid herbs (in our species), with creeping rootstocks and jointed or scapelike stems. *Leaves.*—Entire; petioled; dilated at base or sheathing; without stipules. *Flowers.*—Mostly perfect; furnished with bracts; in dense terminal spikes or racemes. *Calyx and corolla.*—Wanting. *Stamens.*—Three to six or more. *Ovary.*—Superior; one-to several-celled. *Stigmas.*—One to five. *Fruit.*—A capsule or follicle or berry.

An order of about twenty genera and six hundred species, almost all natives of very hot regions. The black and white peppers of commerce are the fruits of *Piper nigrum*. The plants of this order are for the most part pungent, aromatic, astringent, and narcotic, and furnish many drugs, among them cubebs.

Our only genus is *Anemopsis*.

ORDER LX.

Aristolochiaceæ. DUTCHMAN'S-PIPE OR BIRTHWORT FAMILY.

Perennial herbs or shrubs. *Leaves.*—Alternate; entire; mostly cordate-reniform; without stipules. *Flowers.*—Perfect. *Calyx.*—Petaloid; lurid or greenish; with a regular or irregular three-lobed border; the tube more or less adnate to the ovary. *Corolla.*—Wanting. *Stamens.*—Six to twelve; on the ovary and more or less adherent to the styles. Anthers extrorse. *Ovary.*—Six-celled. Styles usually six.

An order of five genera and two hundred species, chiefly of warm countries. The species are many of them medicinal, and in some the flowers are beautiful and ornamental.

We have two genera in California—*Asarum* and *Aristolochia*.

ORDER LXI.

Orchidaceæ. ORCHIS FAMILY.

Perennial herbs, sometimes parasitic. *Roots.*—Often tuberous or thickened. *Stems.*—Simple or scapelike. *Leaves.*—Alternate; sheathing; parallel-veined; sometimes scalelike. *Flowers.*—Perfect; irregular; with parts in threes; usually inverted by the twisting of the ovary. *Perianth segments.*—Six; five similar, and the upper (apparently the lower) dissimilar and called the *lip*. *Stamens.*—One or two; on the ovary; in reality coalescent with the style forming the *column,* which bears on its summit the oblique, concave, viscous stigma, and the anther or anthers. *Ovary.*—Inferior; one-celled.

A very large order containing about four hundred genera and upwards of three thousand species, found in all parts of the world except the coldest, but flourishing most luxuriantly in the tropics, where they are largely epiphytic. They are much cultivated in hothouses, where their great variety of wonderfully beautiful and often grotesque flowers charm the eye or delight the sense with their perfume. Beyond their beautiful flowers the plants of this order are of small importance, the best-known useful product being vanilla, obtained from the fruits (called beans) of various species of *Vanilla,* in largest quantity from Mexico, although found elsewhere.

Of our ten Californian genera, the most important are *Calypso, Corallorhiza, Habenaria, Spiranthes, Goodyera, Epipactis, Cephalanthera,* and *Cipripedium.*

ORDER LXII.

Iridaceæ. IRIS FAMILY.

Perennial herbs with creeping rootstocks or corms, which are more or less acrid. *Leaves.*—Equitant; sheathing; two-ranked; sword-shaped or linear; parallel-veined. *Flowers.*—Perfect; regular; showy; few or solitary; with spathelike bracts. *Perianth.*—Of six segments, in two series. *Stamens.*—Three with extrorse anthers; distinct or united. *Ovary.*—Inferior; three-celled. Style three-cleft; stigma-bearing branches often dilated and petaloid. *Fruit.*—A triangular capsule.

An order of fifty or more genera and over five hundred species, mostly natives of temperate regions, notably South Africa, North and South America, and Europe. The plants of the order are more remarkable for their beautiful flowers than for their economic uses. Well known in our gardens are the gladiolus, crocus, ixia, iris, and tigridia. Orris-root is the product of *Iris Florentina.*

In California we have two genera only—*Iris* and *Sisyrinchium.*

ORDER LXIII.

Liliaceæ. LILY FAMILY.

Mostly herbs. Stems chiefly from coated or scaly bulbs or corms or more or less thickened rhizomes. *Leaves.*—Parallel-veined (rarely net-veined). *Flowers.*—Perfect; regular. *Perianth.*—Corolla-like; six-cleft or divided (the three outer segments sometimes dissimilar and somewhat foliaceous). *Stamens.*—Usually six; opposite the segments (three in *Scoliopus*), though sometimes three with three alternating staminodia. Anthers two-celled. *Ovary.*—Superior; three-celled. *Fruit.*—A capsule or berry.

A large and important order of about one hundred and eighty genera and nineteen hundred species, distributed all over the world. Many are remarkable for the beauty and fragrance of their flowers, and have long been favorites in the garden, such as the lily, tulip, hyacinth, day-lily, lily of the valley, tuberose, agapanthus, smilax, etc. Others are cultivated for food, such as *Asparagus* and various species of *Allium* (onion). Many furnish valuable fibers, such as the New Zealand flax and the yucca; while others are important in medicine, such as aloes and squills.

This order is a marked feature in our flora, and we have several genera peculiar to the State or to western North America.

We have thirty-one genera, most important of which are *Lilium, Fritillaria, Erythronium, Calochortus, Disporum (Prosartes), Clintonia, Scoliopus, Trillium, Veratrum, Zygadenus, Xerophyllum, Muilla, Bloomeria, Brodiæa, Camassia, Chlorogalum, Smilacina, Yucca, Hesperoyucca,* and *Cleistoyucca.*

ORDER LXIV.

Araceæ. ARUM FAMILY.

Smooth perennial herbs. *Leaves.*—Large; radical or alternate. *Flowers.*—Monœcious or diœcious (or sometimes perfect); sessile and crowded on a spadix, which is surrounded by a simple spathe. *Calyx and corolla.*—Wanting; or in perfect flowers four- to six-sepaled. *Stamens.*—Four. *Ovary.*—Superior; two-celled. All the ovaries coalescing in fruit.

An order of twenty-six genera and one hundred and seventy species, mostly of tropical countries. The roots of some are eaten as food in the regions of their growth, while others furnish dangerous poisons or powerful drugs. The well-known calla lily is of this order.

We have in California but one genus, *Lysichiton,* commonly called "skunk-cabbage."

A FEW OF OUR LARGEST AND MOST IMPORTANT GENERA

CEANOTHUS, L. Buckthorn Family.

Shrubs or small trees, sometimes spinescent. *Leaves.*—Opposite or alternate; petioled; variously toothed or entire. *Flowers.*—Blue or white; small, usually not more than two or three lines across; borne in showy thyrsoid or cymose clusters. *Calyx.*—Petaloid; with short tube and five-cleft border, the lobes acute and connivent. *Petals.*—Five; long-clawed; hooded; inserted on the calyx-tube. *Stamens.*—Five; opposite the petals; long-exserted. *Ovary.*—Three-lobed; three-celled. Style short; three-cleft. *Fruit.*—Dry; consisting of three dehiscent nutlets; sometimes crested.

The genus *Ceanothus* is mainly a Western one. Of its thirty or more species, two thirds are found in the region between the Rocky Mountains and the Pacific Ocean.

In California we have about twenty species; and these all hybridize to such an extent, that often the determination of any given species is a very difficult matter. The genus reaches its culmination in the mountains of Santa Cruz County, where there are many beautiful species. Many of the species are commonly known as "California lilac."

LUPINUS, Catullus. Pea Family.

Leaves.—Palmately divided, with from one to sixteen leaflets; stipules adnate; seldom conspicuous. *Leaflets.*—Entire; sessile. *Flowers.* —In terminal racemes, whorled or scattered. *Calyx.*—Deeply bilabiate; upper lip notched; lower usually entire, or occasionally three-toothed or cleft. *Corolla.* — Papilionaceous. *Standard.* — Broad, with sides reflexed. *Wings.*—Falcate; oblong; commonly slightly united at the tip in front of and inclosing the falcate, usually slender, pointed keel. *Stamens.*—Ten; with their filaments united in a tube; of two forms; five with longer and basifixed anthers; the alternate five with shorter and versatile ones. *Pod.*—Compressed; straight; two-valved. Style slender. Stigma bearded.

The lupines are mostly plants of western America. In fact, they are so abundant between the Rocky Mountains and the Pacific Ocean that that territory is known among botanists as the "Lupine Region."

The species, which are very numerous, are difficult of determination, requiring very long technical descriptions, which cannot be given in a work like the present. For this reason we have been able to give but a few of the more easily recognized.

We have in California upwards of forty species. They are of little economic importance, although one or two species have been found very useful in the reclaiming of sand-dunes. Several species have been cultivated for ornament. The leaves are often beautiful and the flower-clusters showy.

A characteristic feature of this genus is that two different forms of stamens alternate with one another in the same flower.

The generic name is supposed to come from the Latin adjective *lupinus,* signifying of the nature of a wolf, and to have been given because of the voracity evinced by the species in exhausting the soil.

ASTRAGALUS, Tourn. Pea Family.

Herbs, or sometimes plants woody at base. *Leaves.*—Alternate; with stipules; unequally pinnate. *Flowers.*—Rather small; chiefly in simple axillary spikes or racemes, upon a commonly elongated peduncle; papilionaceous. *Calyx.*—Five-toothed. *Corolla* and its slender-clawed petals usually narrow. Keel not pointed. *Stamens.*—Nine united; one free. *Ovary.*—One-celled; sometimes apparently two-celled. *Pod.*—Very various; commonly inflated. *Seeds.*—Few to many on slender stalks; generally small for the size of the pod.

The genus *Astragalus* is a very large one, comprising many species in most parts of the world, save Australia and South Africa. About two hundred species are native of North America, most of which are found in the region west of the Mississippi River. Of these several are known as "loco-weed," and are poisonous to sheep and cattle.

"Rattle-weed" is the common name for the plants of this genus, from the fact that the ripened seed make a rattling noise in the dried, inflated pods.

Very few species of this genus have any economic value. *A. gummifer* and some other similar species of western Asia, low, spiny shrubs, yield the gum tragacanth of commerce.

ŒNOTHERA, L.   Evening-Primrose Family.

Herbs, or plants sometimes woody at the base. *Leaves.*—Alternate. *Flowers.*—Axillary or in spikes or racemes. *Calyx-tube.*—More or less prolonged above the ovary with four reflexed segments. *Petals.*—Four; obcordate to obovate; sessile; yellow to white, often tinged with red or turning red in fading. *Stamens.*—Eight; equal; or those opposite the petals shorter. Anthers perfect; two-celled; versatile. *Ovary.*—Four-celled; many-ovuled. Style filiform. Stigma four-lobed or capitate. *Fruit.*—A capsule with the seeds in one or two rows in each cell.

The name *Œnothera* is from two Greek words, meaning *wine* and *a hunt,* or *pursuit.* Mr. Gray tells us that it was given in ancient times to some plant whose roots were eaten to provoke a relish for wine.

This is a large genus, containing a hundred or more species, which are mostly confined to America, about a quarter of them being Californian. Many of them are very beautiful and have long been favorites in gardens. The flowers are yellow or white, and are commonly designated as "evening primroses," as many of them open upon the edge of evening.

GODETIA, Spach.   Evening-Primrose Family.

The genus *Godetia* is closely allied to that of *Œnothera;* but is distinguished from the latter in several points. Its flowers are purple, lilac, or rose-colored—never yellow; the anthers are basifixed—*i. e.* fixed by their bases—not versatile; and the stigma, instead of being capitate, has four linear lobes.

The plants of this genus were formerly included under *Œnothera;* but it has been thought best to put them into a separate genus, which has been named for a Dr. Godet.

There are numerous species, many of them very beautiful and showy. They vary a great deal under different conditions and in different seasons, and are not well understood by botanists as yet.

The genus is confined to the western coast of North America, and is most largely represented in California.

The species flower mostly in late spring and early summer, which has given rise to the pretty name of "farewell to spring" for the plants of this genus.

GILIA, Renz. and Pav.   Phlox or Polemonium Family.

Herbs or plants somewhat shrubby at base. *Leaves.*—Opposite or alternate; simple or compound; without stipules. Many species with showy flowers. All the parts of the flower five, except the pistil, which has a three-celled ovary and a three-lobed style. *Calyx.*—Imbricated in the bud. *Corolla.*—Regular; funnel-form, salver-form, or sometimes short-campanulate or rotate; convolute in the bud. *Stamens.*— Five; on the corolla alternate with its lobes; distinct. Filaments mostly slender; sometimes unequal in length; not bearded at base.

This genus was named in honor of Philip Gil, a Spanish botanist. In America the name is pronounced *jil'i-a,* though according to the rules of the Spanish language *he'li-a* would be the correct pronunciation.

This is a comparatively large genus, comprising about a hundred species, most of which are native to the western parts of the United States. The flowers are often showy and beautiful, and some of them closely resemble the phloxes. A number are cultivated under the botanical name of *Ipomopsis* or *Leptosiphon.*

PHACELIA, Juss.   Baby-eyes or Waterleaf Family.

Herbs, mostly branched from the base and hairy. *Leaves.*—Alternate; the lower sometimes opposite; simple or compound. *Flowers.*— Usually in one-sided scorpioid racemes. *Calyx.*—Deeply five-parted; without appendages. *Corolla.*—From almost rotate to narrowly funnelform; five-lobed; with ten vertical plates or scales at the base within. *Stamens.*—Five; equally inserted low or at the base of the corolla.

Ovary.—One-celled. Styles two; or one which is two-cleft. *Fruit.*—A capsule.

The name *Phacelia* is from a Greek word signifying a *fascicle,* or *bunch,* and refers to the fascicled or clustered flower-racemes.

This genus is closely allied to *Nemophila,* but differs from it in several points. The calyx is not furnished with appendages at the sinuses; the corolla is imbricated in the bud—*i. e.* the lobes overlap one another in the manner of bricks in a wall,—and is not convolute, or rolled up, as in *Nemophila.*

This is mainly a North American genus, having about fifty species, about thirty of which are Californian. Many of the species have beautiful and showy flowers, and are cultivated in gardens. The blossoms are blue, violet, purple, or white, but never yellow (save sometimes in the tube or throat).

Mimulus, L. Figwort Family.

Leaves.—Opposite; simple. *Flowers.*—Axillary on solitary peduncles; sometimes becoming racemose by the diminution of the upper leaves to bracts. *Calyx.*—Tubular or campanulate; mostly five-angled and five-toothed. *Corolla.*—Funnel-form; bilabiate; the upper lip erect, two-lobed; the lower three-lobed; a pair of ridges, either bearded or naked, running down the lower side of the throat. *Stamens.*—Four. Anthers often near together in pairs, with divergent cells. *Ovary.*—Superior; two-celled. Style filiform. Stigma two-lipped, with the lips commonly dilated and petaloid.

The genus *Mimulus* is so named from the shape of the corolla, which is supposed to resemble the gaping countenance of an ape. It comprises forty or fifty species, and affords us some of our most beautiful flowers. The greater number of species and the handsomest are Pacific, and several of our Californian species are especially prized in cultivation.

The plants of the genus are all known as "monkey-flowers." They exhibit an interesting character in the structure and movements of the stigma. It is usually composed of two somewhat expanded lips. These are extremely sensitive, and when touched, or when pollen has been received by them, they close quite rapidly.

ORTHOCARPUS, Nutt. Figwort Family.

Low herbs; almost all annuals. *Leaves.*—Mainly alternate; sessile; often cut into from three to five filiform divisions; the upper passing into the bracts of the dense spike and usually colored, as are the calyx-lobes. *Calyx.*—Short-tubular or oblong-campanulate; evenly four-cleft, or sometimes cleft before and behind and the divisions again cleft. *Corolla.*—Tubular; the upper lip, or galea, little or not at all longer than the lower; small in comparison with the large, inflated, one- to three-saccate lower one, which usually bears more or less conspicuous teeth. *Stamens.*—Four; inclosed in the upper lip. *Ovary.*—Two-celled. Style long. Stigma capitate. *Fruit.*—A capsule.

The genus *Orthocarpus* is mainly Californian, comprising within our borders something less than twenty species. Most of them are to be found from San Francisco northward and in the mountains.

They are closely related to the *Castilleias,* and resemble them closely in habit. The difference between the two genera lies in the relative sizes of the upper and lower lips of the corolla. In *Castilleia* the upper lip is the larger and more prominent; while in *Orthocarpus* the lower is much more conspicuous, often consisting of three inflated sacs.

The species are quite difficult of determination.

"Owl's clover" is a common English name for some of the plants of this genus; while "pelican-flower" is the common name for those belonging to the section with three large inflated divisions to the lower lip of the corolla.

PENTSTEMON, Mitchell. Figwort Family.

Perennial herbs, or rarely shrubby. *Leaves.* — Opposite, rarely whorled; the upper sessile or clasping; the floral gradually or abruptly reduced to bracts. *Flowers.*—Usually red, blue, purple, or white, rarely yellow; in raceme-like panicles. *Calyx.*—Five-parted. *Corolla.* —With a conspicuous and mostly elongated or ventricose tube; the throat swelling out on the lower if on either side; the limb more or less bilabiate, with the upper lip two-lobed and the lower three-cleft, recurved, or spreading. *Stamens.*—Four perfect; a fifth with a bearded filament only. Anther cells mostly united or running together at the summit. *Ovary.*—Two-celled. Style long. Stigma entire.

The name *Pentstemon* is from two Greek words, signifying *five* and *stamen*. It was bestowed upon this genus because the fifth stamen is present, though sterile.

The genus is a large one, comprising seventy species, most of which are North American, though a few are Mexican. It is most abundantly represented in the Pacific States and the States west of the Mississippi. California has over twenty species, many of them very beautiful, a number of them being in cultivation.

"Beard-tongue" is the common English name for the plants of this genus.

From so many charming species it has been very difficult to select; and if the reader finds some beautiful flower of this genus which is unnamed in these pages, he is advised to consult the technical botanies.

CALOCHORTUS, Pursh. Lily Family.

Stem.—Branching; from a membranous-coated, sometimes fibrous-coated corm. *Leaves.*—Few; linear-lanceolate; the radical one or two much larger than those of the flexuous or erect stem. *Flowers.*—Few to many; showy; terminal or axillary, or umbellately fascicled. *Perianth.*—Deciduous; of six more or less concave segments; the three outer lanceolate, greenish, more or less sepal-like; the inner (petals) mostly broadly cuneate-obovate, usually with a conspicuous glandular pit toward the base, which is apt to be hidden by long hairs. *Stamens.*—Six. Anthers erect; basifixed. *Ovary.*—Three-celled; three-angled. Stigmas three; sessile; recurved. *Capsule.*—Three-angled or winged.

The *Calochorti* are the most widely diffused of all the liliaceous plants of the Pacific Coast, and comprise some of the most beautiful flowers in the world. "On the north they reach British America; one species is to be found as far east as Nebraska; and several are natives of northern Mexico; and within these limits no considerable section of country is destitute of some species."* They are so closely allied to the true tulips that the common designation of them as "tulips" is not at all amiss.

* Mr. Carl Purdy.

The name *Calochortus* signifies *beautiful grass.* The members of the genus fall naturally into three general groups:—

First—The GLOBE TULIPS, which have flexile stems, subglobose, nodding flowers, and nodding capsules. Of these there are four — *C. albus, C. amœnus, C. pulchellus,* and *C. amabilis.*

Second—The STAR TULIPS, having low, flexile stems, erect, star-like flowers, with spreading petals, and nodding capsules. They comprise *C. Benthami, C. Maweanus, C. cœruleus, C. apiculatus, C. elegans, C. Tolmei, C. umbellatus,* etc.

Third—The MARIPOSA TULIPS, which are usually tall, fine plants, with stiff, erect stems, having erect, cup-shaped or open-campanulate flowers, usually large and handsome, followed by erect capsules.

They have a few narrow, grass-like, radical leaves, which have usually dried away by the time of flowering, which is in early summer, after the ground has become dry and hard. These inhabit our dry, open hillsides and grassy slopes, loving a stony, clayey, sandy, or volcanic soil. They comprise over thirty different known forms, and others are constantly being discovered.

Among these are *C. Weedii, C. clavatus, C. luteus* and varieties, *C. venustus* and varieties, *C. splendens, C. Catalinæ, C. macrocarpus,* etc.

They have a tendency to hybridize, and the various forms sport and vary, and run into one another in such a wonderful manner that the exact determination of all the species is an impossible task to all but a few experts—and even they are not certain about them all yet. We have given only a few of the commonest or best-characterized species.

Mariposa is the Spanish word meaning *butterfly,* and was applied on account of the marvelous resemblance of the markings of the petals of some of the forms to the wings of that insect.

INDEX TO TECHNICAL TERMS

ENGLISH INDEX TO PLANT FAMILIES

ENGLISH INDEX TO PLANT FAMILIES

LATIN INDEX TO PLANT FAMILIES

LATIN INDEX TO PLANT FAMILIES

INTRODUCTORY

SITUATED on the western verge of the continent, so far removed from the other parts of our country, not only by great distance, but by those mighty natural barriers that traverse the continent from north to south, California is eminently individual in her natural features. Stretching through nine and one half degrees of latitude, with a sea-coast of seven hundred miles, and several mountain ranges, there is probably not another State in the Union that has so wonderful a diversity of climate and vegetation. Her shores, bathed by the warm Japan Current, or Ku-ro Si-wa, which is deflected southward from Alaska, are many degrees warmer than their latitude alone would warrant.

Her general topography is simple and readily understood. The Sierra Nevada, or "snowy range," upon the eastern boundary, with its granite summits and its shoulders clothed with successive belts of majestic coniferous forests, with an occasional snow-peak towering above the range, forms the eastern wall of the great Central Valley, which is inclosed upon the west by the Coast Range, less in height than the Sierra, but equally beautiful, less forbidding, more companionable. The great Central Valley, four hundred and fifty miles long, is drained by two rivers, which meet in its center and break through the Coast Range, delivering their waters to the ocean through the Golden Gate. The Sacramento and San Joaquin rivers receive many important tributaries from the east, fed by the melting snows of the Sierras, and flow through one of the most fertile regions of the world.

The Sierras may be divided into five different belts, of varying altitudes along the length of the range, beginning with the foothill region, which may be termed the chaparral region. This is succeeded by the yellow-pine belt, above which is the sugar-pine, or upper forest, belt, which is in turn succeeded by the sub-alpine, while the alpine dominates all.

The Coast Range is channeled on both sides by many beautiful wooded cañons, affording homes for some of our loveliest flowers. Mr. Purdy writes of it:—This "is not a continuous range, but a broken mass of parallel ridges from forty to seventy miles wide, with many other chains transverse to the general trend of the range, and inclosing numerous valleys, large and small, of widely different altitudes. In the Coast Range there is no warm belt, but isolated warm spots. Climate here can only be ascertained by experience. The geological formation of the ranges and the character of soils constantly vary, and often widely at short intervals. Hence the flora of this region is particularly interesting. It is hardly probable there is a more captivating field for the botanist in the world."

In the north and the south the two great ranges meet in some of the noblest snow-peaks on the continent. Below their southern junction, to the eastward, lies an arid desert region, and above their northern junction extends a dry and elevated plateau to the northeast. Thus there arises a great diversity of natural condition. As all living organisms are greatly influenced by their environment, the flora naturally distributes itself along the lines of climatic variation. Thus we have alpine species on the snowy heights of the Sierras, and sub-alpine forms luxuriating in the meadows fed from their snows; inland species in the Central Valley, and following some distance up its eastern and western walls; the leathery and hardy forms of the wind-swept coast; the curious prickly races of arid regions; delicate lovers of the cool and shaded brook; dwellers in marshes and on lake borders; denizens of dry, rocky hill-slopes, exposed to the glare of the sun; and inhabiters of shaded woods. It may be said that the most characteristically Western plants of our flora are to be found in the Central

Valley, in the lower belts of the Sierras, and in the valleys of the Coast Range, many of them extending beyond our borders, both northward and southward. Many of our alpine species are common to the East, and our maritime flora is of necessity somewhat cosmopolitan, containing many introduced species from various parts of the world.

The climate of California is divided into two seasons—the wet and the dry,—the former extending from October to May, the latter occupying the remaining months of the year. And this climatic division coincides almost exactly with the area of the State. Of course, these dates are not absolute, as showers may occur beyond their limits.

It will be readily seen that the rainy season, or the winter, so-called, is the growing time of our year—the time when the earth brings forth every plant in his kind. On the other hand, the summer is the time of rest. Most of the plant-life having germinated after the first moisture of the fall, grows luxuriantly during the showery months of winter, blossoms lavishly in the balmy sunshine of early springtime, produces seed in abundance by early summer, and is then ready for its annual rest. Instead of shrouding the earth in snow during our period of plant-rest, as she does in more rigorous climes, Nature gently spreads over hill and valley a soft mantle of brown.

When the first shrill notes of the cicada are heard in late spring, we awake to a sudden realization that summer is at hand, and, looking about us, we see that the flowers have nearly all vanished; hill and valley no longer glow with great masses of color; only a few straggling species of the early summer remain; but they too are soon gone, and soft browns and straw-colors prevail everywhere. It is then that the deep, rich greens of our symmetrically rounded live-oaks, so characteristic of this region, show in fine contrast against this delicate background, forming a picture that every Californian dearly loves; the madroño and the laurel spread their canopies of grateful shade; while the redwood affords cool retreats from the summer sun. Then our salt marshes, as though realizing the need of refreshing verdure, put on their most vivid greens; and our chaparral-covered hill-slopes make walls of bronze and olive.

Perhaps no coniferous forests in the world are so beautiful or so attractive as the redwood forests of our Coast Ranges; and they play so important a part in the distribution of our plants, it will not be out of place to devote a little space to them here.

The main redwood belt is of limited range, extending along the Coast from Monterey County to Humboldt County, and nowhere exceeding twenty miles in breadth. Straggling trees may be found beyond these limits, but nowhere a forest growth or trees of great size. In its densest portion, the stately and colossal trees are too close together to permit of a wagon passing between them.

Mr. Purdy writes:—"The redwood is not only a lover of moisture, but to an extent hardly to be believed, unless seen, a condenser and conserver of moisture. Their tops reach high into the sea of vapor, and a constant precipitation from them, like rain, takes place. The water stands in puddles in the roads under them. This causes the densest of undergrowth; hazels, huckleberries, various ceanothi, ferns of large size and in greatest profusion, large bushes of rhododendron, and numerous other plants make the forest floor a perfect tangle in moister portions."

Many charming plants find their homes amid the cool shade of these noble trees. Trillium, and scoliopus, and dog's-tooth violets vie with clintonias and vancouverias in elegance and grace, while little creeping violets, and the lovely redwood-sorrel, and the salal make charming tapestries over the forest floor about these dim cathedral columns.

On the other hand, the open forest belts of the Sierras, which are of far greater extent, present another and quite different flora from that of the Coast Range and the redwood belt. There may be found many interesting plants of the Heath family—cassiope, bryanthus, chimaphila, ledum, various pyrolas, and the snow-plant; there the aconite, false hellebore, eriogonums and gentians, and new and beautiful pentstemons and mimuli and lilies deck the meadows and stream-banks.

After the season of blossoming is over in the lowlands, we may pass on up into the mountains and live again through a vernal springtime of flowers.

Perhaps in no country in the world does the arrival of the spring flowers "so transform the face of Nature as in California." The march of civilization has brought changes in its wake; the virgin soil has been broken and subdued into grain-fields and vineyards; still enough of the lavish blossoming is left us to appreciate Mr. Muir's description of the face of the country as it appeared years ago. He says:—"When California was wild, it was one sweet bee-garden throughout its entire length, north and south, and all the way across from the snowy Sierra to the ocean. . . . The Great Central Plain . . . during the months of March, April, and May was one smooth, continuous bed of honey-bloom, so marvelously rich that in walking from one end of it to the other, a distance of four hundred miles, your foot would press about a hundred flowers at every step. Mints, gilias, nemophilas, castilleias, and innumerable compositas were so crowded together that had ninety-nine per cent of them been taken away, the plain would still have seemed to any but Californians extravagantly flowery. The radiant, honeyful corollas, touching and overlapping and rising above one another, glowed in the living light like a sunset sky —one sheet of purple and gold. . . . Sauntering in any direction, hundreds of these happy sun-plants brushed against my feet at every step and closed over them as if I were wading in liquid gold. The air was sweet with fragrance, the larks sang their blessed songs, rising on the wing as I advanced, then sinking out of sight in the polleny sod; while myriads of wild bees stirred the lower air with their monotonous hum—monotonous, yet forever fresh and sweet as everyday sunshine."

PRELUDE

O LAND OF THE WEST! I know
How the field-flowers bud and blow,
And the grass springs and the grain
To the first soft touch and summons of the rain!
O, the music of the rain!
O, the music of the streams!
—*Ina D. Coolbrith.*

Toward the end of our long cloudless summer, after most other flowers have stolen away, Mother Nature marshals her great order of Compositæ for a last rally; and they come as welcome visitants to fill the places of our vanished summer friends.

Asters and goldenrods, grindelias, lessingias, and the numerour tarweeds, with their cheerful blossoms, relieve the sober browns of sun-dried hill-slopes and meadows, or fringe with color our roadsides and salt marshes.

But even these late-comers weary after a time, and one by one disappear, till there comes a season when, without flowers, Nature seems to be humbled in sackcloth and ashes. The dust lies thick upon roadside trees, a haze hangs like a veil in the air, and the sun beats down with fierce, continued glare.

As this wears on day after day, a certain vague expectancy creeps gradually over the face of things—a rapt, mysterious aspect, foreboding change. One day there is a telltale clarity in the atmosphere. Later, the sky darkens by degrees, and a dull, leaden hue spreads over the vault of heaven. Nature mourns, and would weep. Her heart is full to bursting; still the tears come not. The winds spring up and blow freshly over the parched land. A few hard-wrung drops begin to fall, and at length there closes down a thoroughgoing shower. The flood-gates are opened at last; the long tension is over, and we breathe freely once more.

During this first autumn rain, those of us who are so fortunate as to live in the country are conscious of a strange odor pervading all the air. It is as though Dame Nature were brewing a vast cup of herb tea, mixing in the fragrant infusion all the plants dried and stored so carefully during the summer.

When the clouds vanish after this baptismal shower, everything is charmingly fresh and pure, and we have some of the rarest of days. Then the little seeds, harbored through the long summer in Earth's bosom, burst their coats and push up their tender leaves, till on hillside and valley-floor appears a delicate mist of green, which gradually confirms itself into a soft, rich carpet—and all the world is in verdure clad. Then we begin to look eagerly for our first flowers.

FLOWER DESCRIPTIONS

A FANCY

I think I would not be
A stately tree,
Broad-boughed, with haughty crest that seeks the sky!
Too many sorrows lie
In years, too much of bitter for the sweet:
Frost-bite, and blast, and heat,
Blind drought, cold rains, must all grow wearisome,
Ere one could put away
Their leafy garb for aye,
And let death come.

Rather this wayside flower,
To live its happy hour
Of balmy air, of sunshine, and of dew.
A sinless face held upward to the blue;
A bird-song sung to it,
A butterfly to flit
On dazzling wings above it, hither, thither,—
A sweet surprise of life,—and then exhale
A little fragrant soul on the soft gale,
To float—ah! whither?

—Ina D. Coolbrith.

I. WHITE

White or occasionally or partially white flowers not described in the White Section.

Described in the Yellow Section:—

ANAGALLIS ARVENSIS—Pimpernel.
BRODIÆA LACTEA — White Brodiæa.
CALOCHORTUS WEEDII—Mariposa Tulip.
CUSCUTA—Dodder.
ERIOGONUM URSINUM.
ERYSIMUM GRANDIFLORUM—Cream-colored Wallflower.
ESCHSCHOLTZIA CALIFORNICA—California Poppy.

FLŒRKEA DOUGLASII — Meadow-Foam.
HEMIZONIA LUZULÆFOLIA — Tarweed.
HOSACKIA BICOLOR.
MELILOTUS ALBA — White Sweet Clover.
PTEROSPORA ANDROMEDEA — Pine-Drops.
VERBASCUM BLATTARIA — Moth-Mullein.

Described in the Pink Section:—

APOCYNUM CANNABINUM—American-Indian Hemp.
DODECATHEON CLEVELANDI—Shooting-Stars.
GILIA ANDROSACEA.
LEWISIA REDIVIVA—Bitter-Root.
OXALIS OREGANA — Redwood Sorrel.

PHLOX DOUGLASII--Alpine Phlox.
RHUS INTEGRIFOLIA—Lemonade-Berry.
RHUS LAURINA—Sumach.
SILENE GALLICA.
TRIENTALIS EUROPÆA — Star-Flower.

Described in the Blue and Purple Section:—

BRODIÆA LAXA—Ithuriel's Spear.
CALOCHORTUS CATALINÆ—Catalina Mariposa Tulip.
CALOCHORTUS MAWEANUS—Cat's-Ears.
CALOCHORTUS UMBELLATUS—White Star-Tulip.
CEANOTHUS DIVARICATUS — Wild Lilac.
CEANOTHUS THYRSIFLORUS—California Lilac.
COLLINSIA BICOLOR—Collinsia.

COLLINSIA TINCTORIA — White Collinsia.
DELPHINIUM.
FRITILLARIA LILIACEA — White Fritillary.
IRIS DOUGLASIANA—Douglas Iris.
IRIS MACROSIPHON—Ground Iris.
POLYGALA CORNUTA.
SCUTELLARIA CALIFORNICA—White Skullcap.
TRILLIUM SESSILE—Cal. Trillium.

Described in the Red Section:—

GILIA AGGREGATA—Scarlet Gilia.   AQUILEGIA CÆRULEA.

Described in the Miscellaneous Section:—

CEPHALANTHERA OREGANA—Phantom Orchis.
CYPRIPEDIUM CALIFORNICUM—California Lady's Slipper.

CYPRIPEDIUM MONTANUM—Mountain Lady's Slipper.
DISPORUM MENZIESII — Drops of Gold.

3

TOOTHWORT. PEPPER-ROOT. SPRING-BLOSSOM.

Dentaria Californica, Nutt. Mustard Family.

Roots.—Bearing small tubers. *Stems.*—Six inches to two feet high. *Root-leaves.*—Simple and roundish or with three leaflets. *Stem-leaves.* —Usually with three to five pinnate leaflets, one to three inches long. *Flowers.*—White to pale rose-color. *Sepals and Petals.*—Four. *Stamens.*—Four long and two short. *Ovary.*—Two-celled. Style simple. *Pod.*—Slender; twelve to eighteen lines long. *Syn.*—*Cardamine paucisecta,* Benth. *Hab.*—Throughout the Coast Ranges.

What a rapture we always feel over this first blossom of the year!—not only for its own dear sake, but for the hopes and promises it holds out, the visions it raises of spring, with flower-covered meadows, running brooks, buds swelling everywhere, bird-songs, and the air rife with perfumes.

It is like the dove sent forth from the ark, this first tentative blossom, this *avant courier* of the great army of Crucifers, or cross-bearers, so called because their four petals are stretched out like the four arms of a cross.

It is usually in some sheltered wood that we look for this first shy blossom; but once it has proved the trustworthiness of the skies, it is followed by thousands of its companions, who then come out boldly and star the meadows with their pure white constellations.

The Latin name of this genus (from the word *dens,* a tooth), translated into the vernacular, becomes toothwort, the termination *wort* signifying merely plant or herb.

It was so named because of the toothed rootstocks of many species.

The little tubers upon the root often have a pungent taste, from which comes one of the other common names—"pepper-root." Various other names have been applied to these flowers, such as "lady's smocks," "milkmaids," and "spring blossoms."

TOOTHWORT—*Dentaria Californica.*

ZYGADENE.

Zygadenus Fremonti, Michx. Lily Family.

Bulb.—Dark-coated. *Leaves.*—Linear; a foot or two long; two to twelve lines broad; deeply channeled. *Scape.*—Three inches to even four feet high. *Flowers.*—White. *Perianth Segments.*—Six; three to seven lines long; strongly nerved; bearing at base yellow glands; inner segments clawed. *Stamens.*—Six; shorter than the perianth. *Ovary.*—Three-celled. Styles three; short. *Capsule.*—Three-beaked. *Hab.*—Coast Ranges, San Diego to Humboldt County.

The generic name, *Zygadenus,* is from the Greek, and signifies yoked glands, referring to the glands upon the base of the perianth segments.

We have several species, the most beautiful and showy of which is *Z. Fremonti.* This is widely distributed, and grows in very different situations. In our central Coast Range its tall stems, with their lovely clusters of white stars, make their appearance upon rocky hill-slopes with warm exposure, in the shelter of the trees, soon after the toothwort has sprinkled the fields with its white bloom. In the south it rears its tall stems upon open mesas, unprotected by the shelter of friendly tree or shrub, and in some localities it makes itself at home in bogs. It is possible that the future may reveal the presence of more than one species.

It has sometimes been called "soap-plant"; but this name more appropriately belongs to *Chlorogalum.* It somewhat resembles the Star of Bethlehem of Eastern gardens. The fact that it grows in boggy places has given rise to the name of "water-lily" in certain localities, but this ought to be discountenanced, as it bears not the slightest resemblance to the magnificent water-lily of Eastern ponds.

Another species—*Z. venenosus,* Wats.—is found from Monterey and Mariposa counties to British Columbia. This may be distinguished from the above by its narrow leaves—only two or three lines wide,—usually folded together, and by its smaller flowers, with perianth segments only two or three lines long; and also by the fact that the stamens equal the segments

6

ZYGADENE—*Zygadenus Fremonti.*

in length. The bulb is poisonous, and our Northern Indians call it "death camass," while the farmers in the Sierras call it "lobelia," not because of any resemblance to that plant, but because its poisonous effects are similar to those of the latter. It is fatal to horses, but hogs eat it with impunity, from which it is also known as "hogs' potato." It is found in moist meadows or along stream-banks, in June and July, from Mariposa and Monterey counties northward.

POISON-OAK.

Rhus diversiloba, Torr. and Gray.   Sumach Family.

Shrubs.—Three to fifteen feet high.   *Leaflets.*—One to four inches long.   *Flowers.*—Greenish white; small.   *Sepals and Petals.*—Usually five.   *Stamens.*—As many or twice as many as the petals.   *Ovary.*—One-celled.   Styles three; distinct or united.   *Fruit.*—A small, dry, striate, whitish drupe.   *Hab.*—Throughout California, save in the high Sierras.

The presence of the poison-oak in our woods and fields makes these outdoor haunts forbidden pleasures to persons who are susceptible to it.   It is closely allied to the poison-ivy of the Eastern States, and very similar in its effects.   It is a charming shrub in appearance, with beautiful glossy, shapely leaves; and in early summer, when it turns to many shades of scarlet and purple-bronze, it is especially alluring to the unsuspecting.   It is quite diverse in its habit, sometimes appearing as an erect shrub with slender stems, and again climbing trees or rock surfaces, by means of small aerial rootlets, to a considerable height.   Once established aloft, it often attains a considerable girth, and intermingles its bower of beautiful foliage with that of its host.   Horses eat the leaves without injury; and the honey which the bees distill from its small greenish-white flowers is said to be excellent.

Many low plants seek the shelter of these shrubs, and some of our loveliest flowers, such as Clarkias, Godetias, Collinsias, Brodiæas, and Larkspurs, seem to realize that immunity from human marauders is to be had within its safe retreat.

The remedies for oak-poisoning are numerous; and it may

POISON-OAK—*Rhus diversiloba.*

not be out of place to mention a few of them here. Different remedies are required by different individuals. Any of the following plants may be made into a tea and used as a wash: Grindelia, manzanita, wild peony, California holly, and *Rhamnus Purshiana,* or *Californica.* Hot solutions of soda, Epsom salts, or saltpeter are helpful to many, and the bulb of the soap-root—*Chlorogalum pomeridianum*—pounded to a paste and used as a salve, allowing it to dry upon the surface and remain for some hours at least, is considered excellent. In fact, any pure toilet soap may be used in the same manner.

WAKE-ROBIN.

Trillium ovatum, Pursh. Lily Family.

Rootstock.—Thickened. *Stem.*—Erect; stout; a foot or more high; bearing at summit a whorl of three sessile leaves. *Leaves.*—Rhomboidal; acuminate; netted-veined; five-nerved; two to six inches long. *Flower.*—Solitary; pure white, fading to deep rose; peduncle one to three inches long. *Sepals.*—Three; herbaceous. *Petals.*—One or two inches long. *Stamens.*—Six. *Ovary.*—Three-celled. Stigmas three; sessile. *Capsule.*—Broadly ovate; six-winged. *Hab.*—The Coast Ranges, from Santa Cruz to British Columbia.

The wake-robin is in the vanguard of our spring flowers, and a walk into some high, cold cañon while the days are still dark and short will be amply rewarded by the finding of its white and peculiarly pure-looking blossoms standing upon the bank overlooking the streamlet. The blossoms remain unchanged for a time, and then, as they fade, turn to a deep purplish rose-color.

Our wake-robin so closely resembles *T. grandiflorum,* Salisb., of the Eastern States, that it seems a pity it should have been made into a different species.

BEACH-STRAWBERRY.

Fragaria Chilensis, Ehrhart. Rose Family.

Hab.—The coast, from Alaska to San Francisco and southward.

This beautiful strawberry is found growing near the seashore, where its large, delicious berries are often buried

WAKE–ROBIN—*Trillium ovatum.*

beneath the shifting sand, becoming bleached in color. It sometimes covers acres with its thick, shining, dark-green leaves, among which are sprinkled its large pure-white flowers, an inch or more across.

The wood-strawberry—*F. Californica*—is very common in the Coast Ranges, and in favorable seasons yields quite agreeable fruit, though it is more often dry and flavorless, owing to dry weather at the time of maturing. A beautiful species with glaucous leaves and charming flowers, often double, and luscious though small fruit, is abundant in the Sierras.

MANZANITA. BEARBERRY.
Arctostaphylos manzanita, Parry. Heath Family.

Shrubs three to twenty-five feet high, with purple-brown bark. *Leaves.*—Pale. *Flowers.* — White or pinkish; in crowded clusters. *Corolla.*—Four or five lines long; campanulate. *Stamens.*—Ten, filaments dilated and bearded at base; anthers two-celled, opening terminally, each cell furnished with a long downward-pointing horn. *Ovary.*—Globose; five to ten-celled. Style simple. *Fruit.*—Six lines in diameter, containing several bony nutlets. *Syn.*—*Arctostaphylos pungens,* HBK. *Hab.*—Throughout the State.

Of all our shrubs, the manzanita is the most beautiful and the best known. Sometimes as early as Christmas it may be found in full bloom, when its dense crown of pale foliage, surmounting the rich purple-brown stems, is thickly sown with the little clusters of fragrant waxen bells. After the blossoms have passed away, the shrubs put forth numerous brilliant scarlet or crimson shoots, which at a little distance look like a strange and entirely new kind of blossoming. The manzanita is closely allied to the madroño, and resembles it in many ways, particularly in the annual peeling of its rich red bark and in the form of its flowers.

The Greek generic name, translated into English, becomes "bearberry." The pretty Spanish name—from *manzana,* apple, and the diminutive, *ita,*—was bestowed by the early Spanish-Californians, who recognized the resemblance of the fruit to tiny apples.

MANZANITA—*Arctostaphylos manzanita.*

We have many species of *Arctostaphylos,* but *A. manzanita* is the commonest of them all. It varies greatly in size and habit. In localities most favorable it becomes a large, erect shrub, with many clustered trunks, while in the Sierras it finds but a precarious footing among the granite rocks, often covering their surfaces with its small tortuous, stiff branches. The leaves, by a twisting of their stalks, assume a vertical position on the branches, a habit which enables many plants of dry regions to avoid unnecessary evaporation.

The largest manzanita known is upon the estate of Mr. Tiburcio Parrott, in St. Helena, Napa County, California. It is thirty-five feet high, with a spread of branches equal to its height, while its trunk measures eleven and a half feet in circumference at the ground, soon dividing into large branches. It is a veritable patriarch, and has doubtless seen many centuries. According to an interesting account in "Garden and Forest," it once had a narrow escape from the ax of a woodman. A gentleman who was a lover of trees, happening to pass, paid the woodman two dollars to spare its life.

Years ago no traveler from the East felt that he could return home without a manzanita cane, made from as straight a branch as could be secured.

The berries of this shrub are dry and bony and quite unsatisfactory. They are, however, pleasantly acid, and have been put to several uses. It is said that both brandy and vinegar are made from them, and housewives make quite a good jelly from some species. Bears are fond of the berries, and the Indians eat them, both raw and pounded into a flour, from which mush is made. The leaves made into a tincture or infusion are now an officinal drug, valued in catarrh of the throat or stomach.

From Monterey to San Diego is found *A. glauca,* Lindl., the great-berried manzanita. It closely resembles the above, but its berries are three fourths of an inch in diameter.

Of the same range as the last is *A. bicolor,* Gray, whose

leaves are of a rich, shining green above and white and woolly beneath. Its berries are the size of a pea, yellowish at first, and turning red later.

A. nummularia, Gray, is a beautiful little species, with small, rounded, shining leaves, and exquisite clusters of small pink flowers, found on the southern slopes of Mt. Tamalpais and in the Santa Cruz Mountains.

WATERCRESS.

Nasturtium officinale, R. Br.   Mustard Family.
Hab.—Widely naturalized from Europe.

The common watercress may be found in many of our streams, and can be easily recognized by its pinnate leaves with radish-like pungency and its clusters of small white flowers resembling the candytuft of our gardens.

It has furnished a relish at many a woodland banquet, and it is gathered largely for our markets.   It is not always safe to use the watercress offered for sale in cities, as it is often gathered from unclean places, where the germs of disease are rife.   The plant eaten fresh as a salad or made into a tincture is said to be a valuable stimulant and alterative.

RADISH.

Raphanus sativus, L.   Mustard Family.

Coarse, more or less hispid herbs.   *Roots.*—Tough and stringy. *Leaves.*—Lyrately pinnatifid.   *Flowers.*—Cruciferous; white, rose or lilac.   *Petals.*—An inch or less long.   *Pods.*—Cylindrical; necklace-like; pointed; two and one half inches long.   (See *Cruciferæ.*)   *Hab.*—Introduced; common everywhere.

The wild radish is a very common weed, growing everywhere in our fields and by the roadsides, and its blossoms may be seen at any time of year.   In certain places, where it has been allowed to overrun the ground, I have seen its delicately tinted flowers growing in great masses that might have been considered truly beautiful had they been aught but common weeds.

MAYWEED. CHAMOMILE. MANZANILLO.

Anthemis cotula, L. Composite Family.

Stems.—A foot high or less. *Leaves.*—Alternate; finely dissected into linear lobes; strong-scented. *Flower-heads.*—Long-peduncled; daisy-like; of yellow disk-flowers and white rays. *Involucre.*—Hemispherical; of many imbricated scales. *Hab.*—Introduced; common and wide-spread.

In early summer, after the hills have put on their straw tints, a revival of spring seems to have taken place upon certain distant slopes which have assumed a second verdure. A nearer approach will reveal the arrival of the Mayweed, or chamomile. All summer and late into the fall it tries to recompense us for the absence of most other flowers by producing its little daisy-like flowers in abundance. There is no mistaking its unpleasantly strong-scented herbage for anything else.

In the olden time housewives brewed chamomile tea from its leaves, and the plant has a place among accredited drugs even to the present day. The Spanish-Californians know it as "manzanillo," and use it, dried and powdered, as a remedy for colic. In the Norse mythology this flower was sacred to Baldar, the god of the summer sun, and, with its yellow disk and white rays, it was symbolical of the sun, with its beaming light.

CALIFORNIA SAXIFRAGE.

Saxifraga Californica, Greene. Saxifrage Family.

Leaves.—Few; all radical; oval; one to two inches long, on broad petioles six to twelve lines long. *Scape.*—Six to eighteen inches high. *Flowers.*—White or rose; four or five lines across. *Calyx.*—Deeply five-cleft, with reflexed lobes. *Petals.*—Borne on the calyx. *Stamens.* —Ten. *Ovaries.*—Two; partly united. Styles short. Stigmas capitate. *Syn.*—*S. Virginiensis,* Michx. *Hab.*—Throughout the State.

In the rich soil of cool northward slopes, or on many a mossy bank amid the tender young fronds of the maidenhair, may be found the delicate clusters of our little California saxifrage. The plants are small, with but a few, perhaps only one

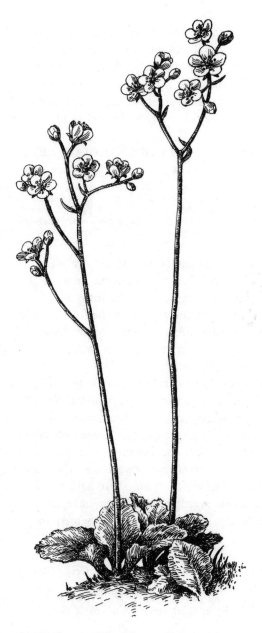

CALIFORNIA SAXIFRAGE—*Saxifraga Californica.*

or two, oval, rather hairy leaves, lying upon the ground, and a slender red scape upholding the dainty cluster of small white flowers. The tips of the calyx-lobes are usually red, and the wee stamens are pink.

We have several species of saxifrage, most of which are plants of exceeding delicacy and grace, and with small flowers.

MINER'S LETTUCE. INDIAN LETTUCE.

Montia perfoliata, Howell. Purslane Family.

Smooth, succulent herbs. *Radical Leaves.*—Long-petioled; broadly rhomboidal; the earliest narrowly linear. *Stems.*—Simple; six to twelve inches high, having, near the summit, a pair of leaves united around the stem. *Flowers.*—White. *Sepals.*—Two. *Petals.*—Five, minute. *Stamens.*—Five. *Ovary.*—One-celled. Style slender. Stigma three-cleft. *Syn.*—*Claytonia perfoliata,* Don. *Hab.*—Throughout California.

Though our Indian lettuce is closely allied to the Eastern "Spring Beauty," one would never suspect it from its outward appearance and habit. The little flower-racemes look as though they might have pushed their way right through the rather large saucer-like leaf just below them. The succulent leaves and stems are greedily eaten by the Indians, from which it is called "Indian lettuce."

Mr. Powers, of Sheridan, writes that the Placer County Indians have a novel way of preparing their salad. Gathering the stems and leaves, they lay them about the entrances of the nests of certain large red ants. These, swarming out, run all over it. After a time the Indians shake them off, satisfied that the lettuce has a pleasant sour taste equaling that imparted by vinegar. These little plants are said to be excellent when boiled and well seasoned, and they have long been grown in England, where they are highly esteemed for salads.

OSO-BERRY.

Nuttallia cerasiformis, Torr. and Gray. Rose Family.

Deciduous shrubs; two to fifteen feet high. *Leaves.*—Broadly oblanceolate; two to four inches long; narrowed into a short petiole. *Flowers.*—White; in short terminal racemes; diœcious; three to eleven

MINER'S LETTUCE—*Montia perfoliata.*

lines across. *Calyx.*—Top-shaped, with five-lobed border. *Petals.*—
Five; inserted with ten of the stamens on the calyx; broadly spatulate.
Stamens.—Fifteen. *Ovaries.*—Five. Styles short. *Fruit.*—Blue-black,
oblong drupes; six to eight lines long. *Hab.*—Chiefly the outer Coast
Ranges from San Luis Obispo to Fraser River.

About the same time that the beautiful leaves of the buckeye are emerging from their wrappings, we notice in the woods
a shrub which has just put forth its clusters of bright-green
leaves from buds all along its slender twigs. Amid their
delicate green hang short clusters of greenish-white flowers.
These blossoms have a delicious bitter fragrance, redolent of
all the tender memories of the springtime.

This shrub is usually mistaken for a wild plum; and the
illusion is still further assisted when the little drupes, like miniature plums, begin to ripen and hang in yellow and purple
clusters amid the matured leaves.

WOOD ANEMONE. WIND-FLOWER.

Anemone quinquefolia, L. Buttercup or Crowfoot Family.

Rootstock.—Horizontal. *Stem.*—Six to fourteen inches high. *Leaves.*
—Radical leaf, remote from the stem; trifid; the segments serrate.
Involucral leaf not far below the flower; three foliolate. *Sepals.*—
Petaloid; five or six; usually bluish outside. *Petals.*—Wanting. *Stamens and Pistils.*—Numerous. *Akenes.*—Two lines long; twelve to
twenty. *Syn.*—*Anemone nemorosa,* L. *Hab.*—The Coast Ranges, in
moist shade.

The delicate blossoms of the wood anemone might at first
be confounded with those of the toothwort by the careless
observer, but a moment's reflection will quickly distinguish
them. The anemone is always a solitary flower with many
stamens, and its petals are of a more delicate texture. It
grows upon wooded banks or cool, shaded flats among the
redwoods.

There are many quaint traditions as to the origin of its
name, and poets have from early times found something ideal
of which to sing in these simple spring flowers.

The generic name has the accent upon the third syllable,

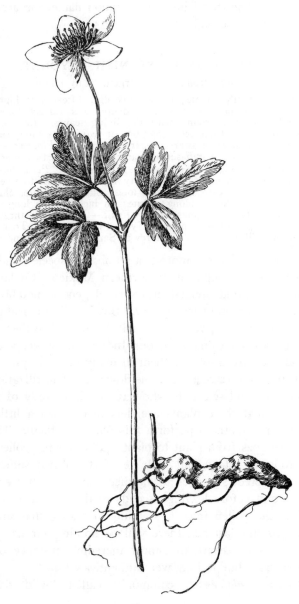

WOOD ANEMONE—*Anemone quinquefolia.*

but, when Anglicized into the common name, the accent falls back upon the second.

WILD DATE. SPANISH BAYONET.

Yucca Mohavensis, Sargent.   Lily Family.

Trunk.—Usually simple; rarely exceeding fifteen feet high; six or eight inches in diameter; naked, or covered with refracted dead leaves, or clothed to the ground with the living leaves.   *Leaves.*—Linear-lanceolate; one to three feet long; one or two inches wide; rigid; margins at length bearing coarse recurved threads.   *Flowers.*—In short-stemmed or sessile, distaff-shaped panicles, a foot or two long; pedicels eventually drooping, twelve to eighteen lines long.   *Perianth.*—Broadly campanulate.   *Segments.*—Six; thirty lines long; six to twelve wide. *Stamens.*—Six; six to nine lines long; filaments white, club-shaped. *Ovary.*—Three-celled; oblong; white; an inch or two long, including the slender style.   Stigmas three.   *Fruit.*—Cylindrical; three or four inches long; pendulous, pulpy.   *Syn.*—*Yucca baccata,* Torr.   *Hab.*— Southern California, from Monterey to San Diego; coast and inland.

The genus *Yucca* comprises a number of species, and reaches its greatest development in northern Mexico.   Of late it has been revised and divided into several genera, notably *Yucca, Hesperoyucca,* and *Cleistoyucca.*   But for all practical purposes the common name, yucca, may still be applied to them all.

They are all valuable to our Indians as basket and textile plants, and are useful to them in many other ways.

Owing to the structure of the flowers, self-fertilization seems impossible, and scientists who have made a study of the subject say that these plants are dependent upon a little white, night-flying moth to perform this office for them.   This little creature goes from plant to plant, gathering the pollen, which she rolls up into a ball with her feet.   When sufficient has been gathered, she goes to another plant, lays her egg in its ovary, and before leaving ascends to the stigma and actually pushes the pollen into it, seeming to realize that unless she performs this last act, there will be nothing for her progeny to eat.   This seems an almost incredible instance of insect intelligence; but it is a well-authenticated fact.

Yucca Mohavensis, commonly called "wild date," or

"Spanish bayonet," is more widely distributed within our borders than either of our other species. Its large panicle of overpoweringly fragrant white waxen bells is a striking object wherever seen. On the coast this yucca is often stemless, but in the interior, where it is more abundant, it rises to a considerable height, and culminates upon the Mojave Desert, where the finest specimens are found.

The fruit, which ripens in August and September, turns from green to a tawny yellow, afterward becoming brownish purple, and eventually almost black. This has a sweet, succulent flesh, and, either fresh or dried, is a favorite fruit among the Indians. Dr. Palmer writes that this is one of the most useful plants to the Indians of New Mexico, Arizona, and southern California. They cut the stems into slices, beat them into a pulp, and mix them with the water in washing, as a substitute for soap.

The leaves are parched in ashes, to make them pliable, and are afterward soaked in water and pounded with a wooden mallet. The fibers thus liberated are long, strong, and durable, and lend themselves admirably to the weaving of the gayly decorated horse-blankets made by the tribes of southern California. They also make from it ropes, twine, nets, hats, hair-brushes, shoes, mattresses, baskets, etc.

FALSE SOLOMON'S SEAL.
Smilacina sessilifolia, Nutt. Lily Family.

Rootstock.—Slender; branching; creeping; scars not conspicuous. *Stem.*—About a foot long (sometimes two); usually zigzag above; leafy. *Leaves.*—Alternate; sessile; lanceolate; two to six inches long; shining above; spreading in a horizontal plane. *Flowers.*—White; few; in a simple terminal raceme, on pedicels two to seven lines long. *Perianth.* —Of six, distinct, spreading segments. *Segments.*—One and one half to four lines long; lanceolate. *Stamens.*—Six; half the length of the segments. *Ovary.*—Three-celled. Style short. *Berry.*—Nearly black; three to five lines through. *Hab.*—Monterey to British Columbia.

The false Solomon's seal is one of the prettiest plants in our woods in March, and in many places it almost hides the ground from view. It has a graceful, drooping habit that shows its handsome, spreading leaves to full advantage, and its few delicate little white blossoms are a fitting termination to the pretty sprays.

S. amplexicaulis, Nutt., is a very handsome, decorative plant, with fine, tall, leafy stem, and large, feathery panicle of tiny white flowers. The broadened white filaments are the most conspicuous part of these blossoms, which are less than a line long. The berries are light-colored, dotted with red or purple.

WOODLAND STAR.

Lithophragma affinis, Gray.   Saxifrage Family.

Stems.—Slender; six to twenty inches high.   *Root-leaves.*—Round-reniform; scalloped; rarely an inch across.   *Stem-leaves.*—Three to five; ternately cleft; variously toothed.   *Flowers.*—White; in a loose raceme; nine lines across.   *Calyx.*—Small; campanulate; five-toothed. *Petals.*—Five; wedge-shaped, with three acute lobes.   *Stamens.*—Ten. Filaments very short.   *Ovary.*—One-celled.   Styles, three, short, stout. Stigmas, capitate.   *Hab.*—Shady places almost throughout the State.

"Star of Bethlehem" is the common name by which many of our children know this fragile flower.   Its slender stems rise from many a mossy bank, upbearing their few delicately slashed, pure-white stars, which seem to shed a gentle radiance about them upon the woodland scene.   They are very satisfactory flowers to gather, and though frail keep well in water.

THIMBLE-BERRY.

Rubus parviflorus, Nutt.   Rose Family.

Stems.—Three to eight feet high.   *Leaves.*—Palmately and nearly equally five-lobed; cordate at base; four to twelve inches broad; the lobes acute; densely tomentose beneath.   *Flowers.*—Few; clustered; white, sometimes pale rose; one to three inches across, with five rounded petals.   *Stamens and Pistils.*—Numerous.   *Fruit.*—Large; red; "like an inverted saucer"; sweet and rather dry.   *Hab.*—Monterey to Alaska.

The thimble-berry is unequaled for the canopy of pure light-green foliage which it spreads in our woods.   It would take the clearest of water-colors to portray its color and texture.   The large white flowers, with their crumpled petals, are

WOODLAND STAR—*Lithophragma affinis.*

deliciously fragrant, but with us are never followed by an edible fruit, probably owing to the dryness of our summer climate. In Oregon and northward the berries are said to be luscious. There the bushes grow in the fir forests, where they seem most at home.

Rubus spectabilis, Pursh., the salmon-berry, has leaves with three leaflets, and large solitary, rose-colored flowers, which are followed by a salmon-colored berry. These shrubs are exceedingly beautiful when in full bloom.

Rubus vitifolius, C. and S., the common wild blackberry, is too well-known to need more than a passing mention.

STRAWBERRY CACTUS.
CALIFORNIA FISH-HOOK CACTUS. LLAVINA.

Mamillaria Goodridgii, Scheer. Cactus Family.

Oval, fleshy, leafless plants; mostly single, though sometimes clustered; three to five inches long; covered with prominences or tubercles. *Tubercles.*—Each bearing a flat rosette of short, whitish spines, with an erect, dark, fishhook-like central one. *Flowers.*—Small; greenish-white. *Outer Sepals.*—Fringed. *Petals.*—About eight; awned. *Stamens.*—Numerous. *Ovary.*—One-celled. Stigmas five or six. *Fruit.*—Scarlet; an inch long. *Hab.*—San Diego and neighboring islands, and southward.

The dry hill-slopes about San Diego afford one of the most interesting fields accessible to civilization,—*i. e.,* within our boundaries,—for the gathering and study of the cacti.

Nestling close to the ground, usually under some shrub or vine, you will find the little fish-hook cactus, one of the prettiest and most interesting of them all. Its oval form bristles with the little dark hooks, each of which emanates from a flat star of whitish spines.

The flowers may be found in April or May, but it is more noticeable when in fruit. The handsome scarlet berries, like old-fashioned coral eardrops, protruding from among the thorns, are easily picked out, and they very naturally find their way to one's mouth. Nor is one disappointed in the expectation raised by their brilliant exterior—for the flavor is delicious, though I cannot say it resembles that of the strawberry, as some aver. To me it is more like a fine tart apple.

COMMON WILD PEA.

Lathyrus vestitus, Nutt. Pea Family.

Stems.—One to ten feet high; slender; not winged. *Leaves.*—Alternate; with small semi-sagittate stipules; pinnate, with four to six pairs of leaflets; tendril-bearing at the summit. *Leaflets.*—Ovate-oblong to linear; six to twelve lines long; acute. *Flowers.*—White, pale rose, or violet; seven to ten lines long. *Lower Calyx-teeth.*—About equaling the tube. *Corolla.*—Papilionaceous; the standard veined with purple in the center. *Stamens.*—Nine united; one free. *Ovary.*—Flattened; pubescent. Style hairy down the inner side. (See *Leguminosæ.*) *Hab.*—Sonoma County to San Diego.

The genus *Lathyrus,* which contains the beautiful sweet-pea of the garden, affords us several handsome wild species, but most of them are difficult of determination, and many of them are as yet much confused. This genus is quite closely related to *Vicia,* but, in general, the leaflets are broader, the flowers are larger, and the style is hairy down the inner side as well as at the tip.

Lathyrus vestitus is the common wild pea. It is quite plentiful, and clambers over and under shrubs, hanging out its occasional clusters of rather large pale flowers.

L. Torreyi, Gray, found from Santa Clara County to Napa in dry woods, is a slender plant, having from one to three small white or pinkish flowers. It is remarkable for and easily distinguished by its very fragrant foliage.

WHITE LAYIA. WHITE DAISY.

Layia glandulosa, Hook. and Arn. Composite Family.

Stems.—Six to twelve inches high; loosely branching; hairy; often reddish. *Leaves.*—Sessile; linear; the upper all small and entire; the lower often lanceolate and incised pinnatifid. *Heads.*—Usually large and showy. *Ray-flowers.*—Bright, pure white, sometimes rose-color; eight to thirteen; three-lobed; an inch or less long; six lines wide. *Disk-flowers.*—Golden yellow; five-toothed. Each scale of the involucre clasping a ray-flower. *Hab.*—Columbia River to Los Angeles.

These white daisies, as they are commonly called in the south, cover the fields and plains in early spring, jostling one another in friendly proximity and stretching away in an endless perspective. They are of a charming purity, and to me are more attractive than their sisters, the tidy-tips.

They love a sandy soil, and I have seen them flourishing in the disintegrated granite of old river-beds, where the dazzling whiteness of the stones was hardly distinguishable from the blossoms. The involucre is thickly studded with curious little glands, resembling small glass-headed pins.

WILD CUCUMBER. BIG-ROOT. CHILICOTHE.
Echinocystis fabacea, Naudin. Gourd Family.

Tendril-bearing vines, ten to thirty feet long. *Root.*—Enormous; woody. *Leaves.*—Palmately five- to seven-lobed; three to six inches broad. *Flowers.*—Yellowish white; monœcious. *Calyx-tube.*—Campanulate; teeth small or none. *Corolla.*—Five- to seven-lobed; three to six lines across. *Staminate Flowers.*—Five to twenty in racemes; their stamens two and a half, with short connate filaments and somewhat horizontal anthers. *Pistillate Flowers.*—Solitary; from the same axils as the racemes. *Ovary.*—Two- to four-celled. *Fruit.*—Two inches long; prickly. *Syn.*—*Megarrhiza Californica,* Torr. *Hab.*—Near the coast, from San Diego to Point Reyes.

The wild cucumber is one of our most graceful native vines. It drapes many an unslightly stump, or clambers up into shrubs, embowering them with its pretty foliage. Seeing its rather delicate ivy-like habit above ground, one would never dream that it came from a root as large as a man's body, buried deep in the earth. From this root, it has received two of its common names, "big-root" and "man-in-the-ground." Sometimes this may be seen upon the ocean beach or rolling about in the breakers, where it has been liberated by the wearing away of the cliffs. It is intensely bitter.

The seeds have a very interesting method of germinating. The two large radical leaves remain underground, sending up the terminal shoot only. They are so tender and succulent that they would be eaten forthwith, if they showed themselves above the ground. An oil expressed from the roasted seeds has been used by the Indians to promote the growth of the hair.

Authorities have differed about the classification of these

WILD CUCUMBER—*Echinocystis fabacea.*

plants, and they have been variously called *Megarrhiza, Micrampelis,* and *Echinocystis,* the latter being latest approved. We have several species. One common in the South is *E. macrocarpa,* Green. This has a large oval, prickly ball, four inches or so long. When mature, this opens at the top, splitting into several segments, which gradually roll downward, like the petals of a beautiful white lily, showing their pure-white inner surfaces and leaving exposed the four cells in the center, with lacelike walls, in which nestle the large, handsome dark seeds. These seeds are often beautifully mottled and colored, and in the early days served the Spanish-Californian children for marbles.

BED-STRAW. GOOSE-GRASS. CLEAVERS.

Galium Aparine, L.   Madder Family.

Climbing by the prickly stem-angles and leaf-margins. *Stems.*— Weak; one to four feet long. *Leaves.*—In whorls of six to eight; linear oblanceolate; one inch long. *Peduncles.*—Elongated; one- to two-flowered. *Flowers.*—Minute; one line across; greenish-white. *Calyx-tube.*—Adnate to the ovary; limb obsolete. *Corolla.*—Mostly four-cleft. *Stamens.*—Four. *Ovary.*—Two-lobed, two-celled. Styles two, short. Stigmas capitate. *Fruit.*—Two or three lines across, covered with hooked bristles. *Hab.*—Throughout the State.

All through our moist woodlands, in early spring, the long stems of the bed-straw may be found, running about upon the ground or entangled amid the stems of other plants. The angles of these weak stems and the leaf-margins and midribs are all clothed with small backward-pointing bristles, which make the plants cling to surrounding objects. The flowers are greenish and minute, and are followed by tiny prickly balls.

A cold infusion of this little plant is used as a domestic remedy in cases of fever, where a cooling drink is desired.

The genus has received the common name of "bed-straw," because it was supposed that one of the species, *G. verum,* filled the manger in which was laid the Infant Jesus. There are a dozen or so species in California.

Very conspicuous all through the south is *G. angustifolium,*

Nutt., often three feet high, sending up very numerous slender, feathery stems from a woody base. This has its small leaves in whorls of four.

G. Nuttallii, Gray, still another species, is common from Marin County to San Diego. This has stems one to three feet high, or clambers higher over bushes. Its leaves are in whorls of four, or, at top, of two, and are two to five lines long. Its minute solitary flowers are followed by a small, smooth, purple berry two lines across.

MOUNTAIN HEART'S-EASE.

Viola Beckwithii, Torr. and Gray.   Violet Family.

Leaves.—Broadly cordate in outline; three-parted; the divisions cleft into linear or oblong segments. *Peduncles.*—About equaling the leaves. *Petals.*—Four to seven lines long; very broad; the upper deep purple, the others lilac, bluish, or white, veined with purple, with a yellowish base; the lateral bearded; the lowest emarginate. *Stigma.*—Bearded at the sides. *Capsule.*—Obtuse. (Otherwise as *V. pedunculata.*) *Hab.*— The central Sierras.

> " By scattered rocks and turbid waters shifting,
>   By furrowed glade and dell,
>   To feverish men thy calm, sweet face uplifting,
>   Thou stayest them to tell
>
> " The delicate thought that cannot find expression—
>   For ruder speech too fair,—
>   That, like thy petals, trembles in possession,
>   And scatters on the air."

The poet, with a delicate insight, has made this mountain flower the reminder to the rugged miner of home and scenes far away. But the vision lasts for a moment only; then, as he brushes away a tear, his uplifted pick—

> " Through root and fiber cleaves—
>   And on the muddy current slowly drifting
>   Are swept thy bruised leaves.
>
> " And yet, O poet! in thy homely fashion.
>   Thy work thou dost fulfill;
>   For on the turbid current of his passion
>   Thy face is shining still.

31

WHITE FORGET-ME-NOT. NIEVITAS.
POP-CORN FLOWER.

Plagiobothrys nothofulvus, Gray.   Borage Family.

Stem or Stems.—Loosely branching, six to eighteen inches high, from a depressed rosette of leaves. *Leaves.*—Whitish, with short, fine pubescence. *Inflorescence.*—Scorpioid. *Calyx.*—Small, five-cleft almost to the middle; deciduous, except at base. *Corolla.*—Five-lobed, with crested throat, white, three lines across. *Stamens.*—Five, on the corolla. *Ovary.* —Four-celled. *Style.*—One. *Fruit.*—Four seedlike nutlets. *Hab.*— Throughout the State, and northward to Washington.

The wild white forget-me-nots are among our most welcome flowers. Though not showy, taken singly, they often cover the fields, presenting the appearance of a light snowfall, from which fact the Spanish-Californians have bestowed the pretty name "nievitas," the diminutive of *nieve,* snow.

Their chief charm often lies in their pure, delightful fragrance, which recalls the days of our careless, happy childhood. Children are keen observers of flowers, and are among their most appreciative lovers, and with them these modest, chaste little blossoms are special favorites.

A rich purple stain or dye is contained in the root and stems.

MIST-MAIDENS.

Romanzoffia Californica, Green.   Baby-eyes or Waterleaf Family.

Leaves mainly radical; rounded and scalloped; six to eighteen lines across; smooth. *Flowers.*—White, pink, or purple; borne on scapes six inches high; in lax racemes. *Calyx.*—Deeply five-parted. *Corolla.* —Funnel-form; five-lobed; four lines long. *Stamens.*—Five. *Ovary.*— Two-celled. *Hab.*—Coast Ranges, from Santa Cruz northward.

In appearance these delicate herbs resemble the saxifrages, and they affect much the same sort of places, decking mossy banks and stream borders with their beautiful scalloped leaves and small white flowers.

The genus was named in honor of Nicholas Romanzoff, a Russian nobleman, who, by his munificence, enabled some noted botanists to visit this coast early in the last century.

WHITE FORGET-ME-NOT—*Plagiobothrys nothofulvus.*

WILD BUCKWHEAT.

Eriogonum fasciculatum, Benth. Buckwheat Family.

Shrubby; very leafy. *Leaves.*—Alternate; much fascicled; nearly sessile; narrowly oblanceolate; acute; tomentose beneath; glabrous above; three to nine lines long. *Flowers.*—White or pinkish; in densely crowded compound clusters; several perianths contained in the small involucres. *Involucres.*—Campanulate; five- or six-nerved and toothed; two lines high. *Perianth.*—Minute; of six nearly equal segments. (See *Eriogonum umbellatum.*) *Hab.*—Santa Barbara and southward; east to Arizona.

The wild buckwheat is a characteristic feature of the southern landscape. It is a charming plant when in full bloom, and its feathery clusters of pinkish-white flowers show finely against the warm olive tones of its foliage. It is a very important honey plant, as it yields an exceptionally pure nectar and remains in bloom a long time. Growing near the sea, it is often close-cropped and shorn by the wind, and then it quite closely resembles the *Adenostoma,* or chamisal.

. Another very widely distributed and common species is *E. nudum,* Dougl. Every one is familiar with its tall, green, naked, rushlike stems, bearing on the ends of the branchlets the small balls of white or pinkish flowers. Its leaves are all radical, smooth green above and densely white-woolly beneath.

SIERRA PLUM. WILD PLUM.

Prunus subcordata, Benth. Rose Family.

Trees or shrubs three to ten feet high, with ash-gray bark and branchlets occasionally spinescent. *Leaves.*—Short-petioled; ovate; sharply and finely serrate; an inch or two long. *Flowers.*—Two to four in a cluster. Pedicels three to six lines long. White; six lines across. *Fruit.*—Red or purple; six to fifteen lines long; fleshy; smooth. (Otherwise as *P. ilicifolia.*) *Hab.*—Mostly eastward of the Central Valley, from San Felipe into Oregon.

The wild plum reaches its greatest perfection in the north, where the shrubs are found in extensive groves covering whole mountain slopes.

The flowers, which are produced before the leaves, from March to May, are white, fading to rose-color. By August

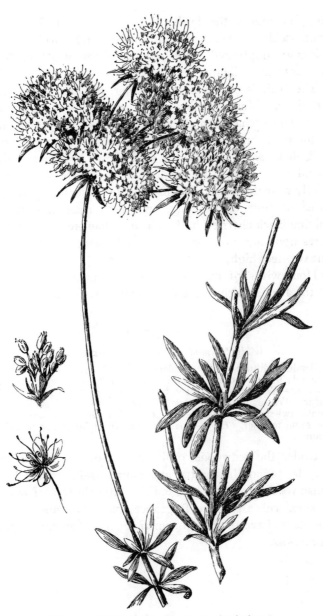

WILD BUCKWHEAT—*Eriogonum fasciculatum.*

and September, the bushes are loaded with the handsome fruit, richly mottled with red, yellow, and purple; and these colors are duplicated in the autumn foliage, which in the north becomes very brilliant.

The fruit is excellent for canning, preserving, and making into jelly. Many families make annual pilgrimages to these wild-plum orchards of the mountains and carry away bushels of the fruit; but even then countless tons of it go to waste.

P. demissa, Walpers,—the wild cherry or choke-cherry,—is found upon mountains throughout the State, but less abundantly near the coast. Its small white flowers grow in racemes three or four inches long, and these ripen into the pretty shining black cherries, half an inch in diameter. It often covers acres upon acres of rough land, and commences to bear when but two feet high.

Housewives of our mountain districts make a marmalade of the fruit, which has a peculiarly delicious tart flavor.

MODESTY.

Whipplea modesta, Torr.   Saxifrage Family.

Slender, diffuse, hairy undershrubs.   *Leaves.* — Opposite; short-petioled; ovate; toothed or entire; an inch or less long; three-nerved. *Flowers.*—White; barely three lines across; in small terminal clusters. *Calyx.*—White; five-cleft.   *Petals.*—Five.   *Stamens.*—Usually ten.   Filaments awl-shaped.   *Ovary.*—Three- to five-celled, globose.   Styles of the same number.   *Hab.*—Coast Ranges from Monterey to Mendocino County.

Under the redwoods, or in moist cañons in their vicinity, may be found this pretty undershrub trailing over banks or brushwood. In April its exquisite little clusters of pure white flowers, with a pleasant fragrance, make their appearance, and the plants have then been sometimes mistaken for a species of *Ceanothus.*

MODESTY—*Whipplea modesta.*

MADROÑO. MADRONE.

Arbutus Menziesii, Pursh. Heath Family.

Shrubs or trees. *Leaves.*—Alternate; petioled; oblong; entire or serrulate; four inches or so long. *Flowers.*—White; waxen; in large clusters. *Calyx.*—Five-cleft; minute; white. *Corolla.*—Broadly urn-shaped; three lines long; with five minute, recurved teeth. *Stamens.*—Ten; on the corolla. Filaments dilated; bearded. Anthers two-celled; saccate; opening terminally; furnished with a pair of reflexed horns near the summit. *Ovary.*—Five-celled. Style rather long. *Fruit.*—A loose cluster of rather large scarlet-orange berries, with rough granular coats. *Hab.*—Puget Sound to Mexico and Texas; especially in the Coast Ranges.

Captain of the Western wood,
Thou that apest Robin Hood!
Green above thy scarlet hose,
How thy velvet mantle shows;
Never tree like thee arrayed,
O thou gallant of the glade!

When the fervid August sun
Scorches all it looks upon,
And the balsam of the pine
Drips from stem to needle fine,
Round thy compact shade arranged,
Not a leaf of thee is changed!

When the yellow autumn sun
Saddens all it looks upon,
Spreads its sackcloth on the hills,
Strews its ashes in the rills,
Thou thy scarlet hose dost doff,
And in limbs of purest buff
Challengest the somber glade
For a sylvan masquerade.

Where, oh where shall he begin
Who would paint thee, Harlequin?
With thy waxen, burnished leaf,
With thy branches' red relief,
With thy poly-tinted fruit,
In thy spring or autumn suit,—
Where begin, and oh, where end,—
Thou whose charms all art transcend?
　　　　　—Bret Harte.

The name "madroño" was applied by the early Spanish-Californians to this tree because of its strong resemblance and close relationship to the *Arbutus unido,* or strawberry-tree, of the Mediterranean countries, called madroño in Spain.

Our madroño, though but a large shrub in the south, increases in size northward, and reaches its maximum development in Marin County, where there are some superb specimens of it. One tree upon the shores of Lake Lagunitas measures more than twenty-three feet in circumference and a hundred feet in height, and sends out many large branches, each two or three feet in diameter.

A large part of the forest growth on the northern slopes of Mt. Tamalpais is composed of it; and as it is an evergreen, it forms a mountain wall of delightful and refreshing greenth the year around. The bark on the younger limbs, which is of a rich Indian red, begins to peel off in thin layers about midsummer, leaving a clear, smooth, greenish-buff surface, and strewing the forest floor with its warm shreds, which, mingling with the exquisite tones of its ripened leaves, which have fallen at about the same time, make a carpet equal in beauty of coloring to that under the English beeches. It is thoroughly patrician in all its parts. The leaves which are clustered at the ends of the slender twigs are rich, polished green above, and somewhat paler beneath.

In the spring it puts forth great panicles of small, white, waxen bells, which call the bees to a sybaritic feast, and in the autumn it spreads a no less inviting repast in its great clusters of fine scarlet berries for the blue pigeons who visit it in large flocks.

The wood of the madrone is hard and close-grained, of a light brown, shaded with red, with lighter-colored sap-wood. It is used in the manufacture of furniture, but is particularly valuable for the making of charcoal to be used in the composition of gunpowder. The bark is sometimes used in tanning leather.

ELLISIA.

Ellisia chrysanthemifolia, Benth. Baby-eyes or Waterleaf Family.

More or less hairy. *Stems.*—Loosely branching; a foot or so high. *Leaves.*—Mostly opposite; auricled at base; twice- or thrice-parted into many short, small lobes. *Flowers.*—In loose racemes; white; three lines or so across. *Calyx.*—Five-cleft; without appendages at the sinuses; almost equaling the corolla. *Corolla*—Open-campanulate; having ten minute scales at base within. *Stamens.*—Five. *Ovary.*—One-celled; globose. Style slender; two-cleft. *Hab.*—San Francisco to San Diego.

These little plants, with delicately dissected leaves, are common in moist, shaded localities; but, unfortunately, their foliage has a very strong odor, which just escapes being agreeable. Their general aspect is somewhat similar to that of some of the small species of *Nemophila;* but the lack of appendages upon the calyx reveals their separate identity. It blooms freely from March to June, and is especially abundant southward.

HELIOTROPE.

Heliotropium Curassavicum, L. Borage Family.

Diffusely spreading; six to twelve inches high. *Leaves.*—Alternate sessile; obovate to linear; an inch or two long; succulent; glaucous. *Flowers.*—Usually white, sometimes lavender; in dense, usually two-forked spikes. *Calyx.*—Five-parted. *Corolla.* — Salver-form; border five-lobed, with plaited sinuses; three lines across. *Stamens.*—Five. Anthers sessile. *Ovary.*—Of four seedlike nutlets. Stigma umbrella-like. *Hab.*—Widely distributed.

This, the only species of true heliotrope common within our borders, is widely distributed over the world. It affects the sand of the seashore or saline soils of the interior. It is in no way an attractive plant, as compared with our garden heliotrope, as its flowers have a washed-out look and are not at all fragrant, while its pale stems and foliage lack color and character.

Its leaves, which contain a mucilaginous juice, are dried and reduced to powder by the Spanish-Californians, who esteem them very highly as a cure for the wounds of men and animals. They blow the dry powder into the wound.

COMMON ELDER.

Sambucus glauca, Nutt. Honeysuckle Family.

Shrubby or arborescent; often thirty feet high; with finely fissured bark. *Leaves.*—Opposite; petioled; pinnate. *Leaflets.*—Three to nine; lanceolate; acuminate; serrate; two inches or so long; smooth. *Flowers.* —Minute; two or three lines across; in large, flat, five-branched cymes; white. *Calyx.*—Five-toothed. *Corolla.*—Rotate; five-lobed. *Stamens.*— Five; alternate with the corolla lobes. *Ovary*—Three- to five-celled. Stigmas of same number. *Berries.*—Small; dark blue, with a dense white bloom. *Hab.*—Throughout the State; common.

The elder is one of our most widely distributed shrubs, and is a familiar sight upon almost every open glade or plain. It is especially abundant in the south. Its flower-clusters, made up of myriads of tiny cream-white blossoms, make a showy but delicate and lacelike mat, while its berries are beautiful and inviting. The bears are especially appreciative of these, and we have sometimes seen their footprints leading along a lonely mountain road to the elder-berry bushes. The fruit is prized by our housewives for pies and preserves, and it would doubtless make as good wine as that of the Eastern species.

Among the Spanish-Californians the blossoms are known as "sauco" and are regarded as an indispensable household remedy for colds. They are administered in the form of a tea, which induces a profuse perspiration. It is said that Dr. Boerhaave held the elder in such reverence for the multitude of its virtues that he always removed his hat when he passed it.

In ancient times the elder was the subject of many strange superstitions. In his interesting book, "The Folk-Lore of Plants," Mr. Thistleton Dyer says that it was reputed to be possessed of magic power, and that any baptized person whose eyes had been anointed with the green juice of its inner bark could recognize witches anywhere. Owing to these magic properties, it was often planted near dwellings to keep away evil spirits. By making a magic circle and standing within it with elder-berries gathered on St. John's Night, the mystic fern-seed could be secured which possessed the strength of forty men and enabled one to walk invisible. This was one of the trees suspected as having furnished wood for the Cross; and to this day the English country people believe themselves safe from lightning when standing under an elder, because lightning never strikes the tree of which the Cross was made.

We have another elder,—*Sambucus callicarpa,* Greene,—not as common as the above, distinguished by its thinner, more pointed leaflets, its ovate clusters of dull white flowers, and its beautiful scarlet berries. This is found along watercourses in the mountains of the Coast Ranges.

COULTER'S SNAPDRAGON.

Antirrhinum Coulterianum, Benth. Figwort Family.

Stems.—Two to four feet high; smooth below. *Leaves.*—Linear to oval; distant. Tendril-shoots long and slender, produced mostly below the flowers. *Flowers.*—White or violet; in densely crowded villous-pubescent spikes, two to ten inches long. (Otherwise as *A. vagans.*) *Hab.*—Santa Barbara to San Diego.

The flowers of this pretty snapdragon are usually white, and the lower lip, with its great palate often dotted with dark color, takes up the larger part of the blossom. They are sometimes violet, however, when they much resemble the flowers of the toad-flax, but are without their long spur.

A. Orcuttianum, Gray, is a similar species, but more slender, with fewer and smaller flowers, whose lower lip is not much larger than the upper, and whose flower-spikes are disposed to have the tortile branchlets in their midst. This is found near San Diego and southward.

HOREHOUND.

Marrubium vulgare, Linn. Mint Family.

The horehound has been introduced from Europe at various points along our Coast, but it is now so abundant as to seem like an indigenous plant. It has many white-woolly, square stems, and roundish, wrinkly opposite leaves, covered beneath with matted, white-woolly hairs. Its small, white, bilabiate flowers are crowded in the axils of the upper leaves so densely as to appear like whorls. It may be known from the other members of the Mint family by its campanulate calyx with ten strong, recurved teeth.

This has long been used in medicine as a tonic, and is especially esteemed by our Spanish-Californians as a remedy for colds and lung troubles.

WILD WHITE LILAC.

Ceanothus velutinus, Dougl.   Buckthorn Family.

Widely branching shrubs, two to six feet or more high.   *Leaves.*— Alternate; petioled; roundish, or broadly ovate; eighteen lines to three inches long; polished, resinous above; somewhat pubescent beneath; strongly three-nerved.   *Flowers.*—White; three lines across; in large, dense, compound clusters four or five inches long and wide.   (See *Ceanothus,* for flower structure.)   *Hab.*—Coast Ranges; Columbia River, southward to San Francisco Bay; also eastward to Colorado.

Its ample bright-green, highly varnished leaves and large white flower-clusters make this a very beautiful species of *Ceanothus.*   The foliage is glutinous with a gummy exudation, which has a rather disagreeable odor.   Yet the shrub would be very handsome in cultivation.   In the Sierras, particularly about the shores of Lake Tahoe, this forms extensive thickets, and is a characteristic feature of the landscape.

Closely associated with this in this mountain region is *Ceanothus cordulatus,* Kellogg, the "snow-bush," which may be easily recognized by its low-spreading habit, generally gray-green aspect, and its thorny widely diverging branchlets.   Its low, thicket-like mats afford shelter for the birds, and, early in the season, it is covered with an abundant feathery white bloom, like a heavy snowfall, on the branches.

WHITE NEMOPHILA.

Nemophila atomaria, Fisch. and Mey.   Baby-eyes or Waterleaf Family.

Corolla.—Pure white, closely dark-dotted nearly to the edge; an inch or less across; densely hairy within the tube.   Scales of the corolla narrow, with long hairs.   (Otherwise as *N. insignis.*)   *Hab.*—Central California.

This delicate *Nemophila* haunts wet, springy places among the hills, and is at its best in early spring.   There are a number of small-flowered forms of *Nemophila* which have been hitherto referred to *N. parviflora,* but which the future will probably prove to constitute a number of species.

N. maculata, Benth., found in middle California and the high Sierras, is a charming form, with large flowers, whose petals bear strong violet blotches at the top.

RATTLE-WEED. LOCO-WEED.

Astragalus leucopsis, Torr. and Gray. Pea Family.

Stems.—A foot or so high. *Leaflets.*—In many pairs; six lines or more long. *Flowers.*—Greenish-white; six lines long; in spikelike racemes an inch or two long. *Calyx.*—With teeth more than half the length of the campanulate tube. *Pod.*—Thin; bladdery-inflated; an inch or more long, on a smooth stalk twice or thrice the length of the calyx-tube. (See *Astragalus.*) *Hab.*—Santa Barbara to San Diego.

These plants are very noticeable and quite pretty, with their pale foliage, symmetrical leaves, and white flowers; but they are dreaded by the farmers of the region of their growth, who aver that they are deadly loco-weeds. It is said that native stock will not touch them; but animals brought from a distance, and unacquainted with them, eat them, with dreadful results of "loco," or insanity.

We have numerous species, all rather difficult of determination.

WILD MORNING-GLORY.

Convolvulus luteolus, Gray. Morning-Glory Family.

Stems.—Twining and climbing twenty feet or more. *Leaves.*—Alternate; sagittate; two inches or so long; smooth. *Peduncles.*—Several-flowered; axillary, with two small linear-lanceolate bracts a little below the flower. *Flowers.*—Cream-color or pinkish, sometimes deep rose. *Sepals.*—Five; without bracts immediately below them. *Corolla.*—Open funnel-form; eighteen lines long; not lobed or angled. *Stamens.*—Five. *Ovary.*—Globose; two-celled or imperfectly four-celled. Style filiform. Stigmas two. *Hab.*—Throughout California.

I remember long stretches of mountain road where the wild morning-glory has completely covered the unsightly shrubs charred by a previous year's fire, flinging out its slender stems, lacing and interlacing them in airy festoons, which are

RATTLE–WEED—*Astragalus leucopsis.*

covered with the fragile flowers in greatest profusion. In these tangles the industrious spiders have hung their exquisite geometrical webs, which catch the glittering water-drops in their meshes. When the sun comes out after a dense, cool fog-bath on a summer morning, nothing more charmingly fresh could be imagined than such a scene.

The common morning-glory of the south—*C. occidentalis,* Gray—is very similar to the above, but may be distinguished from it by the pair of large, thin bracts immediately below the calyx and enveloping it.

Another very pretty species is *C. villosus,* Gray. This is widely distributed, but not very common. Its trailing stems and foliage are of a velvety sage-gray throughout, and its small flowers of a yellowish cream-color. The hastate leaves are shapely, and the whole plant is charming when grown away from dust.

The common European bindweed—*C. arvensis,* L.— is to the farmer a very unwelcome little immigrant. In fields it becomes a serious pest; for the more its roots are disturbed and broken up the better it thrives. But despite its bad character, we cannot help admiring its pretty little white funnels, which lift themselves so debonairly among the prostrate stems and leaves.

In medicine a tincture of the whole plant is valued for several uses.

WOOD-BALM. PITCHER-SAGE.
Sphacele calycina, Benth. Mint Family.

Woody at the base; two to five feet high; hairy or woolly. *Leaves.*—Two to four inches long. *Flowers.*—Dull white or purplish; an inch or more long; mostly solitary in the upper axils. *Calyx.*—Five-cleft. *Corolla.*—Having a hairy ring at base within. *Stamens.*—Four, in two pairs. *Ovary.*—Of four seedlike nutlets. Style filiform. Stigma two-lobed. *Hab.*—Dry hills. San Francisco Bay, southward.

The wood-balm is closely allied to the sages, which fact is betrayed by its opposite, wrinkly, sage-scented leaves; but its flowers have quite a different aspect. These are ample and

PITCHER-SAGE—*Sphacele calycina.*

cylindrical, with a five-lobed border, one of the lobes being prolonged into somewhat of a lip.

The generic name is from the Greek word meaning *sage;* and the specific name, signifying *cuplike,* refers to the shape of the blossoms.

The dwellers among our southern mountains, with that happy instinct possessed by those who live close to the heart of nature, have aptly named this "pitcher-sage."

After the flowers have passed away, the large inflated, light-green calyxes, densely crowded upon the stems, become quite conspicuous.

YUCCA-PALM. TREE-YUCCA. JOSHUA-TREE.
Cleistoyucca arborescens, Trelease. Lily Family.

Scraggly trees; thirty or forty feet high; with trunks one or two feet in diameter. *Leaves.*—Eight inches long; crowded; rigid; spine-tipped; serrulate; the older ones reflexed and sun-bleached, the younger ashy-green. *Flowers.*—In sessile, ovate panicles, terminating the branches. Panicles several inches long. *Perianth.*—Narrowly campanulate; eighteen to thirty lines long. *Fruit.*—Two or three inches long. (Otherwise as *Yucca Mohavensis.*) *Syn.*—*Yucca arborescens,* Trelease. *Hab.*—Southwestern Utah to the Mojave Desert.

The traveler crossing the Mojave Desert upon the railroad has his curiosity violently aroused by certain fantastic tree forms that whirl by the car windows. These are the curious Joshua-trees of the Mormons, which are called in California tree-yucca or yucca-palm. A writer in "The Land of Sunshine" thus aptly characterizes them:—"Weird, twisted, demoniacal, the yuccas remind me of those enchanted forests described by Dante, whose trees were human creatures in torment. In twisted groups or standing isolated, they may readily be imagined specters of the plains."

Mr. Sargent tells us that, though found much to the eastward of our borders, it abounds in the Mojave Desert, where it attains its largest size and forms a belt of gaunt, straggling forest several miles in width along the desert's western rim.

Its flowers appear from March to May, but are not at all

attractive, on account of their soiled white color and disagreeable, fetid odor. "The unopened panicles form conspicuous cones eight to ten inches long, covered with closely overlapping white scales, often flushed with purple at the apex."

The seeds are gathered and used by the omnivorous Indians, who grind them into meal, which they eat either raw or cooked as a mush. The wood furnishes an excellent material for paper pulp, and some years ago an English company established a mill at Ravenna, in Soledad Pass, for its manufacture. It is said that several editions of a London journal were printed upon it, but owing to the great cost of its manufacture, the enterprise had to be abandoned.

The light wood is put to many uses now, and in the curio bazaars of the south it plays a conspicuous part, made into many small articles. By sawing round and round the trunk of the tree, thin sheets of considerable size are procured. A sepia reproduction of one of the old missions upon the ivory-tinted ground of one of these combines sentiment and novelty in a very pretty souvenir. Surgeons find these same sheets excellent for splints, as they are unyielding in one direction and pliable in the other; and orchardists wrap them around the bases of their trees to protect them from the gnawing of rabbits.

SALAL. WINTERGREEN.
Gaultheria Shallon, Pursh. Heath Family.

Shrubby, and one to three or more feet high or prostrate. *Leaves.*—Alternate; short-petioled; ovate to elliptical; pointed; two to four inches long; leathery; bristle-toothed when young; evergreen. *Flowers.*—Manzanita-like; slenderer; glandular-viscid; white or pinkish. *Ovary.*—Five-celled. Style single. *Fruit.*—Black; berry-like; aromatic; edible. (Flower-structure similar to that of *Arctostaphylos manzanita.*) *Hab.*—Coast woods, from Santa Barbara County to British Columbia.

The floor of the redwood forest in our northern coast counties is often carpeted with this little undershrub, while in other places one can wade waist-deep in it. It grows much larger north of us, and upon Vancouver Island it forms dense, impenetrable thickets. Its dark-purple berries have a very agreeable flavor, and form an important article of diet among the Oregon Indians, who call them "salal."

WHITE EVENING PRIMROSE.

Œnothera Californica, Watson.   Evening-Primrose Family.

Hoary pubescent, and more or less villous. *Stems.*—A foot or so high. *Leaves.*—Oblanceolate or lanceolate; sinuately toothed or irregularly pinnatifid; two to four inches long. *Flowers.*—White; turning to rose-color; two inches across. *Ovary and Calyx-tube.*—Over three inches long. *Calyx-lobes.*—One inch long; separate at the tips. (See *Œnothera* for flower-structure.) *Hab.*—Central and southern California; especially about the San Bernardino region; not plentiful.

Perhaps the most beautiful of all our evening primroses is this charming white species. Late in the afternoon the handsome silvery foliage begins to show the great white, opening moons of the fragile blossoms. Their silken texture, delicate fragrance, and chaste look make them paramount among blossoms.

It is a most interesting sight to watch the opening of one of the nodding silvery buds. I sat down by one which had already uplifted its head. The calyx-lobes had just commenced to part in the center, showing the white, silken corolla tightly rolled within. It grew larger from moment to moment, when suddenly the calyx-lobes parted with a jerk, and the petals, freed from their bondage, quickly spread wider and wider, as though some spirit within were forcing its way out, while one after another the calyx-lobes were turned downward with a quick, decisive movement. It was a wonderful exhibition of the power of motion in plants. I could now look within and see a magical tangle of yellow anthers delicately draped with cobwebby ropes of pollen.

The stamens take a downward curve toward the lower petal. The anthers have already opened their stores of golden pollen before the unfurling of the buds, so that the somewhat sticky ropes are all ready to adhere to the first moth who visits the flower in search of the delicious and abundant nectar stored in the depth of the long calyx-tube. The day following their

WHITE EVENING PRIMROSE—*Œnothera Californica.*

opening the blossoms begin to turn to a delicate pink, and the calyx-lobes have a fleshlike look.

EVENING SNOW.

Gilia dichotoma, Benth.   Phlox or Polemonium Family.

Six inches to a foot high; erect; sparsely leaved. *Leaves.*—Opposite; mostly entire; filiform. *Flowers.*—Nearly sessile in the forks, or terminal. *Calyx.*—With cylindric tube five lines long; wholly white, scarious, except the five filiform green ribs, continued into needle-like lobes. *Corolla.*—White; an inch or two across. Anthers linear. *Hab.*—Throughout the western part of the State.

This is one of the most showy of our gilias.   Miss Eastwood writes of it:—"At about four o'clock in the afternoon *Gilia dichotoma* begins to whiten the hillside.   Before expansion the flowers are hardly noticeable; the dull pink of the edges, which are not covered in the convolute corolla, hides their identity and makes the change which takes place when they unveil their radiant faces to the setting sun the more startling.   They intend to watch all night and by sunset all are awake.   In the morning they roll up their petals again when daylight comes on, and when the sun is well up all are asleep, tired out with the vigil of the night.   The odor is most sickening. . . . The same flower opens several times, and grows larger as it grows older."

HEART'S-EASE.

Viola ocellata, Torr. and Gray.   Violet Family.

Stems.—Nearly erect; six to twelve inches high. *Leaves.*—Cordate; acutish; conspicuously crenate. *Petals.*—Five to seven lines long; the upper white within, deep brown-purple without; the others white or yellowish, veined with purple; the lateral with a purple spot near the base and slightly bearded on the claw. (Flower structure as in *V. pedunculata.*) *Hab.*—Wooded districts from Monterey to Mendocino County.

This dainty little heart's-ease has nothing of the gay, joyous, self-assertive look of our yellow pansy, but rather the shy, timid mien belonging to all the creatures of the woodland.   It ventures its pretty blossoms in late spring and early summer.

ICE-PLANT.

Mesembryanthemum crystallinum, L. Fig-Marigold Family.

Procumbent, succulent plants, covered with minute, elongated, glistening papillæ. *Leaves.*—Flat; ovate or spatulate; undulate-margined; clasping. *Flowers.*—White or rose-colored; axillary; nearly sessile; rather small. *Calyx.*—With campanulate tube and usually five unequal lobes. *Petals.* — Linear; numerous. *Stamens.* — Numerous. *Ovary.* — Two- to many-celled. Stigmas five. *Hab.*—The Coast and adjacent islands from Santa Barbara southward; also in the Mojave Desert.

The ice-plant spreads its broad, green leaves over the ground, often making large rugs, which, when reddened by the approach of drouth and glistening with small crystals, produce a charming effect. The flat leaves of this plant are quite unexpectedly different from those of our other species of *Mesembryanthemum*, which are usually cylindrical or three-angled. The leaf-stems and the calyx-tube, in particular, are beautifully jeweled with the clear, glasslike incrustation. The flesh-pink or almost white flowers resemble small sea-anemones, with their single row of tentacle-like petals and hollow tube powdered with the little white anthers.

The plant grows so abundantly in the fields of the southern seasides as to be a dreadful pest to the farmer, and it is very disagreeable to walk through, as it yields up the water of its crystals very readily, and this is said to be of an alkaline quality, which is ruinous to shoe-leather.

This ice-plant grows plentifully in the chalky regions of France, and has there been recommended for use as a food, to be prepared like spinach. It also grows in the Canary Islands.

SQUAW-GRASS. SOUR-GRASS. TURKEY-BEARD.

Xerophyllum tenax, Nutt. Lily Family.

Radical leaves.—Very numerous; two or three feet long; about two lines broad; gracefully flexile; serrulate. *Scape.*—Two to five feet high; with scattered leaves; bearing at top a dense raceme a foot or two long. *Perianth segments.*—Six; spreading rotately; four or five lines long; white. *Stamens.*—Six. *Ovary.*—Three-celled. Styles three; filiform. *Hab.*—Coast Ranges to British Columbia; and northern Sierras.

Often upon high ridges we notice the large clumps of certain plants with long, slender, grasslike leaves, which ray out in every direction like a fountain, and resemble a small pampas-grass before it flowers. We naturally wonder what the plants are, but it may be several years before our curiosity is satisfied. Suddenly some spring we find them sending up tall blossom-shafts, crowned with great airy plumes of pure-white flowers, fully worthy of our long and patient waiting. After putting forth this supreme effort of a lifetime, and maturing its seed, the plant dies.

In the north, where it is sometimes very abundant, and occupies extensive meadows, it is known as "sour-grass." The name "squaw-grass" is also applied there, because the leaves, which are long, wiry, and tough, are used by the Indians in the weaving of some of their finest baskets. Baskets made from them are particularly pliable and durable.

The leaves, with their rough serrulate edges, are not pleasant to handle.

PELICAN-FLOWER. POP-CORN FLOWER.
Orthocarpus versicolor, Greene. Figwort Family.

Slender; seldom branching or more than six inches high. Herbage slightly reddish. *Leaves.*—Cleft into filiform divisions at the apex. *Flowers.*—Pure white, fading pinkish; very fragrant. Lower lip of the corolla with three very large sacs. Folds of the throat densely bearded. (See *Orthocarpus.*) *Hab.*—San Francisco and Marin County.

During the spring the meadows about San Francisco are luxuriantly covered with snowy masses of the fragrant white pelican-flower. Dr. Kellogg saw in these queer little blossoms, with their large pouches and long beaks, something suggestive of the pelican. The name does not apply to all species of *Orthocarpus,* however, as all have not this aspect, only those belonging to a certain section of the genus.

TOLGUACHA. LARGE-FLOWERED DATURA.
Datura meteloides, DC. Nightshade Family.
(For flower structure, see *D. Stramonium.*)

Hab.—Southern California, and northward—at least to Stockton.

The large-flowered datura is a common plant along southern roadsides, producing in early May its enormous white or violet-

PELICAN–FLOWER—*Orthocarpus versicolor.*

tinged funnels, which are sometimes ten inches long. It resembles the common Jamestown-weed, of which it is a near relative, but may be distinguished by its large flower and its cylindrical calyx, which is not angled. It shares with the Jamestown-weed its narcotic poisonous qualities, and is a famous plant among our Indians. Dr. Palmer writes that they bruise and boil the root in water, and when the infusion thus made is cold, they drink it to produce a stupefying effect. In a different degree they administer it to their young dancing-women as a powerful stimulant, and before going into battle the warriors take it to produce a martial frenzy in themselves.

By the Piutes it is called "main-oph-weep." The specific name, *meteloides,* indicates the resemblance of this plant to *Datura Metel,* of India.

SATIN-BELL. LANTERN OF THE FAIRIES. WHITE GLOBE-TULIP.

Calochortus albus, Dougl. Lily Family.

Stem.—One or two feet high; branching. Radical leaves; a foot or two long. *Flowers.*—White. *Sepals.*—Lanceolate. *Petals.*—Twelve to fifteen lines long; pearly white, sometimes lavender-tinged outside; covered within with long, silky white hairs. *Gland.*—Shallow, crescent-shaped, with four transverse scales fringed with short glandular hairs. (See *Calochortus.*) *Hab.*—Coast Ranges and Sierras, San Diego to San Francisco Bay and Butte County.

Just before the oncoming of summer our wooded hill-slopes and cañon-sides entertain one of the most charming of flowers; for the graceful stalks of the satin-bell begin to hang out their delicate white globes. Never was flower more exquisite in texture and fringing—never one more graceful in habit. If fairies have need of lanterns at all, these blossoms would certainly make very dainty globes to hold their miniature lights.

Wherever they grow, these flowers win instant and enthusiastic admiration; and they have received a variety of common names in different localities, being known as "snowy lily-bell," "satin-bell," "hairbell," "lantern of the fairies," and "white globe-tulip."

SATIN-BELL—*Calochortus albus.*

YERBA SANTA. MOUNTAIN BALM.

Eriodictyon Californicum, Greene. Baby-eyes or Waterleaf Family.

Shrubby; three to five feet high. *Leaves.*—Thick; glutinous; smooth above; light beneath, with prominent net-veining; three to six inches long. *Flowers.*—Purple, violet, or white. *Calyx.*—Five-parted. *Corolla.* —Six lines long; four lines across. *Stamens.*—Five; alternate with the corolla-lobes. *Ovary.*—Two-celled. Styles two. *Hab.*—Western California; common on dry hills.

The bitter, aromatic leaves of the yerba santa are a highly valued domestic remedy for colds, and many old-fashioned people would not be without it.

Dr. Bard, one of our most eminent physicians, writes of this interesting little shrub:—"It has been reserved for the Californian Indians to furnish three of the most valuable vegetable additions which have been made to the pharmacopœia during the last twenty years. One, the *Eriodictyon glutinosum,* growing profusely in our foothills, was used by them in affections of the respiratory tract, and its worth was so appreciated by the missionaries that they named it yerba santa, or holy plant."

The other plants referred to by Dr. Bard are the *Rhamnus,* or *Cascara sagrada,* and the *Grindelia.* In the mountains of Mariposa County, it is known as "wild peach," probably because the leaf somewhat resembles the peach-leaf.

Dr. Behr writes that considerable quantities of it are exported, partly for medicinal purposes, and partly as a harmless and agreeable substitute for hops in the brewing of certain varieties of beer, especially porter.

In Ventura County this passes by insensible gradations into *E. tomentosum,* Benth., and there it is difficult to distinguish clearly between the two species.

E. tomentosum, Benth., is found from San Diego probably to Santa Barbara. This comely shrub is so disguised in its woolly coat that one does not at first detect its close relationship to the more common yerba santa. Its broad, oval leaves, ribbed like the chestnut and closely notched, and its generous

YERBA SANTA—*Eriodictyon Californicum.*

clusters of unusually large violet flowers, serve to bewilder us for the moment. The wool upon the foliage gives it a gray-green tone, harmonizing perfectly with the violet flowers. It is specially abundant all over the mesas by the seashore near San Diego.

ALUM-ROOT.

Heuchera Hartwegii, Dougl.   Saxifrage Family.

Rootstock.—Stout.   *Leaves.*—All radical; two to four inches long. *Scapes.*—Often two feet high.   *Flowers.*—White; minute; in loose panicles.   *Calyx.*—Five-toothed; one or two lines long.   *Petals.*—Five; one line long; on the sinuses of the calyx.   *Stamens.*—Five.   *Ovary.*—One-celled. Styles two.   *Syn.*—*Heuchera micrantha,* Dougl.   *Hab.*—Coast Ranges and Sierras from Monterey to British Columbia.

Upon almost any drive or walk along a shaded road we may find the alum-root hanging over a mossy bank. Its large, airy panicle is composed of minute flowers, and appears in early summer. But it is more conspicuous for its exquisite foliage than for its flowers. The leaves are usually mottled in light green and richly veined in dark brown or red, and they often turn to a rich red later in the season.

The root is woody and astringent, to which latter fact the plant owes its English name, which it shares with the other members of the genus. These are very satisfactory plants to bring in from the woods, because they remain beautiful in water for many weeks.

CASCARA SAGRADA.   CALIFORNIA COFFEE.

Rhamnus Californica, Esch.   Buckthorn Family.

Shrubs.—Four to eighteen feet high.   *Leaves.*—Alternate; elliptic to oblong; denticulate or entire; leathery; one to four inches long; six to eighteen lines wide.   *Flowers.*—Clustered; greenish white; small.   *Calyx.* —Five-toothed.   *Petals.*—Five; minute; on the sinuses of the calyx; each clasping a stamen.   *Ovary.*—Two- to four-celled.   Style short. *Fruit.*—Berry-like; black; four to six lines long; containing two or three nutlets, like coffee-beans.   *Hab.*—Throughout California.

Long before the advent of the Spanish, the medicinal virtues of this shrub were known to the Indians, who used it as a remedy for rheumatism and, according to Dr. Bard, to cor-

ALUM-ROOT—*Heuchera Hartwegii.*

rect the effects of an acorn diet. The Mission Fathers afterward came to appreciate its worth so highly that they bestowed upon it the name *Cascara sagrada,* or "the sacred bark." Since those early days the fame of it has spread the world around. No more valuable laxative is known to the medical world to-day, and every year great quantities of it are exported from our shores. Though the shrub is found as far south as San Diego, the bark is not gathered in any quantity south of Monterey, as it becomes too thin southward. The shrub goes under a variety of names, according to the locality in which it is found. In Monterey County it is known as "yellow-boy" or "yellow-root," and in Sonoma County it becomes "pigeon-berry," because the berry is a favorite food of the wild pigeons, and lends to their flesh a bitter taste.

Some years ago quite an excitement prevailed in the State when some visionary persons believed they had found a perfect substitute for coffee in the seeds of this shrub. To be sure, they do somewhat resemble the coffee-bean in form, but the resemblance goes no further; for upon a careful analysis they revealed none of the qualities of coffee, nor upon roasting did they exhale its aroma. After much discussion of the matter and the laying out in imagination of extensive, natural coffee-plantations upon our wild hill-slopes, these hopeful people were destined to see their project fall in ruins.

This shrub is very variable, according to the locality where it grows. Under shade, the leaves become herbaceous and ample, and as we go northward that becomes the prevailing type, and is then called *R. Purshiana,* DC. It is then often very large, having a trunk the size of a man's body. In Oregon it is known as "chittemwood" and "bitter bark," and also as "wahoo" and "bear-wood." The var. *tomentella,* Brew. and Wats., is densely white-tomentose, especially on the under surfaces of the leaves.

EVERLASTING FLOWER. LADY'S TOBACCO.

Gnaphalium decurrens, Ives. Composite Family.

Viscid-glandular under the loose hairs. *Flower-heads.*—In densely crowded, flattish clusters. *Involucre.*—Campanulate; of very numerous, scarious, yellowish-white, oval scales. (Otherwise similar to *Anaphalis margaritacea.*) *Hab.*—From San Diego through Oregon.

The common everlasting flower, or cudweed, is plentiful upon our dry hills, blooming in early summer, where its white clusters are conspicuous objects amid the drying vegetation. In our rural districts it is believed that sleeping upon a pillow made of these flowers will cure catarrhal affections.

The var. *G. Californicum* (*Syn.*—*G. Californicum,* DC.) generally has a bright white involucre, rarely tinged with rose, and obtuse scales.

G. Sprengelii, Hook. and Arn., may be known from the above by its densely gray, woolly herbage, which is not glandular-viscid. It is also common throughout the State.

The beautiful edelweiss of the Alps is a species of *Gnaphalium, G. leontopodium.*

HOLLY-LEAVED CHERRY. ISLAY.

Prunus ilicifolia, Walp. Rose Family.

Evergreen shrubs or small trees; eight to thirty feet high. *Leaves.*—Alternate; holly-like; an inch or two long. *Flowers.*—White; three lines across; in racemes eighteen lines to three inches long. *Calyx.*—Five-cleft. *Petals.*—Five; spreading. *Stamens.*—Twelve to twenty-five. *Ovary.*—Solitary; one-celled. Style terminal. *Fruit.* — A dark-red cherry, becoming black; six lines in diameter. *Hab.*—Coast Ranges, San Francisco into Lower California.

The holly-leaved cherry is a very ornamental shrub, with its shining, prickly evergreen leaves, and it is coming more and more into favor for cultivation, especially as a hedge-shrub. In its natural state it attains its greatest perfection in the mountains near Santa Barbara and southward. On dry hills it is only a shrub, but in the rich soil of cañon bottoms it becomes a tree. Some of the finest specimens are to be found in the gardens of the old missions, where they have been growing probably a century.

Dr. Behr tells us that the foliage, in withering, develops hydrocyanic acid, the odor of which is quite perceptible. The leaves are then poisonous to sheep and cattle.

The shrubs are specially beautiful in spring, after they have made their new growth of bright green at the ends of the branches, and put forth a profusion of feathery bloom. The blossoms have the pleasant, bitter fragrance of the cultivated cherry, and attract myriads of bees, who make the region vocal with their busy hum. The fruit, which ripens from September to December, is disappointing, owing to its very thin pulp, though its astringent and acid flavor is not unpleasant.

It was used by the aborigines as food, however, and made into an intoxicating drink by fermentation. The meat of the stones ground and made into balls constituted a delicate morsel with them.

YERBA BUENA.

Micromeria Douglasii, Benth.   Mint Family.

Aromatic trailing vines. *Stems.*—Slender; one to four feet long. *Leaves.*—One inch long; round-ovate. *Flowers.*—Solitary; axillary; white or purplish. *Calyx.*—Five-toothed; two lines long. *Corolla.*—Five lines long; bilabiate. *Stamens.*—Four; in pairs on the corolla. *Ovary.*—Of four seedlike nutlets. Style filiform. Stigma unevenly two-lipped. *Hab.*—Vancouver Island to Los Angeles County.

The yerba buena is as dear to the Californian as the May-flower to the New Englander, and is as intimately associated with the early traditions of this Western land as is that delicate blossom with the stormy past of the Pilgrim Fathers. Its delicious, aromatic perfume seems in some subtle way to link those early days of the Padres with our own, and to call up visions of the long, low, rambling mission buildings of adobe, with their picturesque red-tiled roofs; the flocks and herds tended by gentle shepherds in cowls; and the angelus sounding from those quaint belfries, and vibrating in ever-widening circles over hill and vale.

Before the coming of the Mission Fathers, the Indians used this little herb, placing great faith in its medicinal virtues,

YERBA BUENA—*Micromeria Douglasii.*

so that the Padres afterward bestowed upon it the name of "yerba buena"—"the good herb." It is still used among our Spanish-Californians in the form of a tea, both as a pleasant beverage and as a febrifuge, and also as a remedy for indigestion and other disorders.

They designate this as "Yerba Buena del Campo"—*i. e.* the wild or field yerba buena,—to distinguish it from the "Yerba Buena del Poso"—"the herb of the well,"—which is the common garden-mint growing in damp places.

Aside from its associations and medicinal virtues, this is a charming little plant. In half-shaded woods its long, graceful stems make a trailing interlacement upon the ground and yield up their minty fragrance as we pass.

MATILIJA POPPY.

Romneya Coulteri, Harv. Poppy Family.

Stems.—Numerous; several feet high. *Leaves.*—Alternate, petioled; the lower pinnatifid, the upper pinnately cut or toothed; glaucous, three to five inches long; sometimes sparingly ciliate, with rigid spinose bristles. *Flowers.*—Solitary; white; five to nine inches across. *Sepals.* —Three; perfectly smooth; caducous. *Petals.*—Six. *Stamens.*—Very numerous. *Filaments.*—Filiform; thickened above; yellow; purple below. *Ovary.*—Seven- to eleven-celled. *Stigmas.*—Several. *Hab.*—Santa Barbara to San Diego.

The Matilija poppy (pronounced ma-til'li-ha) must be conceded the queen of all our flowers. It is not a plant for small gardens, but the fitting adornment of a large park, where it can have space and light and air to rear its imperial stems and shake out its great diaphanous flowers. It is justly far-famed, and by English gardeners, who now grow it successfully, it is regarded as a priceless treasure, and people go from many miles around to see it when it blooms. It is to be regretted that our flowers must go abroad to find their warmest admirers.

This plant was named in honor of Dr. Romney Robinson, a famous astronomer. Its common name was given it because it grows in particular abundance in the Matilija Cañon, some

MATILIJA POPPY—*Romneya Coulteri.*

miles above Ventura in the mountains. Many people have the mistaken idea that it grows only in that region. It is not common, by any means; but it is found in scattered localities from Santa Barbara southward into Mexico. It is very abundant near Riverside, and also upon the southern boundary and below in Lower California, where the plants cover large areas. It not only grows in fertile valleys, but seeks the seclusion of remote cañons, and nothing more magnificent could be imagined than a steep cañon-side covered with the great bushy plants, thickly sown with the large white flowers.

The buds are closely wrapped in three overlapping sepals. These gradually open, and at dawn the buds unfurl their crumpled petals to the day, exhaling a pleasant fragrance. The blossoms remain open for many days.

These plants have long been in use among the Indians of Lower California, who esteem them highly for their medicinal qualities. The seeds require a long period for germination, and they have been known to come at the end of two years. The better method of propagation is from root-cuttings.

The plant has been called "Mission poppy" and "Giant Californian white poppy," but the pretty Indian name cannot be improved upon.

For many years *R. Coulteri* was supposed to be the only species of *Romneya,* but Miss Alice Eastwood has recently discovered and described another, *R. trichocalyx,* Eastwood. This is of somewhat different habit, and spreads by means of stolons, or root offshoots, while *R. Coulteri* is erect and branching. This also has its foliage slashed into long slender segments and its buds covered with appressed bristly hairs. Both species occur in scattered localities from Santa Barbara southward into Lower California.

WHITE SAGE. GREASEWOOD.
Audibertia polystachya, Benth.   Mint Family.

Shrubby, three to ten feet high; many-stemmed. *Leaves.*—Opposite; lanceolate; narrowing into a petiole; several inches long. *Flowers.*

68

—White or pale lavender, in loose panicles a foot or two long. *Calyx.*—Tubular; bilabiate. *Corolla.*—About six lines long, with short tube and bilabiate border. Upper lip small; erect. Lower lip three-lobed; the middle lobe large. *Stamens.*—Two; jointed. *Ovary.*—Of four seed-like nutlets. Style slender. Stigma two-cleft. *Hab.*—Santa Barbara to San Diego.

The classic honey of Hymettus could not have been clearer or more wholesome than that distilled by the bees from the white sage of southern California, which has become justly world-renowned. The plants cover extensive reaches of valley and hill-slopes, and are often called "greasewood."

Certain it is that the white stems have a very greasy, gummy feel and a rank, aggressive odor. In spring the long, coarse, sparsely leafy branches begin to rise from the woody base, often making the slopes silvery; and by May these have fully developed their loose, narrow panicles of pale flowers and yellowish buds.

The structure of these blossoms is very interesting. The long, prominent lower lip curves downward and upward and backward upon itself, like a swan's neck, while the two stamens rising from its surface lift themselves like two long horns, and the style curves downward.

A bee arriving at this flower naturally brushes against the stigma, leaving upon it some of the pollen gained from another flower. Then alighting upon the lower lip, his weight bends it downward, and he grasps the stamens as convenient handles, thus drawing the anthers toward his body, where the pollen is dusted upon his coat as he probes beneath the closed upper lip for the honey in the depths of the tube. The various sages of the south have a very interesting way of hybridizing.

CHAMISAL. CHAMISO. GREASEWOOD.

Adenostoma fasciculatum, Hook. and Arn. Rose Family.

Shrubs two to twenty feet high, with gray, shreddy bark and reddish, slender branches. *Leaves.*—Two to four lines long; linear to awl-shaped; smooth; clustered. Stipules small; acute. *Flowers.*—White; two lines across; in terminal racemose panicles. *Calyx.*—Five-toothed; with bracts below resembling another calyx; tube ten-ribbed. *Petals.*—

Five. *Stamens.*—Ten to fifteen; in clusters between the petals. *Ovary.*—One-celled. *Fruit.*—A dry akene. *Hab.*—Widely distributed.

The chamisal forms a large part of the chaparral of our mountain slopes, and when not in bloom gives to them much the aspect imparted to the Scotch Highlands by the heather. It is an evergreen shrub, with small clustered, needle-like leaves. In late spring it is covered with large feathery panicles of tiny white blossoms, which show with particular effectiveness against the rich olive of its foliage, and furnish the bees with valuable honey material for a considerable season. When interspersed with shrubs of livelier greens, it gives to our hill-slopes and mountain-sides a wonderfully rich and varied character. In the summer of a season when it has flowered freely, the cinnamon-colored seed-vessels blending with the olives of the foliage lend a rich, warm bronze to whole hillsides, forming a charming contrast to the straw tints and russets of grassy slopes, and adding another to the many soft harmonies of our summer landscape. It is most abundant in the Coast Ranges, where, in some localities, it covers mile after mile of hill-slopes with its close-cropped, uniform growth.

When the chaparral, or dense shrubby growth of our mountain-sides, is composed entirely of *Adenostoma,* it is called chamisal.

Another species, *A. sparsifolium,* Torr., found in the south, and somewhat resembling the above, may be known from it by its lack of stipules, its scattered, not clustered leaves, which are obtuse and not pointed, and its somewhat larger flowers, each one pediceled.

This is commonly known among the Spanish-Californians as "Yerba del Pasmo," literally the "herb of the convulsion," and among them and the Indians it is a sovereign remedy for many ailments, being considered excellent for colds, cramps, and snakebites, and an infallible cure for tetanus, or lockjaw. The foliage fried in grease becomes a healing ointment.

The bark of this species is reddish and hangs in shreds.

CALIFORNIA BUCKEYE.
CALIFORNIA HORSE-CHESTNUT.

Æsculus Californica, Nutt. Maple or Soapberry Family.

Shrubs or trees ten to forty feet high. *Leaves.*—Opposite; petioled; with five palmate, stalked leaflets. *Leaflets.*—Oblong; acute; three to five inches long; serrulate. *Flowers.*—White; in a thyrse a foot long; many of them imperfect. *Calyx.*—Tubular; two-lobed. *Petals.*—Four or five; six lines or more long; unequal. *Stamens.*—Five to seven; exserted. Anthers buff. *Ovary.*—Three-celled. *Nuts.*—One to three inches in diameter; usually one in the pod. *Hab.*—Coast Ranges of middle California; also the Sierra foothills.

Our California buckeye is closely allied to the horse-chestnuts and buckeyes of the eastern half of the continent. It is usually found upon stream-banks or the side-walls of cañons, and reaches its greatest perfection in the valleys of our central Coast Ranges. It usually branches low into a number of clean, round, light-gray limbs, which widen out into a broad, dense, rounded head. Its leaves are fully developed before the flowers appear. When in full bloom, in May, it is considered one of the most beautiful of all our American species. Its long, white flower-spikes, sprinkled rather regularly over the green mound of foliage, are very suggestive of a neat calico print. Early to come, the leaves are as early to depart, and by midsummer the beautiful skeleton is often bare, its interlacing twigs making a delicate network against the deep azure of the sky.

Though lavish in its production of flowers, usually but one or two of the large cluster succeed in maturing fruit. By October and November the leathery pods begin to yield up their big golden-brown nuts, which are great favorites among the squirrels. The Indians are said to resort to these nuts in times of famine. Before using them, they roast them a day or two in the ground, to extract the poison.

The inner wood of the root, after being kiln-cured for several weeks, becomes very valuable to the cabinet-maker. It is then of an exquisite mottled green, and when highly polished can hardly be distinguished from a fine piece of onyx.

PUSSY'S-PAWS.

Spraguea umbellata, Torr.   Purslane Family.

Radical leaves.—Spatulate or oblanceolate; six lines to four inches long. *Stem-leaves.*—Similar, but smaller, often reduced to a few bracts. *Scapes.*—Several; two to twelve inches high. *Flowers.*—In dense spikes. *Sepals.*—Two; orbicular; thin; papery; two to four lines across; whitish; equaling the petals. *Petals.*—Four; rose-color. *Stamens.*— Three. *Ovary.*—One-celled. Style bifid. *Hab.*—The Sierras, from the Yosemite to British Columbia.

Pussy's-paws is a very plentiful plant in the Sierras, usually growing upon dry, rocky soil. It varies much in aspect, sometimes sending up a stout, erect flower-scape, and again growing low and matlike with its prostrate flower-stems radiating from the center. It blooms from early summer onward, often almost covering the ground with its blossoms. The flower-clusters grow in a bunch, much like the pink cushions on pussy's feet, whence the pretty common name.

THISTLE-POPPY. CHICALOTE.

Argemone platyceras, Link and Otto. Poppy Family.

Stems.—One to two and one half feet high; hispid throughout, or armed with rigid bristles or prickles. Sap yellow. *Leaves.*—Thistle-like; three to six inches long. *Flowers.*—White; two to four inches in diameter. *Sepals.*—Three; spinosely beaked. *Petals.*—Four to six. *Stamens.*—Numerous. Filaments slender. *Ovary.*—Oblong; one-celled. Stigma three- or four-lobed. Capsule very prickly. *Hab.*—Dry hillsides from central California southward.

The thistle-poppy would be considered in any other country a surpassingly beautiful flower, with its large diaphanous white petals and its thistly gray-green foliage, but in California it must yield precedence to the Matilija poppy. It resembles the latter very closely in its flower, and is often mistaken for it. It may be known by its yellow juice, its prickly foliage, and its very prickly capsules. I believe the flowers are somewhat more cup-shaped than those of *Romneya*.

It affects dry hill-slopes and valleys, often otherwise barren, where it is conspicuously beautiful, and may be found in full bloom in May.

PUSSY'S-PAWS—*Spraguea umbellata.*

RUBY LILY. CHAPARRAL LILY. REDWOOD LILY.
Lilium rubescens, Wats. Lily Family.

Hab.—The Coast Ranges, from Marin County to Humboldt County.

This is the most charming of all our California lilies, even surpassing in loveliness the beautiful Washington lily; and it is said to be the most fragrant of any in the world It resembles the Washington lily; but its flowers are fuller in form, with wider petals and shorter tube, and it has a smaller bulb. It sends up a noble shaft, sometimes seven feet high, with many scattered whorls of undulate leaves, and often bears at the summit as many as twenty-five of the beautiful flowers. These are at first pure white, dotted with purple, but they soon take on a metallic luster and begin to turn to a delicate pink, which gradually deepens into a ruby purple. Mr. Purdy mentions having seen a plant with a stalk nine feet high, bearing thirty-six flowers.

The favorite haunts of this lily are high and inaccessible ridges, among the chaparral, or under the live-oak or redwood. Comparatively few people know of its existence, though living within a few miles of it, because they rarely ever visit these out-of-the-way fastnesses of nature.

Mr. Burroughs has somewhere said: "Genius is a specialty; it does not grow in every soil, it skips the many and touches the few; and the gift of perfume to a flower is a special grace, like genius or like beauty, and never becomes common or cheap." Certainly these blosoms have been richly endowed with this charming gift, and their delicious fragrance wafted by the wind often betrays their presence upon a hillside when unsuspected before, so that one skilled in woodcraft can often trace them by it.

SPANISH BAYONET. OUR LORD'S CANDLE.
Hesperoyucca Whipplei, Engelm. Lily Family.

Without a trunk. *Leaves.*—All radical in a bristling hemisphere; sword-like. *Flower-panicles.*—Distaff-shaped; three or more feet long; at the summit of a leafless bracteate scape, ten or fifteen feet high.

RUBY LILY—*Lilium rubescens.*

Perianth.—Rotately spreading; waxen-white (sometimes rich purple), often green- or purple-nerved. *Filaments.*—Clavate; pure white. Anthers transverse; yellow. Style very thick; three-angled. Stigma stalked; green; covered with tiny prominences. *Fruit.*—A dry capsule. (Structure otherwise as in *Yucca Mohavensis.*) *Syn.*—*Yucca Whipplei,* Torr. *Hab.*—Monterey to San Diego and eastward.

In spring and early summer the chaparral-covered hillsides of Southern California present a wonderful appearance when hundreds of these Spanish bayonets are in bloom. From day to day the waxen tapers on the distant slopes increase in height as the white bells climb the slender shafts. At length each cluster reaches its perfection, and becomes a solid distaff of sometimes two—yes, even six—thousand of the waxen blossoms!

A friend writing of them, once said:—"Nearly every poetaster in the country has sung the praises of the yellow poppies and the sweet little *Nemophilas,* but not one, so far as I know, has ever written a stanza to these grand white soldiers with their hundred swords." There is, indeed, something glorious and warlike about them, as they marshal themselves to the defense of our hillsides.

This surpasses all known species in the height and beauty of its flower-panicles; but, once the season of flowering and fruiting has been consummated, its life mission is fulfilled, and the plant dies. The dead stalks remain standing sometimes for years upon the mountain-sides.

The seeds of this species, as well as those of the tree-yucca, are made into flour by the Indians; and from the leaves they obtain a soft, white fiber, which they use in making the linings of the coarse saddle-blankets they weave from *Yucca Mohavensis.* The undeveloped flowering shoots they consider a great delicacy, either raw or cooked. They gather great numbers of the plants when just at the right stage, and strip off the leaves, leaving round masses. These they prepare after the manner of a clam-bake, and when the pile is pulled to pieces and the product is taken out, it has a faint resemblance to baked sweet apple, and is of about the same consistency. The whole mass is a mixture of sweet, soft pulp and coarse white fibers much like manila rope-yarn.

CLIFF ASTER.

Malacothrix saxatilis, Torr. and Gray. Composite Family.

Stems.—Stout; a foot or two high; woody. *Leaves.*—Lanceolate to spatulate; one or two inches long; entire or pinnatifid; somewhat succulent. *Flower-heads.*—Terminating the paniculate branches; large; two inches or so across; white, changing to rose or lilac; of ray-flowers only. *Involucre.*—Campanulate or hemispherical; six lines high, with many imbricated scales passing downward into loose, awl-shaped bracts. *Hab.*—The Coast, from Santa Barbara southward.

This beautiful plant is a dweller upon the ocean cliffs, and may be seen in abundance from the car-windows just before the train reaches Santa Barbara going north. The stems are woody and very leafy, and the plants are usually covered all over the top with the showy flower-heads.

M. tenuifolia, Torr. and Gray, is a very tall, slender, sparsely leafy plant with fragile, airy white flowers. This is common along the dusty roadsides of the south in early summer.

CALIFORNIA SPIKENARD.

Aralia Californica, Wats. Ginseng Family.

Root.—Thick; aromatic. *Stems.*—Eight to ten feet high. *Leaves.*—Bipinnate; or the upper pinnate, with one or two pairs of leaflets. *Leaflets.*—Cordate-ovate; four to eight inches long; serrate. *Flowers.*—White; two lines long; in globular umbels, arranged in loose panicles a foot or two long. Pedicels four to six lines long. *Calyx.*—Five-toothed or entire. *Petals and Stamens.*—Five. *Ovary.*—Two- to five-celled. Styles united to the middle. *Fruit.*—A purple berry. *Hab.*—Widely distributed; on stream-banks.

In moist, cool ravines, where the sun only slants athwart the branches and a certain dankness always lingers, the California spikenard scents the air with its peculiar odor. It closely resembles *A. racemosa* of the Eastern States, but it is a larger, coarser plant in every way. It throws up its tall stems with a fine confidence that there will be ample space for its large leaves to spread themselves uncrowded. Its feathery panicles of white flowers are followed by clusters of small purple berries, and are rather more delicate than we should expect from so large a plant.

YERBA MANSA.

Anemopsis Californica, Hook.   Yerba Mansa Family.

Rootstock creeping. *Radical leaves.*—Long-petioled; elliptic oblong; two to ten inches long. *Stems.*—Six inches to two feet high. *Flowers.*—Without sepals and petals, sunk in a conical spike six to eighteen lines long; a small white bract under each flower. *Spikes.*—Subtended by from five to eight white petal-like bracts, six to fifteen lines long. *Stamens.*—Three to eight. *Ovary.*—Apparently one-celled. Stigmas one to five. *Hab.*—Southern to central California.

Just as the fervid glow of the sun is beginning to transform the green of our southern hill-slopes to soft browns, the still vividly green lowland meadows suddenly bring forth myriads of white stars, which in their green setting become grateful resting-points for the eye.   These are the blossoms of the famous yerba mansa of the Spanish-Californians.   Among these people the plant is an infallible remedy for many disorders, and so highly do they prize it that they often travel or send long distances for it.

The aromatic root, which has a strong, peppery taste, is very astringent, and, when made into a tea or a powder, is applied with excellent results to cuts and sores.   The tea is also taken as a blood-purifier; and the plant, in the form of a wash or poultice, is used for rheumatism, while the wilted leaves are said to reduce swellings.   In the medical world it is beginning to be used in diseases of the mucous membrane.

SHEPHERD'S PURSE.

Capsella bursa-pastoris, Moench.   Mustard Family.

Stems twelve to eighteen inches high, branching. *Radical leaves.*—Toothed, or incisely lobed with backward-pointing lobes. *Upper leaves.*—Oblanceolate to linear; entire. *Flowers.*—White, minute, cruciferous. *Pods.*—Two lines long, on slender pedicels. *Hab.*—Naturalized all over the world.

Among our commonest and most harmless weeds is the shepherd's purse, which has been introduced from Europe in

YERBA MANSA—*Anemopsis Californica.*

the past. It may be easily recognized by its tiny white cruciferous flowers and its shapely little triangular, flat pods, which have a peppery taste. It is used medicinally, and valued as a remedy for many different maladies. In Europe, a common name for the plant is "mother's heart," and Mr. Johnston says that children play a sort of game with the seed-pouch. "They hold it out to their companions, inviting them to 'take a haud o' that.' It immediately cracks, and then follows a triumphant shout, 'You've broken your mother's heart!' "

Equally common is the *Lepidium,* or pepper-grass, the small round, flat pods of which also have a peppery taste. Both of these belong to the great Mustard family.

MARIPOSA TULIP.

Calochortus venustus, Benth. (and varieties). Lily Family.

Stems.—A foot or two high; branching. *Leaves.*—Narrow; grass-like; channeled; glaucous; decumbent. *Flowers.*—Erect; cup-shaped; white, lilac, pink, claret, magenta, purple, or rarely light yellow; of uniform color or shaded; plain or variously oculated, stained, or blotched. *Petals.*—One or two inches long; slightly hairy below. *Gland.*—Large; roundish; densely hairy. *Capsule.*—Lanceolate; four or five lines broad. (See *Calochortus.*) *Hab.*—Dry sandy soil, in the Coast Ranges and Sierra foothills, from Mendocino County to Los Angeles.

I once emerged from the dense chaparral of a steep hillside upon a grassy slope, where myriads of these lovely flowers tossed their delicate cups upon the breeze. As I passed from flower to flower, I noticed many insect guests regaling themselves upon the nectar. Bees and flies jostled one another and crawled amid the hairs below, and beautifully mottled butterflies hovered over them.

As originally described, this flower was white or pale lilac, with a more or less conspicuous, usually reddish, stain, or blotch, near the top, a brownish spot bordered with yellow in the center, and a brownish striate base. But it varies so widely from this type, in both color and spots, that neither is a reliable character from which to determine the species. Some of the oculated forms of *C. luteus* are so similar that they are

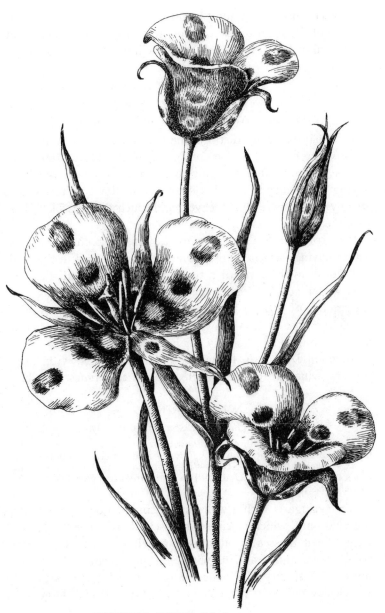

MARIPOSA TULIP—*Calochortus venustus.*

readily confused with this, but a careful examination of the gland and the form of the capsule, together with the character of the soil in which the plants grow, will identify the species.

COMMON NIGHTSHADE.
Solanum nigrum, L.   Nightshade Family.
Hab.—Along streams near the coast.

This may be easily distinguished from *S. Xanti* by its very small white flowers, whose corollas are but three or four lines across and much more deeply and pointedly lobed, the lobes having a tendency to turn backward as the flowers grow older; also by its thinner, duller leaves, and much smaller, black berries, the size of peas.

It is considered a violent narcotic poison, both berries and leaves having caused death when eaten.   It is used in the medical world, in the form of a tincture for various maladies, and it is said that in Bohemia the blossoming plant is hung over the cradles of infants to induce sweet slumber; while in Dalmatia the root is fried in butter and eaten to produce sleep, and is also used as a remedy for hydrophobia.

Solanum Douglasii, Dunal, is a similar species, with larger flowers, which are usually white, though sometimes light blue.

WILD SYRINGA.
Philadelphus, Linn.   Saxifrage Family.

Deciduous shrubs, with opposite, ovate or oblong leaves and abundant clusters of showy white flowers. *Petals.*—Four or five, roundish. *Stamens.*—Twenty to forty. *Styles.*—Three to five, united at base or sometimes nearly to the top. *Ovary.*—Inferior, three- to five-celled. *Hab.*—Widely distributed.

The syringa is such a well-known shrub in our gardens that the wild ones, which resemble it closely, hardly need a description.   Their masses of odorous pure white flowers make them conspicuous and beautiful wherever they occur.   We have a number of species of *Philadelphus* whose differences are not yet clearly defined.   Mr. Galen Clark says in his "Legend of the Yosemite" that the Indians formerly used the wood of the wild syringa for their arrows.

BUTTERFLY TULIP.

Calochortus luteus, var. *oculatus,* Wats. Lily Family.

Similar to *C. venustus,* but with petals differently marked. *Hab.—*Sierras and Coast Ranges, from Fresno County to Shasta County.

Of all our lovely Mariposa tulips, this charming form is perhaps the most like the insect for which it is named. Its creamy or purplish flowers have an exquisitely tinted dark-maroon eye, surrounded by yellow, and it is often streaked in marvelous imitation of the insect's wing. It was doubtless this form Miss Coolbrith had in mind when she wrote the beautiful lines below:

> " Insect or blossom? Fragile, fairy thing,
> Poised upon slender tip and quivering
> To flight! a flower of the fields of air;
> A jeweled moth, a butterfly with rare
> And tender tints upon his downy wing
> A moment resting in our happy sight;
> A flower held captive by a thread so slight
> Its petal-wings of broidered gossamer.
> Are, light as the wind, with every wind astir,
> Wafting sweet odor, faint and exquisite.
> O dainty nursling of the field and sky!
> What fairer thing looks up to heaven's blue,
> And drinks the noontide sun, the dawning's dew?
> Thou winged bloom! thou blossom butterfly!"

WESTERN BOYKINIA.

Boykinia occidentalis, Torr. and Gray. Saxifrage Family.

*Stems.—*Slender; a foot or two high. *Leaves.—*Round-reniform; palmately three- to seven-lobed; one to three inches broad; the lobes coarsely toothed. *Flowers.—*In long-peduncled, loose panicles; white; four lines across; parts in fives. *Calyx.—*With acute teeth. *Petals.—*On the sinuses of the calyx. *Stamens.—*On the calyx, opposite its teeth. Filaments short. *Ovary.—*With its two cells attenuate into the slender styles. *Hab.—*Coast Ranges, from Santa Barbara to Washington.

The tufted leaves and exquisitely delicate saxifrage-like clusters of the *Boykinia* fringe our streams in early summer.

SOAP-PLANT. AMOLE.

Chlorogalum pomeridianum, Kunth. Lily Family.

Bulb.—One to four inches in diameter; densely brown-fibrous. *Leaves.*—Six to eighteen inches long. *Scape.*—One to five feet high; bearing a loosely spreading panicle. *Perianth.*—White; of six spreading, recurved segments nine lines long. *Stamens.*—Six; shorter than the segments. *Ovary.*—Three-celled. Style filiform. Stigma three-lobed. *Hab.*—Widely distributed.

The leaves of the soap-plant have been with us all the spring, increasing in length as the season has advanced. You can easily recognize them, as they resemble a broad, wavy-margined grass, usually lying flat upon the ground, with some of the ragged brown fibers of the bulb showing aboveground, like the fragment of an old manila mat.

In early summer, from their midst begins to shoot a slender stalk. When the process of its growth is complete, it stands from two to five feet high, with slender, wide-spreading branches and rather sparsely scattered flowers.

If you would find its flowers open, you must seek it in the afternoon. At a little distance, it appears as though the truant summer wind had lodged a delicate white feather here and there upon the branches. In themselves, these blossoms are not ill-favored, with their slender, recurved petals; but to us the root is the most interesting part of the plant. This the early Spanish-Californians used extensively in lieu of soap, and esteemed greatly as a hair tonic, and it was known by them as "amole." Even now it is much used among their descendants, and we know of one aged señora over ninety who refuses to use anything else for washing. Her grandsons keep her supplied with the bulbs, which they dig by the sackful from the neighboring hill-slopes and mesas. She takes her linen down to the brookside, and there, in primitive fashion, upon her knees she scours and rinses it till it is as white as the driven snow.

The Indians of the Sierra foothills have a curious use for the bulb. After the June freshets have subsided, many fish

SOAP-PLANT—*Chlorogalum pomeridianum.*

are usually left in small pools in the streams. The squaws go to these pools with an abundance of soap-root, and kneeling upon the banks, rub up a great lather with it. The fish soon rise to the surface stupefied, and are easily taken.

In the Yosemite Valley these plants have far more abundant flowers than our plants in the lowlands.

We are told that in the early days of the gold excitement, when commodities were scarce and brought fabulous prices, the fibrous outer coats of the bulb were used for stuffing mattresses.

The inner portion of the bulb, when reduced to a paste, is said to be an excellent remedy for oak-poisoning, applied as a salve.

This is not the only plant popularly known as soap-plant among us. Several others share the title, among them the goose-foot, the yucca, and the California lilac. There are several other species of *Chlorogalum*.

MOUNTAIN BIRCH. WHITE TEA-TREE. SOAP-BUSH.

Ceanothus integerrimus, Hook. and Arn. Buckthorn Family.

Shrubs or small trees; five to twelve feet high; with cylindrical, usually warty, branches. *Leaves.*—Alternate; on slender petioles two to six lines long; ovate to ovate-oblong; one to three inches long; entire or rarely slightly glandular-serrulate; thin. *Flowers.*—White; sometimes blue; in a thyrse three to seven inches long, one to four thick. *Fruit.*—Not crested. (See *Ceanothus.*) *Hab.*—Mountains from Los Angeles to the Columbia River.

When in flower, this is one of the most attractive of all our *Ceanothi*. It often covers great mountain-sides with its white bloom as with drifted snow. The trip to the Yosemite is often diversified by this beautiful spectacle, which comes as an exhilarating surprise.

Among the mountaineers this shrub is highly valued as forage for their cattle, which they turn upon it after the lowland pastures have dried up.

The young twigs and leaves have the spicy fragrance of the black birch of the Eastern States. The foliage is deciduous, and of rather a pale though bright green. The bark of the root of this shrub is becoming celebrated as a remedy for various disorders, such as malaria, catarrh, and liver trouble.

COMMON WHITE LUPINE.

Lupinus densiflorus, Benth.   Pea Family.

Stems.—Stout; simple below; parted in the middle into numerous wide-spreading branches; two feet high; succulent; sparsely villous. *Flowers.*—In long-peduncled racemes; six to ten inches long; with usually five or six dense whorls. Bracts bristle-like, from a broad base. *Calyx.*—Upper lip scarious; deeply cleft; lower long, toothed. *Corolla.* —White or rose-color; seven lines or so long; the standard dark-dotted. *Pod.*—Two-seeded. *Hab.*—Wide-spread; Sacramento Valley and southward.

In the days when we went fishing in the brook with a pin for minnows, a company of these pretty white lupines in a field represented to our childish fancy so many graceful dames in flounced skirts dancing in a sylvan ballroom.

MEADOW-SWEET.   SPIRÆA.

Holodiscus ariæfolius, Greene.   Rose Family.

Shrubs two to six feet high. *Leaves.*—Alternate; short-petioled; an inch or two long; oval or ovate; crenately lobed above; the lobes often toothed; silky pubescent beneath. *Flowers.*—White; two lines across; in feathery panicles several inches long. *Calyx.*—Five-parted; petaloid. *Petals.*—Five; equaling the sepals. *Stamens.*—About twenty. *Pistils.*— Five; distinct; one-celled. *Syn.*—*Spiræa discolor,* Pursh. *Hab.*—Coast Ranges, mostly from Monterey northward.

Not until midsummer is upon us does the common meadow-sweet make itself noticeable by its large feathery clusters of minute white flowers, which have a pleasant odor, like that of slippery-elm. This was formerly classed as *Spiræa,* but has recently been placed in a separate genus.

We have, however, two species of true *Spiræa* with pink flowers—*S. Douglasii,* Hook., the California hardhack, having its blossoms in long clusters, (found in northern California,) and *S. lucida,* Dougl., having flat-topped flower-clusters, (found in the Sierras).

Another shrub closely allied to all the above is *Neillia opulifolia,* Benth. and Hook., the wild bridal-wreath, or nine-bark. Indeed, this has been classed by some authorities among the *Spiræas*. It may be easily recognized by its hemispherical clusters of white flowers. These clusters are an inch or two across. Though the shrub is quite showy when in bloom, it is almost equally attractive when its carpels are beginning to redden.

CALIFORNIA AZALEA.

Rhododendron occidentale, Gray. Heath Family.

Shrubs two to twelve feet high. *Leaves.*—Clustered at the ends of the branches; obovate to lanceolate; two to four inches long; herbaceous. *Flower-clusters.*—Large, from a special terminal bud. *Calyx.*—Deeply five-cleft. *Corolla.*—With funnel-form tube, and five-cleft border; white; the upper lobe blotched with corn-color; sometimes tinged with pink; glandular-viscid without. *Stamens.*—Five. Anthers two-celled, opening terminally. *Ovary.*—Five-celled. *Capsule.*—Very woody. *Hab.*—Stream-banks throughout the State.

One of the most deservedly admired of all our shrubs is the lovely California azalea. In June and July, the borders of our mountain streams are covered for miles with the bushes, whose rich green foliage is often almost obscured from view by the magnificent clusters of white and yellow, or sometimes pinkish flowers. Its delicious, spicy perfume is always subtly suggestive of charming days spent with rod and line along cool streams, or of those all too brief outings spent far from the haunts of men, in some sequestered mountain-cabin among redwood groves or by rushing waters.

In Oregon it is commonly known as "honeysuckle," and there in the autumn its life ebbs away in a flood of glory, showering the forest floor with flecks of scarlet and crimson. Its root is said to contain a strong narcotic poison, and the leaves are also reputed to be poisonous if eaten, but they are not at all harmful to the touch.

SERVICE-BERRY. JUNE-BERRY.

Amelanchier alnifolia, Nutt. Rose Family.

Deciduous shrubs, three to eight feet high. *Leaves.*—Alternate; petioled; from rounded to oblong-ovate; serrate usually only toward the apex; six to eighteen lines long. *Flowers.*—White, in short racemes. *Calyx-tube.*—Campanulate; limb five-parted. *Petals.*—Five;

CALIFORNIA AZALEA—*Rhododendron occidentale.*

oblong; six lines or so long. *Stamens.*—Twenty; short. *Ovary.*—Three- to five-celled. Styles three to five. *Fruit.*—Small; berry-like; dark purple. *Hab.*—Throughout the State and northward; also eastward to the Western States.

The service-berry seems to be at home throughout our borders, but it reaches its greatest perfection north of us, on the rich bottom-lands of the Columbia River. In spring the bushes are beautiful, when snowily laden with masses of ragged white flowers; and from June to September they are no less welcome, when abundantly hung with the black berries, which usually have a bloom upon them. These berries are an important article of food among our Western Indians, who make annual pilgrimages to the regions of their growth, gathering and drying large quantities for winter use. The drying they effect by crushing them to a paste, which they spread upon bark or stones in the sun. It is said that many a party of explorers, lost in the woods, has been kept alive by this little fruit. In many localities where this shrub is the chief constituent of the underbrush the clearing of the land becomes troublesome, owing to its very tough, large roots.

Almost the same shrub in the Atlantic States is called "shad-bush," because it blooms at about the season when the shad are running up the streams.

VANCOUVERIA. AMERICAN BARRENWORT.

Vancouveria parviflora, Greene. Barberry Family.

Stems.—One or two feet high. *Leaves.*—All radical; twice to thrice ternately compound. *Leaflets.*—One to two inches broad; rich shining green; persisting; undulate and membrane-margined. *Flowers.*—Twenty-five to fifty, in loose panicles; small; with six to nine sepal-like bracts. Parts in sixes, all in front of one another. *Sepals.*—Petaloid; two lines long. *Petals.*—White to lavender. *Stamens.*—Erect; closely appressed to the pistil. *Ovary.*—One-celled. Style stoutish. *Hab.*—Coast Ranges of central California.

There is no more exquisite plant in our coast woods than the American barrenwort, or *Vancouveria*. Its delicate thread-like stems, which are yet strong and wiry, hold up its spreading evergreen leaves, every leaflet in its own place. There is a

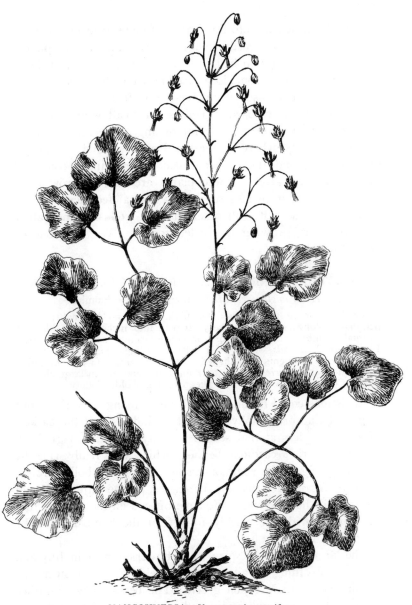

VANCOUVERIA—*Vancouveria parviflora.*

likeness in these leaves to the fronds of our California maiden-hair, and one could easily imagine the maidenhair amplified, strengthened, and polished into this form. Owing to this resemblance, it is in some localities known as "flowering fern." The leaflets are also somewhat ivy-like in form.

In June its delicate, airy panicles of small white blossoms appear. These are especially interesting as belonging to the Barberry family, where all the floral organs stand in front of one another, and the anthers open by cunningly contrived little uplifting valves. These plants are said to grow upon bushy hillsides, in masses sometimes several feet across. But I have never seen it with other than an exclusive and rather solitary habit, growing in shaded forests. We have one or two other species.

CHRISTMAS-BERRY. CALIFORNIA HOLLY. TOYON.

Heteromeles arbutifolia, Rœmer. Rose Family.

Shrubs four to twenty-five feet high. *Leaves.*—Alternate; short-petioled; oblong; serrate; leathery; two to four inches long. *Flowers.*—Small; white; four lines across; in dense terminal panicles. *Calyx.*—Five-toothed. *Petals.*—Five; roundish; spreading. *Stamens.*—Ten; on the calyx. Filaments awl-shaped; flat. *Ovaries.*—Two; one-celled. Styles slender. *Berries.*—Red; four lines in diameter; in large clusters. *Hab.*—Coast Ranges, from San Diego to Humboldt County.

Christmas could hardly be celebrated among us without our beautiful California holly. Florists' windows and the baskets of street-venders at that season are gay with the magnificent clusters of rich cardinal berries, which are really ripe by Thanksgiving. The common name, "California holly," refers more to the berries than to the leaves, as the latter have not the form of holly-leaves. We have often seen the venders mix the berries with the prickly foliage of the live-oak to make them seem more like holly.

The large clusters of spicy white flowers appear in July and August. Nothing in all our flora yields a finer contrast of lavish scarlet against rich green. The berries have a rather pleasant taste, somewhat acid and astringent, and are eaten by the Indians with great relish. The Spanish-Californians used them in the preparation of an agreeable drink.

This is a very handsome shrub in cultivation, and makes an excellent hedge. Its only drawback is that its much-sought berries offer too great attractions to trespassers.

VIRGIN'S BOWER. CLEMATIS.

Clematis ligusticifolia, Nutt. Buttercup or Crowfoot Family.

Nearly smooth. *Stems.*—Woody; sometimes climbing thirty feet. *Leaves.* — Opposite; long-petioled; five-foliolate. *Leaflets.* — Ovate to lanceolate; eighteen lines to three inches long; three-lobed and coarsely toothed; rarely entire or three-parted. *Flowers.*—Diœcious; in axillary panicles. *Sepals.*—Four; petaloid; four to six lines long; thin. *Petals.* —Wanting. *Stamens.*—Numerous. *Pistils.*—Many; becoming long-tailed, silky akenes. *Hab.*—Widely distributed.

The virgin's bower usually looks down upon us from among the branches of some tree, where it entwines itself indistinguishably with the foliage of its host. It climbs by means of the stalks of its leaflets, which wrap themselves about small twigs. This species is not so noticeable during the season of its blossoming as it is later, when the long plumes of its seed have twisted themselves into silvery balls, not unlike the heads of little silky, white poodles. Mrs. Blochman writes that among the Spanish-Californians, it is called "yerba de chivato," and valued as a remedy for barbed-wire cuts in animals. It is used in the form of a wash, and remarkable cures are effected.

Another wide-spread species—*C. lasiantha*, Nutt.—is far more showy than the above. It is found in the Coast Ranges, from Los Angeles to Napa County at least, and in the Sierras to Plumas County. Its long-peduncled flowers are solitary; but they are so numerous and grow so closely together that they make dense masses of white, conspicuous at a long distance. The flowers are larger, the sepals being an inch long, and covered with a silky pubescence, which makes them like soft cream-colored velvet. The three ovate leaflets are also silky.

93

LADIES' TRESSES.

Spiranthes Romanzoffianum, Cham. Orchis Family.

Roots.—Fascicled tubers. *Stems.*—Stout; four to eighteen inches high. *Leaves.*—Oblong-lanceolate to linear. *Spikes.*—One to even ten inches long. *Perianth.*—Yellowish white; four lines long. `Upper sepal and two petals coherent. Lip recurved, bearing a small protuberance on each side at base. *Anther.*—On the face of the short column. *Ovary.*—One-celled. *Hab.*—Through the mountains from Los Angeles northward.

The twisted spikes of these little orchids are interesting, because their ranks remain so clearly defined as they wind about the stem. The plants vary greatly in different seasons as to size, and are usually found in moist places.

TARWEED. MOUNTAIN MISERY.

Chamæbatia foliolosa, Benth. Rose Family.

Shrubby; a foot or two high; branching freely; glandular pubescent throughout; fragrant. *Leaves.*—Alternate; finely dissected; ovate or oblong in outline; two or three inches long. *Flowers.*—White; few in terminal cymes. *Calyx.*—Five-lobed. *Petals.*—Five; spreading; three or four lines long. *Stamens.*—Very numerous; short. *Ovary.*—Solitary. Style terminal. *Fruit.*—A leathery akene. *Hab.*—The Sierras, from Mariposa County to Nevada County.

One of the most conspicuous plants to be met on the way to the Yosemite is the *Chamæbatia.* It is exceedingly abundant, covering considerable areas and filling the air with its balsamic fragrance, strongly suggestive of witch-hazel or tansy, though to many not so agreeable as the latter. It is a beautiful plant, with its feathery leaves and strawberry-like flowers; but by the roadside, where its viscid leaves and stems have caught the dust, it is often but a travesty of itself.

Mrs. Brandegee writes of it:—"Along the line of the railroad in Placer County it is often called 'bear-clover,' perhaps in accordance with our felicitous custom of giving names, because it bears not the least resemblance to clover, and the bear will have nothing to do with it." Another common name for the plant among our mountaineers is "kittikit," possibly taken from the Indians.

LADIES' TRESSES—*Spiranthes Romanzoffianum.*

LARGE-FLOWERED DOGWOOD.

Cornus Nuttallii, Audubon. Dogwood Family.

Shrubs or trees, fifteen to seventy feet high. *Leaves.*—Opposite; obovate; acute at each end; three to five inches long. *Flowers.*—Numerous; small; greenish; in a head surrounded by an involucre of four to six large, yellowish or white bracts, often tinged with red, and eighteen lines to three inches long. *Calyx.*—Four-toothed. *Petals and Stamens.*—Four. *Ovary.*—Two-celled. *Fruit.*—Scarlet; five or six lines long. *Hab.*—The Coast Ranges and Sierras, from Monterey and Plumas counties to British Columbia.

Plants of the genus *Cornus* are known as cornel, or dogwood. Our large-flowered dogwood more nearly resembles the Eastern *C. florida* than any other species, but it is a much handsomer shrub than the latter. It reaches its maximum size in northern Oregon and Washington, where, in the season of its blossoming, it is a sight never to be forgotten. Its masses of large white flowers, like single Cherokee roses, contrast finely with the deep, rich greens of the fir forests, in which it often grows. In its northern range, its leaves turn beautifully, and it becomes one of the most brilliant masqueraders in the autumn pageant.

The wood is very hard, close-grained, and tough, and is used as a substitute for boxwood in the making of bobbins and shuttles for weaving, and also in cabinet-work.

The common dogwood, *Cornus pubescens,* Nutt., var. *Californica,* C. and E., is found on stream-banks throughout the State. It is a shrub from five to fifteen feet high, with purplish branches, ovate leaves, several inches long, small flowers in round-topped clusters without the conspicuous petal-like bracts; and white berries.

C. Canadensis, L., the bunch-berry, is an attractive little plant found in swampy places in Mendocino County and the northern Sierras, and northward and eastward across the continent. It is from three to six inches high, with a whorl of six leaves at the summit and a few scattered ones below. Like *C. Nuttallii,* its flower-clusters are surrounded by white bracts, making them appear like a single flower, though this is much smaller, an inch or so across. The flowers are followed by a pretty cluster of small red berries.

JAMESTOWN-WEED. JIMSON-WEED. THORN-APPLE. COMMON STRAMONIUM.

Datura Stramonium, L. Nightshade Family.

Stems.—Two or three feet high; stout. *Leaves.*—Alternate; ovate; coarsely angled; long-petioled. *Flowers.*—In the forks of the stem; short-pediceled; white. *Calyx.*—Tubular; angled; five-toothed; over an inch long. *Corolla.*—Funnel-form; three inches long; with an expanded five-angled border. *Stamens.*—Five; included. Filaments long and slender; adnate to the corolla below. Style long. *Ovary.*—Two-celled; each cell nearly divided again. *Fruit.*—Larger than a walnut; prickly. *Hab.*—Waste grounds near habitations; introduced.

The jimson-weed, which is a native of Asia, has become quite common in waste places. It is a rank, ill-smelling, nauseating weed, possessing narcotic, poisonous qualities, but its flowers are rather large and showy. The leaves and seeds are made into the drug called "stramonium," which is used as a remedy in neuralgia, spasmodic cough, and other disorders.

As the plant usually grows by roadsides or in the vicinity of dwellings, children are not infrequently poisoned by its fruit and leaves, and it should be weeded out wherever found. The poison manifests itself in dryness of the throat, rapid pulse, and delirium; and even death may ensue, preceded by convulsions and coma.

This plant is also called "mad-apple," "apple of Peru," and "Devil's apple."

It has a near relative — *D. suaveolens,* HBK.,—a large shrub with dark-green leaves and very large, pendulous white flowers. This is common in California gardens, and is known popularly as "floriponda," or "angels' trumpets." It sheds a powerful fragrance upon the air at night, which is not noticeable by day.

MILK-WHITE REIN-ORCHIS.

Habenaria leucostachys, Wats. Orchis Family.

Root.—A fusiform tuber. *Stems.*—One to four· feet high; leafy throughout. *Leaves.* — Lanceolate; diminishing upward. *Flowers.* — Bright white, in a spike. *Perianth segments.*—Two or three lines long. *Lip.*—Four lines long, with a slender spur four to six lines long. *Anther.*—On the column just above the stigma. *Ovary.*—One-celled. *Hab.*—Mountains throughout California.

From July to September we may look for the milk-white rein-orchis in moist meadows. It is especially abundant in the Sierras, where its charmingly fragrant, pure-white spikes are particularly effective against the lush green of the alpine meadows. It is a very decorative plant.

YARROW. MILFOIL.

Achillea millefolium, L. Composite Family.

Stems.—A foot or two high. *Leaves.*—Alternate; sessile; twice-pinnately parted into fine linear, acute, three- to five-cleft lobes; lanceolate in outline; two to four inches long; strong-scented. *Flower-heads.*—Crowded in a flat cluster; white, sometimes pink; four lines across, including the rays; made up of white disk-flowers and obovate white rays. *Hab.*—All around the Northern Hemisphere.

The yarrow, which is a common weed in most countries of the Northern Hemisphere, has long been known to botanists and herbalists, and was formerly in high repute for its many virtues. The leaves steeped in hot water are still considered very healing applications to cuts or bruises; and among the Spanish-Californians the fresh plants are used for stanching the blood in recent wounds.

This plant received the name *Achillea,* because the great hero of the Trojan war was supposed to have been the first to discover its virtues.

In Sweden it is used as a substitute for hops in the brewing of beer. Among the superstitious, even of the present day, it is regarded as a most potent love-charm, when plucked by a love-lorn maiden from the grave of a young man, while repeating the proper formula.

In the spring, the plants first develop a rosette of finely

MILK-WHITE REIN-ORCHIS—*Habenaria leucostachys.*

dissected, feathery leaves, which lie flat upon the ground. Later, when these are well grown, it sends up its tall flower-stalks, crowned with close, flat clusters of small white blossoms.

M. Naudin, who has an intimate knowledge of the plants of dry countries, recommends the yarrow for lawn-making where irrigation is impossible. "It grows freely in the driest of weather, and makes a handsome turf. It must be frequently cut, however, to prevent it from throwing up flower-stems. It will not succeed on a lime-impregnated soil."

Among children the yarrow is commonly known as "old man."

RATTLESNAKE PLANTAIN.

Goodyera Menziesii, Lindl. Orchis Family.

Leaves.—Two or three inches long; leathery; dark green, veined with white. *Scape.*—Six to fifteen inches high, with scattered lanceolate bracts. *Spike.*—Many-flowered. *Perianth.*—White; two to four lines long; downy. Lateral sepals deflexed; upper sepals and two petals coherent. Lip erect, saccate below, concave above, and narrowing into the recurved summit. *Anther.*—On the base of the column behind. *Ovary.*—One-celled. *Hab.*—Mountains, from Marin and Mariposa counties to British Columbia.

The rattlesnake plantain is frequently met under the coniferous trees of our northern woods. Its common name comes from the mottling of its leaves, which is similar to that of the rattlesnake's skin. In midsummer, or later, the plant sends up a stalk of small but shapely little blossoms. These are so modest, one would hardly suspect they belonged to the showy Orchis family.

BUTTON-BUSH.   BUTTON-WILLOW.

Cephalanthus occidentalis, L. Madder Family.

Shrubs eight to ten feet high. *Leaves.*—Opposite, or in whorls of three or four; petioled; ovate to lanceolate; three to five inches long. *Flowers.*—Small; white; in spherical heads an inch in diameter. *Calyx.*—Four-toothed. *Corolla.*—Long funnel-form with four-cleft limb. *Stamens.*—Four; short; borne on the throat of the corolla. *Ovary.*—Two- to four-celled. Style long-exserted. Stigma capitate. *Hab.*—Throughout the State.

The button-bush is a handsome shrub, found upon stream borders, often standing where it roots are constantly under

RATTLESNAKE PLANTAIN—*Goodyera Menziesii.*

water. Its leaves are willow-like, and its spherical flower-heads, poised gracefully at the ends of the branches, resemble small cushions filled with pins. The blossoms often have a jasmine-like fragrance.

A tincture made of the bark is used by physicians as a tonic and laxative and as a remedy for fevers and coughs.

This shrub is especially abundant in the interior, on the lower reaches of the San Joaquin and Sacramento rivers, where it is in bloom from June to August.

WHITE-VEINED SHINLEAF.
Pyrola picta, Smith. Heath Family.

Leaves.—Leathery; dark green, veined with white; one or two inches long. *Scape.*—Four to nine inches high. *Calyx.*—Five-parted. *Petals.* —Six lines or so long; white. *Stamens.*—Ten. Anthers opening terminally. *Ovary.*—Five-celled. Style long; curved. *Hab.*—The middle Sierras and Mendocino County, and northward.

The great coniferous forests of our higher mountains afford homes for many interesting members of the Heath family. A trip to the Sierras in August will yield many a prize to the flower-lover. Pyrolas, with waxen clusters, vie with pipsissi-was; the weird-looking pterospora rears its uncanny, gummy stems, clothed with small, yellowish bells, while an occasional glimpse of a blood-red spike betrays the most wonderful of them all—the snow-plant.

Of the pyrolas we made the acquaintance of three in this region. These pretty plants are called "shinleaf," because the leaves of some of the species were used by the English peasantry as plasters which they applied to bruises or sores. *Pyrola picta,* with its rich leathery, white-veined leaves and clusters of whitish, waxen flowers, was quite plentiful and always a delight to meet. *Pyrola dentata,* Smith, we often found growing with it. This has spatulate, wavy-margined leaves, which are pale and not veined with white, and its scapes are more slender. It never was so attractive or vigorous a plant as the other.

A ramble in the woods one day brought us to the brink of

WHITE-VEINED SHINLEAF—*Pyrola picta.*

a charming stream, whose pure, ice-cold waters babbled along most invitingly. Following its course, we found ourselves in a delightfully cool, moist thicket, where, nestling in the deep shade, we found the beautiful, rich, glossy leaves of *Pyrola rotundifolia,* var. *bracteata,* Gray. The leaves are roundish, of a beautiful, bright chrome-green, highly polished, and the delicate flowers are rose-pink. This is called "Indian lettuce" and "canker lettuce," and a tincture of the fresh plant is used in medicine for the same purposes as chimaphila. *P. aphylla,* Smith, is easily distinguished by the absence of leaves. It has flesh-colored stems, and its flowers are sometimes of the same color, and sometimes white. This is found in the Coast Ranges.

PEARLY EVERLASTING-FLOWER.

Anaphalis margaritacea, Benth. Composite Family.

Stems.—One to three feet high; leafy up to the flowers. *Leaves.*—Alternate; sessile; lanceolate or linear-lanceolate; two to four inches long; white-woolly, at length becoming green above. *Heads.*—Of filiform disk-flowers only. *Involucre.*—Of many rows of pearly white, pointed scales, not longer than the flowers, resembling ray-flowers. *Hab.*—Widely distributed over the northern parts of America and Asia.

Our wild everlasting-flowers are very difficult of determination, and are comprised under at least three genera, *Gnaphalium, Anaphalis,* and *Antennaria.* The word *Anaphalis* is from the same root as the word *Gnaphalium,* and the species have quite the aspect of *Gnaphalium.*

The flowers of the pearly everlasting have a peculiarly pure pearly look before they are entirely open, and their sharp-pointed little scales give them a prim, set look, like very regular, tiny white roses. There is a hint of green in them, but they are never of the dirty yellowish-white of the cudweed, nor have they the slippery-elm-like fragrance of the latter. When fully expanded, the centers are brown. The leaves, which at length become a dark, shining green, make a fine contrast with the permanently white-woolly stems. The flower-clusters are loosely compound.

WASHINGTON LILY. SHASTA LILY.

Lilium Washingtonianum, Kell. Lily Family.

Hab.—Throughout the Sierras, from three to six thousand feet elevation.

I shall never forget the thrill of delight I felt on first beholding this noble white lily, some years ago, in an open fir forest near Mt. Shasta. I had often heard of it, but never dared hope it would be my privilege to gather it for myself in its own native haunts. Since that I have become familiar with it upon the shores of Lake Tahoe and in the Yosemite, where it attains great perfection.

When the plants first emerge from the ground, they are in great danger from the inroads of squirrels and chipmunks, who regard them as luscious morsels. They sit erect, clasp the stem in their fore paws, and nibble it off with great satisfaction.

The blossoms of this species somewhat resemble those of the ruby lily, but the petals have longer claws and are more loosely put together. They are fragrant, but their perfume is not to be compared with that of the ruby lily.

Mr. Purdy once saw, upon a single great mountain-side, ten thousand of these wonderful plants, upbearing their beautiful, pure lilies—a sight outrivaling the poet's vision of the golden daffodils.

The Shasta lily is never found in the Coast Ranges. Another species, *L. Parryi,* Wats., resembling this in the form of its flowers, is found in the San Bernardino Mountains. This is known as the "lemon lily," and has clear yellow flowers, dotted sparingly with deeper yellow. It is a charming flower, and is always found in shaded, springy places in cool cañons.

LABRADOR TEA.

Ledum glandulosum, Nutt. Heath Family.

Shrubs two to six feet high. *Leaves.*—Alternate; short-petioled; oblong or oval; an inch or two long; coriaceous; sprinkled beneath with resin-dots. *Flowers.*—White; in terminal and axillary clusters.

Calyx.—Five-cleft. *Petals.*—Five; three lines long; rotately spreading. *Stamens.*—Four to ten. Anthers opening terminally. *Ovary.*—Five-celled. Style filiform, persistent. *Hab.*—The Coast Ranges, from Mendocino County northward, and through the Sierras.

Our Labrador tea is a comely shrub, found in the mountains at an elevation of four thousand feet and upward. Its small, leathery leaves are miniature copies of those of the California rhododendron, differing from them, however, in the sprinkling of resin-dots upon the under surface.

Upon seeing the flowers of this shrub for the first time, one is apt to imagine it a member of the Rose family, something akin to the cherry, with its clusters of small white flowers of a bitter fragrance; but a glance at the anthers, with their terminal pores, tells the story quickly.

A tea made from the leaves is, with many people, a valued remedy for rheumatism.

This little shrub is much dreaded by sheepmen, who claim that it poisons their flocks. It has been suggested that it would be an excellent thing to have it widely planted as a means of reducing these bands of "hoofed locusts," as Mr. Muir terms them—these marauders who trample down so much beauty, and leave desolation everywhere in their wake.

PIPSISSIWA. PRINCE'S PINE.

Chimaphila Menziesii, Spreng. Heath Family.

Stems.—Six inches high. *Leaves.*—Six to eighteen lines long; dark green, sometimes variegated with white; leathery. *Flowers.*—One to three. *Calyx.* — Five-parted; white. *Petals.* — Five; waxen-white or pinkish. *Stamens.*—Ten. Filaments enlarged and hairy in the middle. Anthers two-celled; opening terminally. *Ovary.*—Five-celled. Style short. Stigma button-like. *Hab.*—The Middle Sierras and Mendocino County.

The prince's pine is a charming little plant, and may be found beneath the undergrowth in the great coniferous woods of the Sierras, where it sits demurely with bowed head, like some cloistered nun engaged with her own meditations. It has an exquisite perfume, like that of the lily of the valley.

The common prince's pine of the Eastern States—*C. um-*

PRINCE'S PINE—*Chimaphila Menziesii.*

bellata—is more rare with us, though it is found through somewhat the same range as the above. It is a more vigorous plant than the other, has from four to seven purplish flowers in the cluster, while its leaves are never spotted.

In the East, from the leaves of this species is manufactured the drug "chimaphila," which is valued as a tonic and astringent, also as a remedy for cataract.

GROUNDSEL-TREE.
Baccharis pilularis, DC. Composite Family.

Evergreen diœcious shrubs, one to twelve feet high, with angled or striate branches. *Leaves.*—Alternate; sessile; obovate; cuneate; obtuse; coarsely toothed; leathery; one inch or less long. *Flower-heads.*—Crowded at the ends of the branchlets; four lines long; one or two across; without ray-flowers. *Involucres.*—Oblong; of many imbricated scales. *Sterile heads.*—With funnel-form, five-lobed corollas. *Fertile heads.*—With filiform corollas, mixed with a dense white silky pappus, which soon elongates. *Hab.*—All along the Coast.

In the fall, the dark-green foliage of the groundsel-tree is relieved by its abundant small white flower-clusters. The flowers of the male shrub are never very beautiful, being usually of a yellowish or dirty white, indeed so little resembling the other, as to appear like a separate species. But when the white silk down of the female shrub is fully expanded, its boughs are laden as with drifted snow. This lavish provision of silk is designed by nature for the wafting abroad of the seed.

It varies greatly in size and habit. Upon exposed, windswept sandhills it is low and close-cropped, but in more favorable localities, where the soil is rich and the climate more genial, it responds graciously to the changed conditions, becoming one of our most picturesque shrubs.

Growing and blooming at the same time with the above, may be found its near relative—*B. Douglasii,* DC. This does not aspire to shrubhood, but its tall stems, with their lanceolate, somewhat glutinous leaves, sometimes reach four feet in height, bearing at summit their pretty ageratum-like, white

BACCHARIS—*Baccharis Douglasii.*

flower-clusters. It loves the sandy soil of creek-banks and low fields, and is abundant from San Francisco to Los Angeles.

Sometimes confounded with this last is *B. viminea,* DC., commonly called "mule-fat," found on stream-banks from Napa County to Los Angeles. It is a willow-like shrub, whose foliage is eaten by horses and mules. Its leaves, acute at both ends, are from one to three inches long. The scales of the involucre are scarious-margined and ciliate, and the receptacle is flat.

LARGE WHITE MOUNTAIN DAISY.

Erigeron Coulteri, T. C. Porter. Composite Family.

Stem.—Six to twenty inches high; leafy; bearing solitary or rarely two or three large, slender-peduncled heads. *Leaves.*—Obovate to oblong; entire or with several sharp teeth; thin. *Flower-heads.*—Of yellow disk-flowers, and usually pure white ray-flowers. *Disk.*—Half an inch wide. *Rays.*—Fifty to seventy; narrowly linear; six lines or more long. *Hab.*—The Sierras; also the Rocky Mountains of Colorado.

" High on the crest of the blossoming grasses,
    Bending and swaying, with face toward the sky,
Stirred by the lightest west wind as it passes,
    Hosts of the silver-white daisy-stars lie."

No fairer sight could be imagined than a mountain meadow filled with these large, pure-white, feathery daisies.

CALIFORNIA FALSE HELLEBORE.

Veratrum Californicum, Durand. Lily Family.

Stems.—Stout; three to seven feet high. *Leaves.*—Oval; narrowing to lanceolate; sessile; sheathing; four to twelve inches long. *Flowers.* —Greenish-white in a large panicle, with usually ascending branches. *Stamens and pistils* in the same flowers, or in separate ones. *Pedicels.*— About two lines long. *Perianth segments.*—Six; spreading; oblanceolate; their bases thickened and green or brownish; upper margins sometimes minutely toothed; three to eight lines long. *Stamens.*—Six. Anthers confluently one-celled. *Ovary.*—Three-celled. Styles three, divergent. *Hab.*—The middle Sierras and Mendocino County northward to the Columbia; also eastward.

The false hellebore may be found in midsummer in the mountains. It grows along watercourses, and often covers rich, moist meadows, where its stems rise from three to seven feet, with their coarsely ribbed, boat-shaped leaves and large panicles of greenish-white flowers. When at its best it is a rather fine, showy thing, but its leaves are often perforated by some insect, and present a ragged, untidy appearance.

The mountaineers commonly call this plant "skunk cabbage," a deplorable misnomer, because it is in no sense merited; and, moreover, we have a plant to which the title more rightfully belongs. The root and young shoots are a violent poison, and are fatal to animals which are unfortunate enough to crop them.

Another species,—*V. fimbriatum,* Gray,—a smaller plant, is found upon the plains in Mendocino County. It may be distinguished from the above by its more slender leaves, its woolly flower-panicle, and its decidedly fringed flower-petals. When it first appears above ground in the spring its shoots are all packed in beautiful, long, green rosettes, which come up side by side. Upon opening one of these rosettes, I found eight successive leaves, one within another, all neatly creased and compactly folded, a miracle of deft workmanship.

VALERIAN.

Valeriana sylvatica, Banks. Valerian Family.

Herbs with opposite leaves. Stems eight to thirty inches high. *Root-leaves.*—Entire and spatulate or oval; or sometimes three-parted. *Stem-leaves.*—Mostly pinnately divided into three to eleven broadly lanceolate or oblong ovate leaflets. *Flowers.*—Small, white, numerous, in terminal racemes or panicles. *Calyx-limb.*—Of numerous plumose bristles; deciduous. *Corolla.*—Salver-form or campanulate funnel-form; three lines long. *Stamens.*—Three; exserted. *Ovary.*—One-celled; inferior. *Hab.*—Throughout the Sierras.

The valerian is one of the earlier flowers to appear in the Sierras, and may be found usually in wet ground. Its blossoms are pretty and feathery, but have not a very agreeable odor. The roots particularly have the strong scent of medicinal valerian, and it is said that some tribes of Indians use them as food.

CASSIOPE.

Cassiope Mertcnsiana, Don. Heath Family.

Small shrubby, alpine, evergreen plants with the aspect of club mosses. *Branches.*—Six to twelve inches high, leafy throughout. *Leaves.*—Closely appressed to stem; overlapping in four ranks, thick, two lines long, keeled on the back. *Flowers.*—Solitary, on slender pedicels; white to rose-color. *Sepals.*—Four or five, membranaceous. *Corolla.*—Campanulate, five-lobed, three lines high, four broad. *Stamens.*—Eight or ten. Anthers with a pair of recurved awns and opening by terminal pores. *Ovary.*—Four- or five-celled. *Style.*—Slender. *Capsule.*—Globular. *Hab.*—The Sierras at ten thousand feet and over, from Mt. Dana to Lassen Peak.

Mr. John Muir says of this little plant:—"Here too . . . I met Cassiope growing in fringes among the battered rocks. . . . Her blossoms had faded long ago, but they were still clinging with happy memories to the evergreen sprays, and still so beautiful as to thrill every fiber of one's being. Winter and summer you may hear her voice, the low, sweet melody of her purple bells. No evangel among all the mountain plants speaks Nature's love more plainly than Cassiope."

GRASS OF PARNASSUS.

Parnassia fimbriata, Banks. Saxifrage Family.

Leaves.—All radical; reniform to cordate-ovate; an inch or more across; long-petioled. *Scape.*—Slender, about a foot high, bearing at summit a solitary white flower. *Calyx.*—Five-parted. *Petals.*—Five; obovate or oblong; four or five lines long; their margins fringed below the middle. *Stamens.*—Five; alternating with clusters of united sterile filaments. *Ovary.*—One-celled. Stigmas three or four: sessile. *Hab.* —The mountains of California.

It is difficult to understand how this plant ever received its common name, as it in no wise resembles a grass. However it may be, it is a charming plant and one full of interest for us, and it is a happy day when we make its acquaintance as we stroll along some mountain brookside.

II. YELLOW

Yellow or occasionally or partially yellow flowers not described in the Yellow Section.

Described in the White Section:—

CALOCHORTUS VENUSTUS—Mariposa Lily, or Tulip.
LILIUM PARRYI—Lemon-Lily.
RAPHANUS SATIVUS—Radish.
VIOLA OCELLATA—Heart's-ease.

Described in the Pink Section:—

LESSINGIA GERMANORUM—Yellow Lessingia.

Described in the Blue and Purple Section:—

FRITILLARIA PUDICA—Yellow Fritillary.
IRIS MACROSIPHON—Ground-Iris.
SISYRINCHIUM CALIFORNICUM—Golden-eyed Grass.
TRILLIUM SESSILE—California Trillium.
POLEMONIUM CARNEUM—Jacob's Ladder.

Described in the Red Section:—

CASTILLEIA LATIFOLIA—Indian Paint-Brush.
CEREUS EMORYI—Velvet Cactus.
PENTSTEMON CENTRANTHIFOLIUS—Scarlet Bugler.

Described in the Miscellaneous Section:—

CYPRIPEDIUM CALIFORNICUM—California Lady's Slipper.

SUN-CUPS.

Œnothera ovata, Nutt. Evening-Primrose Family.

Root.—A thick tap-root. *Leaves.*—All radical; oblong-lanceolate; smooth; ciliate. *Flowers.*—Solitary in the axils; bright golden yellow. *Calyx-tube.*—Filiform; one to five inches long; limb of four lanceolate, reflexed divisions. *Petals.*—Four; three to ten lines long. *Stamens.*— Eight. *Ovary.*—Four-celled; underground. Style filiform. Stigma capitate. *Fruit.*—A ribbed capsule. *Hab.*—Near the coast from San Francisco to Monterey.

This little evening primrose is an exceedingly interesting plant, although it is not of very wide distribution. The flat rosettes of leaves sometimes measure over a foot across, and are thickly sown with the bright golden flowers, large in proportion to the size of the plants. A flower or bud is found in the axil of every leaf, diminishing in size toward the center, one plant sometimes having a hundred blossoms and buds. These flowers are peculiarly fresh and winsome, and were they not so abundant where they grow they would doubtless be considered very beautiful.

A strange feature of the plant is its flower-stem, which is not a flower-stem at all, but a very much prolonged calyx-tube, the seed-vessel being just within the surface of the ground.

We wonder how these imprisoned seeds are going to escape and find lodgment to start new colonies elsewhere. Perhaps the moles and gophers could tell something about it if they would.

The leaves of these little plants are sometimes used for salads.

These blossoms are often erroneously called "cowslips."

COMMON BUTTERCUP.

Ranunculus Californicus, Benth. Buttercup or Crowfoot Family.

Stems.—Slender; branching; six to eighteen inches high. *Radical leaves.*—Commonly pinnately ternate; the leaflets cut into three to seven usually linear lobes. Divisions of the stem-leaves usually narrower. *Flowers.*—Five to ten lines in diameter; shining golden yellow. *Sepals.*—Green; strongly reflexed. *Petals.*—Ten to fourteen; obovate;

SUN–CUPS—*Œnothera ovata.*

each with a small scale at the base. *Stamens.*—Numerous. *Pistils.*—Numerous; on a receptacle. Ovaries flattened. Stigmas recurved. *Hab.*—Throughout western California into Oregon.

> " The buttercup catches the sun in its chalice;
> And there's never a leaf nor a blade too mean
> To be some happy creature's palace."

The first clear, beautiful note of the lark has been heard; skies are blue and fields are green; little frogs are filling the air with their music;—and the buttercups are here. The fields are full of them, and their bright golden eyes, starring the meadows, bring a gladness to the face of nature. The children wade knee-deep in their gold, filling their hands with treasure; and yonder, where their golden masses cover the slopes, King Midas may have passed, transforming the earth with his magical touch.

Because some of the buttercups grow where frogs abound, Pliny bestowed the Latin name *Ranunculus,* meaning "little frog." We have a number of other species of buttercup—some of them denizens of marshy spots; but the common field buttercup is widest-spread and best known.

The Indians, who seem to have a use for everything, parch the seeds of this and beat them to a flour, which they eat without the further formality of cooking. This flour is said to have the peculiar rich flavor of parched corn.

CREAM-CUPS.

Platystemon Californicus, Benth. Poppy Family.

Delicate hairy herbs. *Stems.*—A span or two high. *Leaves.*—Mostly opposite; sessile; two to four inches long. *Flowers.*—Axillary; long-peduncled; an inch or so across. *Sepals.*—Three; falling early. *Petals.*—Six; in two rows; cream-color, often with a yellow spot at base. *Stamens.*—Numerous. Filaments broad; petaloid. *Pistils.*—Six to twenty-five; united in a ring at first; afterward separating. Stigmas terminal. *Hab.*—Throughout California.

The cream-cups are delicate, hairy plants of the early springtime, which often grow in masses and take possession of whole fields. They seem to be more vigorous in the south, and produce larger flowers there than in the north, often

CREAM–CUPS—*Platystemon Californicus.*

having as many as nine petals. The delicate, nodding green buds (like miniature poppy-buds) soon throw off their outer wrappings, and, emerging from captivity, gradually assume an erect position and unfurl their lovely pure straw-colored petals to their widest extent. These blossoms open for several successive days.

The genus takes its name from the flat filaments. The numerous slender pistils are so cleverly joined together into a cylinder that they appear like a hollow, one-celled ovary. But a cross-section will show the separate ovaries under a glass.

Some people like the odor of these flowers; but I must confess to a lack of appreciation of it. I suspect its charm must exist in some pleasant association.

COPA DE ORO. CALIFORNIA POPPY. TOROSA.

Eschscholtzia Californica, Cham. Poppy Family.

Stems.—Twelve to eighteen inches high; branching. *Leaves.*—Alternate; finely dissected; glaucous. *Flowers.*—Two or three inches across; usually orange; but ranging from that to white. Summit of the peduncle enlarging into a cup-shaped torus or disk, upon the upper inner surface of which are borne the calyx, corolla, and stamens. *Calyx.*—A pointed green cap, falling early. *Petals.*—Four. *Stamens.*—Numerous, in four groups, in front of the petals. Anthers linear. *Ovary.*—One-celled. Style short. Stigmas four to six; unequal. *Capsule.*—Cylindrical; ten-nerved; two or three inches long. *Hab.*—Throughout California.

> Thy satin vesture richer is than looms
>   Of Orient weave for raiment of her kings!
>   Not dyes of olden Tyre, not precious things
> Regathered from the long-forgotten tombs
> Of buried empires, not the iris plumes
>   That wave upon the tropics' myriad wings,
>   Not all proud Sheba's queenly offerings
> Could match the golden marvel of thy blooms.
> For thou art nurtured from the treasure-veins
>   Of this fair land; thy golden rootlets sup
>   Her sands of gold—of gold thy petals spun.
> Her golden glory, thou! On hills and plains,
>   Lifting, exultant, every kingly cup
>   Brimmed with the golden vintage of the sun.
> —Ina D. Coolbrith.

CALIFORNIA POPPY—*Eschscholtzia Californica.*

It is difficult to exaggerate the charms of this wonderful flower. When reproduced in countless millions, its brilliant blossoms fairly cover the earth; and far away upon distant mountain-slopes, bright patches of red gold denote that league after league of it lies open to the sun. It revels in the sunshine, and not until the morning is well advanced does it begin to unfurl its tightly rolled petals.

In the early days, when Spanish vessels sailed up and down the newly-discovered coast, the mariners, looking inland, saw the flame of the poppies upon the hills and called this "the land of fire." They said that the altar-cloth of San Pascual was spread upon the hills, and, filled with a devotional spirit, they disembarked to worship upon the shore.

This flower is now cultivated in many parts of the world. But one can form no conception of it, pale and languishing in a foreign garden. One must go to its native hillsides to get any idea of its prodigal beauty.

The common title, "California poppy," though it has been widely used, belongs more properly to another flower, *Papaver Californicum*. The generic name is dissonant and harsh. Why not replace it by one of the more euphonious Spanish titles— "amapola," "dormidera," "torosa," or, most charmingly appropriate of all, "copa de oro,"—"cup of gold"?

There are many forms of *Eschscholtzia,* and of late the original species, *E. Californica,* has been divided into a number of new species, which are, however, difficult of determination.

The Indians of Placer County, it is said, boil the herbage, or roast it by means of hot stones, lay it in water afterward, and then eat it as a green. A drug made from this plant is used in medicine as a harmless substitute for morphine and as a remedy for headache and insomnia, and it has an especially excellent effect with children. The Spanish-Californians make a hair-oil, which they prize highly, by frying the whole plant in olive oil and adding some choice perfume. This is said to promote the growth of the hair and to make it glossy.

MOCK-ORANGE. GOURD. CHILI-COJOTE. CALABAZILLA.

Cucurbita fœtidissima, HBK. Gourd Family.

Stems.—Long; coarse; trailing. *Leaves.*—Alternate; petioled; triangular-cordate; six to twelve inches long; acute; rough. *Tendrils.*—Three- to five-cleft. *Flowers.*—Solitary; yellow; three or four inches long; monœcious. *Calyx-tube.*—Six lines long, equaling the five linear lobes. *Corolla.*—Campanulate; five-cleft to the middle or lower; with recurved lobes. *Stamens.*—In the male flowers two with two-celled anthers, and one with one; in the female all three rudimentary. *Ovary.*—Three-celled. Style short. Stigmas three; two-lobed. *Fruit.*—Orange-like, but with a hard rind. *Syn.*—*C. perennis,* Gray. *Hab.*—San Diego to San Joaquin County.

The rough, ill-smelling foliage of the chili-cojote is a common sight in southern California, where it may be seen trailing over many a field; but woe to the negligent farmer who allows this pest to get a foothold—for it will cost him a small fortune to eradicate it. It sends down into the earth an enormous root, six feet or so long, and often as broad. When the gourds are ripe, these vines look like the dumping-ground for numerous poor, discarded oranges.

Notwithstanding its unsavory character, the various parts of this vine are put to use—specially among the Spanish-Californians and the Indians. The root is a purgative more powerful than croton-oil. When pounded to a pulp, it is used as soap by the Spanish-Californians, who aver that it cleanses as nothing else can; but rinsing must be very thorough—for any particles remaining in the garments prove very irritating to the skin. The leaves are highly valued for medicinal purposes, and the pulp of the green fruit, mixed with soap, is said to remove stains from clothing. The Indians eat the seed, when ground and made into a mush. The early Californian women used the gourds as darning-balls.

This vine is a near relative of the pumpkins and squashes of our gardens.

The flowers are said to be violet-scented.

TREE-POPPY.

Dendromecon rigida, Benth. Poppy Family.

Shrubs two to eight feet high. *Leaves.*—One to three inches long; leathery. *Flowers.*—Solitary; yellow; one to three inches across. *Sepals.*—Two; falling early. *Petals.*—Four. *Stamens.*—Many. *Ovary.* —Linear; one-celled. Stigma two-lobed. *Capsule.*—Eighteen to thirty lines long. *Hab.*—Dry hills from San Diego to Butte County.

The tree-poppy is the only truly shrubby plant in the Poppy family. Its pale leaves are quite rigid, and resemble those of the willow in form. The bright golden flowers are sometimes three inches across, and one can readily imagine the fine effect produced when many of them are open at once upon a hillside. Though found through quite a range, this shrub attains its most perfect development in Santa Barbara County.

CALIFORNIA BARBERRY.

Berberis pinnata, Lag.

Shrubs from less than a foot to five feet high. *Leaves.*—Alternate; pinnate; leathery. *Leaflets.*—Usually five to nine, but sometimes as many as seventeen; nearly sessile; ovate-elliptical to oblong; one to two and a quarter inches long; shining above, paler beneath; repand; prickly toothed. Flower racemes clustered, dense. Filaments with a recurved tooth on each side near the apex. Otherwise as *B. nervosa.* *Hab.*—San Francisco Bay and northward and southward in the Coast Ranges.

The California barberry is a fine shrub, particularly where it grows upon sheltered wooded hillsides. Its handsome holly-like leaves form its chief attraction, as its flowers are not conspicuous for their beauty, although they are interesting in their structure, having the floral organs standing one in front of the other instead of alternating, and the stamens opening by means of little uplifting lids, as in all the members of the Barberry family.

The Oregon grape,—*B. aquifolium,* Pursh.,—closely resembling the above, but having fewer and longer leaflets, with the lower pair distant from the stem, is abundant from Oregon northward, and may extend into our own borders. It is such a beautiful shrub that we have given it a welcome place in our gardens, where it is also known as Mahonia.

TREE–POPPY—*Dendromecon rigida.*

In the spring, when yellow with its masses of flowers, or in its summer dress of rich shining green, or in the autumn, when its foliage is richly toned with bronze or scarlet or yellow, offsetting its fine blue berries, it is equally effective.

Among the northern Indians a decoction made from the root is a favorite tonic remedy, and it has become a recognized drug in the pharmacopœia of our coast, being used as an alterative and tonic. The root is tough and hard, of a bright golden yellow, and intensely bitter. The bark of the root is the part used medicinally.

YELLOW PANSY. JOHNNY-JUMP-UP.

Viola pedunculata, Torr. and Gray. Violet Family.

Stems.—Leafy; two to six inches or more high. *Leaves.*—Alternate; long-petioled; ovate; cuneate; crenate; with lanceolate stipules. *Flowers.*—Large; long-peduncled; deep golden yellow. *Calyx.*—Five-parted. *Petals.*—The two upper tinged with brown outside; the three lower veined with purple; the two lateral bearded; the lower one with a short spur at base. *Stamens.*—Five. Anthers nearly sessile; erect around the club-shaped style. *Ovary.*—One-celled. *Hab.*—Southern to middle California.

Pansies! Pansies! How I love you, pansies!
Jaunty-faced, laughing-lipped, and dewy-eyed with glee;
Would my song might blossom out in little five-leaved stanzas
    As delicate in fancies
    As your beauty is to me!

But, my eyes shall smile on you and my hands infold you,
Pet, caress, and lift you to the lips that love you, so
That, shut ever in the years that may mildew or mold you,
    My fancy shall behold you
    Fair as in the long ago.
              —*Jas. Whitcomb Riley.*

On wind-swept downs near the ocean, on the low hills of the Coast Ranges, or upon the plains of the interior, this charming golden pansy spreads itself in profusion in early spring. It is the darling of the children, who on their way to school gather great handfuls of its brown-eyed blossoms, and among them it is often familiarly known as "Johnny-jump-up." The Spanish-Californian children knew them as "gallitos."

YELLOW PANSY—*Viola pedunculata.*

You may often see myriads of them dancing on their long stems in the breeze, and showing glimpses of red-brown where their purplish outer petals are turned toward you for the moment. In the shelter of quiet woodlands, its stems are longer and more fragile.

TWIN-BERRY.

Lonicera involucrata, Banks. Honeysuckle Family.

Shrubs eight to ten feet high. *Leaves.*—Three inches long or so. *Flowers.*—A pair; at the summit of an axillary peduncle; with a conspicuous involucre of four bracts, tinged with red or yellow. *Calyx.*—Adherent to the ovary; the limb minute or obsolete. *Corolla.*—Tubular; irregular; half an inch or more long; viscid-pubescent; yellowish. *Stamens.*—Five. *Ovary.*—Two- or three-celled. Style filiform. Stigma capitate. *Berries.*—Black-purple. *Hab.*—Throughout the State; eastward to Lake Superior.

A walk through some moist thicket or along a stream-bank in March, will reveal the yellow flowers of the twin-berry amid its ample, thin green leaves. These blossoms are always borne in pairs at the summit of the stem, and are surrounded by a leafy involucre, consisting of two pairs of round, fluted bracts. As the berries ripen and become black, these bracts deepen to a brilliant red and make the shrubs much more conspicuous and ornamental than at blossoming-time.

WATER-HOLLY. MAHONIA.

Berberis nervosa, Pursh. Barberry Family.

Stem.—Simple; a foot or so high; bearing at summit a crown of large leaves, mixed with many dry, chaffy, persistent bracts. *Leaves.*—One or two feet long, with from eleven to seventeen ovate, acuminate, prickly, somewhat palmately nerved leaflets. *Flowers.*—Yellow, in elongated, clustered racemes. Bractlets, sepals, petals, and stamens six, standing in front of one another. Anthers two-celled; opening by uplifting valves. *Ovary.*—One-celled. Style short or none. *Fruit.*—Dark-blue, glaucous berries; four lines in diameter. *Hab.*—Deep coast woods, from Monterey to Vancouver Island.

The water-holly is one of the beautiful plants to be found in our deep coast woods within the cool influence of the sea-fogs. The plants are very symmetrical, with their crown of dark, shining leaves, with numerous prickly leaflets, and in

TWIN–BERRY—*Lonicera involucrata*.

spring, when the long graceful racemes of yellow flowers are produced in abundance, and hang amid and below the leaves, they are very ornamental. The stems are densely clothed with numerous dry, awl-shaped scales, an inch or more long.

SUNSHINE. FLY-FLOWER.

Baeria gracilis, Gray.   Composite Family.

Six inches or so high; branching freely. *Leaves.*—Mostly opposite; linear; entire; an inch or so long. *Flower-heads.*—Yellow; of disk- and ray-flowers. *Rays.*—Ten to fourteen; three or four lines long. *Involucre.*—Campanulate; of a single series of small lanceolate, herbaceous scales. *Hab.*—From San Francisco southward.

Considered singly, the blossom of this plant is a simple, unassuming little flower; but when countless millions of its golden stars stud the nether firmament, it becomes one of the most conspicuous of all our *Compositæ.* It literally covers the earth with a close carpet of rich golden bloom, and other plants, such as scarlet paint-brushes, blue phacelias, and yellow and white tidy-tips, rise out of its golden tapestry. Mile after mile of it whirls by the car-window as we journey along, or long stretches of it gild the gently rounded hill-slopes of the distant landscape.

There are several other species of *Baeria,* but this is the most abundant and wide-spread. In some localities this little plant is so much frequented by a small fly, which feeds upon its pollen, that it is called "fly-flower." It then becomes a serious nuisance to horses and cattle, which grow wild and restive under the persecution of this insect.

In the Spanish playing-cards in the early days, the "Jack of Spades" always held one of these flowers in his hand. By the Spanish-Californians it was called "Si me quieres, no me quieres"—"Love me, love me not,"—because their dark-eyed maidens tried their fortunes upon it in the same manner that our own maidens consult the marguerite.

Growing in brilliant beds by themselves, or intermingling their gold with that of the *Baeria,* the charming feathery blos-

PENTACHÆTA—*Pentachæta aurea.*　SUNSHINE—*Baeria gracilis.*

soms of *Pentachæta aurea,* Nutt., are found in midspring. They have from fifty to seventy rays and their involucres consist of several rows of scarious-margined bracts.

MEADOW-FOAM.

Flærkea Douglasii, Baillon. Geranium Family.

Smooth, succulent herbs. *Stems.*—A foot or so long. *Leaves.*— Much dissected. *Flowers.*—Axillary; solitary. *Sepals.*—Narrow; acute. *Petals.*—Nine lines long or so; yellow, sometimes tipped with white, white, or rose-tinged. *Stamens.*—Ten, in two sets; a gland at the base of those opposite the sepals. *Ovary.*—Of five carpels, becoming distinct. Style five-cleft at the apex. *Syn.—Limnanthes Douglasii,* R. Br. *Hab.*—Oregon to southern California.

When the spring is well advanced, our wet meadows are all a-cream with the meadow-foam, whose dense masses blend exquisitely with the rich red of the common sorrel, which is in blossom at the same time.

This plant is a near relative of the redwood-sorrel, and its flowers are similar in size and veining, and also in their habit of closing at night. It is much admired and has long been in cultivation.

PIMPERNEL. POOR-MAN'S WEATHER-GLASS.

Anagallis arvensis, L. Primrose Family.

Stems.—Prostrate; spreading. *Leaves.*—Usually opposite; sessile; ovate. *Flowers.*—Solitary on axillary peduncles; orange-vermilion (rarely blue or white); six lines or so across. *Calyx* and rotate corolla five-parted. *Petals.*—Rounded; purple at base. *Stamens.*—Five; opposite the petals. Filaments purple, bearded. *Capsule.*—Globose; the top falling off as a lid. *Hab.*—Common everywhere. Introduced from Europe.

The little orange-vermilion flower of the pimpernel is a plain little blossom to the unassisted eye, but it becomes truly regal when seen under a glass, where its rich purple center displays itself in glistening splendor. It is a forcible example of the infinite care bestowed upon all of Nature's children, even to the humblest weeds.

This little plant has come to us from Europe, and it makes itself perfectly at home among us in many widely differing

MEADOW-FOAM—*Flœrkea Douglasii.*

situations. From the fact that it furls its petals upon cloudy days, or at the approach of rain, it is called in England "poor-man's weather-glass."

The plant is an acrid poison and was extensively used in medicine by the ancients. It seems to act particularly upon the nervous system, and was used as a remedy for convulsions, the plague, gout, and hydrophobia.

ENCELIA.

Encelia Californica, Nutt.   Composite Family.

Bushy; two to four feet high; strong-scented. *Leaves.*—Mostly alternate; short-petioled; ovate-lanceolate; an inch or two long. *Flower-heads.*—Solitary; long-peduncled; large. *Disk.*—Eight lines across; of black-purple, tubular flowers, with deep-yellow styles. *Rays.*—Sterile; over an inch long; five lines wide; four-toothed. *Involucre.*—Open-campanulate of several series of coriaceous, imbricated scales. *Hab.*—Santa Barbara to San Diego.

This shrubby *Composita* is quite abundant in the south, and when covered with its large yellow flowers with purple-brown centers is very showy. We have seen mesas covered with the bushes, which have much the same spreading habit as the white marguerite of the garden. It thrives particularly well near the coast, but is also at home upon some of the hills of interior valleys as well. It is quite strong-scented, but the flowers are very handsome, rivaling in decorativeness many of the cherished plants of our gardens.

YELLOW FORGET-ME-NOT.   WOOLLY-BREECHES.

Amsinckia, Lehm.   Borage Family.

Hispid annuals. *Leaves.*—Alternate; oblong-ovate to linear. *Flowers.*—Small; yellow or orange, in coiled spikes or racemes. *Calyx.*—Five-parted; persistent. *Corolla.*—Salver-shaped, or somewhat funnel-form; with five-lobed border; the throat naked or with minute hairy tufts opposite the lobes. *Stamens.*—Five. *Ovary.*—Of four seedlike nutlets. Style filiform. Stigma capitate.

We have several species of *Amsinckia,* all of which have small yellow flowers, resembling in form our little white forget-me-nots. The genus is a western American one, and the species are very difficult of determination. They are all hispid plants, very disagreeable to handle, and are generally of rank growth. They often occur in great masses, when they become rather showy.

The largest-flowered species, which is also the most common one in the south, is *A. spectabilis,* Fisch. and Mey. The corolla of this is often half an inch long and half an inch across, of an orange-yellow, with deeper orange spots in the throat.

TREE-TOBACCO.

Nicotiana glauca, Graham.   Nightshade Family.

Loosely branching shrubs, fifteen feet or so high. *Leaves.*—Alternate; petioled; ovate; smooth. *Flowers.*—Clustered at the ends of the branches. *Calyx.* — Campanulate; five-toothed. *Corolla.* — Tubular; eighteen lines long; with constricted throat; and border shortly five-toothed. *Stamens.*—Five. on the base of the corolla, adnate to the tube below. Anthers with two diverging cells. *Ovary.*—One-celled. Style slender. Stigma capitate; two-lobed. *Hab.*—Throughout southern California and sparingly northward; introduced.

The tall, loosely branching, spreading form of the tree-tobacco is a familiar sight in the south about vacant lots and waste places. Its clusters of long, greenish-yellow flowers hang gracefully from the ends of the slender branches, and the ovate leaves are rather long-stalked. It is supposed to have been introduced from Buenos Aires, and old inhabitants remember the time when but one or two plants were known. In thirty years it has spread rapidly, and is now exceedingly common.

WIND-POPPY. BLOOD-DROP. FLAMING POPPY.

Meconopsis heterophylla, Benth.   Poppy Family.

Smooth herbs. *Stems.*—Slender; a foot or two high. *Leaves.*—Mostly petioled; pinnately divided into variously toothed, oval to linear segments. *Flowers.*—Solitary; on long peduncles; orange-vermilion to scarlet. *Sepals.*—Two; falling early. *Petals.*—Four; two to twelve lines long. *Stamens.*—Numerous. Filaments filiform; purple. Anthers yellow. *Ovary.*—Top-shaped; ribbed; one-celled. Style short. Stigma large; capitate; four- to eight-lobed. *Hab.*—Throughout western California.

The wind-poppy is an exceedingly variable flower. In the central part of the State it is large and showy, its beautiful flame-colored blossoms being two inches across; while in the south it is usually very small, making tiny flecks of red in the grass, for which reason it is there called "blood-drop." It is an exquisite thing. Its petals have the delicate satin texture of the poppy; and their showy orange or scarlet blends suddenly at the center into a deep maroon. The bright-green, top-shaped ovary stands up in the midst of the slender stamens, whose yellow anthers show brilliantly against the dark maroon of the petals.

It blossoms in spring upon open hillsides, seeming to prefer those which are shaded for at least part of the day. It is very fragile, and falls to pieces at a touch, which makes it an unsatisfactory flower to gather.

WHISPERING BELLS.

Emmenanthe penduliflora, Benth. Baby-eyes or Waterleaf Family.

Six inches to a foot high; branched above; hairy; somewhat viscid. *Leaves.*—An inch or more long; pinnatifid. *Flowers.*—Straw-colored; at length pendulous. *Corolla.*—Campanulate; about six lines long. (Flower structure as in *Phacelia.*) *Hab.*—Lake County to San Diego.

In midspring, when passing among the plants upon our dry, open hillsides, our attention is often attracted by a certain delicate, rustling sound, which we find comes from the little papery bells of the dried blossoms of the emmenanthe, which retain the semblance of their first freshness for many weeks.

Though not at first apparent, a little examination will reveal the fact that these plants are very closely related to the phacelias, the chief difference being in the yellow corollas.

YELLOW STAR-TULIP.

Calochortus Benthami, Baker. Lily Family.

Stems.—Several-flowered, very flexuous; three to seven inches high; branching in pairs. *Radical leaf.*—Linear-lanceolate; four lines wide, exceeding the stem. *Stem-leaves.*—Ovate lanceolate; two to four inches long; three to five lines wide. *Flowers.*—Yellow; erect. *Sepals.* —Narrowly ovate; eight to ten lines wide. *Petals.*—Exceeding the sepals a little; clawed; obovate, rounded above; naked. *Gland.*—Covered

WHISPERING BELLS—*Emmenanthe penduliflora.*

above by a crescent-shaped scale, bordered above by short yellow hairs, some of which are club-shaped. *Capsule.*—Nodding; nearly orbicular; six to nine lines long. *Hab.*—Sierra Nevada foothills from Mariposa County to Butte County.

This is a very pretty little star-tulip, with graceful, flexuous stems and erect flowers, whose spreading petals are covered with hairs. Sometimes there is a dark-brown, almost black, spot upon the petals, and when such is the case the plant is called *C. Benthami,* var. *Wallacei.*

CREAM-COLORED WALL-FLOWER.

Erysimum grandiflorum, Nutt.   Mustard Family.

Stems.—Six to eighteen inches high. *Leaves.*—Spatulate or oblanceolate; entire, toothed or lobed; lower long-petioled. *Sepals.*—Four; one pair strongly gibbous at base. *Petals.*—An inch long; longclawed; cream-color or yellowish. *Stamens.*—Six; two shorter. *Ovary.*—One-celled; linear. Style stout; short. Stigma capitate. *Pod.* —Nearly flat; thirty lines or less long. *Syn.*—*Cheiranthus asper,* Cham. and Schlecht. *Hab.*—The seaboard from Los Angeles to Oregon.

Growing along sandy stretches, or upon open mesas by the seashore, we may find the showy blossoms of the cream-colored wall-flower from February to May. These flowers are less stocky and much more delicate than the garden species; and when seen numerously dotting a field carpeted with other flowers, they stand out conspicuously, claiming the attention peculiarly to themselves. They have not the delicious fragrance of the Western wall-flower. At first yellowish, they become pale cream-color after fertilization has taken place.

E. asperum, DC., the Western wall-flower, is widely distributed, and may be known from the above by its four-sided pods, and by its flowers, which are usually orange-color— though they occasionally vary to yellow or purple. These blossoms are especially abundant in the mountains and valleys of the south, where their brilliant orange is conspicuous amid the lush greens of springtime. They are very fragrant, and are favorites among our wild flowers.

CREAM–COLORED WALL–FLOWER—*Erysimum grandiflorum.*

BUR-CLOVER.

Medicago denticulata, Willd.   Pea Family.

Stems.—Prostrate or ascending.   *Leaves.*—Trifoliolate.   *Leaflets.*—
Cuneate-obovate or obcordate; toothed above.   *Flowers.*—Papilionaceous; small; yellow; two or three in a cluster.   *Stamens.*—Nine united,
one free.   *Pods.*—Coiled into two circles; armed with hooked prickles.
Hab.—Common everywhere; introduced.

The bur-clover is a little European weed which has become
very wide-spread and very much at home among us.   It is
an excellent forage-plant, and in late summer, when our cattle
have eaten everything else, they feed upon the little dried burs,
which are very nutritious in themselves.   But these same little
coiled burs, with their numerous firm hooks, work great dam-
age to wool, imbedding themselves in it so firmly as to make
it very difficult to remove them without seriously injuring
its quality.   These plants invade our lawns, where they become
very troublesome, probably brought in the hair of our dogs.

Medicago maculata, Willd., the spotted medick, is very common in some localities about San Francisco Bay, and may be
known by its larger leaflets, an inch across, beautifully blotched
with brown.

COMMON MONKEY-FLOWER.

Mimulus luteus, L.   Figwort Family.

Varying greatly in size.   *Stems.*—One to four feet high.   *Leaves.*—
Mostly smooth; ovate-oval or cordate; coarsely notched.   *Flowers.*—
Yellow.   *Calyx.*—Sharply five-angled; unevenly five-lobed.   *Corolla.*—
One or two inches long; lower lip usually spotted with brown pur-
ple.   *Stamens.*—Four; in pairs.   Anthers with two divergent cells.
Ovary.—Two-celled.   Style long and slender.   Stigma with two rounded
lips.   *Hab.*—Common throughout California.

The bright canary-colored blossoms of the common monkey-
flower are a familiar sight upon almost every stream-bank.
The plant varies greatly in size, according to the locality of
its growth.   I once saw it flourishing in the rich soil of a lake-
shore, where its hollow stems were as large as an ordinary
cane, and its blossoms grotesquely large.

M. moschatus, Dougl., the common musk-plant of cultiva-

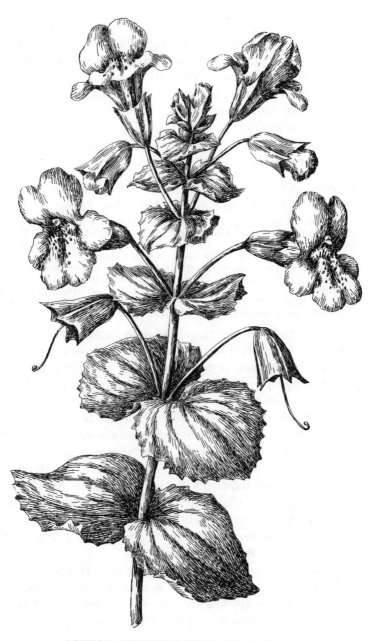

COMMON MONKEY-FLOWER—*Mimulus luteus.*

tion, is usually found along mountain-streams. It may be known by its clammy, musk-scented, light-green herbage. Its flowers are larger than in cultivation.

M. brevipes, Benth., is common from Santa Barbara to San Diego, upon hillsides in spring. It has stems a foot or two high, lanceolate leaves one to four inches long, and large, handsome yellow flowers, having a pair of ridges running down their open throats.

FAWN-LILY. DOG'S-TOOTH VIOLET. CHAMISE-LILY.
Erythronium giganteum, Lindl. Lily Family.

Corm.—Usually elongated. *Leaves.*—Oblong; six to ten inches long; dark green, usually mottled in mahogany and dark brown. *Scape.*—One- to many-flowered. *Perianth.*—Broadly funnel-form, with six deciduous segments; at length revolute to the stem. *Segments.*—Straw-color, with orange base, with often a transverse, brownish band across the base; broadly lanceolate; eighteen lines or so long. *Stamens.*—Six. Filaments filiform. Anthers basifixed. *Ovary.*—Three-celled. Style slender. Stigma three-lobed. *Hab.*—The interior of the Coast Ranges, from Sonoma County to the Willamette Valley.

The dog's-tooth violets expand into larger, finer creations upon our shores than were ever dreamed of elsewhere. They seem to imbibe new vigor in the sweet life-giving air of our Coast Range forests. In southern Oregon, they reach their maximum development, manifesting themselves in numerous beautiful species. With us the common title becomes still more inappropriate than for the Atlantic species—for nothing could be farther from a violet than these large pale flowers, which in reality look far more like lilies. Indeed, in Mendocino County they are commonly known as "chamise-lilies," while in the vicinity of Cloverdale they are called "Easter lilies," according to Professor Setchell. Another name is "Adam and Eve," bestowed because the plant often bears a large and a small flower at the same time.

Personally, I am inclined to favor Mr. Burroughs's suggestion of "fawn-lily." It is both appropriate and pretty. The two erect leaves are like the ears of a fawn; their beautiful mottling is not without a hint of the fawn's spots; and the

FAWN–LILY—*Erythronium giganteum.*

blossom is lily-like. The plant is shy, too, keeping to the seclusion of our deep cañons. In such situations we may find them in groups of a few, or occasionally in beds of hundreds. No more delightful surprise could be imagined than to come suddenly upon such a garden far from the habitations of man. The pale flowers, with orange centers, when fully open, roll their petals back to the stem, like those of the leopard-lily; but in cloudy weather they often maintain a campanulate outline. Plants have frequently been seen with from eight to sixteen flowers upon a stem, the flowers three or four inches across!

These are great favorites in gardens, and in cultivation are known as *E. grandiflorum.* We have several species of *Erythronium,* all of them beautiful.

Œnothera bistorta, Nutt. Evening-Primrose Family.

From several inches to a foot or two high. *Leaves.*—Three or four inches long; denticulate; the upper mostly rounded at base. *Petals.*—Yellow; four to seven lines long; with usually a brown spot at the base. *Stigma.*—Large and spherical. *Capsule.*—Four to nine lines long; a line or so wide; attenuate upward; contorted. (See *Œnothera.*) *Hab.*—Ventura to San Diego.

This is a very common species of evening primrose in the south, and may be found blooming until June. It is very variable in its manner of growth. In moist, shaded localities it becomes an erect plant a foot or two high; while upon open, exposed plains it is often only two or three inches high, but seems almost to emulate the "sunshine" in its attempt to gild the plain with its bright blossoms. It frequently grows in gravelly washes. Its flowers have a peculiarly clean, brilliant, alert look, and may usually be known by the brown spot at the base of the petals. The specific name is in reference to its twice-twisted capsule.

The "beach primrose," *Œ. cheiranthifolia,* var. *suffruticosa,* Wats., often grows in great beds upon the dry sands of the seashore, from Monterey to San Diego. Its decumbent stems are thickly clothed with small, ovate, stemless leaves, and its silvery foliage makes a beautiful setting for its large golden flowers.

CREEPING WOOD-VIOLET.

Viola sempervirens, Greene.   Violet Family.

Stems.—Creeping.   *Leaves.*—Round-cordate; six to eighteen lines broad; finely crenate; often rusty beneath; usually punctate with dark dots. *Peduncles.*—Slender. *Flowers.*—Small; light yellow without and within. (Flower structure as in *V. pedunculata.*) *Syn.*—*Viola sarmentosa,* Dougl. *Hab.*—Coast Ranges, from Monterey to British Columbia.

This modest little violet is found commonly in woods,—often in redwood forests,—where it carpets the ground with its shapely little round leaves.

Its specific name refers to its running habit.

COMMON BLACK MUSTARD.

Brassica nigra, Koch.   Mustard Family.

Stems.—Six inches to twelve feet high. *Lower leaves.*—Lyrate; with large terminal lobes. *Upper leaves.*—Lobed or entire. *Flowers.*—Yellow. *Sepals.*—Four. *Petals.*—Four; three to four lines long. *Stamens.*—Six. *Ovary.*—Two-celled. Style long. *Pod.*—Six to nine lines long, with seeds in one row. *Hab.*—Common everywhere; introduced.

I can give no truer idea of the manner of growth of this common plant in California than by quoting Mrs. Jackson's charming description of it from "Ramona":—

"The wild mustard in southern California is like that spoken of in the New Testament, in the branches of which the birds of the air may rest. Coming up out of the earth, so slender a stem that dozens can find starting-point in an inch, it darts up a slender, straight shoot, five, ten, twenty feet, with hundreds of fine, feathery branches locking and interlocking with all the other hundreds around it, till it is an inextricable network, like lace. Then it bursts into yellow bloom, still finer, more feathery, and lacelike. The stems are so infinitesimally small and of so dark a green, that at a short distance they do not show, and the cloud of blossoms seems floating in the air; at times it looks like a golden dust. With a clear, blue sky behind it, as it is often seen, it looks like a golden snowstorm."

The tall stems are favorite haunts of the red-winged blackbird, who tilts about among them, showing his scarlet wings and occasionally plunging into the depths below, as though he found a spot there much to his mind.

A very superior oil is made from the seed of the mustard, which is one of the strongest antiseptics known. It is especially adapted to the needs of the druggist, because it does not become rancid. The flour of mustard is now much used by surgeons to render their hands aseptic. Tons of the seed are exported from California every year.

STICKY MONKEY-FLOWER. BUSH MONKEY-FLOWER.
Diplacus glutinosus, Nutt. Figwort Family.

Glutinous shrubs two to six feet high. *Leaves.*—Narrowly oblong to linear; one to four inches long; with margins at length rolled backward. *Flowers.*—Corn-color to red; eighteen lines to three inches long. *Calyx.*—Irregularly five-toothed. *Corolla.*—Funnel-form; five-lobed; the lobes gnawed. *Stigma.*—White. *Syn.*—*Mimulus glutinosus,* Wend. *Hab.*—San Francisco to San Diego, and southward.

During a walk upon the hills, at almost any time of year, we may find the corn-colored blossoms of the sticky monkey-flower, but they are most abundant in spring and summer. When in full flower the small bushes are very ornamental, as they are a perfect mass of bloom. They are said to be especially handsome as greenhouse plants.

The flowers vary through a wide range of color, from almost white to a rich scarlet, but the commoner hue is the corn-color. The scarlet-flowered form, found at San Diego, constitutes the var. *puniceus,* Gray. Another form, with red-brown to salmon-colored flowers on very short pedicels, is the var. *linearis,* Gray. The very long-flowered form is the var. *brachypus,* Gray. The sensitive lips of the stigma close upon being touched or after receiving pollen.

STICKY MONKEY–FLOWER—*Diplacus glutinosus.*

ECHEVERIA.

Dudleya lanceolata, Britt and Rose. Stonecrop or Orpine Family.

Fleshy plants, with tufted radical leaves. *Leaves.*—Narrowly lanceolate; the outer ones two to four inches long; acuminate. *Scapes.*—Fifteen inches high; their lower leaves lanceolate; becoming above broadly triangular-ovate, clasping, acute; bearing on their summit a branching flower-cluster. *Calyx.*—Five-parted. *Corolla.*—Cylindrical; of five almost distinct, oblong, acute petals, four to six lines long, reddish-yellow. *Stamens.*—Ten. *Ovaries.*—Five; distinct; one-celled. *Syn.*—*Cotyledon lanceolata,* Benth. and Hook. *Hab.*—Los Angeles to San Diego.

These plants, which are of frequent occurrence in the south, usually affect dry, sandy soils. The fleshy foliage is of a warm tone, owing to a suffusion of pink in the leaves. These have a loose, erect habit, and are not crowded in dense rosettes, as are those of some species, and they are so weak that they pull apart easily. The tall flowering stems have but few leaves, and are sometimes nearly naked.

In early summer these plants put forth a strong effort, quickly sending up several tall, vigorous flower-shoots, drawing upon the nourishment stored in the fleshy leaves, which then become limp and shriveled.

HEN-AND-CHICKENS.

Dudleya Sheldoni, Rose. Stonecrop or Orpine Family.

(For flower structure, see *Dudleya lanceolata.*) *Hab.*—Central California.

These plants are familiar to most of us, as some of the species are extensively cultivated in our gardens as border plants. Their fleshy leaves are often covered with a bloom or a floury powder. Owing to their habit of producing a circle of young plants around the parent, they are commonly called "hen-and-chickens." We have several native species of this genus, formerly called *Cotyledon,* which are usually found upon warm, rocky hill-slopes, or upon rocks near the sea.

D. Sheldoni is a beautiful form, with pointed, ovate leaves, of a light glaucous green, often tinged with pink. Its flowers

HEN-AND-CHICKENS—*Dudleya Sheldoni.*

are yellow, and have their petals distinct almost to the base, and its carpels are distinct. We are told that the Indians make soothing poultices of these leaves.

Another species,—*D. pulverulenta,* Britt and Rose,—found from Santa Barbara to San Diego, is a very beautiful plant. It bears its leaves in a symmetrical rosette, like a diminutive century-plant. These leaves are usually covered with a dense white bloom, and the outer ones are spatulate, abruptly pointed, and two to four inches broad at the tip, while the inner are pointed. The plants are sometimes a foot and a half across, and send up as many as eight of the leafy flowering stems, which look like many-storied, slender Chinese pagodas. The blossoms are pale red.

YELLOW GLOBE-TULIP. DIOGENES' LANTERN.
GOLDEN LILY-BELL.

Calochortus amabilis, Purdy. Lily Family.

Stems.—Stout; forking in pairs; eight to twelve inches high; glaucous. *Radical leaves.*—Ten inches long, four to six lines wide; lanceolate-acuminate. *Flowers.*—Clear yellow; nodding. *Sepals.*—Three. *Petals.*—Three; ovate, with short claw, obtuse at apex; naked, but margined with a close row of short stiff hairs; strongly arched, and with tips overlapping each other; with a deep gland showing on the outside as a knob, and lined within with short stiff hairs, crossing each other. (See *Calochortus.*) *Hab.*—Coast Ranges, from San Francisco Bay to Trinity County.

We have no more charmingly graceful flower than the yellow globe-tulip. A single long grasslike leaf precedes the flexuous stem, with its quaintly arched and delicately fringed blossoms. There is a certain quizzical look about these flowers —something akin to the inquiring look of Diogenes, as he thrust his lantern into all sorts of out-of-the-way places in broad daylight. The margins of the petals look as though they had been snipped into a very fine, delicate fringe, unlike the slender, tapering hairs of *C. alba.*

The Indians are fond of the bulbs, which they eat with great relish, callling them "bo."

Another species,—*C. pulchellus,* Dougl.,—found in the Mt.

148

DIOGENES' LANTERN—*Calochortus amabilis.*

Diablo region, has for many years been confused with the above, but may readily be distinguished by its more globular flowers, its petals, silky-haired within, and of a much lighter canary yellow.

BLADDERPOD.

Isomeris arborea, Nutt. Caper Family.

Shrubby; evil-scented. *Leaves.*—Alternate; compound, with three leaflets. *Flowers.*—With their parts in fours. *Petals.*—Yellow; five to eight lines long. *Stamens.*—Eight; of equal length. *Ovary.*—One-celled. Style short. *Pod.*—Pendulous; inflated; pear-shaped; on a long stalk. *Hab.*—Santa Barbara to San Diego.

This low shrub is somewhat plentiful upon the mesas of the south. Its yellow flowers attract one to it, only to be repulsed by the dreadful odor of its foliage. It certainly ought to have some compensating utility for so repellent a characteristic. The ovary is so long-stalked, even in the flower, that it looks like an abnormal, inflated stigma.

This is the only species of the genus.

YELLOW SAND-VERBENA.

Abronia latifolia, Esch. Four-o'clock Family.

Stems.—Prostrate; rubbery. *Leaves.*—Opposite; unequal; roundish; an inch or so across; petioled; leathery; gummy. *Flowers.*—Yellow; five or six lines long; in dense clusters, subtended by an involucre of five distinct bracts. *Perianth.*—Salver-shaped. Tube green; its base strongly angled or winged. Limb yellow; four- or five-lobed. *Stamens.*—Mostly five, within the perianth. *Ovary.*—One-celled. Style filiform. Stigma club-shaped. *Hab.*—The seashore from Vancouver Island to Monterey.

The fragrant blossoms of the yellow sand-verbena may be found upon the beach at almost any time of year. The stout root, which often becomes several feet long, is sometimes eaten by the Indians.

SEA-DAHLIA.

Leptosyne maritima, Gray. Composite Family.

Leaves.—Alternate; sometimes six inches long· two or three times divided into rather sparse, linear divisions; quite succulent. *Flower-heads.*—Solitary; on naked peduncles from six inches to two feet long; large; three or four inches across; yellow; of disk- and ray-flowers.

YELLOW SAND–VERBENA—*Abronia latifolia.*

Rays. — Narrowly oblong; ten-nerved; three-toothed. *Involucre.* — Double; the outer part of several loose, leafy scales; the inner of eight to twelve erect, more chaffy ones. *Hab.*—The seashore of San Diego and the islands.

On cliffs overlooking the sea, where their merry yellow faces can watch the white-crested breakers as they chase one another ashore in never-ending succession, and where the pelicans sail lazily over in lines, and gulls circle and scream, the sea-dahlias flaunt their large yellow flowers. They closely resemble the yellow single dahlias of our gardens; but the foliage is cut into long lobes, and has the appearance of a coarse, very open lace. The odor of the flowers is not especially agreeable, but the plant merits a place in the garden for its beauty.

TIDY-TIPS. YELLOW DAISY.

Layia platyglossa, Gray. Composite Family.

Stems.—A foot or so high; loosely branching. *Leaves.*—Alternate; sessile; the lower linear and pinnatifid, the upper entire. *Flower-heads.*—Solitary; terminal; of disk- and ray-flowers. *Disk-flowers.*— Yellow, with black stamens. *Rays.*—Bright yellow. tipped with white; six lines long; four lines wide; three-lobed. *Hab.*—Throughout western California; in low ground.

Among the most charming of our flowers are the beautiful tidy-tips. In midspring, countless millions of them lift themselves above the sheets of golden baeria on our flower-tapestried plains. The fresh winds come sweetly laden with their delicate fragrance. Were they not scattered everywhere in such lavish profusion, we would doubtless cherish them in our gardens.

Growing among these blossoms is often found another flower, somewhat similar to them. This is *Leptosyne Douglasii,* DC., the false tidy-tips. It has not the clean, natty appearance of *Layia platyglossa;* for the gradual blending of the light tips into the darker yellow below gives it an indefinite, unattractive look. There is a difference in the involucre, which has two series of bracts; the leaves are parted into linear or filiform divisions, and there are no touches of black among the disk-flowers.

FALSE TIDY–TIPS—*Leptosyne Douglasii.*   TIDY–TIPS—*Layia platyglossa.*

FALSE LUPINE.

Thermopsis Californica, Wats. Pea Family.

Stems.—Two feet tall. *Leaves.*—With leafy stipules an inch long. *Leaflets.*—Three; obovate to oblanceolate; an inch or two long; somewhat woolly. *Flowers.*—Yellow; in long-peduncled racemes. *Calyx.*— Deeply five-cleft; the two upper teeth often united. *Corolla.*—Papilionaceous; eight lines long. *Stamens.*—Ten; all distinct. *Ovary.*—One-celled. *Pod.*—Silky; six- to eight-seeded. *Hab.*—Marin County and southward.

The false lupine very closely resembles the true lupines, but may be distinguished from them by the stamens, which are all distinct, instead of being united into a sheath. Its silvery foliage and racemes of rather large canary-colored flowers are common upon open hill-slopes by April.

FINGER-TIPS.

Stylophyllum edule, Britt and Rose. Stonecrop or Orpine Family.

Plants with cylindrical, fleshy leaves the size of a lead-pencil, growing in tufts often a foot or two across. *Flowering stems.*—A foot or more high. *Flowers.*—Greenish yellow, in structure similar to those of *Dudleya lanceolata.* *Syn.*—*Cotyledon edulis,* Brew. *Hab.*—The Coast at San Diego.

These curious plants are found upon the seashore at San Diego. The young leaves are considered very palatable by the Indians, who use them as a salad.

GOLDEN BUTTERFLY-TULIP.

Calochortus clavatus, Wats. Lily Family.

(See *Calochortus.*)

Hab.—Los Angeles County to San Luis Obispo and El Dorado County.

Ôf all our mariposa tulips, this is the largest-flowered and stoutest-stemmed, and once seen is not readily forgotten. Its magnificent flowers are sometimes five inches across, though not usually so large, and have the form of a broad-based cup. The sturdy, zigzagging stems and glaucous leaves and bracts, combined with the large rich, canary-colored or golden flowers, make a striking plant. The first glance within the cup shows the ring of club-shaped hairs, characteristic of this species, and the anthers radiating starlike in the center; and as the latter are often a dark, rich prune-purple, the effect can readily be imagined.

I saw this charming mariposa blooming in abundance in May near Newhall, where its golden cups were conspicuously beautiful against the soft browns of the drying fields and hillslopes. It is usually found growing upon lava soil.

C. Weedii, Wood., found from San Diego to San Luis Obispo, is a charming species, somewhat similar to the above. Its flowers are yellow, purple, or pure white, and it may be known by several characteristics. Its bulb is heavily coated with coarse fibers; it has a single, long radical leaf, like *C. albus,* but unusual among the mariposas; and its cups are covered all over within with silky hairs, which spring from brown dots on the petals.

BUTTER-AND-EGGS.

Orthocarpus erianthus, Benth.   Figwort Family.

Slender, with many erect branches; stems and bracts usually dark-reddish; soft pubescent. *Corolla.*—Deep sulphur-yellow; the slender falcate upper lip dark purple; the tube very slender, but the sacs of the lower lip large and deep, their folds hairy within. (See *Orthocarpus.*) *Hab.*—Monterey County and northward; very common.

There are many species of *Orthocarpus,* and they are more numerous in middle and northern California and in the Sierras, few of them reaching the south. They are very difficult of determination, and are not well understood by botanists yet.

——— ———

Malacothrix Californica, DC.   Composite Family.

Leaves.—All radical; pinnately parted into very narrow linear divisions. *Scape.*—Six inches to a foot high; bearing a solitary, large, light-yellow head. *Flower-head.*—Composed of strap-shaped ray-flowers only; five-toothed at the apex. *Involucres.*—Of narrow, acute scales in two or three series. *Receptacle.*—Nearly naked. *Hab.*—San Francisco to San Diego, and eastward.

These beautiful *Compositæ* are conspicuous upon our open plains in late spring, and are among the handsomest plants of the family. The fine flowers seem to be sown like disks of light over the flower-carpet of the plain.

BRASS BUTTONS.
Cotula coronopifolia, L.   Composite Family.

Stems.—Six inches to a foot long. *Leaves.*—Alternate; lanceolate or oblong-linear; pinnatifid or entire. *Flower-heads.*—Solitary; yellow; three to six lines across; without rays. *Involucre.*—Of two ranks of nearly equal, scarious-margined scales. *Hab.*—Common everywhere.

These little weeds are natives of the Southern Hemisphere, but are now common everywhere. They affect wet places, and their little flowers, like brass buttons, are very familiar objects along our roadsides. The foliage when crushed gives out a curious odor, between lemon-verbena and camphor.

DEER-WEED.   WILD BROOM.
Hosackia glabra, Torr.   Pea Family.

Woody at base; two to eight feet high; erect or decumbent. *Stems.*—Many; slender; branching; reed-like. *Leaves.*—Sparse; short-petioled; mostly trifoliolate. Leaflets three to six lines long; oblong to linear-oblong; nearly glabrous. *Flowers.*—In numerous small axillary umbels; yellow; four lines long. *Calyx.*—Less than three lines long; five-toothed. *Corolla.*—Papilionaceous. *Stamens.*—Nine united and one free. *Pod.*—Elongated; exserted. Seeds two. (See *Leguminosæ.*) *Hab.*—Common throughout the State.

This graceful, willowy plant, whose slender branches are closely set with small golden-yellow flowers, in which there is often a hint of red, is as ornamental as any of the small-flowered foreign genestas, or brooms, we grow in our gardens; but because it is so very abundant throughout our borders, we have become blind to its merits. It is especially beautiful and symmetrical in the south, where the low, bushy plants often spread over several feet of ground; and on the mesas of Coronado, the plants, growing not far removed from one another, lend to the natural scene the aspect of a garden. There it is in full flower in April; but in the north the blossoms are usually later in arriving, and it is often June before they show themselves; then making whole hill-slopes dull yellow among the chaparral.

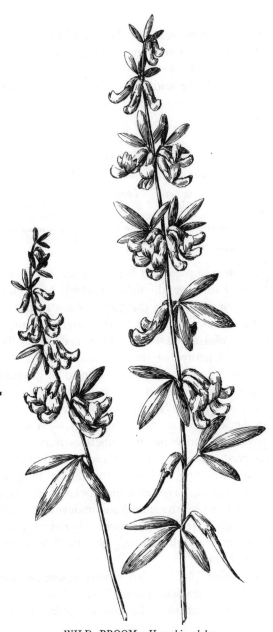

WILD BROOM—*Hosackia glabra.*

It is a great favorite with the bees, and for them holds untold treasure in honey-making sweets. Among the mountaineers it is known as "deer-weed" and "buck-brush," as both deer and stock are said to feed upon it and flourish, when pasturage is scarce, though they rarely touch it when other food is plenty.

GOLDEN STARS.

Bloomeria aurea, Kell. Lily Family.

Bulb.—Six lines in diameter. *Leaf.*—Solitary; about equaling the scape; three to six lines broad. *Scape.*—Six to eighteen inches high. *Flowers.*—Yellow; fifteen to sixty in an umbel. *Perianth.*—About an inch across. *Stamens.*—Six; with cup-shaped appendages. *Ovary.*—Three-celled. Style club-shaped. Stigma three-lobed. *Hab.*—The Coast Ranges, from Monterey to San Diego.

Just as the floral procession begins to slacken a little before the oncoming of summer, the fields suddenly blossom out anew and twinkle with millions of the golden stars of the bloomeria. These plants are closely allied to the brodiæas, and by some authorities are classed as such. They are especially characterized by the structure of the stamens, which rise out of a tiny cup. Under a glass this cup is seen to be granular, somewhat flattened, and furnished with two cusps, or points. The anthers are a very pretty Nile or peacock green.

Another species — *B. Clevelandi,* Wats. — is easily distinguished from the above by its numerous narrow leaves and its green-nerved perianth. This is found at San Diego, upon the mesas in midspring, growing abundantly in spots which, earlier in the season, have been mud-holes. Its open flowers are so outnumbered by the numerous undeveloped green buds, that, even though it grows in masses, it is not very showy, but makes the ground a dull yellow. But its flower-clusters are feathery and delicate.

There is another plant which closely resembles the bloomerias. This is the "golden brodiæa"—*Brodiæa ixioides,* Wats. But the filaments, instead of having a cuplike appendage, are

GOLDEN STARS—*Bloomeria aurea.*

winged, with the little anthers swinging prettily upon their summits. This is found in the Coast Ranges, from Santa Barbara northward, also in the Sierras. It is a beautiful flower; especially when seen starring the velvet alpine meadows in August.

Another plant—*Brodiæa lactea,* Wats.—the "white brodiæa," has flowers similar to the above, but pure white (sometimes lilac), with a green mid-vein. This is common in late spring from Monterey to British Columbia. Its flowers are beautiful and keep a long time in water.

TREFOIL SUMACH. FRAGRANT SUMACH. SQUAW-BERRY.

Rhus Canadensis, var. *trilobata,* Gray. Sumach Family.

Shrubs two to five feet high; spreading. *Leaves.*—Three-foliolate. *Leaflets.*—Sessile; wedge-shaped; six lines to an inch long; pubescent, becoming smooth. *Flowers.*—Yellowish; minute; borne in short, scaly-bracted spikes preceding the leaves. *Fruit.*—Viscid; reddish; two or three lines in diameter; pleasantly acid. *Syn.*—*R. aromatica,* var. *trilobata,* Gray. *Hab.*—Dakota to Texas, and west to California and Oregon.

The dense foliage of these little bushes has a strong odor, which is not altogether agreeable, while their small fruit has a pleasant acid taste, and is much relished by the Indians.

Dr. Edward Palmer writes that this shrub furnishes the Indians of Utah, Arizona, New Mexico, and southern California with one of the most valuable of basket materials. The young twigs, which are much tougher than those of the willow, are soaked, scraped, and split. The baskets are then built up of a succession of small rolls of grass, over which the split twigs are closely and firmly bound. The baskets thus made are very durable, will hold water, and are often used to cook in, by dropping hot stones into them till the food is done. The wood exhales a peculiar odor, which is always recognizable about the camps of these Indians, and never leaves articles made from it.

This is grown in England as an ornamental shrub.

CALIFORNIA COMPASS-PLANT. SUNFLOWER.

Wyethia angustifolia, Nutt. Composite Family.

Stems.—Six inches to two feet high. *Leaves.*—Long-lanceolate; pointed at both ends; the radical and lower ones six to twelve inches long; the upper sessile, shorter, and often broader. *Flower-heads.*—Yellow; composed of ray- and disk-flowers. Plume-like styles of the latter conspicuous. *Ray-flowers.*—Numerous; one inch long; six lines wide; early deciduous. *Involucre.*—Broadly campanulate, of numerous erect, loose, foliaceous, ciliate scales, in several rows. *Hab.*—Monterey, east to the Sierra foothills and north to Oregon.

In late spring our open plains and hillsides are often plentifully sown with the large golden flowers of these California compass-plants, called "sunflowers" by many people. There is a belief prevalent that their erect leaves always stand with their edges pointing north and south, whence the common name. This trait is said to be true of all the species.

W. helenioides, Nutt., has large, broad leaves, which are white-woolly when young. Its flower-heads are often four inches or more across.

This plant is used as a common domestic remedy for coughs and colds by California housewives, and goes under the unmerited name of "poison-weed." It has also been adopted among physicians as an officinal drug. The root, which is slightly bitter and aromatic, is made into a tincture and administered for asthma, throat disorders, and epidemic influenza, with excellent results. It blooms in early spring, and is common upon hillsides.

Another species, very similar to the above, is *W. glabra,* Gray. This may be known by its smooth green leaves, which are often very viscid. It is found from Marin County southward, in the Coast Ranges, and probably northward. A common name for this species is "mule's ears."

W. mollis, Gray, or "Indian wheat," is very abundant in the Sierras, growing all through the open woods, and covering great tracts of dry gravelly soil. Its large, coarse, somewhat woolly radical leaves stand erect and clustered, usually having a flower-staik or two in their midst, bearing some smaller leaves, and several yellow flower-heads, which resemble small sunflowers with yellow centers. It has a strong odor, and gives a characteristic smell to the region where it grows. The common name, "Indian wheat," has been bestowed upon it not because it in the least resembles wheat, but because the Indians gather the seed in great quantities and grind it into a flour. In the spring it is one of the first plants to show itself aboveground, and then its woolly, tightly rolled, sage-green shoots form a beautiful contrast to their deep wine-colored wrappings. These young shoots often peep up from the midst of flattened masses of last year's leaves, laid down and skeletonized by the winter's snows.

CALIFORNIA SLIPPERY-ELM.

Fremontodendron Californica, Coville. Sterculia Family.

Shrubs or trees from two to twenty feet high. *Leaves.*—Alternate; petioled; round-cordate to round-ovate; moderately three- to five-lobed or cleft; woolly or whitish beneath; the larger two inches wide. *Flowers.*—Short-peduncled on very short lateral branches; numerous; one to three inches across; having three to five small bractlets. *Calyx.*—Corolla-like; brilliant gold, five-cleft nearly to the base; the lobes having a rounded, hairy pit at base. *Corolla.*—Wanting. *Filaments.*—United to their middle; each bearing a linear, adnate, curved, two-celled anther. *Ovary.*—Five-celled. Style filiform. *Syn.*—*Fremontia Californica,* Torr. *Hab.*—Dry Sierra foothills, from Lake County southward.

No more beautiful sight is often seen than a slope covered with the wild slippery-elm in blossom. The bushes are almost obscured from view by the masses of large golden flowers. This shrub takes on various forms; sometimes sending out in every direction long slender branches, which are solid wreaths of the magnificent blooms; and again assuming a more erect, treelike habit. It has been hailed with delight in the gardens of our Southern States, and heartily welcomed in France and England. Why do not *we* honor it with a place in our own gardens, instead of giving room to so many far less beautiful exotics?

It flowers in early summer, and its season of bloom is said to last only about two weeks, but the brilliant hibiscus-like

CALIFORNIA SLIPPERY-ELM—*Fremontodendron Californica.*

blossoms, drying upon their stems, maintain for a long time a semblance of their first beauty. The branches are tough and flexible, and are often cut for whips by teamsters. Among the mountaineers it is generally known as "leatherwood." But this name properly belongs to another entirely different plant, *Dirca palustris.*

The bark of the Fremontodendron so closely resembles that of the slippery-elm in taste and other qualities, that it is difficult to distinguish between them; and it is used in the same manner for making poultices.

We are told that this shrub thrives best upon a disintegrated granite soil, and reaches its finest development upon the arid slopes bordering such rainless regions as the Mojave Desert. It was first discovered by General Fremont when crossing the Sierras, about half a century ago, and was named in his honor. It is closely related to the mallows.

DODDER. LOVE-VINE. GOLDEN-THREAD.
Cuscuta, Tourn. Morning-Glory Family.

Leafless plants with filiform, yellow or orange-colored stems; germinating in the soil; soon breaking off and becoming parasitic upon other plants. *Flowers.*—Small; white; densely clustered. *Calyx.*—Usually five-cleft or parted. *Corolla.*—Tubular or campanulate; four-or five-toothed or lobed. *Stamens.*—On the corolla, alternate with its lobes. Filaments with fringed scales below. *Ovary.*—Globose; two-celled. Styles two.

> . . . "while everywhere
> The love-vine spreads a silken snare,
> The tangles of her yellow hair."

Though popularly known as the love-vine, because of its clinging habit, it must be confessed that this pernicious plant in no respect merits the title. On the other hand, it might with propriety be called the octopus of the plant world. If you break a branch from a plant which has become its victim, you can see how it has twined itself about it, drawing its very life-blood from it at every turn, by means of ugly, wartlike suckers.

It is no wonder, however, that people are generally deceived as to the moral character of this plant—for it is indeed a beautiful sight, when it spreads its golden tangle over the chamisal, wild buckwheat, and other plants, often completely hiding them from view.

We have a number of species. *C. salina* often covers our salt marshes with brilliant patches of orange.

YELLOW SWEET CLOVER.

Melilotus Indica, All.   Pea Family.

Syn.—Melilotus parviflora, Desf.   *Hab.—*Widely naturalized from Europe.

In early summer the breezes come laden with fragrance from the sweet clover.   This is easily recognized by its tall stems, its fragrant leaves, with three small, toothed leaflets, and its small crowded racemes of minute yellow flowers a line long.

A white form—*Melilotus alba,* Lam.—is found in the north. Its flowers are vanilla-scented.

This plant is a highly valued remedy in the pharmacopœia for various ailments, and its sweet-scented flowers have been used for flavoring many products, such as Gruyère cheese, snuff, and tobacco.   In Europe the blossoms are packed among furs to give them a pleasant odor and keep away moths.

LARGE YELLOW LUPINE.

Lupinus arboreus, Sims.   Pea Family.

Shrubby; four to ten feet high.   *Flowers.—*Large; in a loose, whorled raceme; sulphur-yellow; very fragrant.   *Leaflets.—*Four to eleven; generally about nine; narrowly lanceolate; nine to twenty lines long. *Pods.—*Two to three inches long; ten- to twelve-seeded; silky pubescent.   (See *Lupinus.*)   *Hab.—*Common from the Sacramento Valley to San Diego.

The large yellow lupine is a common plant upon our windswept mesas, growing in sandy soil.   Its shrubby form, somewhat silvery foliage, and large canary-colored, very fragrant flowers make it always a conspicuous and beautiful plant.

This species and *L. albifrons,* Benth., have been found

extremely useful in anchoring the shifting sands of the dunes near San Francisco. It was accidentally discovered in a deep cutting that these lupines sent their roots down sometimes twenty feet, and the idea was conceived of making use of them in the above manner. Barley, which grows more rapidly than the lupine, was sown to protect the plants while very young. In a single year the lupines covered the sands with a dense growth, two or three feet high, sufficient to prevent them from shifting during the severest storms, and to allow of the subsequent planting of various pines, willows, and other trees. Thus the way was prepared for one of the most beautiful of pleasure-grounds—Golden Gate Park of San Francisco, which can hardly be rivaled anywhere for natural situation and diversity of scene.

One of our handsomest species is *L. Stiveri,* Kell., found in the Yosemite Valley. Its blossoms have yellow standards and rose-colored wings.

ST. JOHN'S-WORT.

Hypericum concinnum, Benth. St. John's-wort Family.

Stems.—Three to eighteen inches high; branching from a woody base. *Leaves.*—Opposite; often in four ranks; linear to oblong; six lines to an inch or more long; usually folded; translucently dotted. *Flowers.*—Golden yellow; over an inch across. *Sepals.*—Five. *Petals.* —Five; margins black-dotted. *Stamens.*—Numerous; in three bunches. *Ovary.*—Usually three-celled. Styles three. *Hab.*—Central California.

Just as spring is merging into summer, we may look for the bright golden flowers of our common St. John's-wort. The numerous stamens give these blossoms a feathery appearance, and the leaves often group themselves characteristically in four ranks upon the stems.

All the plants of the genus are known as St. John's-wort, because certain of the species were supposed to flower upon the anniversary of this saint. Perhaps there are no other plants around which tradition has thrown such a glamour. Mr. Dyer says, in his interesting book, "The Folk-Lore of

ST. JOHN'S-WORT—*Hypericum concinnum.*

Plants," that the St. John's-wort was supposed to be an excellent amulet against lightning, and that it had the magic property of revealing the presence of witches; whence in Germany it was extensively worn on St. John's Eve, when the air was supposed to be peopled with witches and evil spirits, who wandered abroad upon no friendly errands. In Denmark it is resorted to by anxious lovers who wish to divine their future.

GOLDEN DICENTRA.

Dicentra chrysantha, Hook. and Arn.   Bleeding-heart Family.

Stems.—Glaucous and smooth; two to five feet high.   *Leaves.*—The larger ones a foot long or more; finely dissected into small linear lobes.   *Flowers.*—Erect; yellow; six to nine lines long; in a loose terminal panicle a foot or two long.   *Sepals.*—Two; small; caducous. *Corolla.*—Flattened and cordate; of two pairs of petals; the outer larger, saccate at base, and with spreading tips; the inner much narrower, spoon-shaped, their tips cohering and inclosing the anthers and stigma.   *Stamens.*—Six.   *Ovary.*—One-celled.   Style slender.   Stigma two-lobed.   *Hab.*—Dry hills, Lake County to San Diego.

The arrangement of the essential organs in the genus *Dicentra* is very curious and interesting.   The six stamens are borne in two companies of three each, which stand in front of the outer petals, and have their filaments more or less united at the base.   The central stamen in each group has a two-celled anther, while its neighbor on either hand has but a one-celled anther.   The stigma-lobes often bend downward prettily, like the flukes of a little anchor.

To this genus belongs the beautiful Oriental bleeding-heart of the garden; and we have two or three interesting native species.

D. chrysantha is usually a somewhat coarse plant, lacking the grace of *D. formosa,* the California bleeding-heart.   The pale leaves, which are minutely and delicately dissected, are suggestive of the fronds of certain Japanese ferns.   But the flower-stalks are often stiff and sparsely flowered, and the blossoms, which are erect, not pendulous, have an overpowering narcotic odor, much like that of the poppy.   These plants may be found upon dry hillsides or in sandy washes in early summer, where the brilliant yellow blossoms are quite conspicuous. One view of these flowers is not unlike the conventionalized tulip.

This species is said to thrive well in cultivation and make a very effective plant when grown in rich garden soil.

CALIFORNIA DANDELION.

Troximon grandiflorum, Gray.   Composite Family.

Herbs with woody tap-root and milky juice. *Leaves.*—All radical; lanceolate or oblanceolate; mostly laciniately pinnatifid. *Scapes.*—One to two and one half feet high. *Heads.*—Solitary; two inches or so across; of strap-shaped yellow rays only. *Involucre.*—Of several series of imbricated scales, the outer foliaceous and loose. *Receptacle.*— Mostly naked; pitted. *Akenes.*—Two lines long; tapering into a filiform beak six or eight lines long, surmounted by a tuft of silk. *Hab.*—Washington to southern California near the Coast.

The common dandelion of the East has found it way into our lawns, but it never adapts itself as a wild plant to the vicissitudes of our dry summer climate. Nature has given us a dandelion of our own, of a different genus, which is quite as beautiful, though its flowers are not so vivid a gold. They are larger than those of the Eastern plant, and are borne upon taller stems. In early summer the large, ethereal globes of the ripened seed are conspicuous objects, hovering over our straw-tinted fields.

Mr. Burroughs writes of the dandelion:—"After its first blooming, comes its second and finer and more spiritual inflorescence, when its stalk, dropping its more earthly and carnal flower, shoots upward and is presently crowned by a globe of the most delicate and aerial texture. It is like the poet's dream, which succeeds his rank and golden youth. This globe is a fleet of a hundred fairy balloons, each one of which bears a seed which it is destined to drop far from the parent source."

If gathered just before they open and allowed to expand in the house, these down-globes will remain perfect for a long time and make an exquisite adornment for some delicate vase.

We have several other species of *Troximon,* but this is our finest.

STONECROP.

Sedum spathulifolium, Hook. Stonecrop or Orpine Family.

Leaves.—Alternate; fleshy; spatulate; six to ten lines long; sessile; crowded in rosettes at the ends of the decumbent branches. *Scapes.*—Four to six inches high. *Flowers.*—In compound, one-sided, loose cymes; their parts four or five; pale-yellow. *Sepals.*—United at base. *Petals.*—Lanceolate; three lines long. *Stamens.*—Twice the number of the petals. *Pistils*—Equaling the number of the petals; attenuate into the short styles. *Ovaries.*—One-celled. *Hab.*—Middle California to Vancouver Island.

Blooming somewhat earlier than the "hen-and-chickens," but in similar situations, the stonecrop often clothes rock-masses with beautiful color. The common name, "orpine," was given on account of the yellow, or orpine, flowers; and the name "stonecrop," from its always growing in stony places.

———— ————

Hosackia bicolor, Dougl. Pea Family.

Smooth throughout; erect; two feet high. *Leaves.*—With rather large, scarious, triangular stipules; pinnate. *Leaflets.*—Five to nine; obovate or oblong; six to twelve lines long. *Peduncles.*—Three to seven-flowered; naked or with a small scarious, one- to three-leaved bract. *Flowers.*—Seven lines long. *Calyx-teeth.*—Triangular; half as long as the tube. *Standard.*—Yellow; wings and keel white. *Stamens.*—Nine united; one free. *Pod.*—Linear; nearly two inches long; acute. *Hab.*—Middle California to the State of Washington.

The yellow and white blossoms of this pretty *Hosackia* are quite showy, and are usually found upon low ground near the seaboard.

Another similar species, also having a yellow standard and white wings and keel, is *H. Torreyi,* Gray. This is more or less silky pubescent; its wings are not spreading, its leaflets are narrower, and the bract of the umbel is sessile. This is found along shaded stream-banks both in the higher Coast Ranges and in the Sierras, and blooms in summer.

H. gracilis, Benth., with the standard yellow and the wide-spreading wings and shorter keel of rose-color, occurs in moist meadows along the coast from Monterey to the Columbia River. It blooms by the middle of April.

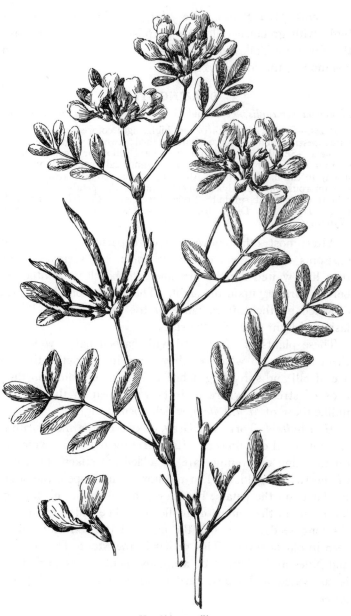

Hosackia gracilis.

H. crassifolia, Benth., a very large species, two or three feet high, with greenish-yellow or purplish flowers, is abundant in the Yosemite Valley about the borders of meadows. It is also common in the foothill region.

BLAZING-STAR.

Mentzelia lævicaulis, Torr. and Gray. Loasa or Blazing-star Family.

Stems.—Stout; two or three feet high; light colored. *Leaves.*—Alternate; sessile; lanceolate; sinuate-toothed; two to eight inches long. *Flowers.*—Sessile, on short branches; light yellow or cream-color; three or four inches across. *Calyx-tube.*—Cylindrical; naked; limb five-cleft nearly to the base. *Petals.*—About ten; oblanceolate; acute. *Stamens.*—Numerous on the calyx; almost equaling the petals. *Ovary.*—One-celled; truncate at summit. Style three-cleft. *Capsule.*—Fifteen lines long. *Hab.*—San Diego to the Columbia River, and eastward to Wyoming.

After most other flowers have departed, the magnificent blossoms of the mentzelia come forth. It seems as though they had waited for the firmament to be clear of other stars before bursting upon the sight. Their enormous blossoms are crowned by the soft radiance of the long stamens, "like the lashes of light that trim the stars."

These plants are furnished with barbed hairs, which cause them to cling to whatever they come in contact with. They are of tall and spreading habit, and are often found in the dry beds of streams, where their flowers open in the daytime— unlike those of *M. Lindleyi,* which open at night.

M. Lindleyi, Torr. and Gray, is one of the most brilliantly radiant of all our flowers. Its charming blossoms, which open on the edge of evening, are of a delicate silken texture, and of the richest gold. When the flowers first open, the stamens lie flat upon the petals; but they gradually rise up, forming a large tuft in the center of the flower. The faded sepals crown the long seed-vessels, like the flame of the conventional torch seen in old pictures. This grows in the Monte Diablo Range; and Niles and Alum Rock are convenient places to find it. It is cultivated in Eastern gardens under the name of *Bartonia aurea.*

BLAZING–STAR—*Mentzelia Lindleyi.*

SKUNK-CABBAGE.

Lysichiton Kamtschatcensis, Schott. Arum Family.

Rootstock.—Thick; horizontal. *Leaves.*—All radical; oblong-lanceolate; acute; one to three feet or more long; three to ten inches broad; narrowed to a short petiole or sessile. *Flowers.*—Small, crowded on a spadix, at the summit of a stout peduncle becoming six to twelve inches long. *Spadix.*—With an erect, spoon-shaped spathe, one and one-half to two feet long; bright yellow. *Perianth.*—Four-lobed. *Stamens.*—Four. Filaments short, flat. *Ovary.*—Conical; two-celled. Stigma depressed. *Fruits*—Fleshy, coalescent and sunk in the rachis. *Hab.*—Peat bogs; from Mendocino County northward to Alaska; also, perhaps, in the Rocky Mountains.

In our northwestern counties, before the frost is entirely out of the ground, the leaves of the skunk-cabbage may be seen pushing their way up through the standing water of marshy localities. They soon attain a great size, and resemble the leaves of the banana-tree. They are of a rich velvet-green, slightly mottled, and are said to rival some of the tropical productions of our greenhouses.

There seems to be a difference of opinion as to the disagreeableness of these leaves. I suspect the odor lies mostly in the slimy, soapy sap, and is not very noticeable if they are not bruised or cut.

When the plants are in bloom, in May and June, they are very handsome, the large spoon-shaped, golden spathes being conspicuous at some distance. As this spathe withers away, the flower-stalk continues to grow, and its little greenish-yellow blossoms become brown.

The peppery root is highly esteemed for medicinal purposes, and is gathered and made into a salve, which is considered a specific for ringworm, white swelling, inflammatory rheumatism, etc. The root is said to enter largely into the composition of a patent medicine called "Skookum."

The late Mr. Johnson, of the U. S. Forestry Department in Oregon, told me that the bears are very fond of this root, and dig industriously for it, often making a hole large enough to bury themselves, and he mentioned having seen whole fields plowed up by them in their search for it.

This plant belongs to the same family as the skunk-cabbage of the East and the calla-lily. It has been found in the Santa Cruz Mountains.

PRICKLY-PEAR. TUNA.

Opuntia Engelmanni, Salm. Cactus Family.

Erect, bushy, spreading shrubs without leaves, with flattened stems produced in successive, compressed oval joints. *Joints.*—Six to twelve inches long; studded sparsely with bundles of stout spines. *Flowers.*— Solitary; sessile; yellow or red; about three inches across. *Sepals, petals, and stamens.*—Numerous in many series, their cohering bases coating the one-celled ovary and forming a cup above it. *Petals.*— Spreading. Style one, with several stigmas. *Fruit.*—Purple; oval; pulpy; juicy; two inches long. *Hab.*—Southern California, Los Angeles, San Diego, etc.

The genus *Opuntia* is divided into two sections, consisting respectively of flat-stemmed and cylindrical-stemmed plants, the former commonly known as "prickly-pear," or "tuna," the latter as *Cholla cactus.*

Of the former, *O. Engelmanni* is our commonest wild species. It is the one seen from the car-windows growing in great patches upon the Mojave Desert, and it is abundant upon dry hills all through the south. There are two varieties of it— var. *occidentalis,* Engelm., the form prevalent in the interior, and var. *littoralis,* Engelm., found upon the sea-coast from Santa Barbara to San Diego.

These plants have a very leathery, impermeable skin, from which evaporation takes place but slowly, which enables them to inhabit arid regions. The fruit is sweet and edible, and the Indians, who are especially fond of it, dry large quantities for winter use. They make of the fresh fruit a sauce, by long-continued boiling, which they regard as especially nutritious and stimulating after it is slightly fermented. They also roast the leaves in hot ashes and eat the slimy, sweet substance which is left after the outer skin and thorns have been removed.

Cattle-men of the southern plains plant the different species as hedges about their corrals, and feed the succulent joints to their stock after burning off the spines.

Several Mexican species were planted in the early days about the Missions by the Padres, as defensive hedges, and remnants of these redoubtable fortifications, ten to fifteen feet high, are still to be seen stretching for miles through our southern fields.

In Mexico the *Opuntia tuna* is largely cultivated for the rearing of cochineal insects.

VENEGASIA.

Venegasia carpesioides, DC. Composite Family,

Several feet high; leafy to the top. *Leaves.*—Alternate; slenderly petioled; cordate or ovate-deltoid; crenate; two to four inches long; thin. *Flower-heads.*—Large; two inches across, including the rays; yellow; slender-peduncled; composed of ray- and disk-flowers. *Rays.*—Over an inch long; six lines wide; two- or three-toothed; fertile; about fifteen. *Involucre.*—Broad; of many roundish-green scales; becoming scarious inward. *Hab.*—Coast, Santa Barbara and southward.

This plant, with its ample thin leaves and large yellow flowers, would arrest the attention anywhere. It often grows under the shade of trees in cool cañons, where its blossoms brighten the twilight gloom. It is an admirable plant, and has but one drawback—its rather unpleasant odor. It is the only species of the genus which was named in honor of an early Jesuit missionary, Michael Venegas. It is especially abundant and beautiful about Santa Barbara.

CANCER-ROOT. NAKED BROOM-RAPE.

Aphyllon fasciculatum, Gray. Broom-rape Family.

Leafless parasitic plants. *Stems.*—Scaly; thickened and knotty below, and bearing on their summits few or many clustered, one-flowered peduncles of about the same length. *Flowers.*—Yellowish; sometimes purplish or reddish outside. *Calyx*—Slenderly five-toothed. *Corolla.*—Tubular; over an inch long, with five spreading lobes; somewhat bilabiate. *Stamens.*—Four; in pairs; included. *Ovary.*—One-celled. Style slender. Stigma two-lobed. *Hab.*—Throughout California, eastward to Lake Superior.

There are about half a dozen species of cancer-root known upon our Coast, all strange-looking, leafless plants, of very

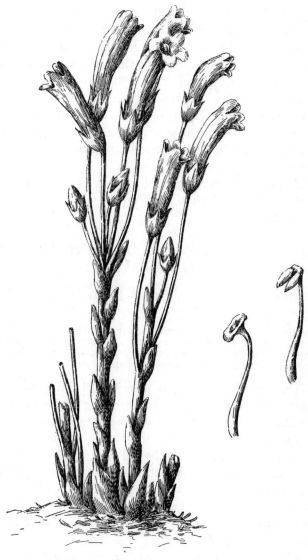

CANCER–ROOT—*Aphyllon fasciculatum.*

doubtful moral character—for I fear it must be confessed they are thieves. Stealthily sending their roots down and imbedding them in the roots of their victims, they draw from them the nourishment needed for their sustenance. But they have been overtaken by the proper retributive punishment— for having no longer any need of organs for the elaboration of nourishment, they are denied green leaves, the most beautiful adornment of many plants; and even the flowers of some of them seem to us to have a sickly, unwholesome hue. However, it must be acknowledged that these plants are quite interesting, despite their evil ways.

A. fasciculatum usually blooms in early summer, on dry, rocky hills, and is parasitic upon the roots of sagebrush, wild buckwheat, etc.

YELLOW MARIPOSA TULIP.

Calochortus luteus, Dougl. Lily Family.

Stems.—Four to twelve inches high; bearing a single bulblet inclosed in the stem-sheath. *Leaves.*—Very narrow; one to three lines wide. *Flowers.*—Erect; cup-shaped; yellow; comparatively small; not oculated, but the petals striated with brown lines, especially on the middle third. *Gland.*—Transversely oblong to lunate; densely hairy with orange-colored ascending hairs, with scattered spreading hairs about it. *Capsule.*—Broad at the base; tapering upward. *Hab.*—Clay soil; Coast Ranges from Mendocino County to San Diego.

The typical *C. luteus,* as described above, is the least beautiful of all the mariposa tulips, being lower of stature and smaller of flower than most of the others; but among its varieties may be found some of the most charming flowers of the genus, the true butterfly-tulips of the early Spanish, often oculated and marked in a wonderful manner. In color and marking they often run closely into forms of *C. venustus,* the only constant characters by which to distinguish them being found in the shape of the gland and the capsule and the character of the soil in which they grow.

There are two well-marked varieties—*citrinus* and *oculatus* —besides numerous other forms, where the species seems to have run riot in color and marking. The var. *citrinus* is a strong, vigorous-growing plant, with flowers of a deep lemon-yellow, with a large, distinct, very dark maroon eye on each petal. It is exceedingly beautiful.

FALSE PIMPERNEL.

Hypericum anagalloides, Cham. and Schlecht. St. John's-wort Family.

Stems.—Numerous; weak; low; spreading; rooting at the joints. *Leaves.*—Two to six lines long; oblong to round; clasping. *Flowers.* —Three or four lines across; salmon-colored. *Stamens.*—Fifteen to twenty. *Capsule.*—One-celled. *Hab.*—Lower California to British Columbia, eastward into Montana.

In moist places the prostrate stems of this little plant often make dense mats.

Its specific name indicates its resemblance to the *Anagallis,* or pimpernel. In fact, one might easily imagine it a pimpernel with salmon-colored flowers.

SILVER-WEED. CINQUEFOIL.

Potentilla Anserina, L. Rose Family.

Stems.—Prostrate. *Leaves.*—All radical; a foot or so long; pinnate, with seven to twenty-one leaflets with smaller ones interposed. *Leaflets.* —Sessile; oblong; toothed; shining green; silvery beneath. *Flowers.*— Bright yellow; long-peduncled; solitary; an inch across. *Sepals.*—Five; with five bractlets between. *Petals.*—Five. *Stamens.*—Twenty to twenty-five. *Pistils.*—Numerous; on a hairy receptacle. *Hab.*—Throughout North America.

The bright golden blossoms of the silver-weed are common in moist places, haunting stream-banks, lingering about stagnant ponds, or even pushing their way up amid the grasses of our salt marshes. The white under-surfaces of the leaves are responsible for one of the common names of this plant. The root has been used in the tanning of leather.

P. glandulosa, Lindl., is found upon dry hillsides. It is one or two feet high, and is an ill-smelling, somewhat sticky plant, with glandular hairs. The stems are leafy, and the small flowers, like pale-yellow strawberry-blossoms, are produced in loose clusters. The corolla scarcely exceeds the calyx. The leaves, which have from five to nine leaflets, have not the silvery under-surface of those of *P. Anserina*. We have a number of other species.

GUM-PLANT. GRINDELIA. AUGUST-FLOWER.

Grindelia cuneifolia, Nutt. Composite Family.

Bushy; two to four feet high; smooth. *Leaves.*—Cuneate-spatulate to linear-oblong; leathery; three or four inches long. *Flower-heads.*—Solitary; terminating the branches; yellow; composed of disk- and ray-flowers. *Rays.*—One inch long. *Involucre.*—Hemispherical; of numerous scales, with spreading tips. *Buds.*—Covered with a milky gum. *Syn.—Grindelia robusta,* var. *angustifolia,* Gray. *Hab.*—From Santa Barbara northward.

The grindelias are especially characteristic of the region west of the Mississippi River, and are all known as "gum-plants," or "resin-weeds," owing to the balsamic exudation which is found mostly upon the flower-heads. We have several species, all of which are rather difficult of determination.

Before the occupation of California by the whites, the value of these plants was known to the Indians, who used them in pulmonary troubles, and as a wash in cases of oak-poisoning or other skin-diseases. They are now made into a drug by our own people, who use them in the same manner as the aborigines.

By the middle of August our salt marshes are gay with the bright yellow flowers.

Every year men are sent out to gather the plant. Only about five or six inches of the tops of the branches are cut, as the resin is found mostly there in the form of a white gum. Tons of these shoots are shipped East annually, to be returned to us later in the form of the medicine called "grindelia."

Grindelia hirsutula, Hook. and Arn., is a pretty species, flowering in early summer upon hill-slopes. This may be known by its reddish stems and more slender and fewer ray-flowers.

GRINDELIA—*Grindelia cuneifolia.*

SULPHUR-FLOWER.

Eriogonum umbellatum, Torr. Buckwheat Family.

Leaves.—All radical; obovate to oblong-spatulate; two inches or less long; mostly smooth above; sometimes woolly below. *Scapes.*—Three to twelve inches high. *Flowers.*—Sulphur-yellow; two or three lines long; many contained in each little top-shaped involucre, on threadlike stems. *Involucres.*—Two lines or so long; deeply cleft, the lobes becoming reflexed. *Perianth.*—Six-parted. *Stamens.*—Nine. *Ovary.*—Triangular; one-celled. *Styles.*—Three. Stigmas capitate. (See illustration of *Eriogonum fasciculatum,* for flower structure.) *Hab.*—Mountains of middle and northern California, and eastward.

Large companies of the sulphur-flower may be seen in the Sierras in July and August, where it covers open, dry, rocky slopes, making brilliant masses of color.

Growing with this is often found another species,—*E. ursinum,* Wats.,—with flowers of a beautiful translucent cream-color, often tinged with pink.

COMMON EVENING PRIMROSE.

Œnothera biennis, L. Evening-Primrose Family.

Stems.—Stout; usually simple; one to five feet high; more or less hairy. *Leaves.*—Mostly sessile; lanceolate to oblong; two to six inches long; denticulate. *Flowers.*—Golden yellow; in a leafy spike; erect in the bud. *Calyx-tube.*—Twelve to thirty lines long. *Petals.*—Six to nine lines long. *Stigma-lobes.*—Linear. *Capsule.*—An inch or less long. (See *Œnothera.*) *Hab.*—Throughout the United States.

The common evening primrose is a very wide-spread plant in the United States, and it has long been in cultivation in Europe. Its flowers open suddenly at night, and, according to tradition, with a popping noise. Referring to this, the poet Keats speaks of—

> "A turf of evening primroses,
> O'er which the mind may hover till it dozes;
> O'er which it well might take a pleasant sleep,
> But that 't is ever startled by the leap
> Of buds into ripe flowers."

These blossoms were believed to be luminous at night, shining by the sunlight stored during the daytime.

The young roots, which are edible, are excellent, either pickled or boiled, having a nutty flavor. In Germany and

SULPHUR-FLOWER—*Eriogonum umbellatum.*

France these are used, either stewed or raw, in salads, like celery; and the young mucilaginous twigs are also used in the same way. A tincture of the whole plant is a valued remedy in medicine for many disorders. Our California plants are mostly of the var. *hirsutissima,* Gray, having very large flowers and a hairy capsule. A synonym for this form is *Œnothera Hookeri,* Torr. and Gray.

WILD BOUVARDIA.

Gilia grandiflora, Gray.   Phlox or Polemonium Family.

Stems.—Erect; a foot or two high. *Leaves.*—Two or three inches long; linear or oblong-lanceolate; sessile. *Flowers.*—Salmon-color; crowded at the summit of the stem. *Calyx.*—With obconic tube and broad, obtuse lobes. *Corolla.*—Narrowly funnel-form, with tube an inch long, and five-lobed border almost as broad. (See *Gilia.*) *Syn.*—*Collomia grandiflora,* Dougl. *Hab.*—Widely distributed.

This plant was formerly placed in the genus *Collomia;* but that genus was not well founded, and all its species have now been transferred to *Gilia.* From the resemblance of its showy buff or salmon-colored flowers to the bouvardias of our gardens, these plants are popularly known as "wild bouvardia." The blossoms are found in early summer, and grow usually in dry places, exposed to the sun.

LITTLE ALPINE LILY.

Lilium parvum, Kell.   Lily Family.

Bulbs.—Small; of short, thick, jointed scales. *Stems.*—Slender; eighteen inches to six feet high. *Leaves.*—Scattered, or in whorls; two to five inches long; an inch or less broad; rich green. *Flowers.*—Orange-vermilion, dotted with purple; two to fifty; scattered or somewhat whorled. *Capsule.*—Sub-spherical; six to nine lines long. *Hab.*—The high Sierras, from Yosemite Valley to Lake Tahoe.

Passing from the parched and dusty plains of our central valleys in July and August, we are transported as though upon the magic tapestry of Prince Houssain into a heavenly region of springtime, where the streams, fed by the snow lying in shadowy mountain fastnesses, gush through plushy emerald meadows, starred with millions of daisies and bordered by lux-

LITTLE ALPINE LILY—*Lilium parvum.*

uriant tangles of larkspurs, columbines, monk's-hoods, lupines, and a thousand other charming plants—a veritable flower-lover's paradise.

Here from the thickets, standing with their roots in the rich, loamy soil of the brookside, gleam the small orange blossoms of the little alpine lily—little only in flower, for the slender stems often rise to a height of six feet, producing several whorls of rich green leaves. These lilies are but an inch or an inch and a half long, with their perianth-segments yellow to orange below and deeper orange-vermilion above, their tips only being rolled backward. Often there are a great many buds and blossoms on one plant.

TARWEED. WILD COREOPSIS.
Madia elegans, Don. Composite Family.

Usually viscid throughout. *Stems.*—Three to six feet high. *Leaves.*—Crowded at the base of the stem; six to ten inches long; small above. *Flower-heads.*—Of both ray- and disk-flowers. *Rays.*—Twelve to fifteen; one inch long; three-lobed at the apex; yellow, sometimes with a dark-red base. *Involucre.*—With one series of scales, each clasping a ray. *Hab.*—Throughout California, and in Oregon and Nevada.

This is one of the most beautiful of all our tarweeds. Its golden, coreopsis-like flowers open after sunset, and close at the first warmth of the morning rays.

All the madias are used medicinally by old Spanish settlers.

Madia sativa, Molina, the Chile tarweed, is one of our most troublesome species, because its viscid secretion is so very abundant. The plants are tall, but the flowers are inconspicuous, owing to the smallness or absence of the rays. It is native of Chile as well as of California.

An oil of excellent quality was made from its seeds in that country before the olive was so abundant.

GOLDEN YARROW.
Eriophyllum confertiflorum, Gray. Composite Family.

White-woolly plants, at length smooth. *Stems.*—A foot or two high. *Leaves.*—Cuneate in outline; divided into three to seven narrow linear divisions. *Flowers.*—Golden yellow; in densely crowded flat-topped

TARWEED—*Madia elegans.*

clusters. *Heads.*—Small; of disk- and ray-flowers. *Rays.*—Four or five; broadly oval or roundish; one and one-half to two lines long. *Involucre.*—Oval; of about five thin bracts; two lines long. *Hab.*— From San Francisco to the Sierras, and southward to San Diego.

In early summer many a dry, rocky hill-slope is ablaze with the brilliant flowers of the golden yarrow. The brown-mottled butterfly may often be seen hovering over it, or delicately poising upon its golden table, fanning his wings.

E. arachnoideum, F. and M., is a very handsome species with solitary golden flower-heads an inch or so across. Its leaves are broader and not so finely divided, and some of the upper ones are linear and entire. This is found near the coast from Santa Cruz to Mendocino County. Its leaves are conspicuously white-woolly beneath.

LEOPARD-LILY. TIGER-LILY.
Lilium pardalinum, Kell. Lily Family.

Bulbs consisting of forking rhizomes, covered with small erect imbricated scales; often forming matted masses. *Stems.*—Three to ten feet high. *Leaves.*—Usually whorled, with some scattered above and below; lanceolate; three to seven inches long. *Flowers.*—Few to many; long-pediceled. *Perianth segments.*—Six; two or three inches long; six to nine lines wide; strongly revolute; with orange base and reddish or scarlet tips; spotted or dotted with purple on the lower half. *Stamens.*—Six. Anthers versatile. *Ovary.* — Three-celled. Style club-shaped. Stigma capitate. *Capsule.*—Eighteen lines or more long. *Hab.* —Stream-banks and wet meadows in the outer Coast Ranges and in the Sierras.

The leopard-lily often grows in clumps and colonies of several hundred, and is always found in the rich soil of stream-banks or of wet, springy places. Most of us have been familiar with these spotted beauties from our childhood, with their delicately swinging anthers full of cinnamon-colored pollen.

A friend writing us from near Mt. Shasta, one July, said:— "I wish you could have seen the *grove* of tiger-lilies we saw near the place where we rested and lunched. They sprang from a velvet bed of mosses and ferns, under the shadow of a great rock, that towered at least a hundred feet above them. Out of the rock sprang two streams of living water, ice-cold, which crossed the trail and dashed over a rock below. Upon one plant we counted twenty-five buds and blossoms, while a friend counted thirty-two upon another."

Under extraordinarily favorable conditions, this lily has been known to reach a height of ten feet.

YELLOW POND-LILY.

Nuphar polysepalum, Engelm. Water-Lily Family.

Leaves.—Six to twelve inches long; three fourths as wide; obtuse; deeply cleft at base; floating or erect. *Flowers*—Floating; three to five inches across. *Sepals.*—Eight to twelve; petaloid; bright yellow, sometimes greenish without. *Petals.*—Twelve to eighteen; small; about equaling the stamens, and resembling them. *Stamens.*—Numerous; red; recurved in age; pollen yellow. *Ovary.*—Large; eight- to twenty-celled. Stigma button-shaped; many-rayed; four lines to an inch across. *Hab.* —From Colorado to central California, and northward to Alaska.

Most of us are familiar with the yellow water-lily, and have seen its pretty shield-shaped leaves floating upon the surface of some glassy pond, starred with its large golden flowers. The latter are sometimes five inches across and quite showy. Sometimes entire marshes are covered with the plants. The large seeds are very nutritious, and form an important article of diet among the northern Indians.

HUMBOLDT'S LILY. TIGER-LILY.

Lilium Humboldtii, Roezl and Leichtlin. Lily Family.

Bulbs.—Large; often weighing over a pound; with scales two or three inches long. *Stems.*—Stout; purplish; three or four feet high; eight- or ten-flowered, or more. *Leaves.*—Wavy-margined; roughish. *Flowers.*—Large; six to eight inches in diameter; golden yellow; spotted with pale purple, turning to red or brown *Segments.*—Having papillose prominences near the base. (Otherwise like *L. pardalinum.*) *Hab.*—The foothills of the Sierras; southward to San Diego.

This wonderful lily, at first glance, resembles the common leopard- or tiger-lily—*L. pardalinum*—and it is found sometimes in the same regions as the latter, but never in the same kind of localities. It affects the loose soil of dry, upland woods, but never grows in wet or boggy places, and no finer sight could be imagined than a cañon-side covered with these golden lilies nodding on their tall stems. Its flowers are larger than those of *L. pardalinum,* and have more of a golden hue and less of red in them. Its time of blossoming is in July. A plant was once known which had fifty buds and blossoms, thirty of which were open at once!

PINE-DROPS.

Pterospora andromedea, Nutt.   Heath Family.

Stems.—One to three feet high.   *Bracts.*—Crowded at base; scattered above.   *Calyx.*—Five-parted.   *Corolla.*—Three lines long; yellowish. *Stamens.*—Ten.   Anthers tailed; opening lengthwise!   *Ovary.*—Five-celled.   Style short.   Stigma five-lobed.   *Hab.*—Throughout California, and across the continent.

In our walks in the mountains, we occasionally encounter the flesh-colored wands of this curious plant. The colorless leaves are reduced to mere bracts, and the stems are densely clothed above with the little yellowish waxen bells. The whole plant is very viscid and disagreeable to handle.

Though rare, it is found all across the continent. In the East it grows only under pine-trees, upon whose roots it is supposed to be parasitic, while in California it is said to be found under both oaks and pines.

There is but a single species in this genus. The seed is furnished with a broad membranous wing, which has given rise to the name *Pterospora,* derived from two Greek words, meaning *wing* and *seed.* When mature, the tall dark-red stems, with their pretty seed-vessels, often persist in a dried state until the following season, and are then beautiful adornments in our mountain cabins, and are certainly more agreeable to gather than when fresh.

COMMON SUNFLOWER.

Helianthus annuus, L.   Composite Family.

Hispid, coarse plants.   *Stems.*—Several feet high.   *Leaves.*—Mostly alternate; petioled; deltoid-ovate to ovate-lanceolate; acuminate; three to seven inches long; three-ribbed at base.   *Flower-heads.*—Large; three or four inches across, including the rays; solitary; composed of yellow ray-flowers and purple-brown, tubular disk-flowers.   *Involucre.* —Of several series of imbricated, ovate, acuminate scales.   *Disk.*—

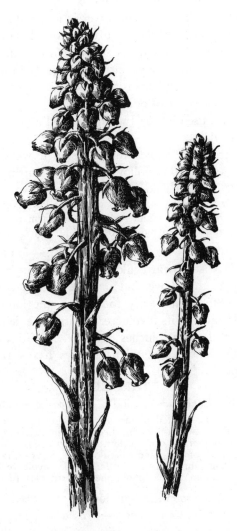

PINE–DROPS—*Pterospora andromedea.*

An inch or so across. *Hab.*—Plains and open places; north-central and southern California, and eastward.

The stately form of the sunflower is a common sight in the south, where whole fields are often covered with the plants. Their season of blossoming is supposed to be in the autumn, but we have seen them blooming just as gayly in March. This wild sunflower of the plains is believed to be the original parent of the large sunflower of our gardens.

Its seeds are used by the Indians as food and in the preparation of hair-oil.

Popular tradition makes this blossom a worshiper of the sun, and it is believed to follow him with admiring glances.

> "The lofty follower of the sun,
> Sad when he sets, shuts up her hollow leaves,
> Drooping all night, and when he warm returns,
> Points her enamored bosom to his ray."

Another species,—*H. Californicus,* DC.,—found from San Francisco Bay southward, along streams, has something the same habit as the above, but may be known from it by its slender, smooth stems, leafy to the top, the long, sprawling, awl-shaped bracts of its involucre, and its more delicate flowers, about two and a half inches across. The disk-corollas are slightly pubescent below. This species has a rather strong balsamic odor.

TARWEED.

Hemizonia luzulæfolia, DC. Composite Family.

Glandular, strong-scented plants. *Stems.*—Loosely branching; slender; six inches to two feet high. *Leaves.*—Linear; very small above; elongated and withering early below. *Flower-heads.*—White or light yellow; composed of ray- and disk-flowers. *Rays.*—Six to ten; two to five lines long; three-lobed. *Scales* of the involucre each clasping a ray. *Hab.*—Common throughout the western part of the State.

Under the common designation of "tarweed," plants belonging to two different genera—*Madia* and *Hemizonia*—and comprising thirty or forty species, may be found. They are mostly annuals or biennials, with viscid, heavily scented foliage, which make themselves conspicuous in late summer and

TARWEED—*Hemizonia luzulæfolia.*

through the autumn. The hemizonias are distinctively Californian; while the madias we have in common with Chile. Their viscid exudation is particularly ruinous to wool and clothing, but alcohol is a solvent for it, and will generally remove it.

We wonder how these plants, which flourish in our driest seasons, can extract so much moisture from the parched earth, and of what practical use this resinous secretion can be in their economy. Though some of them are described as having a disagreeable odor, many of them have a very pleasant balsamic fragrance, which gives our summer and autumn atmosphere a peculiar character of its own. Whole fields and hillsides are tinged with their warm olive foliage, or are yellow with their golden flowers, which appear like a fall revival of the buttercups. The flowers open mostly at night or in early morning, closing in bright sunshine.

Hemizonia luzulæfolia is a common species, whose flowers have the odor of myrrh.

MOTH-MULLEIN.

Verbascum Blattaria, L. Figwort Family.

Stem. — Tall and slender. *Leaves.* — Alternate; oblong; crenate-toothed; nearly smooth; the upper ovate, acute, clasping. *Flowers.*— Yellow or white; purple-tinged; an inch or so across; in a terminal raceme; the pedicels much exceeding the calyx-lobes. *Calyx.*—Five-parted. *Corolla.*—Wheel-shaped, with five rounded, somewhat unequal lobes. *Stamens.*—Five. Filaments violet-bearded. Anthers confluently one-celled. Pollen orange-colored, copious. *Ovary.*—Two-celled. Style slender. *Hab.*—The upper Sacramento Valley, central California, etc.; naturalized from Europe.

The mulleins are natives of Europe, which have found their way across the water to us. Two or three species are now common in some localities. The moth-mullein is so called because its blossoms have the appearance of a number of delicate moths resting upon the stem. This is a tall, green plant.

Another species—*V. Thapsus,* L.—is also quite common. In the Sacramento Valley its tall, woolly tapers may be seen leaning in every direction, giving the fields a disorderly appearance. This plant abounds throughout Europe and Asia, and was well known to the ancient Greeks and Romans, who made lampwicks of its dried leaves and utilized its stalks, dipped in tallow, for funeral torches. In medieval Europe it was called "hag-taper," because it was employed by witches in their incantations. In Europe at the present time it is known as the "American velvet-plant," because of a mistaken idea that it is a native of this country.

CALIFORNIA GOLDENROD.

Solidago Californica, Nutt. Composite Family.

Stem.—Rather stout; low or tall. *Leaves.*—Oblong, or the upper oblong-lanceolate, and the lower obovate. *Flowers.*—In a dense, pyramidal panicle, four to twelve inches long, with mostly erect racemose branches. *Heads.*—Three or four lines long; yellow. *Rays.*—Small; seven to twelve; about as many as the disk-flowers. *Hab.*—Throughout California, to Nevada and Mexico.

Our State is not so rich in goldenrods as New England, yet we have several rather pretty species. *Solidago Californica* is found upon dry hills, and blooms from July to October. It is said to thrive well under cultivation.

It differs from the "Western goldenrod" in having its flowers in a pyramidal cluster.

WESTERN GOLDENROD.

Solidago occidentalis, Nutt. Composite Family.

Smooth throughout. *Stems.*—Paniculately branched; two to six feet high. *Leaves.*—Linear; entire; obscurely three-nerved; two to four inches long; one to three lines wide. *Flower-heads.*—In numerous small, flat clusters, terminating the slender branchlets; three lines long; yellow. *Rays.*—Sixteen to twenty; not surpassing the eight to fourteen disk-flowers. *Involucre.*—Of imbricated scales; the outer successively shorter. *Hab.*—Near the Coast, from southern California to British America.

The Western goldenrod, with its slender, willowy stems and small flower-clusters, may be found in wet places in late summer and early autumn. Its blossoms are acacia-scented.

CREOSOTE-BUSH. GOBERNADORA. HIDEONDO.

Larrea Mexicana, Moricand. Creosote-Bush Family.

Ill-smelling, resinous shrubs, four to ten feet high; diffusely branched.
Leaves.—Opposite; with two unequal leaflets. *Leaflets.*—Three to six
lines long; pointed; sessile. *Flowers.*—Solitary; yellow. *Sepals.*—Five;
silky; deciduous. *Petals.*—Five; three or four lines long. *Stamens.*—
Ten; on a small ten-lobed disk. Filaments winged below. *Ovary.*—
Five-celled; Style slender. *Hab.*—Inland deserts of the southern part
of the State.

The most plentiful shrub growing in our southern desert
regions is the creosote-bush, so called because its sticky leaves
burn with a black smoke and a rank odor, between creosote
and carbolic acid.

These shrubs often cover vast tracts of arid soil, and in
places are the only growth to be seen. The evergreen foliage
is of a warm olive tone, and is borne at the ends of many slender, grayish branches. The small, stemless, opposite leaves,
each divided almost to its base into two leaflets, spread butterfly-like upon the slender branchlets. The leaf-nodes are swollen
into small, warty prominences, which are especially resinous.

In many localities, especially in Arizona, the branches of
this shrub are thickly incrusted with a certain gummy substance, which careful examination has proved to be almost
identical with the East Indian shellac of commerce. This is
caused by an insect of the genus *Coccus,* who stings the young
twigs, at the same time laying its eggs in them, causing them to
exude the gum. Could this gum be collected in sufficient quantities, it would doubtless prove a valuable article of commerce,
probably not inferior to the East Indian lac. Dr. Edwd.
Palmer writes that it is extensively used by our Indians as a
cement with which to fasten their flint arrow-heads to the
shafts, to mend broken pottery, and to make water-tight their
baskets, woven of grass and roots. The plant yields a greenish-
yellow dye, with which they paint their persons and color their
fabrics; but garments so dyed are said to emit a disagreeable
odor always upon being heated.

A lotion made by steeping the branches in water is said to be an excellent remedy for sores; while the leaves dried and reduced to powder are effectively used for the same purpose. Some of our pharmacists say that the plant is a valuable remedy for rheumatism.

By the Spanish-Californians this shrub is known as "gobernadora" and "hideondo"; and by the American settlers of the desert it is known by several uncomplimentary names, among them the meaningless one of "greasewood."

It blossoms in early summer.

BALSAM-ROOT.

Balsamorrhiza sagittata, Nutt.   Composite Family.

Leaves.—All radical; four to nine inches long, on stalks still longer; entire; cordate-sagittate or deltoid-hastate; silvery woolly. *Flowers.*— Solitary or sometimes two or three at summit of the scape; golden yellow. *Heads.*—Large, two inches or more across, composed of both disk- and ray-flowers. *Hab.*—The eastern side of the Sierras, eastward to beyond the Rocky Mountains.

The balsam-root is often found growing with the Indian wheat, but may be distinguished from it by its sagittate leaves and tall leafless flower-stems.

We have several species of *Balsamorrhiza,* all having thick roots, with resinous bark with the flavor of turpentine.

In Oregon the Indians cook these roots for food after removing the outer bark, and call the product "pash" or "kayoum."

" Springing in green valleys,
    And on the mountains high,
And in the silent wilderness
    Where no man passeth by."

III. PINK

Pink or occasionally or partially pink flowers not described in the Pink Section.

Described in the White Section:—

ACHILLEA MILLEFOLIUM—Yarrow.
CALOCHORTUS VENUSTUS—Mariposa Tulip.
CASSIOPE MERTENSIANA—Cassiope.
CHIMAPHILA MENZIESII—Prince's Pine.
CONVOLVULUS LUTEOLUS—Wild Morning-glory.
GAULTHERIA SHALLON—Salal.
LATHYRUS TORREYI.
LATHYRUS VESTITUS—Common Wild Pea.
LAYIA GLANDULOSUM—White Daisy.
LILIUM RUBESCENS—Ruby Lily.
MALACOTHRIX SAXATILIS.
MESEMBRYANTHEMUM CRYSTALLINUM—Ice-Plant.
ŒNOTHERA CALIFORNICA—White Evening Primrose.
ORTHOCARPUS VERSICOLOR—Pelican Flower.
PYROLA APHYLLA.
RAPHANUS SATIVUS—Radish.
RHODODENDRON OCCIDENTALE—California Azalea.
RUBUS SPECTABILIS—Salmon-Berry.
SPIRÆA LUCIDA—Pink Spiræa.
SPIRÆA DOUGLASII—Californian Hardhack.
SPRAGUEA UMBELLATA—Pussy's-Paws.

Described in the Yellow Section:—

HOSACKIA GRACILIS.

Described in the Blue and Purple Section:—

CALOCHORTUS SPLENDENS—Mariposa Tulip.
CALOCHORTUS UNIFLORUS.
TRILLIUM SESSILE—California Trillium.

Described in the Red Section:—

GILIA AGGREGATA—Scarlet Gilia.

Described in the Miscellaneous Section:—

CYPRIPEDIUM CALIFORNICUM—California Lady's Slipper.
GOMPHOCARPUS TOMENTOSUS—Hornless Woolly Milkweed.
RUMEX HYMENOSEPALUS—Wild Pie-Plant; Canaigre.

RED-STEMMED FILAREE. ALFILERILLA. CLOCKS. PIN-CLOVER.

Erodium cicutarium, L'Her. Geranium Family.

Leaves.—Chiefly radical in a depressed rosette; six to ten inches long; dissected into narrow toothed lobes. Stem-leaves smaller. *Flowers.*—Pink; four to eight in an umbel; parts in fives. *Petals.*—Three lines long. *Stamens.*—Five perfect, with flattened filaments; five reduced to mere scales. *Carpels* and styles one or two inches long; separating upward from a central axis into twisted, bearded tails. *Hab.*—Throughout the State.

The name "alfilerilla" is Spanish, coming from *alfiler,* a needle, and refers to the long, slender beak of the carpels. By corruption it has become "filaree."

This plant is found in abundance everywhere, and is one of our most valuable forage-plants. It varies greatly in size, and becomes very rank in growth where the soil is rich. Ordinarily, it makes its appearance soon after the beginning of the rainy season, as a rosette of leaves lying upon the ground, and later it sends up its reddish stems. Its seed-vessels look like a group of fantastic, long-billed storks, and the long beaks of the carpels, as they separate from the central axis, begin to curl about any convenient object. They are thus widely disseminated in the hair of animals and the clothing of people. Children call them "clocks," and love to stand the seed up in their clothing and watch the beaks wind slowly about, like the hands of a timepiece.

We have several other species of *Erodium.* *E. moschatum,* L'Her., is a coarser plant whose foliage has a musky fragrance, especially when wilted. It is also a valuable forage-plant, and is commonly known as "musky filaree" or "green-stemmed filaree," or "musk clover."

E. Botrys, Bertoloni, is a very abundant plant. Its flowers are larger, six lines across, and are pink, strongly veined with wine-color. The beaks of its carpels are sometimes four inches long.

RED–STEMMED FILAREE—*Erodium cicutarium.*

REDWOOD-SORREL.

Oxalis Oregana, Nutt. Geranium Family.

Herbs with sour juice. *Leaves.*—With three leaflets; petioles two to even twelve inches long. Leaflets one or two inches broad; usually light-blotched. *Scapes.*—One to six inches long; one-flowered. *Sepals.* —Five. *Petals.*—Five; nine to twelve lines long; white or rose-colored, often veined with darker color; usually having an orange spot at base. *Stamens.*—Ten. *Ovary.*—Five-celled. Styles five. *Hab.*—Coast woods, from Santa Cruz to Washington.

In deep woods, "where no stir nor call the sacred hush profanes," the beautiful leaves and delicate flowers of the redwood-sorrel cover the ground with an exquisite tapestry, which catches the shimmer of the sunlight as it shifts down through the tall trees. If the goddess Nanna in passing left the print of her pretty fingers upon the clover, perhaps some wood-nymph may have touched the leaves of this charming plant. Each day as twilight deepens, the leaflets fold gently together and prepare to sleep.

The small yellow oxalis—*O. corniculata,* L.—becomes a troublesome weed in our lawns.

ROCK-CRESS.

Arabis blepharophylla, Hook. and Arn. Mustard Family.

Stems.—Four to twelve inches high. *Radical leaves.*—Broadly spatulate; one or two inches long. *Cauline leaves.*—Oblong; sessile. *All leaves.*—Ciliate. *Flowers.* — Purplish-pink. *Sepals.* — Four; generally colored. *Petals.*—Four; six to nine lines long; clawed. *Stamens.*— Six; two shorter. *Ovary.*—Two-celled. Stigma button-shaped. *Pod.*— Linear; an inch or more long; flattened. *Hab.*—The Coast, from San Francisco to Monterey.

The bright magenta-colored blossoms of the rock-cress may be looked for in early spring along the hills of the Coast Ranges. This plant is said to be very beautiful in cultivation. The generic name was bestowed because many of the well-known species are natives of Arabia, while the formidable specific name means "eyelash-leaved," referring to the ciliate leaves.

REDWOOD-SORREL—*Oxalis Oregana.*

WILD HOLLYHOCK.

Sidalcea malvæflora, Gray.   Mallow Family.

Stems.—Several; eight inches to two feet long. *Leaves.*—Round in outline; variously lobed and cut. *Flowers.*—Pink; in terminal racemes. *Calyx.*—Five-cleft without bractlets. *Petals.*—Five; united at base; one inch long. *Stamens.*—United in a column; in two series.   Anthers one-celled. *Ovaries.*—Three to ten in a ring; separating at maturity. Styles as many; filiform. *Hab.*—The Coast from San Diego to Mendocino County.

In early spring the graceful sprays of the *Sidalcea* bend over our meadows everywhere, making them bright with their pink blossoms, which the children call "wild hollyhocks."   The stamens of these flowers are especially pretty and interesting if examined with a glass.   By a careful dissection, the stamen-column is found to be double, its outer part bearing five bunches of stamens.   The anthers are one-celled and of a beautiful rose-pink.   They may be seen best by pulling apart one of the unopened buds.

There are two kinds of these plants, one having large pale-pink flowers, which are perfect; the other bearing smaller deep rose-pink blossoms, in which the anthers are only rudimentary.

There are quite a number of species of *Sidalcea* in California, but they are very difficult of determination for the non-botanist.

REDBUD.   JUDAS-TREE.

Cercis occidentalis, Torr.   Pea Family.

Small trees or shrubs. *Leaves.*—Alternate; slender-petioled; round-cordate; palmately veined; smooth; about two inches in diameter. *Flowers.*—Rose-color; papilionaceous; clustered in the axils. *Petals.* —Four lines long; the standard smaller and inclosed by the wings. *Stamens.*—Ten; all distinct. *Ovary.*—One-celled. *Pods.*—Two or three inches long; thin. *Hab.*—Mt. Shasta to San Diego.

By April, or earlier, our interior hills and valleys begin to show the rosy blossoms of the Judas-tree.   The leafless branches are wreathed with the abundant flowers, which gives the shrub the appearance of a garden fruit-tree.   When seen later, in its full summer foliage, it is almost equally attractive.   Its shapely

WILD HOLLYHOCK—*Sidalcea malvæflora.*

leaves are then diversified by the clusters of long purple pods, which hang gracefully among them.

The Indians find the slender twigs of this shrub very useful in their basket-making. By means of the thumb-nail or flints, they split them into threads, which they use as woof.

A closely allied species of *Cercis,* growing in Palestine, had, according to tradition, white flowers, until the arch-traitor Judas hanged himself from its limbs, when it blushed pink for very shame.

In medieval Europe the Judas-tree was believed to be a favorite rendezvous for witches, and it was considered dangerous to approach one at nightfall.

HUCKLEBERRY.

Vaccinium ovatum, Pursh. Heath Family.

Evergreen shrubs, three to eight feet high. *Leaves.*—Ovate to oblong-lanceolate; leathery; smooth and shining. *Flowers.*—In axillary clusters; small; pinkish. *Calyx.*—Minutely five-toothed. *Corolla.*—Campanulate; two or three lines long. *Stamens.*—Ten; anthers opening terminally. *Ovary.*—Globose; five-celled. Style filiform. *Berries.*—Small; reddish, turning black. *Hab.*—The Coast Ranges from Monterey to Vancouver Island.

When in bloom our California huckleberry is a delightful shrub. Its leaves, which are of a particularly rich, shining green, are set at a characteristic angle to the red stems, contrasting finely with their warm tones; and the effect is heightened by the clusters of small pink and white waxen bells scattered here and there amid the foliage.

The huckleberry is at its best upon the high ridges of the Coast Ranges, where it becomes especially luxuriant in the fog-nurtured region of the northern portion of the redwood belt. There its abundant berries become juicy and delicious, and are much sought for preserving and pie-making. Its branches, when cut, keep admirably in water and are favorite greens for household decoration.

HUCKLEBERRY—*Vaccinium ovatum.*

STAR-FLOWER. CHICKWEED-WINTERGREEN.

Trientalis Europæa, var. *latifolia,* Torr. Primrose Family.

Root.—Tuberous. *Stem.*—Four to eight inches high; with a whorl of oval, pointed leaves one to four inches long. *Flowers.*—White or pink; eight lines across. *Calyx* and rotate corolla seven-parted, sometimes six- to nine-parted; divisions pointed. *Stamens.*—As many as the corolla-lobes, and opposite them. *Ovary.*—One-celled. Style filiform. *Hab.*—The Coast Ranges, from Monterey northward, also in the Sierras.

In April and May, as we walk through shaded woods, we begin to notice a trim little plant three or four inches high, with very slender stem, bearing at its summit a number of pretty leaves of varying size. A little later, we find among them one or two delicate pink, starry flowers on very slender, threadlike stems.

The generic name is from the Latin *triens,* and is in allusion to the height of the plant, which is the third part of a foot.

CLINTONIA.

Clintonia Andrewsiana, Torr. Lily Family.

Leaves.—Radical; oblong; six inches to one foot long; two to four wide. *Flower-stem.*—One or two feet high; with one leafy bract. *Flowers.*—Pink; many; in a terminal compound cluster on pedicels an inch or less long. *Perianth.*—Campanulate; four to seven lines long. *Segments.*—Six; gibbous at the base. *Stamens.*—Six. *Ovary.*—Two- or three-celled. *Fruit.*—Beautiful, large, dark-blue berries. *Hab.*— The Coast Ranges, from Santa Cruz to Humboldt County.

This is one of the most distinguished-looking plants of our deep coast woods, Its large leaves, of a rich polished green, arrange themselves symmetrically around the short stem, seeming to come from the ground—and so fine are they, that if no blossom appeared, we should feel the plant had fulfilled its mission of beauty. But in April a blossom-stalk shoots up from their midst, bearing upon its summit a cluster of deep rose-colored, nodding bells. These are succeeded later by a bunch of superb dark-blue berries, which might be made of lapis lazuli or the rarest old delft china. I remember a beautiful spot upon the Lagunitas Creek, where the stream, flowing

over a brown, pebbly bottom, passes among the redwoods
where their tall shafts make dim cathedrals aisles,—

> . . . "forest-corridors that lie
> In a mysterious world unpeopled yet."

Here little yellow violets and the charming wood-sorrel carpet
the ground, the fetid adder's-tongue spreads its mottled leaves,
while groups of the lovely *Clintonia* put the finishing touches
to an already beautiful scene.

LEMONADE-BERRY. MAHOGANY.

Rhus integrifolia, Benth. and Hook. Sumach Family.

Evergreen shrubs two to six feet high, becoming small trees southward. *Leaves.*—Alternate; short-petioled; one to three inches long;
rigid; leathery; ovate. *Flowers.*—Of two sexes, also some perfect; in
short, dense terminal clusters one to three inches long; rose-colored or
white. *Sepals, petals, and stamens.*—Four to nine; usually five. *Petals.*—
Rounded; ciliate; one or two lines across. Ovary.—One-celled. Stigmas three. *Fruit.*—Flat; one-seeded; six lines across; red; viscid and
acid. *Hab.*—The Coast from Santa Barbara to San Diego.

Growing everywhere upon the southern coast in great
abundance, this shrub forms low, dense, wind-shorn thickets.
Farther inland it rises to a height of several feet, with tough,
India-rubber-like branches, and in Lower California it becomes
a small tree. In its better estate it is very ornamental, especially in spring, when sprinkled with its clusters of small pink
flowers. The little drupes are covered with an acid, oily substance, and have long been used by the Indians and Mexicans
in the preparation of a lemonade-like drink. These people are
so fond of this fruit that they dry it for winter use, grinding
and roasting it as we do coffee. The wood of these shrubs is
of a dark-red color, which is responsible for the common name,
"mahogany."

Another *Rhus* very common in the valleys of southern
California is *R. laurina,* Nutt., usually called "sumach." It
is an evergreen shrub, with smooth, lanceolate leaves, two or
three inches long, exhaling a rather strong odor, considered by
some like bitter almonds, and bearing dense clusters of small

white flowers in midsummer. Its small drupes are only a line or two across. They are also coated with a waxen substance, and yield a pungent oil.

In the mountains from Santa Barbara to San Diego is found another species—*R. ovata,* Wats. This has large leathery, pointed leaves, and is known as "lemonade-and-sugar-tree," as the acid berries are coated with a sweet, waxen substance, which the Indians value as sugar. Its leaves resemble in form those of the lilacs of our gardens.

SHOOTING-STARS. WILD CYCLAMEN. MAD VIOLETS.
Dodecatheon Meadia, L.   Primrose Family.

Leaves.—All radical; tufted; from obovate to lanceolate. *Scape.*—Three to fifteen inches high; umbel two- to twenty-flowered. *Calyx.*—Deeply five-cleft, the divisions reflexed in flower, erect in fruit. *Corolla.*—With extremely short tube, and an abruptly reflexed five-parted limb; white, rose-color, or purple. *Stamens.*—Five; opposite the corolla-lobes. Filaments short; united. Anthers standing erect around the long style, forming a beak; violet. *Ovary.*—One-celled. *Hab.*—Throughout the continent; exceedingly variable.

The shooting-star is one of our prettiest spring flowers, which arrives a little before the baby-eyes and just as the brakes are unrolling their green crosiers. There is something particularly pleasing in these blossoms. It seems as though Nature had taxed her ingenuity to produce something original when she fashioned them. The name *Dodecatheon,* from the Greek, is entirely a fanciful one, and means "the twelve gods."

Formerly *D. Meadia,* L., was considered the only species, embracing many widely varying forms; but of late botanists have made several of the forms into separate species.

D. Hendersoni (Gray), Ktz., is the species prevalent in our central and northern Coast Ranges. This has ovoid or obovoid, very obtuse, entire leaves, with broad petiole, equaling the blade, two inches long. Its flower-stem is from eight to twelve inches high, bearing a cluster of bright rose-purple flowers. The corolla has a short, dark-maroon tube, encircled by a band of yellow, sometimes merging into white. The

SHOOTING-STARS—*Dodecatheon Hendersoni*, var. *cruciata*.

variety *cruciata*, with very slender stems and the flower parts in fours, is common in the Bay region, and southward possibly to Santa Barbara. Its blossoms have a strong odor, suggestive of a tannery. In this species the capsule opens at the top, splitting into a number of little teeth, which soon turn downward.

D. Clevelandi, Greene, is a beautiful species found in the south. It sends up a tall shaft, crowned with a large cluster of beautiful blossoms, varying from a delicate lilac to pure white. The petals are ringed below with pale yellow, and the beak of the flower is a rich prune-purple. There is a certain generous, fine look about these flowers, although they are exquisitely delicate. Their charm is completed by a delicious perfume, like that of the cultivated cyclamen.

In midsummer the wet meadows of the Sierras, particularly in the Yosemite region, are rosy with these flowers, which are peculiarly beautiful against the lush green grasses.

Among the children the various forms are known by a number of names, such as "mad violets," "prairie-pointers," "mosquito-bills," and "roosters'-heads." The latter is said to be the designation of prosaic little boys who see in these blossoms gaming possibilities, and who love to hook them together and pull to see which head will come off first.

PRICKLY PHLOX.

Gilia Californica, Benth. Phlox or Polemonium Family.

Stems.—Woody; two or three feet high. *Leaves.*—Alternate; palmately three- to seven-parted, with spreading, needle-like divisions, two to four lines long. *Flowers.*—Solitary, at the ends of the branchlets; rose-pink or lilac, with a white eye. *Calyx.*—Five-toothed. *Corolla-limb.*—An inch and a half across. (See *Gilia.*) *Hab.*—Dry hills from Monterey to San Bernardino.

I hardly know how to describe these delightful flowers. At a little distance the plant-stems have almost the look of a cactus, so densely are they clothed with the small, rigid leaves. Nor does a closer acquaintance serve to lessen the likeness—for in our breathless haste to take possession of the beautiful

PRICKLY PHLOX—*Gilia Californica.*

blossoms we are quite certain to have their prickly character impressed upon the hands as well as upon the sight. The texture of the flowers is of the finest silk, with an exquisite sheen; and they have a delicate fragrance. Growing at the tips of the numerous branchlets, they often form large masses of rich rose-colored bloom, which are especially brilliant and showy against the warm foliage.

In some localities they are called "rock-rose," an unfortunate name in two respects: it has long belonged to a yellow flower of an entirely different family—*Helianthemum;* and these blossoms do not in the least resemble a rose.

CALIFORNIA FOUR-O'CLOCK.

Mirabilis Californica, Gray. Four-o'clock Family.

Stems.—From a woody base; a foot or two long. *Leaves.*—Ovate; six to fifteen lines long; rather thick. *Flowers.*—Magenta-colored; one to three in a campanulate, calyx-like, five-toothed involucre. Involucres nearly sessile. *Perianth.*—Six lines long; open funnel-form; five-lobed. *Stamens.*—Five. Anthers yellow. *Ovary.*—Globose; one-celled. Style filiform. Stigma capitate. *Hab.*—Southern California and eastward.

When the heat of the day is over and the morning-glories are folding together their faded chalices, the bright little four-o'clocks begin to open their myriad magenta-colored eyes upon the closing day, and they, together with the evening primroses, will keep the vigils of the night. These diaphanous little flowers, with their long stamens resting on the lower side of the perianth, are like diminutive azaleas.

They are very puzzling, and the part that baffles the young botanist is the calyx, which, as it sometimes has two or three corollas within it, cannot be considered a calyx at all, but must be called an involucre. In reality the corolla is absent, and the calyx, which is colored like a corolla, is called a perianth. This appears to sit upon the top of the round ovary, but in reality a green continuation of it is drawn down tightly over the ovary.

CALIFORNIA FOUR-O'CLOCK—*Mirabilis Californica.*

BEACH MORNING-GLORY.

Convolvulus Soldanella, L.   Morning-Glory Family.

Stems.—A foot or less long; trailing. *Leaves.*—Kidney-shaped; long-petioled; leathery; an inch or two broad. *Flowers.*—Pink to lavender; one to nearly three inches across, with a pair of thin bracts just below the calyx, partly enveloping it. (Otherwise as *C. luteolus.*) *Hab.*—The seashore from Puget Sound to San Diego.

The beach morning-glory trails its stems over the shifting sands of the seashore, making clusters of beautiful foliage, over which the large, delicate flowers raise their exquisite satin funnels.

CALYPSO.

Calypso borealis, Salisb.   Orchis Family.

Bulb.—Small; solid. *Stem.*—Three to six inches high. *Leaf.*—An inch or two long. *Sepals* and petals light to deep rose-color; six to nine lines long. *Lip.*—Brownish pink, mottled with purple. *Style.*—Petaloid, oval, and concave, bearing the hemispherical anther on its summit underneath. *Hab.*—The northern Coast Ranges; also across the continent.

It has never been my good fortune to find this rare and exquisite little orchid, but beautiful specimens have been sent from the redwoods of Sonoma County and from Oregon.   The books speak of it as growing in bogs; but I am told by those who gathered them that the little plants sit lightly upon the layer of needles that carpet the forest-floor.   The roots scarcely penetrate the soil, so that the plants are easily disengaged without digging.

Nature produced a perfect work when she fashioned this little plant, so simple, so charming in every way, with its one dainty leaf and one unique blossom.   The form of the column is peculiarly interesting, being that of a curving concave petal, bearing the anther, in the shape of a hollow hemisphere, on its upper edge.

THE PRIDE OF CALIFORNIA.

Lathyrus splendens, Kell.   Pea Family.

Stem.—Climbing; six to ten feet. *Leaflets.*—About eight; scattered; very variable; linear to lanceolate or oblong; acute; mucronate; strongly three- to five-nerved. *Tendrils.*—Two- to five-parted. *Stipules.*—

CALYPSO—*Calypso borealis.*

Small; semi-sagittate. *Peduncles.* — Stout; usually seven- to ten-flowered. *Flowers.* — Very large; brilliant crimson. *Calyx.* — Five-toothed; eighteen-nerved. *Standard and keel.*—An inch or more long. *Pods.*—Three inches long; smooth; compressed; ten- to twenty-seeded. *Hab.*—Parts of San Diego County, and southward.

Clambering over our wild shrubs, this wonderful pea gives them the appearance of being loaded with a magnificence of bloom quite unwonted. The blossoms are the richest and most gorgeous of crimsons throughout, and have such a superb air that it is difficult to believe they are not the product of centuries of careful selection by the gardener. The long standard turns back over the stem, continuing the gracefully outlined keel in a long compound curve. The blossoms hang from the stem in charming abandon, like a flock of graceful tropic-birds poising upon the wing before taking flight, or like a fleet of gayly decked pleasure-barges, with canopies thrown back, fit for the conveyance of a Cleopatra.

WILD PORTULACA.

Calandrinia caulescens, HBK.; var. *Menziesii,* Gray. Purslane Family.

Decumbent, branching herbs, mostly smooth. *Leaves.*—Alternate; linear to oblanceolate; one to three inches long. *Flowers.*—In loose racemes; rose-color or magenta; about an inch across. *Sepals.*—Two; keeled. *Petals.*—Mostly five. *Stamens.*—Four to eleven. *Ovary.*—One-celled. Style slender. Stigma three-cleft. Seeds black, shining, lens-shaped. *Hab.*—From Lower California to Vancouver Island.

The wild portulaca is very abundant, and in seasons favorable to its development is a very noticeable little plant. Its succulent stems have a spreading habit and bear many satiny flowers of a deep purplish-pink, which open in the bright sunshine. The petals, which are veined with a slightly darker color, become white toward the center, and the little anthers are full of orange-colored pollen. These blossoms have a delicate, somewhat musky perfume.

Cattle are fond of the herbage, and the plants are considered excellent as pot-herbs and for salads. The seeds, which are a favorite food of the wild doves, are very pretty, being lens-shaped, black, and shining, with a granular surface.

WILD PORTULACA—*Calandrinia caulescens.*

FLOWERING CURRANT. INCENSE-SHRUB.

Ribes glutinosum, Benth.   Saxifrage Family.

Shrubs six to fifteen feet high. *Leaves.*—Three- to five-lobed; glutinous when young; one to one and one half inches broad. *Flowers.*—Rose-pink to pale pink; in long drooping racemes. *Calyx.*—Petaloid; five-lobed. *Petals and stamens.*—Five on the calyx. *Ovary.*—One-celled. Styles two; more or less united. *Berries.*—Blue, with a dense bloom; glandular-hispid. *Syn.*—*Ribes sanguineum,* Pursh., var. *glutinosum,* Brew. and Wats. *Hab.*—The Coast Ranges; more common southward.

In early winter in the south, and somewhat later northward, the wild currant becomes a thing of beauty hardly to have been expected. The young foliage, of a clear brilliant green, is gayly decked with the long clusters of peculiarly fresh pink blossoms, which seem like the very incarnation of the spirit of Spring, producing a certain *éblouissement,* which quickens our sense into an anticipation of beauty on every side.

We are made aware of a strong, heavy fragrance emanating from this shrub, for which its numerous glands are responsible, and which has gained for it the popular name of "incense-shrub" in some localities.

The fruit, which ripens toward fall, is dry and bitter, or insipid.

The genus *Ribes* includes the currant and the gooseberry, and furnishes us with several charming shrubs in California.

WILD GERANIUM.

Geranium incisum, Nutt.   Geranium Family.

Stems.—A foot or two high; branching loosely; hairy and glandular-pubescent, with enlarged joints. *Leaves.*—Two to five inches broad; palmately cut, nearly to the base, into five to seven narrow segments. *Flowers.*—Rose-pink; over an inch across. *Sepals.*—Five; five or six lines long. *Petals.*—Five; roundish. *Stamens.*—Ten; in two sets. *Carpels.*—Five. *Styles.*—Five; united almost to their summits around a central axis, and at maturity separating elastically from it, with their respective carpels, forming coils or tails. *Hab.*—Yosemite Valley and northward in the Sierras.

The pretty blossoms of the wild geranium grow abundantly in the rich soil of the valley floor in the Yosemite, and are sure to attract the attention of the passer-by.

FLOWERING CURRANT—*Ribes glutinosum.*

They share with the erodiums the curious form of the seed-vessels, which when immature resemble long-billed cranes or storks. Hence the generic name, which comes from the Greek word meaning a crane.

GROUND-PINK. FRINGED GILIA.

Gilia dianthoides, Endl. Phlox or Polemonium Family.

One to six inches high. *Leaves.*—Six lines or so long; linear to filiform. *Flowers.*—Rose or lilac, blending inward to white, with darker color or yellow in the throat. *Calyx.*—Five-cleft. *Corolla.*—Nine to twelve lines across; fringed. (See *Gilia.*) *Hab.*—From Santa Barbara to San Diego.

In March our southern meadows and hill-slopes are all aglow with the lovely flowers of this charming little *Gilia.* The plants are tiny, often no more than an inch high, but are ambitious out of all proportion to their size, covering themselves with blossoms exquisitely delicate in texture, form, and coloring, which literally carpet the earth with an overlapping mosaic.

It is a wonderful thought that upon every one of these countless millions of little flowers that clothe the fields Nature has bestowed such care that each is a masterpiece in itself.

COMMON FLEABANE.

Erigeron Philadelphicus, L. Composite Family.

Hairy, perennial herbs. *Stems.*—One to three feet high; leafy to the top. *Root-leaves.*—Spatulate or obovate. *Stem-leaves.*—Oblong; sessile, with broad clasping base; irregularly toothed. *Flower-heads.*—In a loose corymb. *Disks.*—Yellow; three or four lines across. *Rays.*—Innumerable; very narrow; flesh-color to rose-purple; about three lines long. *Hab.*—Widely distributed on the Pacific and Atlantic coasts.

The feathery, daisy-like flowers of the common fleabane are of frequent occurrence in moist meadows or along the roadsides in spring. The ray-flowers are so narrow as to form a delicate fringe around the disk.

The common name arose from the belief that these plants were harmful to fleas.

FRINGED GILIA—*Gilia dianthoides.*

TURKISH RUGGING.

Chorizanthe staticoides, Benth.   Buckwheat Family.

A foot high or more, with widely spreading branches. *Leaves.*—All radical; oblong; obtuse; twelve to thirty lines long, including petioles. *Involucres.*—Loosely clustered; sessile; one-flowered; campanulate; with six bristle-like teeth. *Perianth.*—Pink; two lines long; six-lobed; not fringed. *Stamens.*—Mostly nine; on the perianth. *Ovary.*—One-celled. Styles three. Stigmas capitate. *Hab.*—From Monterey to San Diego.

In late spring the dry, open hills of the south are overrun with the soft lavender of the chorizanthe. The flowers are small, but the whole plant is purplish, and the stems are quite as productive of color as the blossoms. In fact, the whole plant seems to consist of a scraggly interlacement of slender branches and small flowers, as the leaves, which nestle close to the ground, are not very noticeable.

CANCHALAGUA.   CALIFORNIA CENTAURY.

Erythræa venusta, Gray.   Gentian Family.

Six inches to two feet high. *Leaves.*—Six to twelve lines long; pale apple-green. *Calyx.*—Usually five-parted. *Corolla.*—Bright pink, with yellow or white center; an inch or so across. *Stamens.*—Five; anthers spirally twisted after shedding the pollen. *Ovary.*—One-celled. Style slender. Stigmas two. *Hab.*—From Plumas County southward; more abundant southward.

Just as our attention has been called afresh to the fields by the sudden appearance of the "golden stars," or bloomeria, in late spring, we find, as we stoop to gather them, a charming pink flower nestling close to the earth amid the grasses. Though low of stature, these firstlings of the season atone for it by brilliancy of color, and their pink blossoms have a peculiarly clean, fresh, wide-awake appearance, reminding one of a rosy-faced country wench.

While enjoying their bright beauty, we do not for a moment suspect that we are paying homage to the famous "canchalagua" of the Spanish-Californians. No well-regulated household among these people is without bundles of these herbs strung upon the rafters—for they are considered by them

CANCHALAGUA—*Erythræa venusta.*

an indispensable remedy for fevers; also, an excellent bitter tonic, and are said to possess rare antiseptic properties. These little plants are very abundant in and near the Yosemite Valley, where they make bright beds of color in midsummer.

FALSE MALLOW.

Malvastrum Thurberi, Gray.   Mallow Family.

Shrubby at base; three to fifteen feet high; densely tomentose. *Leaves.*—An inch or two across; thick. *Flowers.*—Clustered in the axils of the leaves; or in an interrupted naked spike. *Calyx.*—Five-lobed; with one to three bractlets. *Petals.*—Five, about six lines long; rose-purple. *Stamens.*—United in a column. *Ovaries.*—Numerous; united in a ring. Styles united at base. Stigmas capitate. *Hab.*—The southern Coast Ranges and islands of the Coast.

Upon the mesas of the south we often see a shrubby member of the Mallow family, with long, wandlike branches ornamented with closely set, pink flowers, of delicate texture and pleasant perfume. This is the false mallow. It is a very handsome and noticeable shrub when in full bloom. The anthers are golden brown, and the stigmas are spherical instead of filiform. Upon the seashore it blooms much earlier than in the valleys inland.

MESEMBRYANTHEMUM. FIG-MARIGOLD.

Mesembryanthemum æquilaterale, Haworth.   Fig-marigold Family.

Succulent plants. *Stems.*—Elongating; forming large mats. *Leaves.* —Opposite; sessile; fleshy; three-angled; two inches or more long; oblong. *Flowers.*—Terminal; solitary; fifteen lines to two inches across; pink. *Calyx.*—With top-shaped tube and five-lobed border. *Petals.*—Very numerous; linear. *Stamens.*—Innumerable. *Ovary.*—Four- to twenty-celled. Stigmas six to ten. *Hab.*—The Coast, from Point Reyes southward.

The fig-marigold is a very common plant upon our seashore. It seems to flourish best toward the south, where it covers large tracts of sand with its succulent foliage, making mats of pleasant verdure in otherwise sandy wastes. Its stems often trail many yards down the cliffs, making beautiful natural draperies, decked with myriads of the pink blossoms. Because it is capable of withstanding the drouth in the most

FALSE MALLOW—*Malvastrum Thurberi.*

remarkable manner, it has been planted to produce verdure where irrigation is impossible. The very numerous slender petals give the flower the appearance at first sight of a composita. The fruit is pulpy and full of very small seeds, like the fig, and has a suggestion of the flavor of the Isabella grape.

Many species of *Mesembryanthemum* are cultivated in our gardens, mostly as border-plants. The genus is a large one, most of the species being native of southern Africa, and it is supposed that the three species now common upon our Coast were introduced in the remote past without the agency of man.

SMALL GILIA.

Gilia androsacea, Steud. Phlox or Polemonium Family.

Stems.—Three to twelve inches high; erect; spreading. *Leaves.*—Opposite; sessile; palmately five- to seven-parted; seemingly whorled. *Flowers.*—In terminal clusters. *Corolla.*—Salver-shaped; rose-pink, lilac, or white, with a yellow or dark throat; its tube filiform, about an inch long; limb eight to ten lines across. Filaments and style slender; exserted. (See *Gilia.*) *Hab.*—Throughout the western part of the State; into the Sierra foothills.

The delicate flowers of this little plant may be found nestling amid the grasses of dry hill-slopes in late spring, often making charming bits of color. It is usually rather a low plant, but in specially favorable situations it rises to a foot in height. Its fragile flowers vary from pure white to lilac and a lovely rose-pink, and look like small phloxes.

BROWNIES.

Mimulus Douglasii, Gray. Figwort Family.

Flowering at half an inch high; later becoming a span high. *Leaves.*—Ovate or oblong; three- to five-nerved at base; narrowed into a short petiole. *Flowers.*—Rich maroon, with deeper color in the throat and some yellow below. *Calyx.*—Five-toothed. *Corolla.*—An inch to eighteen lines long; with dilated throat. Lower lip much shorter than the ample, erect, upper one; sometimes almost wanting. (See *Mimulus.*) *Hab.*—Throughout California.

This little mimulus is quite common upon gravelly or stony hills. Its pert little maroon flowers, with their very long tubes and erect lobes, so ridiculously out of proportion

SMALL GILIA—*Gilia androsacea.*

to the size of the tiny plant, give it the look of some very important small personage.

BITTER-ROOT. SPAT'LUM. TOBACCO-ROOT.

Lewisia rediviva, Pursh.   Purslane Family.

Root.—Very thick.   *Leaves.*—Clustered; linear-oblong; one or two inches long.   *Scapes.*—One-flowered; one or two inches long; jointed in the middle, with a whorl of five to seven scarious bracts at the joint. *Sepals.*—Six to eight; six to nine lines long; scarious-margined. *Petals.*—Twelve to fifteen; rose-color, sometimes white; oblong; eight to sixteen lines long; rotately spreading in sunshine.   *Stamens.*—Forty or more.   *Ovary.*—One-celled.   Style three- to eight-parted nearly to the base.   *Hab.*—The mountains of California, northward and eastward.

Within our borders this little plant is not abundant, but must be sought upon mountain heights.   Formerly it was supposed not to occur south of Mt. Diablo, but it has since been found in the mountains of the southern part of the State and at intermediate points.   It is very abundant in Montana, where it has been adopted as the State flower.

The plants are very small, being but an inch or two high, but the flowers are handsome and showy, and the delicate rose-colored corollas, which are often two inches across, are of an exquisite silken texture.   The root is remarkably large and thick for so small a plant, and it contains a nutritious, farinaceous matter, much esteemed by the Indians for food.   Among them it is known as "spat'lum," and they gather large quantities of it, which they store in bags for future use.

This was the "racine-amère," or "bitter-root," of the early French settlers.   It is also known as "tobacco-root," because when boiled it has a tobacco-like odor.

The specific name, *rediviva,* was bestowed because of the wonderful vitality of these plants.   It is known upon good authority that specimens which had been drying for two years in an herbarium continued to produce leaves, and at last, when taken out and planted, went on growing and blossomed!

This genus is an exception to the other members of the Purslane family, in having more than two sepals.

SPINELESS TUNA.

Opuntia basilaris, var. *ramosa,* Parish.   Cactus Family.

Low; spreading; branching freely above. *Joints.*—Flat; smooth; without large spines, but with close tufts of minute bristles; obovate or fan-shaped; five to eight inches long; nearly as wide at the top. *Flowers.*—Large; brilliant rose-magenta; two or three inches long. *Fruit.*—Dry; sub-globose. (Flower-structure as in *O. Engelmanni.*) *Hab.*—The southern deserts and San Bernardino Mountains.

In the arid regions of the southern interior, this opuntia is a very common one, and its large, brilliant rose-magenta flowers attract the attention wherever seen.   They are very tempting blossoms, and it is hard to resist them, even though we know the penalty will be the conversion of thumbs and fingers into pin-cushions for innumerable, minute, tormenting thorns.

SNOW-BERRY.

Symphoricarpus racemosus, Michx. Honeysuckle Family.

Shrubs two to four feet high. *Leaves.*—Opposite; short-petioled; cuneate to oblong; entire or lobed; nine to eighteen lines long; herbaceous. *Flowers.*—Small; mostly in terminal clusters. *Calyx.*—Adnate to the ovary; with five-toothed border. *Corolla.*—Campanulate; five-lobed; three lines long; waxen; pinkish; very hairy within. *Stamens.*—Five; on the corolla. *Ovary.*—Four-celled. *Berries.*—Waxen-white; six lines in diameter. *Hab.*—Widely distributed.

In early winter the pure-white clusters of the snow-berry, on their almost leafless stems, make flecks of light through the dun woods.   At this season of few woodland attractions, these berries, together with the trailing sprays of the fragrant yerba buena and the long graceful leaves of the iris, are about the only trophies to be obtained upon a walk.   In early spring, when their slender twigs first begin to leaf out, these little shrubs are among the most delicate and airy of growing things, and make a tender veil of green through the shadowy woodland.   The blossoms, which arrive rather late, are inconspicuous.

TREE-MALLOW.

Lavatera assurgentiflora, Kell.   Mallow Family.

Shrubs.—Six to fifteen feet high.   *Leaves.*—Alternate; three to nine inches across.   *Flowers.*—Pink, veined with maroon.   *Calyx.*—Five-cleft, with an involucel below, like a second calyx.   *Petals.*—Twelve to eighteen lines long.   *Filaments.*—Numerous; united in a column. *Styles.*—Numerous; filiform.   *Carpels.*—One-seeded, in a ring around an axis; separating at maturity.   *Hab.*—The islands off the Coast; cultivated on the mainland north to Mendocino County.

The lavateras are Old-World plants, with the exception of a few species which are natives of the islands of our southern coast.   In the early days the Padres planted the above species (*L. assurgentiflora*) plentifully around the old Missions, and thence it has spread and become spontaneous in many localities.   It can be seen in San Francisco, planted as wind-break hedges about the market-gardens, where it thrives luxuriantly as long as it is protected from cattle.

The leaves and twigs abound in mucilage, and are very fattening and nutritious food for sheep and cattle, who are very fond of it.

WILD HONEYSUCKLE.

Lonicera hispidula, Dougl.   Honeysuckle Family.

Woody; climbing and twining.   *Leaves.*—Opposite; short-petioled; oval; pale; one to three inches long; the upper pairs uniting around the stem.   *Flowers.*—Pink; in spikes of several whorls.   *Calyx.*—Minute; growing to the ovary; border five-toothed.   *Corolla.*—Tubular; six lines to an inch long; bilabiate; the lips strongly revolute; the upper four-lobed, the lower entire.   *Stamens.*—Five; much exserted. *Ovary.*—Two- or three-celled.   Style slender.   Stigma capitate.   *Berries.*—Scarlet; translucent.   *Hab.*—Throughout the State.

In early summer the climbing honeysuckle with its pale foliage flings its long arms over neighboring trees and shrubs, showing glimpses here and there of small pinkish flowers.   But it is far more noticeable in the fall, when its long pendulous branches are laden with the fine clusters of translucent, orange-red berries.   It is quite variable and has many forms, which are all considered varieties of the one species.

Another species—*Lonicera conjugialis,* Kellogg—grows in

TREE-MALLOW—*Lavatera assurgentiflora.*

the form of a very leafy shrub, and is found in the Sierras from Mariposa County northward. Its opposite ovate leaves are thin and pointed, and its small dark-red flowers are borne in pairs at the summit of a slender, wiry peduncle in the axils of the leaves.

These little flowers are quite irregular, the upper lip of the corolla being four-notched and the ovaries of the pair are joined solidly together, whence it receives its specific name.

PINK PAINT-BRUSH. ESCOBITA.
Orthocarpus purpurascens, Benth. Figwort Family.

Stems.—Six to twelve inches high. *Leaves.*—Variously parted into filiform divisions. *Bracts.*—About equaling the flowers; tipped with crimson or pale pink. *Corolla.*—About an inch long; the lower lip only moderately inflated and three-saccate; the upper long, hooked, bearded, crimson. *Stigma.* — Large. (See *Orthocarpus.*) *Hab.*— Widely distributed.

The bright-magenta tufts of the pink paint-brush are often so abundant that they give the country a purplish hue for miles at a stretch. The Spanish-Californians have a pretty name for these blossoms, calling them "escobitas," meaning "little whisk-brooms."

O. densiflorus, Benth., is a very similar species; but its corolla has a straight upper lip, without hairs. This is commonly known as "owl's clover."

CLARKIA.
Clarkia elegans, Dougl. Evening-Primrose Family.

Stems.—One to six feet high; simple or branching. *Leaves.*—Alternate; broadly ovate to linear; dentate; an inch or more long. *Petals.* —About nine lines long; with long, slender claws and rhomboidal blades; pink. *Stamens.*—Eight; all perfect. Filaments with a hairy scale at base. *Stigma.*—Four-lobed. *Capsule.*—Six to nine lines long; sessile. (Otherwise as *C. concinna.*) *Hab.*—Widely distributed.

This plant is a very common one along our dusty roadsides in early summer, and it shows a facility in adapting itself to quite a range of climate and condition. It grows from six inches to six feet high, is nearly smooth or quite hairy, and

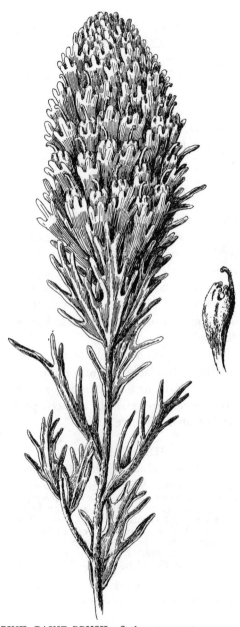

PINK PAINT-BRUSH—*Orthocarpus purpurascens.*

has rather large flowers or quite small ones. Its scarlet stamens, purple-pink petals, and often deeper purple sepals make an odd combination of color. It often grows in showy masses, making patches of glowing color under the shade of trees.

CHAPARRAL PEA.

Xylothermia montana, (Nutt.) Greene. Pea Family.

Evergreen, much branched, spiny shrubs, four to seven feet high. *Leaves.*—With from one to three leaflets. *Leaflets.*—Three to nine lines long. *Flowers.*—Magenta-colored; solitary; nearly sessile; seven to nine lines long; papilionaceous. *Stamens.*—All ten distinct. *Pod.*—One-celled; two inches long. *Syn.*—*Pickeringia montana,* Nutt. *Hab.*—The Coast Ranges, from Lake County to San Diego.

Upon wild mountain-slopes where are heard the flutelike notes of a certain shy bird that rarely comes near habitations, the chaparral pea often makes dense, impenetrable thickets. It would be impossible to mistake it for any other shrub, with its solitary magenta-colored pea-blossoms, which often cover the bushes with a mass of color. Its green branchlets terminate in long, rigid spines, which are often clothed with small leaves nearly to the end.

Woe to him who tries to penetrate the chaparral when it is composed of this formidable and uncompromising shrub! The result is quite likely to be a humiliating progress upon hands and knees before he can extricate himself, probably with torn garments and scratched visage.

HEDGE-NETTLE.

Stachys bullata, Benth. Mint Family.

Rough, pubescent herbs. *Stem.*—Ten to eighteen inches high; four-angled. *Leaves.*—Opposite; ovate or ovate-oblong; cordate; coarsely crenate; wrinkly veined; petioled; an inch or two long. *Flowers.*—Pinkish; in a narrow, interrupted spike. *Calyx.*—Five-cleft. *Corolla.*—Eight lines long; bilabiate. Upper lip erect; lower deflexed, of three unequal lobes, spotted with purple. *Stamens.*—Four. Filaments hairy. Anthers divergently two-celled. *Ovary.*—Of four seedlike nutlets. Style filiform. Stigma two-cleft. *Hab.*—Throughout the State.

The hedge-nettles are common weeds, of which we have several species. *S. bullata,* so called on account of its leaves,

CHAPARRAL PEA—*Xylothermia montana.*

which look as though blistered, is the most wide-spread. It is quite variable in aspect, and we are constantly meeting it in new guises and being deceived into believing it something finer than it really is, through some subtle change in its usually homely little pink flowers.

TWINING HYACINTH, OR TWINING BRODIÆA.

Brodiæa volubilis, Baker. Lily Family.

Coated corm about one inch in diameter. *Leaves.*—All radical; broadly linear; a foot or more long. *Scape.*—Twining; two to even twelve feet long; naked. *Umbel.*—Many-flowered. *Perianth.*—Five to eight lines long; rose-color without, whitish within. *Stamens.*—Three; alternating with three notched staminodia. Filaments winged; very short. *Ovary.*—Three-celled. Style short. Stigma capitate. *Syn.*—*Stropholirion Californicum,* Torr. *Hab.*—Sierra foothills, from Mariposa County northward.

In this plant we see the brodiæa disporting itself in a very odd manner, having vinelike aspirations. It produces several long leaves, which lie prostrate upon the ground, and then the stem puts in its appearance and commences a wonderful series of evolutions not to be outdone by any contortionist. It twists and clambers and climbs, reaching a height of five or six feet, often having expended twice that amount of stem in its convolutions.

During this remarkable process, which consumes from two to four weeks, the terminal bud has remained dormant. But it now commences to grow, and in a couple of weeks the flower-cluster is complete in all its beauty. It is sometimes six inches across.

It often happens that before the flower has blossomed the stem is broken off at the ground. Strangely enough, this seems not to matter at all, for it grows on and perfects its flowers just as though nothing had occurred. People often bring the stem indoors and allow it to climb up over the curtains, where they can watch the interesting process of its growth. These plants are quite abundant along the stage routes to the Yosemite Valley.

TWINING BRODIÆA—*Brodiæa volubilis.*

CALIFORNIA ROSE-BAY.

Rhododendron Californicum, Hook. Heath Family.

Evergreen shrubs three to fifteen feet high. *Leaves.*—Four to six inches long; leathery. *Flowers.*—Rose-pink; in large clusters. *Calyx.* —Small; with rounded lobes. *Corolla.*—Broadly campanulate; two inches or so across; slightly irregular; with wavy-margined lobes; the upper spotted within. *Stamens.*—About equaling the corolla. Style crimson. Stigma funnel-form. (Otherwise as *R. occidentale.*) *Hab.* —From British Columbia to Marin County.

In our northern counties the rugged mountain-sides are often densely covered with the lovely rose-bay, which in early summer presents an appearance it would be impossible to rival. When the foliage, which is very rich in both quality and hue, is thickly massed with the great glowing flower-clusters, the sight is worth a pilgrimage to see. It is a shrub so beautiful, we marvel it is not generally cultivated in gardens.

The bees are very fond of the blossoms, but popular tradition ascribes a poisonous quality to the honey made from them.

We have noticed no perfume in these flowers, but the leaves are often quite pleasantly fragrant.

COMMON WILD ROSE.

Rosa Californica, Cham. and Schlecht. Rose Family.

Erect shrubs three to eight feet high. Prickles few; stout; recurved; mostly in pairs beneath the entire stipules. *Leaves.*—Alternate; pinnate; with five to seven leaflets. *Leaflets.*—Ovate or oblong; serrate. *Flowers.*—Few to many in clusters; pale-pink. *Calyx.*—With urn-shaped tube and five-cleft border, whose lobes are foliaceously tipped. *Petals.*—Five; six to nine lines long. *Stamens.*—Very numerous. *Ovaries.*—Several; bony; in, but free from, the calyx-tube. *Hips.*— Many; four or five lines through. *Hab.*—From San Diego to Oregon.

The wild rose is one of the few flowers that blooms cheerfully through the long summer days, lavishing its beautiful clusters of deliciously fragrant flowers as freely along the dusty roadside as in the more secluded thicket. In autumn it often seems inspired to a special luxuriance of blossoming, and it lingers to greet the asters and mingle its pink flowers and brilliant scarlet hips with their delicate lilacs.

R. gymnocarpa, Nutt., "the redwood-rose," is exquisitely

CALIFORNIA ROSE–BAY—*Rhododendron Californicum.*

dainty. This is found in shady places under the trees. It blooms earlier than the common species, and is neither so abundant nor so fragrant. Its flowers are barely an inch across and of a bright pink. The prickles are straight, and the calyx-lobes are without leafy tips, while the leaflets are small and shapely.

BEAUTIFUL CLARKIA.

Clarkia concinna (F. and M.), Greene. Evening-Primrose Family.

Stems.—Several inches to two feet high. *Leaves.*—One or two inches long. *Flowers.*—Axillary; sessile; parts in fours. *Calyx.*—Red-pink; tube an inch or more long. *Petals.*—Rose-pink; six lines to over an inch long. *Ovary.*—Four-celled. *Syn.—Eucharidium concinnum,* Fisch. and Mey. *Hab.*—The Coast Ranges, from Santa Barbara to Mendocino County.

In June these charming blossoms may be found in the company of the maidenhair fern fringing the banks of shady roads, or standing in glowing masses under the buckeye-trees. In them Nature has ventured upon one of those rather daring color combinations of which we would have hardly dreamed, and the result is delightful. The petals are bright rose-pink, while the sepals are of a red pink.

SPREADING DOGBANE.

Apocynum androsæmifolium, L. Dogbane Family.

Erect; one to three feet high; spreading. *Leaves.*—Opposite; short-petioled; ovate or roundish; an inch or two long. *Flowers.*—Clustered; pink. *Calyx.*—Five-cleft. *Corolla.*—Campanulate; three or four lines long; with five revolute lobes; having a small scale at base, opposite each lobe. *Stamens.*—Five; on the corolla. Filaments short. Anthers erect around the stigma. Style none. *Ovaries.*—Two; becoming a pair of long pods. Seeds silky-tufted. *Hab.*—Widely distributed in the United States.

The small pink flowers of the spreading dogbane may be found all through the summer, often upon our driest hillsides. The shapely little blossoms are of a flesh-tint without, richly veined with deeper pink within, and quite fragrant. The plants have a milky juice and a tough fiber in the stem, similar to that in the American-Indian hemp. The plant was formerly

BEAUTIFUL CLARKIA—*Clarkia concinna.*

supposed to be poisonous to dogs, from which fact it received its generic name, which translated gives the common English name "dogbane." It is used in medicine as a remedy for rheumatic gout. The very long pods seem absurdly out of proportion to the small flowers.

A. cannabinum, L., the American-Indian hemp, is also found within our borders, but it grows along stream-banks and in marshy places. It has oblong, pointed leaves, and small greenish-white flowers, only two lines long, whose close cylindrical corollas hardly surpass the calyx. The yellowish-brown bark of this plant is very tough and fibrous, and at the same time soft and silky. Our Indians have always found it of the utmost value in the making of ropes, lariats, nets, mats, baskets, etc., and before the coming of the white man they even made certain articles of clothing of it. A tincture made from the root is a recognized drug in the pharmacopœia. Professor Thouin, of Paris, says that a permanent dye may be obtained from a decoction of it, which is brown or black, according to the mordant used.

FIRECRACKER FLOWER.

Brodiæa coccinea, Gray. Lily Family.

Leaves.—Grasslike, a foot or two long. *Scape.*—One to three feet high; six- to fifteen-flowered. *Perianth.*—An inch or two long; rich crimson; the limb of six green or yellowish oblong lobes. *Stamens.*—Three; on the perianth. Filaments adnate to its tube. Anther tips exserted. *Staminodia.*—Three; broad; short; white; on the throat of the perianth, alternating with the stamens. *Ovary.*—Three-celled. Style exserted. Stigma three-lobed. *Syn.*—*Brevoortia coccinea,* Wats. *Hab.*—The mountains from Mendocino County to Shasta County.

When our northern valleys have become parched by the first heat of summer, many beautiful flowers are still to be found in deep cañon retreats, where the streams, overarched by great shadowing oaks, gush downward through leafy copses of hazelwood and thimble-berry by beds of moss and fern. Upon the walls of such charming gorges the firecracker flower rears its slender stem and shakes out its bunch of brilliant crim-

FIRECRACKER FLOWER—*Brodiæa coccinea.*

son blossoms. These are a prophetic symbol of our national holiday rather than an aid to its celebration—for they have often passed away before the Fourth of July.

GODETIA. FAREWELL TO SPRING.
HERALD OF SUMMER.

Godetia amœna, Lilja. Evening-Primrose Family.

Stems.—One to three feet high; sometimes stout. *Leaves.*—Linear to linear-lanceolate; entire; an inch or two long; distant. *Flowers.*—Often nodding in the bud. *Calyx-tube.*—Two to four lines long. *Petals.*—Deep rose-color, sometimes yellowish at base with a dark spot; nine to fifteen lines long. *Capsules.*—Smoothish; eight to eighteen lines long; its sides two-ribbed; sessile or short-pediceled. (See *Godetia.*) *Hab.*—From the Columbia River southward to Ventura.

In early summer the rosy flowers of this godetia make bright masses of color along dry banks and hill-slopes. Its blossoms are very variable as to marking. Sometimes the petals have a bright crimson blotch at the base and sometimes they are without it, both forms often occurring upon the same plant. In some seasons all the flowers are without the blotch.

G. grandiflora, Lindl., found in Humboldt and Mendocino counties, is probably the most showy species we have. The plants are a foot or two high and covered all over with the wonderful flowers, which are often four inches across. These are delicate pink, blotched with rich crimson.

G. Bottœ, Spach., is an exquisite species found in the Coast Ranges, from Monterey to San Diego. Its very slender stems lift the fragile, satiny cups above the dried grasses in charming companies. These blossoms also vary much. Among the prettiest forms is one which is pale rose or lilac, blending to white at the center, delicately striate with purple-dotted lines, and having a rich purple spot in the center. This often grows with the lilac butterfly-tulip, *Calochortus splendens,* and at a little distance is so similar it is difficult to distinguish it from the lily. But the lily rarely or never grows in throngs. The capsules of this species have pedicels from three to nine lines long.

FAREWELL TO SPRING—*Godetia amœna.*

BLEEDING-HEART.

Dicentra formosa, DC.   Bleeding-heart Family.

Leaves.—Ternately dissected, with toothed leaflets.   *Scapes.*—Six inches to two feet high.   *Flowers.*—Rose-colored to pale pink, sometimes almost white or yellowish; nodding.   (Floral structure as in *D. chrysantha.*)   *Hab.*—The Coast Ranges and Sierras, from middle California to British Columbia.

The bleeding-heart is a rather shy flower, and never makes itself common enough to dull our enthusiasm for it.   It fully merits its specific name, for it is a plant of elegant form throughout, from its shapely divided leaves to its graceful clusters of pendent hearts.   It is found in the woods of our Coast Ranges, but may be seen to best advantage when nestling amid the lush grasses of Sierra meadows.

INDIAN RHUBARB.   UMBRELLA-PLANT.

Peltiphyllum peltatum, Engler.   Saxifrage Family.

Rootstock.—Thick; creeping.   *Leaves.*—Radical; long-petioled; a foot or more across when mature; nine- to fourteen-lobed; centrally depressed.   *Scapes.*—One to three feet high.   *Calyx.*—Five-lobed.   *Petals.* —Five; roundish; three lines or more long; purplish-pink.   *Stamens.*— Ten.   *Ovaries.*—Two; distinct.   Stigmas capitate or reniform.   *Syn.*— *Saxifraga peltata,* Torr.   *Hab.*—The Sierras, from Mariposa County to Mt. Shasta; also Mendocino County.

Upon the borders of our swift-flowing mountain streams, where the water-ouzel flies up and down all day, sometimes filling the air with melody as he passes, may be seen the large lotus-like leaves of this great saxifrage.   They stand with their dark, warm stems in the water; or, poising upon the brink, they lean gracefully over it, making myriad reflections in the brown depths below, while every passing breeze awakens a quick response among them.

Early in the season, before the coming of the leaves, these plants send up tall stems with dense, branching clusters of handsome purplish-pink flowers.   The leaves, small at first, continue to grow until late summer, when they have reached their perfection; after which they begin to deepen into the richest of autumn hues.

BLEEDING–HEART—*Dicentra formosa.*

This plant is commonly called "Indian rhubarb," because the Indians are extravagantly fond of the stalks of the leaves and flowers. It is now cultivated in Eastern gardens, where it thrives in artificial ponds.

GREAT WILLOW-HERB. FIREWEED.

Epilobium spicatum, Lam. Evening-Primrose Family.

Stems.—Often four to seven feet high. *Leaves.*—Scattered; willow-like. *Flowers.*—Purplish-pink; an inch or more across. *Calyx-tube.*—Linear; limb four-parted; often colored. *Stamens.*—Eight. Anthers purplish. *Ovary.*—Four-celled. Seeds silky-tufted. *Syn.*—*E. angusti-folium,* L. *Hab.*—The Sierras; eastward to the Atlantic; also in the North Coast mountains. Found also in Europe and Asia.

This plant has received one of its English names because its leaves are like those of the willow and its seeds are furnished with silken down, like the fluff on the willow.

It is our finest and most showy species of epilobium, and is also found in the Eastern States, where it is still known by a former name—*E. angustifolium,* L. Owing to the fact that it grows with special luxuriance in spots which have been recently burned over, it is commonly known as "fireweed." It may be found in perfection in the Sierras in August, where its great spikes of large pink flowers make showy masses of color along the streams and through the meadows, commanding our warmest admiration.

In the fall the tall, pliant, widely branching stems of the "autumn willow-herb"—*E. paniculatum,* Nutt.—stand everywhere by the roadside. The small pink flowers, half an inch across, terminate the almost leafless stems, and later are replaced by the dry, curled remains of the opened capsules and the feathery down of the escaping seeds.

COMMON CATCH-FLY.

Silene Gallica, L. Pink Family.

Hairy. *Stems.*—Generally several. *Leaves.*—Spatulate; six to eighteen lines long. *Flowers.*—In terminal, one-sided racemes; four or five lines long; short-pediceled. *Petals.*— Pale rose-color or almost

GREAT WILLOW-HERB—*Epilobium spicatum.*

white; barely exceeding the calyx. (Flower structure as in *S. Californica.*)

This little weed has come to us from Europe, and it is now so widely distributed, both near the sea and inland, that it is hard to believe it is not native. The slender racemes are from two to four inches long, and the little flowers vary from white to pale pink. They can boast none of the showy beauty of their relatives, the Indian pink and the Yerba del Indio.

ALPINE HEATHER.

Bryanthus Breweri, Gray. Heath Family.

Dwarf evergreens; six inches to a foot high; woody. *Leaves.*— Alternate; linear; three to seven lines long. *Flowers.*—Purplish-rose; on glandular pedicels. *Calyx.* — Five-toothed; small. *Corolla.* — Saucer-shaped; six lines or so across. *Stamens.*—Seven to ten. Anthers two-celled; opening terminally. *Ovary.*—Five-celled. Style slender. Stigma capitate. *Hab.*—The high Sierras.

This little plant, to which Mr. Muir fondly alludes in his charming book, "The Mountains of California," may be found blooming in July and August in the Sierras. Sometimes it nestles in rocky crevices in the cool drip of the snow-banks, and again it ventures boldly out into the openings, where it spreads its rich carpet, covered with a wealth of rosy bloom. From the abundance of this little heathling about its shores, one of our mountain lakes has received the name of "Heather Lake."

PINK MONKEY-FLOWER.

Mimulus Lewisii, Pursh. Figwort Family.

Stems.—Slender; eighteen inches or so high. *Leaves.*—Sessile; oblong-ovate to lanceolate; denticulate; somewhat viscid. *Peduncles.* —Elongated. *Corolla.*—Eighteen lines to two inches long; with tube exceeding the calyx and five ample spreading ciliate lobes; rose-color or paler, with usually a darker stripe down the center of each lobe. Ridges of lower lobe yellow and spotted; bearded. *Stamens.*—Included. (See *Mimulus.*) *Hab.*—The Sierras, from central California northward and eastward to Montana.

One of the most beautiful of all our monkey-flowers is this charming species, which is found along the cold streams of the

ALPINE HEATHER—*Bryanthus Breweri.*

Sierras. Its large flowers have a fragile, delicate look, and the light stems and leaves are of an exquisite green.

I remember coming upon a delightful company of these blossoms, in a little emerald meadow upon the margin of one of those alpine lakelets which nestle among the granite crags. They seem the most fitting flowers for just such a high, pure atmosphere.

ALPINE PHLOX.

Phlox Douglasii, Hook. Phlox or Polemonium Family.

Plants forming cushion-like tufts; three or four inches high. *Leaves.*—Needle-like; six lines or less long; with shorter ones crowded in the axils. *Flowers.*—Pink, lilac, or white; sessile; terminating the branchlets. *Calyx.*—Five-cleft. *Corolla.*—Salver-form; with five-lobed border. *Stamens.*—Five; on the tube of the corolla. *Ovary.*—Three-celled. Style three-lobed. *Hab.*—The Sierras, from Mariposa County northward and eastward.

This delightful little phlox grows abundantly in the open forests of the Sierras at an altitude of from five to ten thousand feet. Its charming low mats are often over a foot in diameter, and sometimes cover the ground with their beautiful bloom. It also loves the open sunhsine of cool mountain heights, and with its cushiony tufts clothes many a bit of granite soil with beauty. There it seems undaunted by its stern surroundings and lifts its innocent eyes confidingly to the skies which bend gently over it—those skies

"So fathomless and pure, as if
All loveliest azure things have gone
To heaven that way—the flowers, the sea,—
And left their color there alone."

PRIDE OF THE MOUNTAINS.

Pentstemon Menziesii, var. *Newberryi,* Gray. Figwort Family.

Stems.—Six inches to a foot high; woody at base. *Leaves.*—Ovate, obovate, or oblong; an inch or less long; leathery. *Peduncles.*—Usually one-flowered, forming a short, glandular-pubescent raceme. *Corolla.*—Bright rose-pink; an inch long. *Anthers.*—White-woolly; with divergent cells. (See *Pentstemon.*) *Hab.*—The high Sierras of central California.

This charming pentstemon is one of the most gracious flowers to be found in the Sierras in late summer. Upon banks

ALPINE PHLOX—*Phlox Douglasii.*

overhanging the streams, or growing at great heights under the open sky, it makes many a rock-shelf gay with its brilliant pink blossoms. We wonder how it can possibly subsist upon the hard, glittering granite; but there the mystery of its life continues from day to day, and there it cheerfully produces its masses of bright flowers, which gladden the weary climber to these snowy heights.

This species of pentstemon is well marked by its white-woolly anthers, which almost fill the throat. Northward it passes into the typical *P. Menziesii,* which has flowers from violet-blue to pink-purple.

SIERRA PRIMROSE.

Primula suffrutescens, Gray. Primrose Family.

Leaves.—Wedge-shaped, an inch or so long; clustered at the ends of the branches. *Flower-stems.*—Several inches high. Umbel several-flowered. *Calyx.*—Five-cleft. *Corolla.*—Salver-shaped; an inch or less across; deep rose-color, with a yellow eye. *Stamens.*—High on the corolla-throat opposite its lobes. *Ovary.*—One-celled. Style slender. *Hab.*—The Sierras.

If one takes his alpenstock in hand and climbs to the snow-line in late summer, he is apt to be rewarded by the charming flowers of the Sierra primrose. The little plants grow in the drip of the snow-banks, where the melting ice gradually liberates the tufts of evergreen leaves. The glowing flowers look as though they might have caught and held the last rosy reflection of the sunset upon the snow above them.

ALPINE WILLOW-HERB. ROCK-FRINGE.

Epilobium obcordatum, Gray. Evening-Primrose Family.

Stems.—Decumbent; three to five inches long. *Leaves.*—Opposite; ovate; sessile; four to ten lines long. *Flowers.*—One to five; bright rose-pink; over an inch across. *Calyx.*—With linear tube and four-cleft limb. *Petals.*—Four; erect and spreading; obcordate. *Stamens.* —Eight; four shorter. Filaments slender; exserted. *Ovary.*—Linear, four-celled. Style filiform; much exserted. Stigma four-lobed. Seeds silky-tufted. *Hab.*—The Sierras, from Tulare County northward.

Though low of stature, this little willow-herb is a charming plant, with large rosy flowers. At an elevation of eight thou-

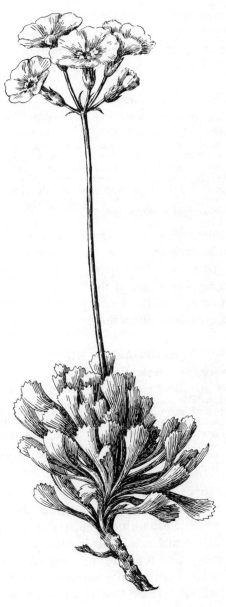

SIERRA PRIMROSE—*Primula suffrutescens.*

sand feet or more in the mountains, it nestles amid the rocks, fringing their crevices with a profusion of brilliant bloom. Though it often costs a hard climb up rocky crags to secure it, we feel well repaid by its bright beauty.

LESSINGIA.

Lessingia leptoclada, Gray.   Composite Family.

Finely white-woolly. *Stems.*—From a few inches to two feet high, with numerous, almost filiform branchlets, bearing few or solitary heads of pink or white flowers. *Lower leaves.*—Spatulate; sparingly toothed; withering early. *Upper leaves.*—Lanceolate, or linear and entire; sessile; uppermost diminished into remote, subulate bracts. *Heads.*—Five- to twenty-flowered. Of tubular disk-flowers only. Outer flowers much larger. *Involucre.*—Silky hairy; broadly campanulate; with imbricated, appressed bracts. *Hab.*—Wide-spread.

In late summer the pink lessingia is apparent along dry roadsides or embankments, where its blossoms make charming masses of soft color. It is quite abundant in the Yosemite, especially in the lower end of the valley.

L. Germanorum, Cham., found plentifully from San Diego to San Francisco, has yellow flowers.

ELEPHANTS' HEADS.

Pedicularis Grœnlandica, Retz.   Figwort Family.

Stems.—Tall and slender; smooth. *Leaves.*—Alternate; lanceolate in outline; pinnately parted into linear-lanceolate, serrate divisions; diminishing upward into the flower-bracts. *Flowers.*—Pink; in a dense spike several inches long. *Calyx.*—Five-toothed. *Corolla.*—With short tube and bilabiate limb. Upper lip with a long beak, like an elephant's trunk; lower three-lobed, deflexed. *Stamens.*—Four. Filaments and style filiform; sheathed in the beak. *Ovary.*—Two-celled. *Hab.*—The Sierras, from King's River northward; and eastward to Hudson's Bay.

No more curious flower could be found than this little denizen of our alpine meadows. Its tall pink spikes attract one from a distance, and astonish one upon nearer acquaintance by the wonderful resemblance of their blossoms to many small elephants' heads. The forehead, the long ears hanging at the sides of the head, and the long, slender, curving trunk are all perfectly simulated. These flowers have a pleasant perfume.

LESSINGIA—*Lessingia leptoclada.*

Another species—*P. attollens,* Gray—often found growing with the above, is similar to it in general structure, but its leaves are more dissected, its flower-spike is rather woolly, and its beak is only two or three lines long. These blossoms bear no resemblance to the elephant.

SPANISH CLOVER.

Hosackia Purshiana, Benth. Pea Family.

Soft-woolly throughout. *Stems.*—Erect or loosely spreading over the ground. *Leaves.*—Sessile. *Leaflets.*—One to three; ovate to lanceolate; three to nine lines long. *Flowers.*—Yellowish-pink; solitary; two or three lines long. Peduncles usually exceeding the leaves; with a single leaflet below the flower. *Calyx-teeth.*—Linear; much exceeding the tube, about equaling the corolla. *Pod.*—Narrow; twelve to eighteen lines long; five- to seven-seeded. *Hab.*—Throughout the State.

This little plant is very abundant and wide-spread. It makes its appearance after the drouth sets in, and often spreads over the ground in considerable patches. Its woolly or silky foliage has a pale cast, and its small, solitary, pinkish flowers, which are quite numerous, are not unattractive.

IV. BLUE AND PURPLE

Blue or purple or occasionally or partially blue or purple flowers not described in the Blue and Purple Section.

Described in the White Section:—

ANTIRRHINUM COULTERIANUM—Coulter's Snapdragon.
AUDIBERTIA POLYSTACHYA—White Sage.
CALOCHORTUS LUTEUS OCULATUS—Butterfly Tulip.
CALOCHORTUS VENUSTUS—Mariposa Tulip.
CASSIOPE MERTENSIANA—Cassiope.
CEANOTHUS INTEGERRIMUS—Mountain Birch; Tea-Tree; Soap-Bush.
ERIODICTYON CALIFORNICUM—Yerba Santa.
ERIODICTYON TOMENTOSUM—Yerba Santa.
LATHYRUS VESTITUS—Common Wild Pea.
MALACOTHRIX SAXATILIS.
MICROMERIA DOUGLASII—Yerba Buena.
RAPHANUS SATIVUS—Radish.
SOLANUM DOUGLASII—Nightshade.
SPHACELE CALYCINA—Pitcher-Sage.
VIOLA BECKWITHII—Mountain Heart's-ease.

Described in the Yellow Section:—

ANAGALLIS ARVENSIS—Pimpernel.
CALOCHORTUS WEEDII—Mariposa Lily, or Tulip.
HOSACKIA CRASSIFOLIA.

Described in the Pink Section:—

CONVOLVULUS SOLDANELLA—Beach Morning-glory.
DODECATHEON MEADIA—Shooting-Stars.
ERIGERON PHILADELPHICUS—Common Fleabane.
GILIA ANDROSACEA.
GILIA CALIFORNICA—Prickly Phlox.
GILIA DIANTHOIDES—Ground Pink.
PENTSTEMON MENZIESII—Pride of the Mountains.
PHLOX DOUGLASII—Alpine Phlox.

Described in the Red Section:—

AQUILEGIA CÆRULEA.

Described in the Miscellaneous Section:—

DARLINGTONIA CALIFORNICA—California Pitcher-Plant.
DIPSACUS FULLONUM—Teasel.

FETID ADDER'S-TONGUE.

Scoliopus Bigelovii, Torr.   Lily Family.

Leaves.—Two; oval-elliptical to narrowly oblanceolate; four to fifteen inches long; blotched with brown.   *Flowers.*—Three to twelve; on lax pedicels three to nine inches long.   *Sepals.*—Whitish, veined with purple; spreading.   *Petals.*—Erect; narrowly linear; wine-color without.   *Stamens.*—Three.   *Ovary.*—One-celled; three-angled.   Stigma three-lobed.   *Hab.*—The Coast Ranges from Marin to Humboldt County.

When the first white blossoms of the toothwort are making their appearance in moist woodlands, we may be sure that the fetid adder's-tongue is already pushing its shining green leaves aboveground away up in the cold cañons of north hill-slopes; and unless we hasten, we shall be too late to see its curious flowers.   I have often arrived only in time to find its fruit, which resembles a beechnut in shape.   When the flowers first open they stand erect, held in the shining chalice formed by the two sheathing green leaves.   Later the leaves open out, showing their beautiful blotched surfaces, and the three-angled flower-stems become limp and twisted.   The petals stand erect, and are so slender as to resemble three linear stigmas.   The little oval anthers are green before opening, but soon become golden with the discharging pollen.

These flowers are elegant in appearance, and suggestive of orchids; but unfortunately they have a very offensive odor, like that of the star-fishes found upon our beaches, which makes us quite content to leave them ungathered.   But the large yellow slug has no such aversion to them, and we have often seen him banqueting upon them.   Indeed, he is so fond of them that the flowers are often entirely gone from the stems.

CALIFORNIA LILAC. SOAP-BUSH.

Ceanothus divaricatus, Nutt.   Buckthorn Family.

Tall, almost arborescent shrubs; with very divergent and rigid branches.   Twigs cylindrical; smooth; mostly very pale.   *Leaves.*—Alternate; short-petioled; ovate; four to ten lines long; three-nerved; somewhat leathery.   *Flowers.*—In a narrowly oblong, dense cluster two or three inches long; pale blue to white.   *Capsule.*—Two or three

FETID ADDER'S-TONGUE—*Scoliopus Bigelovii.*

lines in diameter; not lobed; scarcely crested. (See *Ceanothus.*) *Hab.*
—Chiefly the southern Coast Ranges.

This species of California lilac is very abundant in the south,
and is specially characterized by its widely branching habit
and its round, pale-green twigs. The flowers are usually light
blue; but in some localities they are pure white. Near Santa
Barbara, in January, the mountain-slopes are often snowy with
them.

Dr. Gregg, of San Diego, while hunting one day in Lower
California, just over the border, had his attention called to the
wild lilac by his old Mexican guide, who assured him that the
blossoms in themselves were excellent soap. Taking a hand-
ful of them down to the stream, he rubbed them vigorously
between his wet hands, and found to his astonishment that they
made an excellent lather, with a pleasant fragrance of winter-
green. I have since proved the fact for myself. A more
delightful way of performing one's ablutions can hardly be
imagined than at the brookside with so charming a soap. It
is very cleansing and leaves the skin pleasantly soft.

It was probably the blossoms of *C. integerrimus* he used, as
that shrub is called "soap-bush" in that region; but I have
since tried the experiment upon *C. divaricatus* and some other
species with perfect success, from which I suspect this may be
a generic characteristic.

HOUND'S-TONGUE.

Cynoglossum grande, Dougl. Borage Family.

Stem.—Two feet or so high. *Leaves.*—Alternate; long-petioled;
ovate-oblong; pointed; usually rounded at base; often a foot long.
Flowers.—Bright blue; in a terminal panicle. *Calyx.*—Deeply five-
cleft. *Corolla.*—Rotate; with short tube and five-lobed border; having five beadlike crests in the throat. *Stamens.*—Five; on the corolla,
alternate with its lobes. *Ovary.*—Four-lobed. Style undivided. *Fruit.*
—Four prickly nutlets. *Hab.*—From Marin County to Washington.

Among the first plants to respond to the quickening influence of the early winter rains, is the hound's-tongue, whose
large, pointed leaves begin to push their way aboveground

HOUND'S-TONGUE—*Cynoglossum grande.*

usually in January. At first these are often quite velvety beneath and of a pinkish hue, and hold hidden within their midst the well-formed buds which a few warm, sunny days will call forth. The flowers, at first pink, become bright blue after fertilization has taken place.

The favorite haunts of this welcome blossom are half-shaded woods, where it rears its tall stalk in almost sole possession at this early season.

The common name is a translation of the generic name, which is derived from two Greek words, signifying *dog* and *tongue,* bestowed because of the shape of the leaves. In the olden times a superstition was rife that if a person laid the hound's-tongue beneath his feet it would prevent dogs from barking at him.

The distribution of the seed is most cunningly provided for, as the upper surfaces of the nutlets are covered with tiny barbs, which a magnifying-glass reveals to be quite perfect little anchors, admirably adapted for catching in the hair of animals.

CALIFORNIA TRILLIUM.

Trillium sessile, var. *Californicum,* Wats. Lily Family.

Rootstock.—Like a small turnip. *Stems.*—Usually several from the same root; a foot or so high. *Leaves.*—Three at the top of the stem; three to eight inches long. *Flowers.*—White to deep wine-color. *Petals.*—One to four inches long. (Otherwise as *T. ovatum.*) *Hab.*—From San Luis Obispo to Oregon.

We begin to look for the California trillium early in the spring. Little companies of the plants may be seen upon low flats under the trees, where the soil is rich. The small, turnip-like tubers usually send up several stems, which lean gracefully away from one another. The large leaves are often like pieces of decorated china that have been several times through the kiln. They have various superimposed blotchings, the latest of which are dark, sharp, cuneiform characters, mysterious hieroglyphs of Nature, which might reveal wondrous secrets, could we but decipher them. The blossoms have a strong,

CALIFORNIA TRILLIUM—*Trillium sessile*, var. *Californicum.*

heavy fragrance, and are exceedingly variable in color, ranging from pure white to lilac, deep wine, and even black-purple. These plants are much admired in the East and in Europe, where they are cultivated in the garden.

BRODIÆA. CLUSTER-LILY. WILD HYACINTH.
Brodiæa capitata, Benth. Lily Family.

Corm.—Small; scaly-coated. *Leaves.*—Linear; a foot or more long; passing away early. *Scapes.*—Four inches to over two feet high. *Flowers.*—Deep violet to white; six to ten lines long. *Bracts.*—Sometimes deep, rich purple. *Perianth.*—With oblong tube and campanulate, six-parted limb. *Stamens.*—Six; on the corolla; the inner with an appendage on each side; the outer naked. *Ovary.*—Three-celled. Style stout. Stigma three-lobed. *Hab.*—Throughout California.

This beautiful brodiæa grows all over the hills in early spring, and steals into cultivated fields, where it luxuriates in the freshly stirred soil and lifts its fine violet-colored clusters above the waving grain. It holds quite as warm a place in our affections as the more gorgeous poppy. These blossoms will keep a long time after being gathered, and are used every year in lavish profusion in the decorations of the flower carnivals.

The little bulbs, eaten raw, are quite palatable, and are eagerly sought by the children, who call them "grass-nuts." The early Spanish-Californians also appreciated them, and knew them as "saitas." They have a number of other common names, such as "Spanish lily," "cluster-lily," "wild hyacinth," and "hog-onion"; but I must protest against the injustice of this latter, and beg all flower-lovers to discountenance it.

Closely resembling the above, is *B. multiflora, Benth.* It has, however, but three stamens, the other three being represented by staminodia, which are entire and of the same length as the stamens.

B. congesta, Smith, another similar species, is often four feet tall. It also has three stamens and three staminodia; but the latter are deeply cleft and exceed the anthers. This is called "ookow" by the Indians.

268

BRODIÆA—*Brodiæa capitata.*

BROWN LILY. MISSION-BELLS. BRONZE-BELLS.
RICE-ROOT.

Fritillaria lanceolata, Pursh. Lily Family.

Stem.—A foot or two high. *Leaves.*—In scattered whorls; lance-olate; two to five inches long. *Flowers.*—One to several; open campanulate; greenish or black-purple; variously checkered or mottled. *Perianth-segments.*—Strongly arched, with a large oblong nectary. *Stamens.*—Six. *Ovary.*—Three-celled. *Hab.*—The Coast Ranges from Santa Cruz northward into Marin County.

> " 'Neath cloistered boughs each floral bell that swingeth
>
> Makes Sabbath in the fields, and ever ringeth
> A call to prayer."

One of the oddest and most beautiful flowers of our rich woodlands is the brown lily, or fritillary. It is unrivaled in elegance, for every line of its contour is a study in grace. Nor do its charms cease with stem and leaf and flower; for, hidden away in the rich leaf-mold, is one of its most beautiful features, its bulb. This is pure, shining white, conical in form, and surrounded by many tiny bulblets, like grains of rice, which crumble away from it at a touch. If you go into the woods in early spring, you will often see certain handsome, broad, shining, solitary leaves, a foot or less long, close to the ground, and you will wonder what they are. Often near them there are many tiny leaves of the same sort pushing their way aboveground; and sometimes among them all there is a solitary strong scape, with unfolding leaves and a promise of flowers. This is a colony of the beautiful brown lilies. The tiny leaves are the product of the little rice-grains, and are probably now seeing the light for the first time. Between these and the large leaves the breadth of the hand, are many sizes, in all stages. The broad leaves may be from bulbs four or five years old, but they will send up no blossom-stalk this year; for there is rarely or never a radical leaf and a blossom-stalk from the same bulb at once.

When the plant is about to flower, the bulb sends up a tall stalk, with here and there a whorl of shining leaves, hanging at

BROWN LILY—*Fritillaria lanceolata.*

the summit its string of pendent bronze-bells. These are mottled and checkered, and are of varying shades, from dull green to black-purple, and often have a beautiful bloom upon them. Their modest colors blend so nicely into the shadowy scene about, that it is difficult to see them unless the eye is somewhat practiced.

Following the inflorescence comes a beautiful and unique seed-vessel, curiously winged and angled, and of a delicate, papery texture when mature. It contains the thin, flat seeds, neatly packed in six ranks.

The flowers are usually an inch long, though they are sometimes two inches long. A plant was once found three and a half feet high, with a chime of nineteen bells.

BLACK LILY. CHOCOLATE-LILY.
Fritillaria biflora, Lindl. Lily Family.
Hab.—The Coast Ranges, from San Diego to Mendocino County.

We have a number of species of *Fritillaria,* most of them with beautiful flowers. They fall naturally into two groups, according to the character of the bulb; *F. lanceolata* and *F. biflora* being types of the two groups.

F. biflora, the black, or chocolate, lily, is the species common in the south, and blooms early. It closely resembles *F. lanceolata,* but can always be distinguished by its bulb, which is composed of several erect, short, easily separable scales. Its specific name is an unfortunate one; for, far from being confined to two flowers, it often has as many as ten.

F. pluriflora, Torr., the pink fritillary, found upon the upper Sacramento, has flowers of a uniform reddish-purple, without mottling or spots. It has a comparatively large bulb, an inch or so long, formed of separate scales, which often has below it a fleshy tap-root.

F. pudica, Spreng., found on the eastern slopes of the Sierras, has solitary yellow flowers.

F. liliacea, Lindl., is our only white species. This is found upon the hills of San Francisco, at Mare Island, at Point Richmond, and in the Sacramento Valley. It has a whorl of leaves near the ground and two or three greenish-white, nodding flowers. It is exceedingly local.

LARGE-FLOWERED PHACELIA.

Phacelia grandiflora, Gray. Baby-eyes or Waterleaf Family.

Coarse, glandular-viscid plants; one to three feet high. *Leaves.*—Round-ovate; irregularly toothed; sometimes three or four inches long. *Flowers.*—Lavender to white; variously streaked and veined with purple. *Corolla.*—Rotate; two inches across; without scalelike appendages in the throat. *Filaments.*—Long; purple. Anthers large; versatile. Style two-cleft. (See *Phacelia.*) *Hab.*—From Santa Barbara to San Diego.

This is the largest-flowered of all our phacelias. Its tall stems are abundantly covered above with the fine-looking blossoms. These are very attractive to the uninitiated, who usually rushes forward in breathless haste to possess himself of these new-found treasures and is rarely satisfied with less than a large bunch of them. But woe lies in wait for him. The innumerable glands, covering the whole plant, readily yield up their viscid fluid, which in a few moments turns everything with which it comes in contact to a deep red-brown, like iron-rust. If he escape with ruined clothing and hands the color of a red Indian, he will have come off well—for the plant poisons some people.

Another species—*P. viscida,* Torr.—found in about the same range as the above, resembles it closely. It is a foot or so high, branching from the base, and has blue flowers with purple or white centers, and only half the size of the above.

GREEN-BANDED MARIPOSA. NOONA.

Calochortus macrocarpus, Dougl. Lily Family.

Hab.—Sandy deserts of northeastern California to eastern Washington and into Idaho.

Nature has sent this, one of the finest and most elegant of all our mariposas, to beautify the arid sagebrush deserts of our northeastern boundary. In Europe it is admired beyond all our other species, and there is a great demand for the bulbs. Its large flowers are of a beautiful lilac, similar in tone to the Marie Louise violet, and each pointed petal has a green band running down its center.

Among the Indians of their native region the rather large bulbs of these plants are known as "noonas," and regarded as a priceless delicacy. Even those who have never experienced the bliss of tasting them know them by reputation as the acme of all that is delicious. When Mr. Johnson, of Astoria, wished to secure a number of the bulbs for the European market, he hired the squaws to dig them, but found that they ate them as fast as they dug them; and it was only by offering them most liberal stores of bacon and flour he could induce them to restrain their appetites and part with the treasure.

VIOLET NIGHTSHADE.

Solanum Xanti, Gray.   Nightshade Family.

Herbaceous nearly to the base; viscid-pubescent, with jointed hairs. *Stems.*—Several feet high.   *Leaves.*—Two inches or less long; sometimes with lobes at the base; thin.   *Flowers.*—An inch or so across. *Calyx.*—Five-parted.   *Corolla.*—Violet, with green spots ringed with white at the base.   *Stamens.*—Five.   Filaments short.   Anthers erect; opening terminally.   *Ovary.*—Two-celled.   Style filiform; exserted. *Berries.*—Purple; six lines in diameter.   *Hab.*—Southern California, northward to Santa Barbara, and occasional in the Sierras.

These plants are especially abundant in the south, where one encounters them upon every roadside. The clusters of violet flowers are very handsome, and often have the perfume of the wild rose.

Another species—*S. umbelliferum,* Esch.—is so nearly like the above as to be often confounded with it. But it has smaller, thicker leaves, the hairs are branched, and it is more woody below, with shorter flowering branches.

We once saw, in an ideal Japanese villa among the redwoods, a rustic arbor over which had been trained the rough, woody stems of one of these nightshades. The genius of these wise little people, who had adapted this pretty woodland

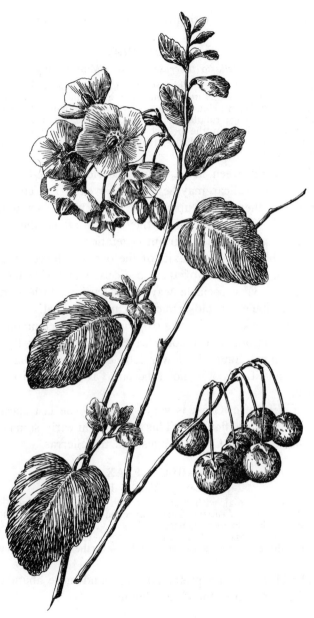

VIOLET NIGHTSHADE—*Solanum Xanti.*

climber to sylvan cultivation, seemed to us worthy of emulation.

SKULLCAP.

Scutellaria tuberosa, Benth. Mint Family.

Stems.—Several inches high, or at length trailing, and a foot long; from small tubers. *Leaves.*—One inch long and less; not aromatic. *Flowers.* — Axillary; blue-purple. *Calyx.* — Bilabiate. *Corolla.* — Six lines or more long; tubular; bilabiate. *Stamens.*—Four; in pairs; ascending; contained in the helmet. *Ovary.*—Of four seedlike nutlets. Style filiform. *Hab.*—Hillsides, from San Diego northward; probably throughout the State.

The bright-green herbage and the rich purple-blue flowers of the little skullcap may be looked for early in February. In the north they grow upon dry, stony hill-slopes under the chaparral, while southward they often affect the walls of cañons, among moist, luxuriant vegetation.

Though borne in the axils of the opposite leaves, the pretty blossoms, by a twist of their pedicels, stand side by side in pairs, in a very sociable way. The curious little two-lipped calyx resembles an old-fashioned Quaker bonnet.

Another species—*S. angustifolia,* Pursh.—common in the Sierras, has linear to oblong leaves, an inch long; flowers an inch or more long, the lower lobe of whose corolla is hairy within, and the root is not tuberous. It is otherwise like the above.

S. Californica, Gray, is very similar to the last species, but has cream-white flowers. This is found in early summer upon dry banks in the Coast Ranges and the Sierras.

BLUE FLAX.

Linum Lewisii, Pursh. Flax Family.

Smooth, perennial, with stems twelve to thirty inches high; leafy below, lax above. *Leaves.*—Linear-lanceolate; five to nine lines long. *Flowers.*—Blue; in loose clusters. *Sepals.*—Five; small. *Corolla.*—Six to nine lines across. *Petals.*—Five. *Ovary.*—Ten-celled. *Styles.*—Five. Capsule three or four lines long. *Hab.*—Northern Coast Ranges, and the Sierras.

The blue flax is a pretty flower, found more abundantly in the Sierras than in the Coast Ranges.

SKULLCAP—*Scutellaria tuberosa.*

CORAL-ROOT.

Corallorhiza Bigelovii, Wats.   Orchis Family.

Leafless plants, with coral-like roots. *Scapes.*—Flesh-colored; six to twenty-four inches high, with two to four scarious, sheathing bracts. *Flowers.*—Few to many; sessile. *Perianth.*—Of six segments.   The five upper yellowish, striped with purple. The lip yellowish, tipped with deep red-purple. *Anther.*—One; resting upon the column like a lid; falling early. *Ovary.*—One-celled. *Hab.*—Central and northern Coast Ranges and Sierras.

The coral-root is very rare in some localities, and one may not meet it more than a few times. But there are favored spots where its flesh-colored stems rear themselves luxuriantly. One year I saw a magnificent bunch of them being taken to San Francisco to furnish a rare and costly decoration for some festive occasion. Some of the stems were two feet tall and thickly covered above with the odd flowers, making a cluster which it would be difficult to equal for quiet elegance of coloring.

The plants are often found in redwood groves or upon wooded hill-slopes of north exposure, where the dull stems and flowers blend so nicely into the dead needles and leaves upon the ground that it is difficult to detect their presence.

As its name indicates, the root is the counterpart of a spray of branching coral.

Another species—*C. multiflora,* Nutt.—has stems of a colder purple; and the lip of the flower is white, spotted with purple, somewhat fan-shaped and three-lobed.

JACOB'S LADDER.   GREEK VALERIAN.

Polemonium carneum, Gray.   Phlox or Polemonium Family.

Stems.—One to two feet; lax; diffusely branching. *Leaves.*—Alternate; pinnate. *Leaflets.*—Sessile; thin; seven to seventeen; ovate to ovate-lanceolate; twelve to fifteen lines long. *Flowers.*—Loosely clustered on slender pedicels. *Calyx.*—Campanulate; five-cleft; four lines long, increasing in size with age. *Corolla.* — Broadly funnel-form; salmon-color to purple; eight to twelve lines long; the limb as broad expanded. *Stamens.*—Five, on the corolla, included. *Ovary.*—Three-celled. Style three-cleft. *Fruit.*—A capsule. *Hab.*—Coast Ranges, from Marin County to Siskiyou County.

This beautiful flower is found in the woods of our Coast

CORAL-ROOT—*Corallorhiza Bigelovii.*

Ranges in April and May. It is rather rare and quite variable, as its flowers range from salmon-color to purple.

Polemonium cæruleum, Linn., is said to be found in the high Sierras. This has tall stems, and the corolla varies from bright blue to white.

CALIFORNIA LILAC. BLUE MYRTLE. BLUE-BLOSSOM.

Ceanothus thyrsiflorus, Esch.   Buckthorn Family.

Varying from small, prostrate shrubs in exposed places, to erect shrubs or small trees. *Branches.*—Strongly angled; not spiny. *Leaves.*—Elliptical; twelve to eighteen lines long; three-nerved; smooth and shining above. *Flowers.*—Bright to pale blue, rarely white; in dense clusters about three inches long, terminating the usually elongated, somewhat leafy peduncles. *Capsules.*—Globose; two lines in diameter; smooth, not crested; slightly lobed. (See *Ceanothus.*)   *Hab.*—Near the coast, from Monterey northward into Oregon.

In the spring our chaparral-covered slopes begin to take on a bluish tinge, like the misty smoke of distant camp-fires, for which the blossoms of the California lilac are responsible. This is a graceful evergreen shrub, with rich, shining leaves, among which the abundant feathery clusters of tiny blue flowers find a charming setting. The blossoms are deliciously fragrant, filling the cool air with perfume.

This shrub is never found far away from the coast, and it reaches its greatest beauty in Mendocino County, where it becomes a tree, sometimes thirty-five feet high. Its wood is exceedingly brittle. In early days it used to be cultivated in San Francisco gardens before it was crowded out by foreign shrubs, often far less worthy.

It is known in some localities as "blue myrtle," and in others as "blue-blossom." The name "California lilac," by which it is most often known, is more generally and more appropriately applied to this species of ceanothus than to any of the others.

The dark seeds are a favorite food of the quail.

CALIFORNIA LILAC—*Ceanothus thyrsiflorus.*

BLUE LARKSPUR. ESPUELA DEL CABALLERO.
Delphinium, Tourn. Buttercup or Crowfoot Family.

California is rich in beautiful larkspurs, but the species are very difficult of determination and not well defined as yet. We have two well-marked scarlet species; but confusion still reigns among the blue and the white. Some of the latter are poisonous to sheep and cattle, causing great losses to the herds every year in some localities.

Among the blue larkspurs are some of our handsomest spring flowers. Their slender wands, covered with magnificent large blossoms, rise abundantly on every side upon some of the mesas of our seashore, making charming flower-gardens upon the plains. They are so lavishly bestowed that every comer may gather his fill and still none be missed. In color they are matchless—of the richest of Mazarin blue and purple-blue.

Other species are to be found upon the slopes of interior valleys and scattered all through the Coast Ranges and the Sierra foothills. In midsummer, which is the vernal springtime of the mountains, many lovely species deck the alpine meadows and brooksides.

The Spanish-Californians have a pretty title for these blossoms—"espuela del caballero"—"the cavalier's spur."

PURPLE NEMOPHILA.
Nemophila aurita, Lindl. Baby-eyes or Waterleaf Family.

Stems.—One to three feet long; square; angled; weak; very brittle; with backward-pointing, hooked bristles. *Leaves.*—All with a dilated, clasping, eared base or winged petiole; above deeply pinnatifid into five to nine oblong or lanceolate, downward-pointing lobes. *Corolla.*— Violet; an inch or so across. (Otherwise as *Nemophila insignis.*) *Hab.*—From San Francisco to San Diego.

The purple nemophila is most abundant in the south, growing everywhere in early springtime upon hillsides partially shaded. Its long, coarse, hispid stems run riot over small undershrubs or dead or unsightly brushwood, often completely

BLUE LARKSPUR—*Delphinium.*

covering them with a mound of foliage thickly sown with the dull-purple flowers.

At first it is difficult to realize that this plant of coarse habit belongs to the sisterhood of baby-eyes, those delicate, ethereal favorites of the springtime. In fact, one's first impression of it is that it is some new species of nightshade. One learns, however, to have a fondness for these blossoms and a growing desire to gather them; but their tangling, quarrelsome habit forbids one, if any other flowers are in question.

It is said that the dark-eyed señoritas of early days decked their ball-dresses with sprays of this flower, which clung gracefully to the thin fabrics.

CAT'S-EARS. PUSSY'S-EARS.

Calochortus Maweanus, Leicht. Lily Family.

Hab.—The Coast Ranges from San Francisco Bay northward into Oregon.

This is an exceedingly pretty little calochortus, much resembling *C. Benthami* in form, but having pure-white or purplish-blue flowers, which are also covered with hairs and delicately fringed with hairs on the margin. Its stems are low, slender, and graceful, without bulblets at the base; its petals are six to eight lines long; and the gland upon the petals has a transverse scale covering its upper portion.

This plant belongs to the section of *Calochortus* whose species are known as "star-tulips." In the Coast Ranges, in early spring, the blossoms are found in moist meadows near the sea, where they nestle amid the grasses.

The children are especially fond of them, and know them as "cat's-ears" and "pussy's-ears."

C. uniflorus, Hook. and Arn., found in wet meadows from Monterey northward, has lilac to rose-purple flowers. Its petals are hairy on the lower third, and its stems bear small bulblets at the base underground.

C. umbellatus, Wood., is very similar to *C. Maweanus;*

CAT'S-EARS—*Calochortus Maweanus.*

but its pure-white petals are almost without hairs, and its stem is without bulblets. This is found blooming in March and April on the low mountains of Contra Costa and Marin counties.

GROUND-IRIS.

Iris macrosiphon, Torr.   Iris Family.

Almost stemless plants, often forming mats. *Rhizome.*—Slender. *Radical leaves.*—Grasslike; six to fifteen inches long. *Buds.*—One or two; borne in sheathing bracts. *Flowers.*—On short pedicels; deep purple-blue, marked with white. *Perianth.*—With slender tube one to three inches long. *Stamens.*—Three; borne under the petaloid divisions of the style. *Ovary.*—Three-celled. *Capsule.*—Oblong-ovoid; shortly acute at each end; one inch long. Seeds in two rows in each cell; compressed and angled. *Hab.*—The Coast Ranges, from San Mateo to Trinity County.

When spring is at its height, this charming little iris may be found upon sunny, open hillsides among the unrolling crosiers of the common brake. There is something peculiarly captivating about these blossoms, with their satisfying richness of hue and perfect symmetry of form, added to which is a sweet, delicate perfume, an ideal exhalation of the springtime.

As the buds unfold beautifully in water, it is better to gather buds than flowers, as the latter are too fragile to carry without breaking.

I. longipetala, Herb., is the common bog-iris of our central coast. It grows in large clumps in wet places, and while not a delicate flower, it has a certain brave, hardy look as it stands out upon the wind-swept mesas of the Coast. Its stems are rather stout, a foot or two high, and have from three to five large lilac flowers. The sepals are veined with deeper lilac and blotched with orange.

TOAD-FLAX.

Linaria Canadensis, Dumont.   Figwort Family.

Stems.—Slender; six inches to two feet high. *Leaves.*—Mostly alternate on the flowering stems, but smaller and broader ones often opposite or whorled on the procumbent shoots; linear; smooth. *Flowers.*—Blue; in terminal racemes; like those of antirrhinum, but

GROUND-IRIS—*Iris macrosiphon.*

the tube furnished with a long, downward-pointing spur at base. *Hab.*
—Throughout California.

The delicate blue flowers of the toad-flax are not uncommon in spring, and the plants are usually found in sandy soil. The little blossoms are very ethereal and have a sweet perfume. I once saw a deep-blue band upon a mesa near San Diego which vied in richness with the ultramarine of the sea just beyond. It stretched for some distance, and at last curved around and crossed the road over which I was passing, when it proved to be made up of millions of these delicate flowers. The color effect seemed cumulative, for the mass was so much richer and deeper than the individual flowers.

WILD HELIOTROPE. VERVENIA.

Phacelia ramosissima, Dougl. Baby-eyes or Waterleaf Family.

Divergently branching, straggly herbs; rough and hairy. *Leaves.*—Pinnately divided. *Flowers.*—Bright violet-blue; in clustered, scorpioid racemes. *Calyx-lobes.* — Linear-spatulate to obovate. *Corolla.* — Six lines long. *Style.*—Two-cleft. *Ovary.*—One-celled. *Hab.*—Throughout the western part of the State.

The wild heliotrope is one of the most abundant flowers of midspring, especially in the south. It affects the gravelly banks of streams or the sandy soil of mesas; or grows all along the railroad embankments, making great mounds of foliage, thickly sown with the bright violet-blue blossoms; or it may often be seen clambering up through small shrubs, seeming to seek the support of their stiff branches. It is needless to say that this is not a true heliotrope, but belongs to the closely allied genus, *Phacelia.* Among the Spanish-Californians it is known as "vervenia."

It is a very important honey-plant.

P. Douglasii, Torr., is a species with lavender corolla with much the aspect of the baby-blue-eyes. This is common in the western part of the State, south of Monterey, and is found sparingly north of that point.

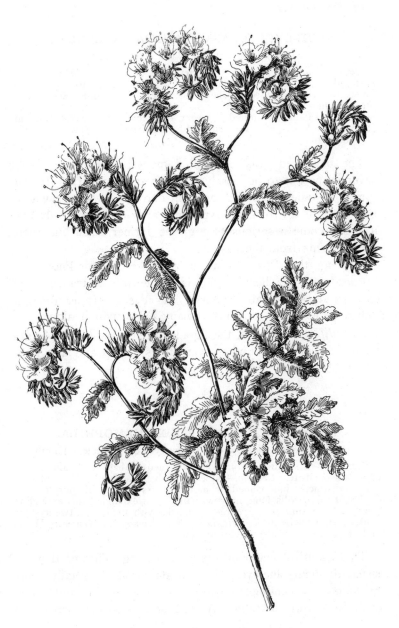

WILD HELIOTROPE — *Phacelia ramosissima.*

BLUE-EYED GRASS. AZULEA. VILLELA.

Sisyrinchium bellum, Wats. Iris Family.

Leaves.—Radical; grasslike; shorter than the stems. *Stems.*—Flat; clustered; six to eighteen inches high. *Flowers.*—Four to seven; contained in two nearly equal sheathing bracts. *Perianth.*—Six-parted; purplish-blue, with yellow center; six lines to an inch across. *Stamens.* —Three. Filaments united. *Ovary.*—Three-celled. Style filiform. Stigma spindle-shaped; three-cleft after fertilization. *Hab.*—Throughout California.

The blue-eyed grass is such a modest flower one would never suspect it to be closely allied to the regal iris. In late spring its quiet stars are found in our meadows everywhere. In the south it grows so luxuriantly and so determinedly that it has become a serious pest to the farmer, crowding more useful plants from the pasture.

Among the Spanish-Californians the plant is known as "azulea" and "villela," and is made into a tea which is considered a valuable remedy in fevers. It is thought that a patient can subsist for many days upon it alone.

S. Californicum, Ait., the "golden-eyed grass," with bright yellow flowers, is found in wet places all up and down the Coast, also in the Sierras.

BABY-EYES. BLUE-VEINED NEMOPHILA.

Nemophila intermedia, Bioletti. Baby-eyes or Waterleaf Family.

Leaves.—With petioles somewhat widened at base and ciliate; the upper all opposite. *Corolla.*—Nine to twelve lines wide; light blue to white; distinctly blue-veined or more or less sown with purple dots. Scales of the corolla long, narrow, hairy, with expanded tips extending nearly to the sinuses. *Ovary.*—Rounded; with twelve to twenty-four ovules. (Otherwise as *N. insignis.*) *Syn.*—*Nemophila Menziesii,* Hook. and Arn. *Hab.*—Rather wide-spread.

This beautiful nemophila is a more fragile flower than its sister, the baby-blue-eyes. Its delicate corolla is usually white in the center, blending to azure-blue upon the rim, and dotted and veined with the same. At its best, it is an inch across. It

BLUE–EYED GRASS—*Sisyrinchium bellum.*

affects the borders of moist woodlands, rarely venturing far out into the openings. There it nestles amid the tender herbage, often producing its ethereal flowers in such profusion that it seems as though bits of the sky had fallen to earth. In the south these blossoms do not seem so truly at home—for they are never so large nor so fine.

CALIFORNIA MILKWORT.

Polygala Californica, Nutt. Milkwort Family.

Stems.—Two to eight inches high. *Leaves.*—Six to twelve lines long. *Flowers.*—Rose-purple. *Sepals.*—Five; two of them large and spreading like wings; six lines or less long. *Petals.*—Three; united to each other and to the stamen-tube; the middle one hooded above and beaked. *Stamens.*—Eight. Filaments united into a sheath, which is open above. Anthers one-celled; opening terminally. *Ovary.*—Two-celled. Style enlarging upward; curved like a button-hook. *Pod.*—Rounded; flat; three or four lines across. *Syn.*—*P. cucullata,* Benth. *Hab.*—The Coast Ranges southward to Santa Barbara and beyond.

In late spring the little flowers of the milkwort are common upon dry hill-slopes in the shade of the trees. The small plants have a very grown-up look, as though their age might be greater than indicated by their stature. At first glance one is quite certain to mistake these plants for members of the Pea family, as the blossoms have wings and a keel like the papilionaceous flower. But a careful counting of sepals, petals, and stamens will reveal their separate identity.

A curious feature of this plant is the fact that it bears another kind of flower near the root. This is without petals, and is destined, for some strange reason, to bear the seed. The upper flowers seem mostly for show, though one does occasionally mature fruit.

P. cornuta, Kell., found in the Sierras, is a larger plant, with greenish-white flowers.

BIRD'S-EYES.

Gilia tricolor, Benth. Phlox or Polemonium Family.

Stems.—Slender; branching; six inches to a foot or more high. *Leaves.*—Twice pinnately parted into narrow linear lobes. *Corolla.*—Six lines long; with yellow tube; funnel-form throat, marked with deep

CALIFORNIA MILKWORT—*Polygala Californica.*

violet-purple; and lilac or white limb. (See *Gilia.*) *Hab.*—Throughout western California.

Whole slopes are often carpeted with this dainty gilia, producing an effect which has been described as like light chinchilla. The little blossoms have a peculiarly fresh and winsome look, and are called "bird's-eyes" by the children. The corollas are delicate lilac, blending into white toward the center, while the throat has five purple spots within, which give way to bright gold below.

WILD CANTERBURY-BELL.

Phacelia Whitlavia, Gray. Baby-eyes or Waterleaf Family.

A foot or so high; very hairy and glandular. *Leaves.*—Alternate; petioled; ovate or deltoid; toothed; twelve to eighteen lines long. *Flowers.* –Purple. *Calyx.*—Five-parted. *Corolla.*—An inch or more long. *Stamens.*—Five; on the base of the corolla; appendaged at base; long-exserted, with the two-cleft style. *Ovary.*—Two-celled. *Syn.*—*Whitlavia grandiflora,* Harv. *Hab.*—From Los Angeles to San Bernardino.

The wild Canterbury-bell is one of the most charming flowers to be found anywhere. It affects the rich soil of half-shaded hill-slopes in the vicinity of streams, where it opens its beautiful fragile bells. Its stems are very brittle, and the blossoms fall early, the lower ones usually having passed away before the upper buds have emerged from the coil. The exceedingly long stamens and style give these blossoms an elegant, airy look.

P. Parryi, Torr., is another beautiful species, found from Los Angeles to San Diego. It resembles the above in foliage, color of blossoms, and the long stamens; but the form of the flowers is that of the nemophila.

LILAC SAND-VERBENA. WILD LANTANA.

Abronia villosa, Wats. Four-o'clock Family.

Plants with more or less glandular-villous pubescence. *Stems.*—Prostrate. *Leaves.*—Rarely an inch long. *Peduncles.*—One to three inches long; five- to fifteen-flowered. *Involucral bracts.*—Lanceolate; three or four lines long. *Perianth.*—Lilac; four or five lines across;

WILD CANTERBURY-BELL—*Phacelia Whitlavia.*

with obcordate lobes. (Otherwise as *A. latifolia.*) *Hab.*—San Diego and eastward; also in southern deserts.

The charming flowers of the lilac sand-verbena are not found upon the immediate sea-beach, but always a little withdrawn from it, where the soil is more firmly established, yet within sight and sound of the waves. The blossoms have a delicate beauty, not shared by our other species of *Abronia,* and somewhat resemble our garden verbenas. They are sometimes called "wild lantana."

A. umbellata, Lam., is common all up and down our coast, often making masses of deep pink on the beach; while *A. maritima,* Nutt, is found from Santa Barbara to San Diego. The latter is a very stout, coarse, viscid plant, with small, very deep magenta flowers.

BABY-BLUE-EYES.   CALIFORNIA BLUEBELLS.
MARIANAS.

Nemophila insignis, Dougl.   Baby-eyes or Waterleaf Family.

Tender, more or less hairy herbs. *Stems.*—Branching; six to twelve inches long. *Leaves.*—Pinnately parted into five to nine small, oblong, entire or two- to five-lobed divisions. *Calyx.*—Five-parted, with five extra, alternating, reflexed lobes. *Corolla.*—An inch or more across; from azure-blue, with a large, well-defined white center, more or less dotted, to deep blue. The throat furnished with ten short, wide, hairy scales, or plates. *Stamens.*—Five; on the corolla. *Ovary.*—One-celled. Style two-cleft. *Hab.*—Throughout California.

When skies are smiling and the earth is already clothed with a luxuriant and tender herbage, we find upon some balmy morning that the baby-eyes have opened in gentle surprise upon the lovely world. The spring breezes blow over no more beautiful and ethereal flowers than these. Companies of them open together, dotting the sward and luring us on from one to another, the one just beyond always seeming a little brighter blue or a little more captivating than those near at hand, till we are beguiled into filling our hands with them.

These delicate blossoms vary greatly in size and color. The largest and finest I ever saw grew upon the flower-sprinkled

BABY–BLUE–EYES—*Nemophila insignis.*

slopes of Lake Merced, near San Francisco. There the perfect azure corollas were an inch and a half across, with the large white circle in the center well defined.

Under southern skies it becomes a deep Yale blue, with the texture of tissue-paper, and with dark red-brown anthers.

From the campanulate, half-opened buds, it has been called "California bluebell," and among the Spanish-Californians it is known as "Mariana."

INNOCENCE. COLLINSIA.
Collinsia bicolor, Benth. Figwort Family.

Stems.—A foot or so high. *Leaves.*—The lower oblong; the upper ovate-lanceolate. *Calyx.*—Unequally five-cleft. *Corolla.*—Nine lines long. Upper lip lilac or white; lower of three lobes; the middle folded into a keeled sac containing the stamens and style; the two lateral rose-purple. *Stamens.*—Four; in two pairs on the corolla. Upper filaments bearded. *Ovary.* — Two-celled. Style filiform. *Hab.*— Throughout western California.

Where spreading trees cast a dense shade and the moisture still lingers, companies of lovely collinsias stand amid the fresh green grasses, their delicate, many-storied blossoms swaying upon the idle breezes. In the north these are in the rear guard of spring flowers, and make their appearance just before the godetias bid farewell to spring; but in the south they come earlier. They vary much in color, from the typical rose-purple and white or lilac to all white.

We have a number of species; but *C. bicolor* is the most showy and wide-spread. A white-flowered species, *C. tinctoria,* Hartweg, is very beautiful and abundant in the Yosemite Valley. It has a glandular pubescence that stains the fingers.

CAMASS. KAMASS. WILD HYACINTH.
Camassia esculenta, Lindl. Lily Family.

Bulbs coated. *Leaves.*—Radical; six or eight; grasslike; three to eight lines broad; usually shorter than the scape. *Scape.*—Twelve to twenty-four inches high; loosely ten- to twenty-flowered. Pedicels three to twelve lines long. *Flowers.*—From dark blue to nearly white; seven to fifteen lines long or more; an inch or so across. *Perianth.*— Of six distinct, oblanceolate, three- to seven-nerved segments. *Stamens.*

COLLINSIA—*Collinsia bicolor.*

—Six; shorter than the segments. Anthers yellow. *Ovary.*—Three-celled. Style filiform; about equaling the perianth; slightly three-cleft at the summit. *Hab.*—Wet meadows and marshes, from central California to Washington.

In some localities these plants are found covering meadows and marshy tracts in great profusion. They bear beautiful clusters of showy blue flowers, somewhat like the hyacinth in habit, and have long been favorites in European gardens. We are especially interested in them, however, on account of the bulbs, which are about an inch in diameter and very nutritious. Grizzly bears, when more plentiful in the early days, were particularly fond of them; and the northern Indians to-day value them very highly as an article of diet, calling them "kamáss." Indeed, the Nez Percé Indian war in Idaho was caused by encroachments upon the territory which was especially rich in these bulbs. The plants are more abundant north of us than with us.

Mr. Macoun gives a most interesting account in "Garden and Forest" of the preparation of kamáss among the Indians, which is a very important and elaborate performance. He says, in substance:—For some days beforehand the squaws were busily engaged in carrying into camp branches of alder and maple, bundles of skunk-cabbage (*Lysichiton*), and a quantity of a black, hairlike lichen, which grows in profusion upon the western larch. A hole ten feet square and two feet deep was then dug, and a large fire was made in this, in which they heated a great many small boulders to the glowing point. They then piled maple and alder boughs over these to the depth of a foot or more, tramped them down, and laid over them the leaves of the skunk-cabbage. Thin sheets of tamarack bark were spread over the steaming green mass, and upon these were placed the bulbs in large baskets. The black lichen was laid over the uncovered bark, and the remaining bulbs were spread on this. The whole was then covered with boughs and leaves as before, and sand was sprinkled on to the depth of four or five inches, and on the top of the whole a larger fire than before was built. The sun was just setting when this was lighted, and it burned all night. The oven was left for a day to cool. When opened, the bulbs in the baskets were dissolved to a flour, from which bread could be made; while those on the lichen had become amalgamated with it, forming a substance resembling plug-tobacco, which could be broken up and kept sweet a long time.

When boiled in water, the bulbs yield a very good molasses, much prized by the Indians, and used by them upon important festival occasions.

There is a white-flowered form of this same species, whose bulb is said to be poisonous.

DOUGLAS IRIS.
Iris Douglasiana, Herb. Iris Family.

Rhizomes.—Stoutish; clumps not dense. *Radical leaves.*—Strongly ribbed underneath; dark, shining green above; one to three feet long; three to eight lines broad; flexile; rosy pink at base. *Stems.*—Simple; two- or three-flowered. *Flowers.*—On pedicels six to eighteen lines long; deep reddish-purple, lilac, or cream. *Perianth-tube.*—Six to twelve lines long. *Capsule.*—Narrowly oblong; acutely triangular; twenty lines long. Seeds nearly globular. (Otherwise as *I. macrosiphon.*) *Hab.*—The coast, from Santa Cruz to Marin County.

On account of the bright and varied hues of its flowers, the genus *Iris* was named for the rainbow-winged messenger of the gods. In France it is known as "fleur-de-lis," a name whose origin has caused endless discussion and has been accounted for in many ways. There are many species, all of them beautiful. Orris-root is the product of the lovely white Florentine iris.

In California we have several comparatively well-known species, and a number of others which are without names as yet; but the Douglas iris is probably our most beautiful. It thrives well upon open mesas or upon well-drained hill-slopes in the shelter of the chaparral. But it is found at its best in the rich soil of moist woodlands, whose seclusion seems the most fitting abode for so aristocratic a flower. There, surrounded by the delicate greenery of fern-fronds and a hundred other tender, springing things, it seems to hold a sylvan court, receiving homage from all the other denizens of the wood. There is a certain marked and personal individuality about these flowers which makes encountering them seem like meeting certain distinguished personages. In the shade of deep woods the flowers are usually cream-white, while in open chaparral or on grassy slopes they are more apt to be lilac.

CHIA. SAGE.

Salvia Columbariæ, Benth. Mint Family.

Stems.—Six inches to two feet high. *Leaves.*—Wrinkly; one to several inches long. *Flowers.*—Blue; in interrupted whorls. *Whorls.*— Twelve to eighteen lines in diameter; subtended by numerous, ovate-acuminate bracts. *Calyx.*—Bilabiate; upper lip arching, and tipped with two short bristles; lower, of two awnlike teeth. *Corolla.*—Three or four lines long; bilabiate. Upper lip erect; notched or two-lobed. Lower deflexed; with three lobes, the central much larger. *Stamens.*— Two. Filaments two; short; apparently forked—*i. e.* bearing on their summit a cross-bar having on one end a perfect anther-cell and on the other a dwarfed or rudimentary one. *Ovary.*—Of four seedlike nutlets. Style slender. *Hab.*—Throughout the State, especially southward.

This rough-leaved sage is quite common, especially southward, and grows upon dry hillsides or in sandy washes, where it blossoms in early spring. Its small bright-blue flowers are borne in an interrupted spike, consisting of from one to four button-like heads. Each of these heads has below it a number of leafy bracts, which are often of a bright wine-color, and form a rather striking contrast to the blue flowers.

After the blossoms have passed away, the dried stems and heads remain standing all over the hills, shaking out the little gray seed in abundance. These seeds have been for centuries an article of economic importance to the aborigines and their descendants. Dr. Rothrock writes that among the Nahua races of ancient Mexico the plant was cultivated as regularly as corn, and was one of their most important cereals. Quantities of the seed have been found buried beneath groves which

CHIA—*Salvia Columbariæ.*

must be at least several hundred years old. It was in use among the Indians of California before the occupation of the country by the whites, being known among them as "chia."

Dr. Bard writes of these seeds:—"They were roasted, ground, and used as food by being mixed with water. Thus prepared, it soon develops into a mucilaginous mass, larger than its original bulk. Its taste is somewhat like that of linseed meal. It is exceedingly nutritious, and was readily borne by the stomach when that organ refused to tolerate other aliment. An atole, or gruel, of this was one of the peace-offerings to the first visiting sailors. One tablespoonful of these seeds was sufficient to sustain for twenty-four hours an Indian on a forced march. Chia was no less prized by the native Californian, and at this late date it frequently commands six or eight dollars a pound."

When added to water, the seeds make a cooling drink, which assuages burning thirst—a very valuable quality on the desert.

BLUE GILIA.

Gilia achilleæfolia, Benth. Phlox or Polemonium Family.

Stems.—Stoutish; a foot or more high. *Leaves.*—Alternate; dissected into linear segments. *Flowers.*—In capitate clusters an inch and a half across; deep to lighter blue. *Calyx.*—Five-toothed. *Corolla.*—Four lines long; broadly funnel-form, with obtuse lobes. *Stamens.*—Exserted. Anthers nearly white. (See *Gilia.*) *Hab.*—Hills and sandy ground throughout western California.

This pretty gilia is quite common about San Francisco in springtime, and often makes masses of bright deep blue over the fields.

It varies a great deal according to the soil and locality of growth. The flowers of some forms of it at a little distance resemble those of *Brodiæa capitata.*

CHICORY. SUCCORY. WILD BACHELOR'S-BUTTON.

Cichorium Intybus, L. Composite Family.

Stems.—Two to five feet high; much branched. *Leaves.*—Alternate; the lower oblong or lanceolate, partly clasping, sometimes sharply incised; the upper reduced to bracts. *Flower-heads.*—Bright blue;

BLUE GILIA—*Gilia achilleæfolia.*

sessile; two or three together in the axils of the leaves or terminal; of ray-flowers only. *Rays.*—Ten lines long; about two wide; notched at the tip. Bracts of the involucre in two series; green. *Hab.*—Escaped from cultivation in many places.

The most careless observer will some day have his attention startled into activity by a certain tall, fine plant growing along the roadside, bearing beautiful ragged blue flowers closely set to its stem. This is a stranger from over the seas, whose native home is England; and, like all English, it is an excellent colonist, having pushed its way into most parts of the civilized world. It has become quite plentiful among us in the last few years, and whole fields may often be seen covered with its lovely bright-blue blossoms, which are known as "ragged sailors," and "wild bachelor's-buttons." They open in the early morning, closing by midday. In Europe a popular belief is rife that they open at eight o'clock in the morning and close at four in the afternoon.

> "On upland slopes the shepherds mark
> The hour when, to the dial true,
> Cichorium to the towering lark
> Lifts her soft eye, serenely blue."

The plant is useful in several ways. Its root is boiled and eaten as a vegetable; the leaves, when blanched, make an excellent salad; and the whole plant was formerly employed in medicine, and is still considered a valuable remedy for jaundice. But the most common use of it is as a substitute for coffee, or as an adulterant of it. The fleshy, milky root is dried, ground, and roasted, and though it has neither the essential oil nor the delicious aroma of coffee, it is not an unpleasant beverage, and its cheapness brings it within the reach of the very poor.

The chicory industry has grown to be of considerable importance in California of late. The plants are grown in reclaimed tule land near Stockton, where there is a factory for the conversion of the root into the commercial article.

LARGE MOUNTAIN FORGET-ME-NOT.

Lappula velutina, Piper.   Borage Family.

Herbs, one to three feet tall, clothed throughout with a dense velvety pubescence.   *Lower leaves.* — Spatulate-oblanceolate; acutish; about three inches long.   *Stem-leaves.*—Numerous; mostly sessile by broad bases; oblong linear or lanceolate.   *Flowers.*—In clusters; sky-blue; eight lines across.   *Fruit.*—Clothed all over with prickles.   (For flower-structure, see *Cynoglossum grande.*)   *Hab.*—The Sierras, notably the Tahoe region.

In open woods of the Sierras these flowers are abundant and beautiful, and in clearings often make the ground blue with their charming hue, which is of the pure azure of summer skies.   The individual flowers resemble those of the hound's-tongue in structure, but are larger, and the large clusters are dense instead of loose.   The whole plant, instead of being smooth, is velvety pubescent, and the leaves are crowded on the stem.   There is often found growing with this a white-flowered species, *Lappula Californica,* Piper.

The small-flowered, blue forget-me-not — *Lappula nervosa,* Piper—is also abundant in the same regions.   It is tall and straggly of habit, with slender leaves, flowers three lines or less across, and is more often found in moist places or near water.   Its turquoise-blue flowers are followed by very troublesome little burs, which catch in the hair of sheep and are much dreaded by sheep-herders.   This is often called "stickseed."

SPEEDWELL.   BROOKLIME.

Veronica alpina, Linn.   Figwort Family.

Stems.—Simple; prostrate below, and ascending above; a span or more long.   *Leaves.*—Opposite; oval or roundish; entire; sessile; six lines long.   *Flowers.*—Small; blue, veined with darker blue; in a terminal raceme.   *Calyx.*—Four-parted.   *Corolla.*—Rotate; four-parted; somewhat irregular; three lines across.   *Stamens.*—Two; exserted.   *Style.* — Filiform.   *Stigma.* — Capitate.   *Ovary.* — Two-celled.   *Hab.*— Throughout the higher Sierras and eastward across the continent at similar elevations.

The little speedwell furnishes one of the dainty surprises of our mountain brooksides and meadows, and its interesting little blossoms afford us a moment's joy before they fall from their stems.

BLUE-AND-WHITE LUPINE.
Lupinus bicolor, Lindl.   Pea Family.

Stems.—Stoutish; six to ten inches high; silky. *Leaves.*—Alternate; with small stipules. *Leaflets.*—Five to seven; linear-spatulate; one inch long. *Flowers.*—Four or five lines long; blue and white; the white changing to red-purple after fertilization. Upper calyx-lip bifid; lower twice as long; entire. *Keel.*—Falcate; acute; ciliate toward the apex. *Pod.* — Small; about five-seeded. (See *Lupinus.*)   *Hab.* — Western central California.

In late spring the open fields about San Francisco take on a delicate, amethystine tinge, due to the blossoms of the blue-and-white lupine. After fertilization has taken place, the white in these blossoms turns to deep red, and this admixture gives the general lilac tone to the mass.

CATALINA MARIPOSA TULIP.
Calochortus Catalinæ, Wats.   Lily Family.

Stems.—A foot or two high; loosely branching; bulbiferous at the base. *Leaves and bracts.*—Linear-lanceolate. *Flowers.*—Erect; eighteen lines or so long. *Sepals.*—Green without; scarious-margined; whitish within; with purple spot at base; one inch long; acute. *Petals.*—White, tinged with lilac to lilac-purple; with garnet base; bearing an oblong gland covered with hairs. Filaments garnet. *Capsule.*—Narrowly oblong; three-sided; obtuse; an inch or two long. Seeds flat; horizontal. (See *Calochortus.*)   *Hab.*—From San Luis Obispo County to San Bernardino; and the islands off the coast.

This is one of the earliest mariposas to bloom in the south. Its beautiful, stately white cups have a garnet base within, and this, with its oblong, obtuse capsule and horizontal seeds, clearly identifies it. These blossoms are favorite resting-places for the bees, who are often beguiled into them from their labors and lulled to a gentle slumber. We have frequently startled the little truants from these siestas, and with amusement watched them struggling for a moment before regaining consciousness and whizzing away once more upon their round of duties.

This may be designated our maritime calochortus, as it is found mostly near the Coast or upon its islands.

C. splendens, Dougl., found in the Coast Ranges from Lake

BLUE–AND–WHITE LUPINE—*Lupinus bicolor.*

County to San Diego, is sometimes confused with the above, as well as, in the south, with *Godetia Bottæ*. It is a beautiful flower, whose petals are a clear rose-lilac without spots or marks, with long, whitish, cobwebby hairs on their middle third. Its anthers are purple or lilac, three to six lines long.

ITHURIEL'S SPEAR. BLUE MILLA.

Brodiæa laxa, Wats. Lily Family.

Corm.—Small; fiber-coated. *Leaves.*—Usually two; radical; linear; channeled. *Scapes.*—Six inches to two feet high. *Umbels.*—Of ten to thirty or more purple or violet, or even white, flowers. *Pedicels.*—One to three inches long. *Perianth.*—Twelve to twenty lines long. *Stamens.* Six; in two rows; the upper opposite the inner lobes of the perianth. *Ovary.*—Three-celled; on a stalk six lines long. *Hab.*—From Kern County to northern Oregon.

After the delicate collinsias have stolen away, the beautiful flowers of Ithuriel's spear begin to claim our attention in open grassy spots on the borders of rich woodlands. The common name is a happy one; for there is something commanding about this tall blossom-crowned shaft. It will perhaps be remembered that the angel Ithuriel possessed a truth-compelling spear. When Satan, disguised, went to the Garden of Eden to tempt Eve, Ithuriel and Zephon were sent to expel him.

> . . . "him there they found,
> Squat like a toad, close at the ear of Eve,
> Assaying by his devilish art to reach
> The organs of her fancy, and with them forge
> Illusions as he list, phantasms, and dreams;
>
> . . . .
>
> Him thus intent Ithuriel with his spear
> Touched lightly; for no falsehood can endure
> Touch of celestial temper, but returns
> Of force to its own likeness: up he starts
> Discovered and surprised."

DOG-VIOLET.

Viola canina, var. *adunca,* Gray. Violet Family.

Stems.—Leafy; several from the rootstocks. *Leaves.*—Ovate; often somewhat cordate at base; acute or obtuse; six to eighteen lines long;

ITHURIEL'S SPEAR—*Brodiæa laxa.*

obscurely crenate. Stipules foliaceous; narrowly lanceolate; lacerately toothed. *Flowers.*—Violet or purple; rather large. Lateral petals bearded. Spur as long as the sepals; rather slender; obtuse; hooked or curved. (Otherwise as *V. pedunculata.*) *Hab.*—The Coast Ranges, from San Francisco to Washington.

> . . . "violets
> Which yet join not scent to hue
> Crown the pale year weak and new."

Nestling amid the grasses on many a moist mesa by the sea, the modest flowers of the dog-violet may be found at almost any time of year. They vary greatly in the length of their stems, according to the season and the locality of growth.

BEACH-ASTER. SEASIDE DAISY.

Erigeron glaucus, Ker. Composite Family.

Six to twelve inches high, having a tuft of radical leaves and some ascending stems. *Leaves.*—Obovate or spatulate-oblong; one to four inches long; pale; somewhat succulent; slightly viscid. *Flower-heads.* —Composed of dull-yellow disk-flowers and bright-violet ray-flowers. *Disk.*—Eight lines or so across. *Rays.*—Six or eight lines long; narrow; numerous; in several rows. *Hab.*—The coast, from Oregon to southern California.

Almost anywhere upon our Coast, "within the roar of a surf-tormented shore," we can find the beautiful blossoms of the beach-aster. We may know them by their resemblance to the China asters of our gardens, though they are not so large. They present a most delightful combination of color in their old-gold centers, violet rays, and rather pale foliage.

THISTLE-SAGE.

Salvia carduacea, Benth. Mint Family.

Leaves.—All radical; thistle-like; with cobwebby wool. *Stems.*—Stout; a foot or two high. *Flower-whorls.*—An inch or two through. *Calyx.*—Bilabiate; with five spiny teeth. *Corolla.*—Lavender; an inch long. Upper lip erect; two-cleft. Lower fan-shaped; white-fringed. *Stamens.*—On the lower lip. Proper filaments very short, with one short and one long fork, each bearing an anther-cell. (Otherwise like *S. Columbariæ.*) *Hab.*—Western and southern California.

Upon the dry, open plains of the south the charming flowers of the thistle-sage make their appearance by May. Upon the train we pass myriads of them standing along the

BEACH–ASTER—*Erigeron glaucus.*

embankments, and seeming to beckon mockingly at us, well knowing the train almost never stops where we can get them.

These plants present the most remarkable blending of the rigid, uncompromising, touch-me-not aspect and the ethereal and fragile. In each of the several stories of the flower-cluster there are usually a number of the exquisitely delicate flowers in bloom at once, standing above the hemisphere of densely crowded, spiny calyx-tips. Nothing more airy or fantastic could well be imagined than these diaphanous blossoms. The upper lip of the corolla stands erect, its two lobes side by side, or crossed like two delicate little hands. The lower lip has two small and inconspicuous lateral lobes and one large central one, which is like the ruff of a fantail pigeon and daintily fringed with white. The color combination in these blossoms is charming. To the sage-green of the foliage and the lilac of the blossoms is added the dash of orange in the anthers that puts the finishing touch. The whole plant has a heavy, dull odor of sage.

This species is also sometimes called "chia," and its seeds are used in the same manner as those of our other salvia, but to no such extent.

VIOLET BEARD-TONGUE.

Pentstemon heterophyllus, Lindl. Figwort Family.

Woody at base; many-stemmed. *Stems.*—Two to five feet tall. *Leaves.*—Lanceolate or linear; or the lowest oblong-lanceolate; diminishing into narrow floral bracts. *Panicle.*—Narrow. Pedicels one- to three-flowered; short and erect. *Corolla.*—Rose-purple, or violet suffused with pink; an inch or more long; ventricose-funnel-form above the narrow, slender tube. (See *Pentstemon.*) *Hab.*—Western California, specially southward.

The beautiful flowers of the violet beard-tongue are often seen among the soft browns of our dusty roadsides in early summer. They are truly charming flowers, and we marvel how any one can pass them by unnoticed. I have seen them especially showy in the southern part of the State, in Santa Barbara and Ventura counties, where the plants often spread

AZURE BEARD–TONGUE—*Pentstemon azureus.*

over two or three feet, sending up innumerable slender flower-covered wands. The undeveloped buds are of a characteristic greenish-yellow tone, making an unusual contrast to the expanded flowers and the rather pale foliage. The structure of the anthers is quite interesting, each cell consisting of a little bag with bristly margins, the two together being heart-shaped in outline.

P. azureus, Benth., or the "azure beard-tongue," is very similar to the above, growing from one to three feet high; but it is smooth and glaucous; its leaves are inclined to have a broader base, and its flowers are usually larger, azure blue, approaching violet, sometimes having a red-purple tube, while its border is often an inch across. This is found throughout the State, but is more common in the interior and in the Sierras. Its buds are not yellow.

WILD GINGER.

Asarum caudatum, Lindl. Birthwort Family.

Rootstocks.—Creeping; aboveground. *Leaves.* — Alternate; two to four inches long; heart-shaped; not mottled; shining green. *Flowers.*—Raisin-colored. *Perianth.*—With spherical tube and three long-pointed lobes, thirty lines long. *Stamens.*—Twelve. Filaments more or less coherent in groups, adherent to the styles, and produced beaklike beyond the anthers. *Ovary.*—Six-celled. Styles united; equaling the stamens. *Hab.*—The Coast Ranges, from Santa Cruz to British Columbia.

The beautiful long-stemmed leaves of the wild ginger stand upon the borders of many a shaded cañon stream, seeming to enjoy the gossiping of the brook as it gurgles by. The leaves and roots of these plants are aromatic, and the former when crushed emit a pleasant fragrance, similar to that of the camphor-laurel. The branching rootstocks, creeping along the surface of the ground, grow from their tips, which are swathed in the undeveloped silky leaves.

In the spring a warm hue comes among these closely folded leaves, and presently a curious dull-colored bud begins to protrude its long tip from their midst. This bud looks as though some worm had eaten off its end; but we soon see that its

WILD GINGER—*Asarum caudatum*.

blunt appearance is due to the fact that the long prongs of the sepals are neatly folded in upon themselves, like the jointed leg of an insect. It must require considerable force in the flower to unfurl them. When at length expanded, these blossoms have the look of some rapacious, hobgoblin spider, lurking for its prey.

Another species,—*A. Hartwegi,* Wats.,—the "Sierra wild ginger," is easily distinguished from the above by its white-mottled leaves, which grow in clusters, and by its smaller flowers. It blooms later than the other, its flowers lasting into July. These plants are closely related to the "Dutchman's pipe."

COMMON MILKWEED. SILKWEED.

Asclepias Mexicana, Cav. Milkweed Family.

Stems.—Three to five feet high; slender. *Leaves.*—Mostly whorled and fascicled; linear-lanceolate; short-petioled; two to six inches long. *Peduncles.*—Erect; slender; often in whorls. *Flowers.*—Very small and numerous; in umbels; white and lavender. *Corolla-lobes.*—Two lines long. *Anthers.*—Twice the filament column in length. *Horns.*—Awl-shaped; arising from below the middle of the ovate hoods, and conspicuously curved over the stigma. *Pods.*—Slender; spindle-shaped. (Structure otherwise as in *Gomphocarpus.*) *Hab.*—Throughout the State, and beyond its borders.

This is one of our most widely distributed milkweeds. and may be found blossoming along our dusty roadsides and through the fields in early summer. Its stems are tall and wandlike, with long, narrow leaves, and its little blossoms are very trim. Its distaff-shaped pods, with their beautiful silken down, are familiar objects, much beloved by children, and are sought by older people, who utilize them in many dainty ways.

Asclepias speciosa, Torr., the form common in the Yosemite Valley, is a tall plant with large opposite, ovate, sessile, somewhat woolly leaves. Its leathery pods are interestingly poised on a curiously bent stem, giving them the look of some grotesque bird with large head and slender neck. Mr. Galen Clark tells us in his "Legends of the Yosemite" that the Indians formerly made from the tough, flexible bark of this

COMMON MILKWEED—*Asclepias Mexicana.*

plant a strong twine which they used for fish-lines and for the warp in their fur blankets.

This plant is much admired in Europe, where it is cultivated under the name of *A. Douglasii.*

FALSE INDIGO. LEAD-PLANT.
Amorpha Californica, Nutt. Pea Family.

Shrubs three to over eight feet high. *Leaves.*—Mostly alternate; with stipules; pinnate. *Leaflets.*—One inch long; five to nine or more pairs. *Flower-spikes.*—Two to six inches long. *Flowers.*—Black-purple; two and a half lines long. *Calyx.*—Half as long. *Corolla.*—With only one petal! (the standard); this erect and folded. *Stamens.*—Slightly united at base; exserted. *Ovary.*—One-celled. *Pod.*—Three lines long. (See *Leguminosæ.*) *Hab.*—The Coast Ranges, from Marin County to San Diego.

This shrub or small tree is remarkable for its sickeningly fragrant foliage. The small blossoms, taken individually, are inconspicuous, but when seen in masses, sprinkling the foliage with black and gold, they are quite effective. The generic name comes from the Greek word signifying *deformed,* in reference to the defective corolla.

BLACK SAGE. BALL-SAGE.
Audibertia stachyoides, Benth. Mint Family.

Shrubby; three to eight feet high; with herbaceous flowering branches. *Leaves.*—Opposite; oblong-lanceolate; tapering into a petiole; crenate. *Flowers.*—In interrupted spikes, having from three to nine dense, rather remote, headlike, bracteate whorls. *Calyx.*—Bilabiate; each lip with two or three awned teeth. *Corolla.*—Lavender; six lines long; bilabiate. Upper lip erect; emarginate; lower deflexed; three-lobed. *Stamens.*—Two sterile; two perfect on jointed filaments. *Ovary.* —Of four seedlike nutlets. Style slender. Stigma two-cleft. *Hab.*— From San Francisco Bay to San Diego.

We have but two or three true sages, or salvias, in California; but the plants of the closely allied genus *Audibertia* are with perfect propriety called sages, as they manifest all the characteristics of that genus, differing only in the structure of the stamens. There are a number of species of *Audibertia,* all of them important honey-plants. They are particularly abundant in the south, where they form a characteristic feature in the landscape, often covering whole hill-slopes.

A. stachyoides frequently forms dense thickets over vast reaches of mountain-sides, and when in full bloom is very noticeable. Its specific name is a happy one, denoting its resemblance to the stachys, or hedge-nettle. But its pointed leaves, shrubby habit, and rank odor, together with its more numerous flower-whorls, proclaim its separate identity.

A. nivea, Benth., found from Santa Barbara to San Diego, has larger spikes of rich, warm lilac flowers. Nothing could be more charming than the soft lavender billows of it undulating over slope after slope of wild mountain-side.

CALIFORNIA LOBELIA.

Bolelia pulchella, Greene. Lobelia Family.

Stems.—Three to six inches high. *Leaves.*—Alternate; sessile; linear; obtuse; passing into flower-bracts above. *Flowers.*—Racemose; blue. *Calyx-tube.*—Very long and slender; adnate to the ovary; its limb of five slender divisions. *Corolla.*—With short tube and bilabiate border. The smaller lip of two narrow spreading or recurved divisions; the larger three-lobed; broader than long; nine or ten lines by five or six lines. All the lobes intense blue; the large centers mostly white. *Stamens.*—Five; united into a curved tube. *Capsule.*—Splitting at the sides. *Syn.*—*Downingia pulchella,* Torr. *Hab.*—Nearly throughout the State.

These little lobeliaceous plants are very common, especially upon the plains of the interior, and may be found growing in wet places, where they often make the ground blue. The showy, white-centered flowers are familiar along the roadsides upon the borders of puddles. The blossoms, which are really stemless, appear to have stems of considerable length, owing to the very long, slender ovary and calyx-tube. They are cultivated for ornament under the name of *Clintonia pulchella.*

We have one other species in the northern part of the State. It is a larger plant, sometimes a foot tall, with ovate to lanceolate leaves. This is *B. elegans,* Torr.

BLUE-CURLS. VINEGAR-WEED.

Trichostema lanceolatum, Benth. Mint Family.

Glandular and pubescent weeds one or two feet high; branching from the base. *Leaves.*—Opposite; sessile; crowded; lanceolate or ovate-lanceolate; gradually acuminate; densely pubescent; several-nerved; an inch or more long. *Flowers.*—Blue; in axillary, short-peduncled, dense clusters. *Calyx.*—Five-cleft. *Corolla.*—Six lines long; with filiform tube, which is bent abruptly downward and backward upon itself, and five-lobed border. *Stamens.*—Four; of two lengths. Filaments filiform; spirally coiled, in bud, but long-exserted and curving upward in flower. *Ovary.*—Of four seedlike nutlets. Style long; filiform; two-cleft at the tip. *Hab.*—Throughout western California.

Of all the plants of our acquaintance, the common blue-curls is the most aggressive and ill-smelling. Its odor is positively sickening. Some years ago, when it was first new to me, I brought some of it down from Sonoma County upon the train, and, even though it had been carefully wrapped, I was obliged to deposit it in the wood-box, as far as possible from the passengers.

The generic name comes from two Greek words, signifying *hair* and *stamen,* and was bestowed on account of the capillary filaments. The common name also refers to the long, curling blue stamens.

This species blossoms late in summer, and grows upon very dry ground, where it seems almost a miracle for any plant to thrive.

ROMERO. WOOLLY BLUE-CURLS.
Trichostema lanatum, Benth. Mint Family.

Shrubby; two to five feet high. *Leaves.*—Opposite and fascicled in the axils; an inch or so long; green above; white-woolly beneath. *Flowers.*—Blue; in terminal clusters sometimes a foot long; covered with dense violet wool. *Calyx.*—Five-toothed. *Corolla.*—Nearly an inch long; with tube half its length and border violet-shaped. *Stamens and style.*—Two inches long. *Ovary.*—Of four seedlike nutlets. *Hab.*—From San Diego to Santa Barbara.

When the first scorching winds of the desert have withered and laid low the lovely flowers of the southern plains, the romero is just coming into bloom upon dry hillsides. Its shrubby form, with densely crowded leaves, becomes conspicuous by reason of its long spikes of purple-woolly buds and blossoms. This inflorescence is an exquisite thing, more like the production of a Paris milliner than a guileless creation of nature. The individual blossoms have much the look of alert little blue violets wearing long, elegant lilac aigrets. Both leaf

ROMERO—*Trichostema lanatum.*

and flower have a pleasant aromatic fragrance, entirely unlike the dreadful odor of the common blue-curls.

Among the Spanish-Californians it is known altogether by the musical name of "romero," and is one of their most highly valued medicinal herbs, being considered a panacea for many troubles. Fried in olive oil, it becomes an ointment which alleviates pain and cures ulcers; dried and reduced to powder, it is a snuff very efficacious for catarrh; and made into a tincture, it is used as a liniment. This plant is also sometimes called "black sage."

HARVEST BRODIÆA. LARGE-FLOWERED BRODIÆA.

Brodiæa grandiflora, Smith. Lily Family.

Corm.—Fibrous-coated. *Leaves.*—Narrowly linear; somewhat cylindrical. *Scape.*—Four to twelve inches high. *Pedicels.*—Three to ten, rarely one; unequal. *Perianth.*—Violet; waxen; ten to twenty lines long; broadly funnel-form; six-cleft; lobes recurving. *Stamens.*—Three; opposite the inner segments. *Staminodia.*—Three; strap-shaped; entire; white; erect; about equaling the stamens. *Ovary.*—Sessile; three-celled. Style stout. Stigma three-lobed. *Hab.*—From Ventura to the British boundary in the Coast Ranges and Sierras.

In the latter part of May and early in June, just as the grain is mellowing in the fields, the dry grasses of our hill-slopes and roadsides begin to reveal the beautiful blossoms of the "harvest brodiæa." Seen at its best, this is one of our finest species. It sends up a scape a foot high, bearing from five to ten of the large lily-like, violet flowers. They are somewhere described as varying to rose. I have never seen them of this color, though a flash of them caught when riding by a field is often suggestive of a pink flower.

These plants vary considerably in size, in some localities blooming when but an inch or two high, and in others having their tall scape crowned with as many as ten of the fine blossoms. These have their segments nerved with brown upon the outside. The clear-white stamens stand opposite the outer segments, alternating with the white staminodia. The leaves have dried away before the coming of the blossoms.

HARVEST BRODIÆA—*Brodiæa grandiflora.*

B. terrestris, Kell., common throughout central California, is always found in sandy soil. Its perianth is less than an inch long, and its staminodia are yellow, with inrolled edges. This is clearly distinguished by these characteristics, added to the fact that its flower-cluster has no common stalk or scape, but seems to sit upon the ground, giving the separate flowers the appearance of coming from the ground.

VIOLET SNAPDRAGON.

Antirrhinum vagans, Gray. Figwort Family.

Herbs with prehensile branchlets. *Leaves.*—Alternate; short-petioled; lanceolate to oblong-ovate; entire; an inch long. *Flowers.*—Six lines long; lavender. *Sepals.*—Five; upper one large, oblong; the others small, linear. *Stamens.*—Four; in pairs; on the corolla. Filaments slender. Anthers with two diverging cells. *Ovary.*—Two-celled. Style awl-shaped. *Hab.*—Throughout the western part of the State.

When the first dryness of summer is beginning to make itself felt, the tall wandlike sprays of the little lilac snapdragon begin to appear along our dusty roadsides. A curious feature of this plant is to be found in the long threadlike branchlets produced in the axils of the leaves. These are like so many little arms, apparently waving about in aimless abandon, but in reality vigilant of any opportunity to grasp some convenient object of support.

Another species—*A. glandulosum,* Lindl.—is common from Santa Cruz southward. This may be known by its pink and yellow flowers, its very viscid, leafy stems, three to five feet tall, and its lack of prehensile branchlets. This has somewhat more the look of the familiar garden species. Its anthers are arranged like teeth in the roof of its mouth, and the children, by slightly pinching the sides of its funny little countenance, can make it open its mouth in quite a formidable manner.

Sir John Lubbock, writing of the fertilization of flowers, says of our large garden species:—"Thus the *Antirrhinum,* or snapdragon, is completely closed, and only a somewhat powerful insect can force its way in. The flower is in fact a strongbox, of which the humble-bee only has the key."

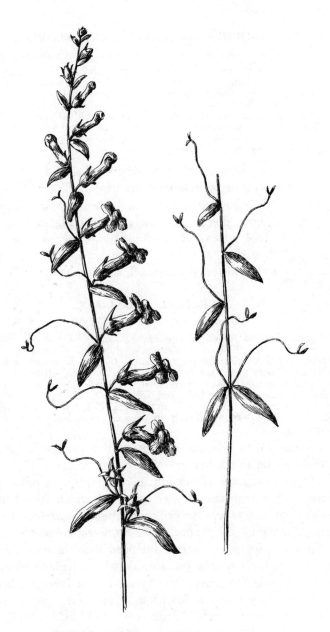

VIOLET SNAPDRAGON—*Antirrhinum vagans.*

CALIFORNIA HAREBELL. BELLFLOWER.

Campanula prenanthoides, Durand.　Harebell or Campanula Family.

Stems.—Several inches to two feet high.　*Leaves.*—Alternate; ovate-oblong to lanceolate; one inch or less long.　*Flowers.*—Blue; on recurved pedicels.　*Calyx.*—Growing to the ovary below; with five awl-shaped teeth.　*Corolla.*—Five to eight lines long; with short tube and slender, spreading, recurved lobes.　*Stamens.*—Five.　*Ovary.*—Three-to five-celled.　Style club-shaped; much exserted.　Stigma becoming three-lobed.　*Hab.*—Coast woods from Monterey to Mendocino County, and through the northern Sierras.

The fragile blossoms of the harebell lurk in the seclusion of our cool cañons or peer down at us from the banks of shaded mountain roads toward the end of July.　We almost wonder that this ethereal flower dares delay its coming so long when outside its cool retreat all is parched and dry.　Owing to its deeply slashed corolla, it has a more airy and delicate aspect than its English sister, the harebell, so often celebrated by the poets.

SELF-HEAL. HEAL-ALL.

Brunella vulgaris, L.　Mint Family.

Stems.—Six to fifteen inches high.　*Leaves.*—Opposite; petioled; ovate or oblong.　*Flowers.*—In a dense, short spike, with broad, leafy bracts; purple, violet, or rarely white.　*Calyx.*—Bilabiate; upper lip with three short teeth; the lower two-cleft.　*Corolla.*—Bilabiate; upper lip arched, entire; lower three-lobed; deflexed.　*Stamens.*—Four; in pairs.　Filaments two-forked; one fork naked, the other bearing the two-celled anther.　*Ovary.*—Of four seedlike nutlets.　Style filiform; two-cleft above.　*Hab.*—Widely distributed over the northern hemisphere.

From April to July the blossoms of the self-heal, or heal-all, may be found in the borders of woods or in open grounds.

The generic name is thought to come from the old German word, *braune,* a disease of the throat, for which this plant was believed to be a cure.　According to the old doctrine of signatures, plants by their appearance were supposed to indicate the diseases for which nature intended them as remedies, and in England the *Brunella* was considered particularly efficacious in the disorders of carpenters and common laborers, because its corolla resembled a bill-hook.　Hence it was commonly called "carpenter's herb," "hook-heal," and "sicklewort."

328

CALIFORNIA HAREBELL—*Campanula prenanthoides.*

PENNYROYAL. POLÉO.
Monardella villosa, Benth.   Mint Family.

Stems.—Woody; branching from below; a foot or two high. *Leaves.*—An inch or less long; toothed or entire; veins conspicuous. *Flowers.*—White to deep lilac; in a dense head subtended by a number of ovate, green bracts. *Calyx.*—Tubular; five-toothed; four lines long. *Corolla.*—Nine lines long; with filiform tube and bilabiate border. Upper lip two-cleft; lower cleft into three linear divisions. *Stamens.*—Four; in pairs; exserted. Anther-cells divergent. *Ovary.*—Of four seedlike nutlets. *Hab.*—Throughout the State; common.

Owing to their resemblance to the *Monarda,* or horse-mint of the East, these Western plants have been given the diminutive of its name—*Monardella.*

In early summer the blossoms, which are generally purple, are conspicuous in our drying woods. The herbage is pleasantly fragrant. The more hairy form, which suggested the specific name, is found in the south.

Another species,—*M. lanceolata,* Gray,—common in the Sierras and south to San Diego, is a very handsome plant with lanceolate or oblong-lanceolate, entire leaves, an inch or two long, and having its bright rose-colored or purple corollas sometimes dark-spotted. This is known among the Spanish-Californians as "poléo" (pennyroyal), and is valued as a remedy for various ailments.

M. odoratissima, Benth., found abundantly in the Sierras, and known as "wild pennyroyal," is a bushy, many-stemmed plant, whose flowers usually have a faded lavender hue. But the plant is exceedingly fragrant, perfuming the air all about.

SQUAW'S CARPET.   MAHALA MATS.
Ceanothus prostratus, Benth.   Buckthorn Family.

Hardy, evergreen, trailing shrubs, carpeting the ground. *Leaves.*—Opposite; short-petioled; obovate or spatulate; cuneate; leathery; several-toothed above; three to twelve lines long. *Flowers.*—Violet-blue; in loose clusters on stout peduncles. *Fruit.*—With thick, often red, flesh; with three large wrinkled, somewhat spreading horns from near the apex, and low intermediate crests. (See *Ceanothus.*) *Hab.*—The Sierras and northern Coast Ranges.

Upon half-shaded slopes in the Sierras, where great firs rear their noble shafts, forming an open forest, this little trailing

PENNYROYAL—*Monardella villosa.*

shrub makes a clean, delightfully springy carpet underfoot. Early in the season it is an exquisite thing, when sprinkled with its feathery clusters of violet-blue flowers, and it is no less attractive in late summer, when its odd scarlet fruit studs the rich green foliage.

The children of our mountain districts know it as "squaw's carpet" and "mahala mats." Among the Digger Indians the word "Mahala" is applied as a title of respect to all the women of the tribe indiscriminately, and they always refer to one another as "Mahala Sally," "Mahala Nancy," etc.

LUCERN. ALFALFA. CHILEAN CLOVER.

Medicago sativa, L. Pea Family.

Perennials, with roots sometimes reaching down eight or ten feet. *Stems.*—Two to four feet high. *Leaflets.*—Three; toothed above. *Flowers.*—Violet. *Calyx.*—Five-toothed. *Corolla.*—Papilionaceous; six lines long. *Stamens.*—Nine united; one free. *Pod.*—Spirally coiled; without spines. *Hab.*—Usually escaped from cultivation.

The value of this little plant has been known for many centuries. It was introduced into Greece from Media, whence it received the name "medicago," and was cultivated several centuries before Christ. It has reached us through Mexico and Chile, where it is called "alfalfa" and "Chilean clover."

It is but sparingly naturalized among us, but on account of its very nutritious herbage it is largely cultivated for feed. Its very deep root enables it to seek moisture from perennial sources, and to thus withstand the dryness of our summers. It requires considerable care to start the plants; but once established, the roots will continue under favorable circumstances to produce crops of herbage almost indefinitely. When grown upon good soil and irrigated, it will yield several crops a year. When cured for hay, it is cut just before flowering. But it is of greatest value for feeding green to dairy cows and other animals. An alfalfa field is a beautiful and grateful sight amid the drouth of our late summer. In Chile sprays of this plant are laid about in the houses to drive away fleas.

ALFALFA—*Medicago sativa.*

ACONITE. MONK'S-HOOD. FRIAR'S-CAP. BLUEWEED.

Aconitum Columbianum, Nutt. Buttercup or Crowfoot Family.

Stems.—Two to six feet high. *Leaves.*—Alternate; palmately three-
to five-cleft, three to five inches across. *Flowers.*—From blue to almost
white; in a terminal cluster. *Sepals.*—Five; petaloid; very irregular;
the upper one helmet-shaped. *Petals.*—Two to five; the upper two
stamen-like, concealed within the helmet; the lower three minute or
obsolete. *Stamens.*—Numerous. Filaments short. *Pistils.*—Usually
three; becoming divergent follicles. *Syn.*—*A. Fischeri,* Reichb. *Hab.*—
The Sierras and the northern Coast Ranges.

The blossoms of the monk's-hood, or aconite, may be found
with those of the tall blue larkspur and the little alpine lily
along our mountain streams in late summer. Owing to the
shape of the upper sepal, these flowers have received several
of their common names, such as "helmet-flower," "friar's-cap,"
and "monk's-hood."

The genus *Aconitum* has been known from remote times
and noted for the poisonous qualities of its species. From the
roots and leaves of *A. napellus,* the officinal species, supposed
to be native of Britain, is made the powerful drug, aconite.
Our own species is also poisonous, and among the mountaineers
it is called "blueweed," and remembered only for its disastrous
effect upon their sheep, who are sometimes driven to eat it
when other feed is scarce. The helmet varies greatly in breadth
and length.

TALL MOUNTAIN LARKSPUR.

Delphinium scopulorum, var. *glaucum,* Gray.
Buttercup or Crowfoot Family.

Mostly smooth; more or less glaucous. *Stems.*—Two to six feet
high. *Leaves.*—Palmately five- to seven-parted; the divisions slashed
into sharp-pointed lobes. *Flowers.*—Blue; in narrow, slender racemes;
on rather short, slender pedicels. *Sepals.*—Rather narrow; six lines
long or less; minutely tomentose. Spur crapy; rather slender. *Ovaries.*
—Smooth. (Flower-structure as in *D. nudicaule.*) *Syn.*—*D. scopulorum,* Gray. *Hab.*—The Sierras, at about six thousand feet; from the
San Bernardino Mountains to the Yukon River.

By July and August the slender spires of the tall mountain
larkspur are conspicuous along the watercourses of the Sierras,

MONK'S-HOOD—*Aconitum Columbianum.*

where they are usually found in the company of their near relatives, the monk's-hoods and the gay scarlet columbines. A ramble down one of these mountain streams affords a succession of most delightful surprises. Willow copses, alternating with tangles of larkspur, great willow-herb, and monk's-hood, are followed by open, velvety meadows, starred by white and blue daisies, or diversified by the pure spikes of the milk-white rein-orchis, or the lovely blossoms of the pink mimulus; while further down, the stream perchance suddenly narrows and deepens, flowing by some jutting rock-wall, resplendent with crimson pentstemons or brilliant sulphur-flowers.

BLUE GENTIAN.

Gentiana calycosa, Griseb. Gentian Family.

Stems.—Six to twelve inches high. *Leaves.*—Eighteen lines to less than an inch long. *Flowers.*—Deep, rich blue. *Corolla.*—An inch or two long; plaited into folds between the lobes; the sinuses with two long, tooth-like appendages; the lobes green-dotted. *Stamens.*—Five; alternate with the corolla-lobes. Filaments flattened and adnate to the corolla below. *Ovary.*—One-celled. Style awl-shaped. Stigma two-lobed. *Hab.*—The Sierras.

This genus was named for Gentius, an ancient king of Illyria, who is said to have discovered the medicinal virtues of these plants. The drug called "gentian," a bitter tonic, is made from the root of a German species,—*G. lutea,*—with yellow flowers.

All the gentians are natives of the cooler portions of the world, inhabiting northern latitudes and mountain heights. We have several fine species, which are found in the Sierras and the northern Coast Ranges.

G. calycosa is a truly beautiful flower, rivaling the sky with its deep-blue blossoms, which are to be found in the fall in many an alpine meadow, called by Mr. Muir "gentian-meadows."

BLUE GENTIAN—*Gentiana calycosa.*

COMMON ASTER.

Aster Chamissonis, Gray. Composite Family.

Stems.—Two to five feet high; loosely branching. *Leaves.*—Alternate; sessile; lanceolate; three to six inches long; the upper becoming small or minute. *Flower-heads.*—Five or six lines long; composed of yellow disk-flowers and violet or purple rays. *Rays.*—Twenty to twenty-five; half an inch long. *Involucre.*—Campanulate; of many small imbricated scales. *Hab.*—Throughout California.

We have not as many species of *Aster* as are found in the Eastern States, but we have some very beautiful ones. *A. Chamissonis* is one of our commonest and most wide-spread species. Its blossoms begin to appear in late summer and linger along through the fall. Many species of *Erigeron* (very closely allied to *Aster*) are called "asters" among us, and comprise some of our most charming flowers. These are found chiefly in the mountains, though *E. glaucus* is found upon the sea-beach and ocean cliffs.

LAVENDER MOUNTAIN DAISY.

Erigeron salsuginosus, Gray. Composite Family.

Stems.—A foot or two high. *Radical and lower leaves.*—Spatulate to nearly obovate; tapering into a margined petiole. *Upper leaves.*—Ovate-oblong to lanceolate; sessile. *Uppermost leaves.*—Small and bract-like. *Flower-heads.*—Solitary; large; of yellow disk-flowers and lavender rays. *Disk.*—Over half an inch across. *Rays.*—Fifty to seventy; six lines or more long; rather wide. *Bracts of the involucre.*—Numerous; loosely spreading. *Syn.*—*Aster salsuginosus,* Richardson. *Hab.*—Sierra meadows, at an altitude of from six to ten thousand feet.

Of all the beautiful flowers of the Sierras, not one lingers so fondly in the memory, after our return to the lowlands, as this exquisite lavender daisy. Late in the summer it stars the alpine meadows with its charming flowers, or stands in sociable companies on those natural velvet lawns of the mountains. It resembles the feathery, white mountain daisy, and grows in the same region; but its rays are wider and give the blossoms a somewhat more substantial look.

COMMON ASTER—*Aster Chamissonis.*

MOUNTAIN BLUEBELLS. SMOOTH LUNGWORT.
Mertensia Siberica, Don. Borage Family.

Smooth, rather succulent, herbs, a foot or more high. *Leaves.*—Alternate; ovate-lanceolate or oblong; two to five inches long; minutely ciliate. *Flowers.*—Nodding. *Calyx.*—Five-parted. *Corolla.*—Salverform or somewhat funnel-form, with rounded lobes; half an inch or less long; blue. *Stamens.*—Five; exserted. Filaments broader than the anthers. *Ovary.*—Four-lobed. Style filiform exserted. Stigma minutely capitate. *Fruit.*—Four wrinkled nutlets. *Hab.*—The Sierras.

The handsome blossoms of the mountain bluebell are to be found along water-courses at considerable elevations. These are not true bluebells, or campanulas, but belong to the genus *Mertensia* of the Borage family. Plants of this genus are commonly called "smooth lungwort" to distinguish them from the rough plants of the genus *Pulmonaria,* or common lungwort.

V. RED

Red or occasionally or partially red flowers not described in the Red Section.

Described in the Yellow Section:—

ANAGALLIS ARVENSIS—Pimpernel.

MECONOPSIS HETEROPHYLLA—Wind-Poppy.

DIPLACUS GLUTINOSUS—Sticky Monkey-Flower.

DUDLEYA PULVERULENTA (Syn.—*Cotyledon pulverulenta.*)

OPUNTIA ENGELMANNI—Prickly Pear.

Described in the Pink Section:—

LONICERA CONJUGIALIS—Bush Honeysuckle.

INDIAN WARRIOR.

Pedicularis densiflora, Benth.   Figwort Family.

Root woody.   *Stems.*—Six to twenty inches high.   *Leaves.*—Alternate; oblong-lanceolate; pinnate; leaflets lobed and toothed; diminishing into the flower-bracts.   *Calyx.*—Campanulate; five-toothed.   *Corolla.*—Club-shaped, bent downward above the calyx and oblique to it; one inch long; the two upper lobes united and containing the stamens; the three lower mere teeth.   *Stamens.*—Four.   Style filiform; exserted.   *Ovary.*—Two-celled.   *Hab.*—Throughout western California.

These blossoms, which come early in the season, seem "warmed with the new wine of the year."   They often stand in little companies in openings among the trees, and the rays of the afternoon sun slanting in upon them brighten and vivify them into a rich, warm claret-color.   The leaves, finely dissected, like certain fern-fronds, are often of a bronze tone, which harmonizes finely with the flowers.

To the casual observer, this flower resembles the Indian paint-brush.   In reality, it belongs to a closely allied genus. But in this blossom the bracts do not constitute the brilliant part of the inflorescence, and the calyx, instead of being the showy, sheathing envelop it is in the paint-brush, is quite small and inconspicuous.

Mrs. Blochman has quaintly and aptly alluded to the corolla of this flower as a long and slender mitten, just fit for some high-born fairy's hand.

Among the children of our mountain districts this flower is known as "Indian warrior."

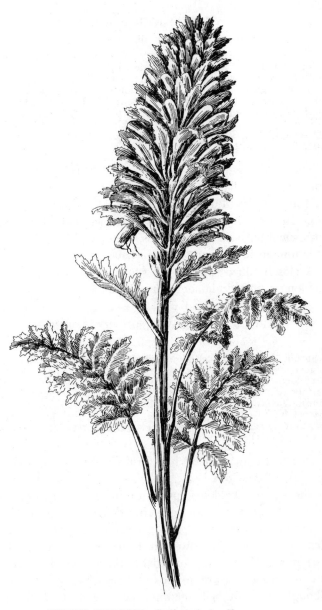

INDIAN WARRIOR—*Pedicularis densiflora.*

WILD GOOSEBERRY.

Ribes Menziesii, Pursh. Saxifrage Family.

Shrubs two to six feet high, with naked glandular-bristly or prickly branches and stout triple thorns under the fascicled leaves. *Peduncles.* —With one or two drooping, fuchsia-like flowers. *Calyx.*—Half an inch long; garnet; the five oblong lobes somewhat longer than the tube, but hardly longer than the stamens, which surpass the five white petals with inrolled edges. Styles exserted. Anthers sagittate. *Berry.* —Four to six lines in diameter; thickly covered with long prickles. (Otherwise as *Ribes glutinosum.*) *Hab.*—From San Diego to Humboldt County; also in the Sierras.

The wild gooseberry, considered as a fruit, is very disappointing, as its large, prickly berries are composed mostly of skin and seeds. But as an ornamental shrub it is very pleasing. In February its long, thorny branches are densely clothed with small but rich green leaves, under which hang the perfect little miniature red-and-white fuchsias.

A closely allied species—*R. subvestitum,* Hook. and Arn.— has long exserted filaments and glandular-prickly berries.

FUCHSIA-FLOWERED GOOSEBERRY.

Ribes speciosum, Pursh. Saxifrage Family.

Shrubs six to ten feet high, with spreading branches, armed with large triple thorns. *Leaves.*—Evergreen; three- to five-lobed; an inch or so long. *Flowers.*—Bright cardinal; an inch long. *Calyx.*—Petaloid; its tube adnate to the ovary; the limb is usually five-cleft (sometimes four). *Petals.*—On the sinuses of the calyx. *Stamens.*—As many as the petals; twice the length of the calyx. *Ovary.*—One-celled. Style two-cleft. *Fruit.*—A dry, densely glandular berry. *Hab.*—From Monterey to San Diego.

One of the most charming shrubs to be found in the southern part of the State is the fuchsia-flowered gooseberry. Early in the season the long sprays of its spreading branches are thickly hung with the beautiful drooping cardinal flowers, which gleam against the rich green of the glossy leaves. The stems often rival the flowers in brilliance of coloring, but they harbor a multitude of formidable thorns which serve to cool our impetuous desire to possess ourselves of the blossoms. Though far more brilliant than the flowers of *R. subvestitum,*

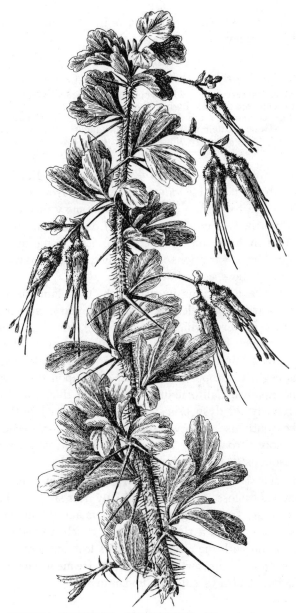

FUCHSIA-FLOWERED GOOSEBERRY—*Ribes speciosum.*

these are not so truly counterparts in miniature of the garden fuchsia as they.

WILD PEONY.

Pæonia Brownii, Dougl. Buttercup or Crowfoot Family.

Coarse, leathery herbs, with woody roots. *Stems.*—Stout; branched; ten to eighteen inches high. *Leaves.* — Alternate; once- or twice-ternately compound; the leaflets ternately lobed. *Flowers.*—Solitary. *Sepals.*—Green; often with leaflike appendages. *Petals.*—Five to ten; dark red. *Stamens.*—Numerous. *Pistils.*—Two to five; becoming leathery follicles. *Hab.*—Almost throughout California.

Our wild peony, which is the only species of North America, grows through a wide range of territory, from the hot plains of the south to the region of perpetual snow in the mountains of the north. As might be expected, it manifests considerable variation in form and character. Indeed, some authors have thought these variations sufficiently marked to warrant the division of the species into two.

After the first rains in the south, the plant pushes up its broad, scarlet-tipped leaves, and by January, or earlier, produces its flowers, which are deep red, shading almost into black, an inch or so across, and quite fragrant. These blossoms are at first erect; but as the seed-vessels mature, the stems begin to droop, till the fruit rests upon the ground.

The Spanish-Californians consider the thick root an excellent remedy for dyspepsia, when eaten raw; while the Indians of the south use it, powdered or made into a decoction, for colds, sore throat, etc. In the north its leaves are reputed to be poisonous to the touch.

In some localities it is known as "Christmas-rose." In the mountains it blossoms in June and July near snow-banks. There, as it emerges from the ground, its shoots and the under surfaces of its leaves are of a rich wine-color, which makes a charming combination with the olive tones of its leaf-surfaces. During the early stages of its growth it is liable to frequent covering by the snow, but it always emerges undaunted.

WILD PEONY—*Pæonia Brownii.*

CALIFORNIA FIGWORT.   CALIFORNIA BEE-PLANT.

Scrophularia Californica, Cham.   Figwort Family.

Stems.—Two to five feet high; angled.   *Leaves.*—Oblong-ovate or oblong-triangular; two or more inches long.   *Flowers.*—Small; dull red; three to five lines long; in loose terminal panicles.   *Calyx.*—Five-lobed.   *Corolla.*—Bilabiate; upper lip four-lobed; lower of one lobe. *Stamens.*—Four perfect; in pairs; and a fifth scalelike, rudimentary one. *Ovary.*—Two-celled.   Style exserted.   *Hab.*—Almost throughout the State.

The tall stems of the California figwort are common along roadsides, and become especially rank and luxuriant where the soil has been freshly stirred.   The plants are so plentiful and so plebeian in appearance, that we are apt to class them in the category of weeds; but the fact that their little corollas are almost always stored abundantly with honey for the bees, saves them from this reproachful title.

They are cultivated by the keepers of bees.   The odd little dull-red or greenish flowers have a knowing look, which is enhanced by two of the stamens, which project just over the lower rim of the corolla, like the front teeth of some tiny rodent.

FALSE ALUM-ROOT.   FRINGE-CUPS.

Tellima grandiflora, R. Br.   Saxifrage Family.

Radical leaves.—Long-petioled.   *Stem-leaves.*—With shorter petioles; round-cordate; variously lobed and toothed; very hairy, with coarse, bristle-like hairs; two to four inches across.   *Stems.*—One to three feet high.   *Flowers.*—In long racemes; on short pedicels; green or rose-color.   *Calyx.*—Campanulate; five-toothed; ribbed; three to six lines long; adnate to the ovary below.   *Petals.*—Five; short-clawed; slashed above; two or three lines long; on the calyx.   *Stamens.*—Ten; very short.   *Ovary.*—One-celled; with a disklike summit, tapering into two stout styles with large capitate stigmas.   *Hab.*—From Santa Cruz to Alaska.

This plant closely resembles the alum-root in habit and appearance, and its leaves are prettily blotched in the same manner.   It grows along rich banks by shaded roads, and blooms from early spring onward.   Its tall racemes of either rose-colored or greenish, obscure flowers look rather like the promise of something to come than a present fulfillment.   The petals are small and inconspicuous at a distance; but when

CALIFORNIA BEE-PLANT—*Scrophularia Californica.*

closely examined, reveal a delicacy and beauty of form entirely unsuspected.

INDIAN PAINT-BRUSH. SCARLET PAINT-BRUSH.

Castilleia latifolia, Hook. and Arn. Figwort Family.

Hairy, at least above; six inches to two feet high. *Leaves.*—Laciniate-cleft or incised; sometimes entire; two inches or so long; mostly alternate. *Flowers.*—With conspicuous colored bracts. *Calyx.*—Tubular; about equally cleft before and behind; tinged with scarlet or yellow. *Corolla.*—Tubular; six lines to over an inch long; the upper lip equaling the tube; the lower very short; three-toothed; the whole tinged with red or yellow. *Stamens.*—Four; inclosed in the upper lip. *Ovary.*—Two-celled. Style long; exserted. *Hab.*—The coast and vicinity, from Mendocino County to Monterey.

Scarlet flowers are so rare, and nature is so chary of that beautiful hue, that these blossoms are especially welcome. Their dense tufts make brilliant dashes of color, which are very noticeable amid the vivid greens of springtime. Strange to say, most of their brilliancy is due not to the corollas, but to the large petal-like bracts under the flowers and to the calyxes.

In the vicinity of the seashore these blossoms may be found at almost any time of the year, while inland they have their season of bloom in the spring, resting for the most part during the summer.

We have many species of *Castilleia,* closely resembling one another. In mountain meadows several are very abundant.

They are known in some localities as "Indian plume."

C. latifolia is in every way a larger and more showy flower than the closely allied species, *C. coccinea,* Spreng., of the East, commonly but most inappropriately known as "painted cup."

C. foliolosa, Hook. and Arn., may be easily recognized by its white-woolly stems and foliage.

SCARLET FRITILLARY.

Fritillaria recurva, Benth. Lily Family.

Bulb as in *F. lanceolata. Stems.*—Eight to eighteen inches high; one- to nine-flowered. *Flowers.*—Scarlet outside; yellow, spotted with scarlet, within. *Perianth.* — Campanulate; urn-shaped. *Segments.*—Twelve to eighteen lines long; with recurved tips. *Stamens and style.*

INDIAN PAINT-BRUSH—*Castilleia latifolia.*

Not quite equaling the segments. *Capsule.*—Rather obtusely angled. (Otherwise as *F. lanceolata.*) *Hab.*—The Sierras, from Placer County northward into Oregon.

The scarlet fritillary is, without doubt, one of the most beautiful of all our species. It usually has from one to nine blossoms on the stalk, but it has been known to have as many as thirty-five! These flowers are somewhat baffling to the young botanist, who is apt to believe them to be some species of lily. And, indeed, he is not far wrong, as the two genera are very closely allied. They may, however, be distinguished easily when we remember that in *Fritillaria* the style is often three-cleft and the perianth segments have a circular honey-bearing gland or pit and the flowers are medium in size; while in *Lilium* the style is entire, the nectary is in the form of a lengthened groove, and the flowers are, with two exceptions in our flora, very large and showy.

F. coccinea, Greene, is another beautiful scarlet-and-yellow species, found in the mountains of Sonoma and Napa counties. This has from one to four flowers, which are an inch long, with simple campanulate outline, without recurving tips.

NORTHERN SCARLET LARKSPUR.
CHRISTMAS-HORNS.

Delphinium nudicaule, Torr. and Gray. Buttercup or Crowfoot Family.

Stems.—A foot or two high; naked or very few-leaved. *Leaves.*—One to three inches in diameter; deeply three- to five-cleft, or barely parted into obovate or cuneate divisions. *Flowers.*—Scarlet; in loose, open racemes; on pedicels two to four inches long. *Sepals.*—Five; petaloid; the upper prolonged upward into a spur containing the smaller spurs of the two upper petals. Spur six to nine lines long. *Petals.*—Usually four; the two lateral small, not spurred. *Stamens.*—Many. *Pistils.*—Mostly three; becoming divergent follicles. *Hab.*—The Coast Ranges from San Luis Obispo to Oregon.

Though not so intensely brilliant and striking as the southern scarlet larkspur, this is a delightful flower, the sight of which gracing some rocky cañon-wall or making flecks of flame amid the grass, gives us a thrill of pleasure. It would require no great stretch of the imagination to fancy these blossoms a

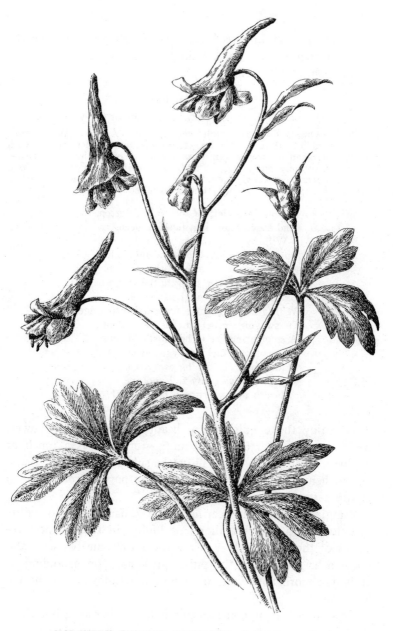

NORTHERN SCARLET LARKSPUR—*Delphinium nudicaule.*

company of pert little red-coated elves clambering over the loose, slender stems. In our childhood we used to hear them called "Christmas-horns."

COLUMBINE.

Aquilegia truncata, Fisch. and Mey. Buttercup or Crowfoot Family.

Stems.—One to three feet high; very slender. *Leaves.*—Mostly radical; divided into thin, distant leaflets. *Flowers.*—Scarlet; tinged with yellow; eighteen to twenty-four lines across. Parts in fives. *Sepals.*—Petaloid; rotately spreading. *Petals.*—Tubular; produced into long spurs or horns. *Stamens.*—Numerous on the receptacle; much exserted. *Pistils.*—Five; simple. *Hab.*—Almost throughout California.

> Sprung in a cleft of the wayside steep,
> And saucily nodding, flushing deep,
>   With her airy tropic bells aglow,—
> Bold and careless, yet wondrous light,
> And swung into poise on the stony height,
>   Like a challenge flung to the world below!
> Skirting the rocks at the forest edge
> With a running flame from ledge to ledge,
> Or swaying deeper in shadowy glooms,
> A smoldering fire in her dusky blooms;
> Bronzed and molded by wind and sun,
> Maddening, gladdening every one
> With a gypsy beauty full and fine,—
> A health to the crimson columbine!
> —*Elaine Goodale.*

To enjoy the exquisite airy beauty of this lovely flower, we must seek it in its own haunts—for there is a touch of wildness in its nature that will not be subdued; nor will it submit to being handled or ruthlessly transported from its own sylvan retreat.

Fringing the stream, peering over the bank, as if to see its own loveliness reflected there, or hiding in the greenest recesses of the woodland, it is always a welcome blossom, and the eye brightens and the pulse quickens upon beholding it. It is far more abundant in mountain meadows than in the lowlands.

This species is at home throughout our borders; but there

COLUMBINE—*Aquilegia truncata.*

is another form which is said to be found occasionally in our very high mountains—*A. cærulea,* James. This is plentiful in the Rocky Mountains, and is the State flower of Colorado. Its blossoms, which are blue or white, are large and magnificent, with slender spurs an inch and a half or two inches long.

CLIMBING PENTSTEMON. SCARLET HONEYSUCKLE.
Pentstemon cordifolius, Benth.   Figwort Family.

Woody at base, with long, slender branches, which climb over other shrubs. *Leaves.*—Cordate or ovate; an inch or less long. *Calyx.*—Campanulate; five-parted. *Corolla.*—Bright scarlet; eighteen lines long. Sterile stamen bearded down one side. (See *Pentstemon.*) *Hab.*—From Santa Barbara to San Diego.

In spring we notice in the borders of southern woodlands and along the roadsides certain long, wandlike branches with beautiful heart-shaped leaves, which are suggestive of those of the garden fuchsia. Our curiosity is naturally aroused and we wonder what blossom is destined to grace this elegant foliage. Early summer solves the mystery by hanging the tips of these wands with brilliant scarlet blossoms, in every way satisfying the earlier promise. These flowers often look down at us in a sort of mocking, Mephistophelian manner, as they hang amid the rich greens of other shrubs and trees. Seen with a glass, they are quite glandular. The fifth stamen looks like a very cunning little golden hearth-brush.

HUMMING-BIRD'S SAGE.
Audibertia grandiflora, Benth.   Mint Family.

Coarse plants, with woolly stems; one to three feet high. *Leaves.*—Opposite; wrinkly; white-woolly beneath; crenate; the lower three to eight inches long; hastate-lanceolate; on margined petioles; upper sessile; pointed. *Inflorescence.*—Over a foot long, with many large, widely separated whorls of crimson flowers. *Corollas.*—Eighteen lines long. *Stamens and style.*—Much exserted. *Flower-bracts.*—Ovate; sharp-pointed; often crimson-tinged. (Otherwise as *A. stachyoides.*) *Hab.*—The Coast Ranges, from San Mateo southward.

This, the largest-flowered of all our *Audibertias,* becomes especially conspicuous by April and May in southern woodlands, where its large, dark flower-clusters may be seen in

CLIMBING PENTSTEMON—*Pentstemon cordifolius.*

little companies amid the shadows. The leaves and bracts are quite viscid, and have a rather rank, unpleasant odor; but the flowers are not without a certain comeliness. The long, crimson trumpets are arranged in whorls about the stems, projecting from many densely crowded bracts. Tier after tier of these whorls, sometimes as many as nine, mount the stems. The bracts and stems are usually of a rich bronze, which harmonizes finely with the color of the flowers. The joint in the filament is quite conspicuous in this species.

"Humming-birds that dart in the sun like green and golden arrows" seem to be the sole beneficiaries of the abundant nectar in these deep tubes.

CALIFORNIA SWEET-SCENTED SHRUB.
WESTERN SPICE-BUSH.

Calycanthus occidentalis, Hook. and Arn. Sweet Shrub Family.

Shrubs. — Six to twelve feet high. *Leaves.* — Ovate to oblong-lanceolate; three to six inches long; dark green; roughish. *Flowers.*—Wine-colored (sometimes white); solitary; two inches or so across. *Sepals, petals, and stamens.*—Indefinite, passing into each other; all coalescent below into the cuplike calyx-tube, on whose inner surface are borne the numerous carpels. *Petals.*—Linear-spatulate, usually tawny-tipped. Carpels becoming akenes. *Hab.*—From the lower Sacramento River northward.

This is one of our most beautiful shrubs. Upon the banks of streams, or often upon a shaded hillside where some little rill trickles out from a hidden source, it spreads its branches and lifts its canopy of ample leaves. There is a pleasant fragrance about the whole shrub, and the leaves, when crushed, are agreeably bitter. From April to November the charming flowers, like small wine-colored chrysanthemums, are produced; and these are followed by the prettily veined, urn-shaped seed-vessels, which remain upon the bushes until after the next season's flowers appear, by which time they are almost black. It is from these cuplike seed-vessels that the genus takes its name, which is derived from two Greek words, meaning *flower* and *cup.*

CALIFORNIA SWEET-SCENTED SHRUB—*Calycanthus occidentalis.*

INDIAN PINK.

Silene Californica, Durand.   Pink Family.

Root.—Deep.   *Stems.*—Several; procumbent or sub-erect; leafy. *Leaves.*—Ovate-elliptic or lanceolate; eighteen lines to four inches long.   *Flowers.*—Brilliant scarlet; over an inch across.   *Calyx.*—Five-toothed.   *Petals.*—Five; long-clawed; the blades variously cleft, and with two erect toothlike appendages at the throat.   *Stamens.*—Ten; exserted with three filiform styles.   *Ovary.*—One-celled.   *Hab.*—Widely distributed in California, but not plentiful.

The Indian pink is one of the most beautiful of our flowers, and it appeals to the æsthetic sense in a way few flowers do. Its brilliant scarlet blossoms brighten the soft browns of our roadsides in early summer, and gleam amid the green of thickets like bits of fire.   Its corolla is elegantly slashed, and it is altogether a much finer flower than the southern form, *S. laciniata.*   Its rather broad leaves are often quite viscid to the touch, in which respect it shares in the character from which the genus was named—in allusion to Silenus, the companion of Bacchus, who is described as covered with foam.

S. laciniata, Cav., is a similar species found from central California southward.   It is usually a taller plant, with many stems and narrow leaves.   It is also quite viscid, and many small insects, mostly ants, are almost always to be seen ensnared upon its stems.   We are at a loss to account for this until we remember what Sir John Lubbock says in this connection.   He suggests that ants are not very desirable visitors for promoting cross-fertilization among plants, as their progress is slow, and they cannot visit many plants far apart.   On the other hand, winged insects, such as bees, butterflies, and moths, making long excursions through the air, are admirably adapted for bringing pollen from distant plants.   Hence plants spread their attractions for such insects, while they often contrive all sorts of ingenious devices for keeping undesirable ones, like ants, away from their flowers.

The Spanish-Californians call this plant "Yerba del Indio," and make it into a tea which they esteem as a remedy for all

INDIAN PINK—*Silene Californica.*

sorts of aches and pains, and use as a healing application to ulcers.

Another species—*S. Hookeri,* Nutt.—is easily known by its large pink flowers, often two and a half inches across, and delicately slashed. This is found in our northernmost counties, growing upon wooded hillsides, where its charming flowers show to excellent advantage.

COAST LILY.

Lilium maritimum, Kell. Lily Family.

Bulb.—Conical; twelve to eighteen lines thick, with closely appressed scales. *Stem.*—One to five feet high; slender. *Leaves.*—Seldom, if at all, whorled; linear or narrowly oblanceolate; obtuse; one to five inches long. *Flowers.*—One to five; deep blood-red; spotted with purple; long-pediceled; horizontal. *Perianth-segments.*—Six; lanceolate; eighteen lines long; the upper third somewhat recurved. *Hab.*—Near the Coast, from San Mateo to Mendocino County.

The little coast lily is found most abundantly in the black peat bogs of Mendocino County, though it ranges southward to San Mateo County and northward to Humboldt County.

Mr. Purdy says of it:—"It is seldom seen farther than two miles from the ocean. On the edges of the bogs the lily is often a dwarf, blossoming at three or four inches. In the bogs it roots itself in the tufts, and becomes a lovely plant five feet high with ten or fifteen fine blossoms."

The leaves are dark, glossy green, and the blossoms are more cylindrical than funnel-form, the three inner segments spreading more than the outer, which remain almost erect. The little oval anthers, with cinnamon-colored pollen, almost fill the narrow tube and conceal the fact that the segments are yellow below and more decidedly spotted.

CHOLLA-CACTUS.

Opuntia prolifera, Engelm. Cactus Family.

Leafless, spiny, arborescent shrubs, three to ten feet high, with elongated, cylindrical joints, covered with oblong tubercles which bear from three to eight spines. Longest spines twelve to eighteen lines long. *Stems.*—Two to seven inches thick. *Flowers.*—Purplish-red; densely clustered at the ends of the branches. *Sepals, petals, and stamens.*—Many. *Ovary.*—One-celled. Style one. Stigmas several. *Fruit.*—Green; obovate; concave on the top; having no spines, only bristles; usually sterile; often producing other flowers. *Hab.*—From Ventura to San Diego and southward.

Upon dry hills, even as far north as Ventura, the cholla-cactus is a familiar feature of the landscape. In many places it forms extensive and impassable thickets, which afford an asylum to many delicate and tender plants that retire to it as a last refuge from sheep and cattle.

The young joints, which are clustered at the ends of the branches, are from three to nine inches long. By means of their barbed spines, these adhere to any passing object, and as they break off very readily, they are thus often transported to a distance. As they root easily, this seems to afford a means of propagation, in the absence of seed—for the fruit is usually seedless.

The spines are quite variable in length, the longest being sometimes an inch and a half. Each one is covered by a papery sheath, which slips off easily.

Upon the ground about these shrubs may usually be found the skeletons of old branches. These are hollow cylinders of woody basket-work, which are quite symmetrical and pretty.

O. serpentina, Engelm., found at San Diego, and often growing with the above, resembles it somewhat, but may be known by its much longer spines, which are from three to nine inches long, and by its greenish-yellow flowers. The plants are usually found near the seashore and scattered—*i. e.* never forming thickets.

Upon the sea-coast at San Diego is found another plant similar to the above,—*Cereus Emoryi,* Engelm.,—the "velvet cactus." Instead of being covered with tubercles, these plants have from sixteen to twenty vertical ribs, upon which are borne the bunches of slender spines. These spines are from a quarter of an inch to one and three-quarters inches long, and without barbs. The flowers are greenish-yellow, and not particularly pretty or attractive.

SCARLET BUGLER.

Pentstemon centranthifolius, Benth.   Figwort Family.

Very glaucous and smooth. *Stem.*—One to three feet high. *Leaves.*—Ovate-lanceolate; mostly sessile; the upper cordate-clasping; thick. *Panicles.*—Narrow; a foot or two long. *Corolla.*—Bright scarlet; an inch or more long; hardly bilabiate. (See *Pentstemon.*) *Hab.*—From Monterey to Los Angeles.

The tall spires of the scarlet bugler are such familiar sights along southern roadsides and sandy washes that people almost forget the enthusiastic admiration their bright beauty first elicited. It is said that acres of mountain lands are sometimes a solid mass of vermilion during the blooming season of this lovely plant.

The panicle is often two feet long, with its string of scarlet horns. The individual flowers bear quite a likeness to those of the honeysuckle, common in Eastern gardens, and by those who encounter the plant for the first time, it is usually spoken of as "honeysuckle." The blossoms are sometimes yellow near San Bernardino.

P. Bridgesii, Gray, met more frequently in the Yosemite than elsewhere, though it occurs in the Sierras from the Yosemite southward, is a very similar plant to the above. But it differs in having its corolla quite distinctly bilabiate, though of the same general tubular, funnel-form shape.

LARGE VETCH.

Vicia gigantea, Hook.   Pea Family.

Climbing. *Stems.*—Five to fifteen feet long. *Leaves.*—Alternate; pinnate; terminated by a tendril. *Leaflets.*—Ten to thirteen pairs; linear-oblong; obtuse; mucronulate; one or two inches long. *Stipules.*—An inch long; semi-sagittate. *Racemes.*—Dense; one-sided; five to eighteen-flowered. *Flowers.*—Dull red. *Corolla.*—Papilionaceous; six or seven lines long. Petals not spreading. *Stamens.*—Nine united; one free. *Style.*—Hairy all around under the stigma. *Pod.*—An inch or so long. (See *Leguminosæ.*) *Hab.*—From San Francisco Bay northward to Sitka.

This vine is usually found in moist places. Its blossoms are never attractive—for they have a faded, worn-out look,

SCARLET BUGLER—*Pentstemon centranthifolius.*

even when they are fresh. The pods are black when ripe, and the seeds are said to be edible.

SCARLET GILIA.

Gilia aggregata, Spreng. Phlox or Polemonium Family.

Stems.—One to three feet high. *Leaves.*—Pinnately parted into seven to thirteen linear, pointed divisions. Upper leaves more simple. *Flowers.* —In a loose panicle. *Calyx.*—Deeply five-cleft; glandular. *Corolla.*— Scarlet, pink, or rarely even white; with funnel-form tube, one inch long; and rotately spreading five-lobed border. Lobes three to six lines long. (See *Gilia.*) *Hab.*—Throughout the Sierras.

The scarlet gilia is a familiar flower in the Sierras in late summer, growing everywhere in dry places. It may be easily recognized by its rich, glossy, flat, green leaves, pinnately divided into linear divisions, its tall, loosely branching habit, and its bright, delicate scarlet flowers, standing out horizontally from the stem. The corolla-lobes are often flesh-pink or yellowish within, splashed or streaked with scarlet. The whole plant is quite viscid.

SCARLET MONKEY-FLOWER.

Mimulus cardinalis, Dougl. Figwort Family.

Stout; viscid; hairy. *Stems.*—One to five feet high. *Leaves.*— Sessile; ovate to ovate-lanceolate; ragged-margined; several-nerved; two or three inches long. *Peduncles.*—Three inches long. *Corolla.*— Scarlet; two inches or more long. Upper lip erect; its two lobes turned back. Lower lip three-lobed; reflexed. *Stamens.*—Exserted. (See *Mimulus.*) *Hab.*—Throughout Oregon and California along water-courses.

One day in June, when riding upon the shores of Bolinas Bay, I came upon a spot where a cañon stream flowed out upon a little flat at tide-level, making a small fresh-water marsh, in which mint, bulrushes, and scarlet mimulus were striving for the mastery. But the mimulus was the most wonderful I ever saw. It stood four or five feet high—a patch of it—strong and vigorous, and covered with its handsome, large scarlet flowers, a sight to be remembered. This species is often culti-vated in gardens.

SCARLET GILIA—*Gilia aggregata.*

SNOW-PLANT.

Sarcodes sanguinea, Torr. Heath Family.

Fleshy, glandular-pubescent plants; six inches to over a foot high; bright red; without green foliage; having, in place of leaves, fleshy scales, with glandular-ciliate margins. *Flowers.* — Short-pediceled. *Sepals.*—Five. *Corolla.*—Six lines long; campanulate; with five-lobed limb. *Stamens.*—Ten. Anthers two-celled; opening terminally. *Ovary.*—Five-celled; globose. Style stout. Stigma capitate. *Hab.*—Throughout the Sierras, from four to nine thousand feet elevation.

I shall never forget finding my first snow-plant. It was upon a perfect August day in the Sierras. Following the course of a little rill which wound among mosses and ferns through the open forest where noble fir shafts rose on every hand, I came unexpectedly upon this scarlet miracle, standing in the rich, black mold in a sheltered nook in the wood. A single ray of strong sunlight shone upon it, leaving the wood around it dark, so that it stood out like a single figure in a *tableau vivant.* There was something so personal, so glowing, and so lifelike about it, that I almost fancied I could see the warm life-blood pulsing and quivering through it. I knelt to examine it. In lieu of leaves, the plant was supplied with many overlapping scalelike bracts of a flesh-tint. These were quite rigid below and closely appressed to the stem, but above they became looser and curled gracefully about among the vivid red bells.

I had heard that the plant was a root parasite; so it was with much interest and great care I dug about it with my trowel. But I failed to find its root connected with any other. I have since learned that it is now considered one of those plants akin to the fungi, which in some mysterious way draw their nourishment from decaying or decomposing matter.

I carried my prize home, where it retained its beauty for a number of days. I afterward found many of them. They gradually follow the receding snows up the heights; so that late in the season one must climb for them. They often grow in clusters, and I have counted as many as fifteen springing up together.

SNOW-PLANT—*Sarcodes sanguinea.*

The name "snow-plant" is very misleading, because from it one naturally expects to find the plant growing upon the snow. But this is rarely or never the case, for it is *after* the melting of the snow that it pushes its way aboveground.

Late in the season the plant usually has one or more well-formed young plants underground at its base. These are all ready to come forth the next season at the first intimation that the snow has gone, which easily accounts for its marvelously rapid growth. By the end of August, the seed-vessels are well developed, and as large as a small marble, but flattened; and by that time the plants have lost their brilliant coloring, and become dull and faded.

It is said that the stems have been boiled and eaten, and found quite palatable; but this would seem to the lover of the beautiful like eating the showbread from the ark of Nature's tabernacle.

SOUTHERN SCARLET LARKSPUR.

Delphinium cardinale, Hook.   Buttercup or Crowfoot Family.

Stems.—Three to ten feet tall. *Leaves.*—Large; five- to seven-lobed nearly to the base, the lobes three- to five-cleft, with long-pointed segments. *Flowers.*—Large. *Sepals.*—Lanceolate; eight lines or more long; rotately spreading; the spur an inch or more long; pointed. *Upper petals.*—Orange, tipped with red; pointed; standing prominently forward. (Otherwise as *D. nudicaule.*) *Hab.*—The mountains, from Ventura County to San Diego.

During all the long springtime, Nature has been quietly making her preparations for a grand floral *denouement* to take place about mid-June. If we go out into the mountains of the south at that season, we shall be confronted with a blaze of glory, the like of which we have probably never witnessed before. This is due to the brilliant spires of the scarlet larkspur, which sometimes rise to a height of ten feet!

One writer likens the appearance of these blossoms, as they grow in dense masses, to a hill on fire; and Mr. Sturtevant writes:—"To come upon a large group of these plants in full bloom for the first time, is an event never to be forgotten. I first saw a mass of them in the distance from the top of a hill. Descending, I came upon them in such a position that the rays of the setting sun intensified the brilliancy of their fiery orange-scarlet color. I gathered a large armful of stalks, from three to seven feet high, and placed them in water. They continued to expand for several weeks in water."

There is a general resemblance between this and the northern scarlet larkspur, but the clusters of this are far larger and denser, and the individual flowers are finer. The half-opened buds more resemble the open flowers of *D. nudicaule;* but the fully expanded flowers have the form of some of the finest of the blue larkspurs.

The plants affect a sandy soil or one of decomposed granite.

WESTERN CARDINAL-FLOWER.
Lobelia splendens, Willd. Lobelia Family.

Stems.—Two to four feet tall; slender, smooth or nearly so. *Leaves.*—Alternate; mostly sessile; lanceolate or almost linear; glandular-denticulate. *Flowers.*—In an elongated, wandlike raceme; cardinal red. *Calyx.*—Five-cleft. *Corolla.*—With straight tube, over an inch long and split down the upper side; border two-lipped; upper lip with two rather erect lobes; lower spreading and three-cleft, with lobes three to six lines long. *Stamens.*—Five; united into a tube above. Anthers somewhat hairy. *Ovary.*—Two-celled. Style simple. Stigma two-lobed. *Hab.*—San Diego, San Bernardino, and Los Angeles counties, and eastward to Texas.

The Western cardinal-flower quite closely resembles *L. cardinalis* of the East, differing from it in a few minor points only. I have never been fortunate enough to see it; but I am told that it is a magnificent plant, and that from July to September many a wet spot in our southern mountain cañons is made gay with its brilliant blossoms.

Of the Eastern plant Mr. Burroughs writes:—"But when vivid color is wanted, what can surpass or equal our cardinal-flower? There is a glow about this flower, as if color emanated from it as from a live coal. The eye is baffled and does not seem to reach the surface of the petal; it does not see the texture or material part as it does in other flowers, but rests in a steady, still radiance. It is not so much something colored as it is color itself. And then the moist, cool, shady places it affects usually, where it has no rivals, and where the large, dark shadows need just such a dab of fire! Often, too, we see it double, its reflected image in some dark pool heightening its effect."

HUMMING-BIRD'S TRUMPET. CALIFORNIA FUCHSIA.
Zauschneria Californica, Presl. Evening-Primrose Family.

Woody plants, more or less villous. *Stems.*—Much branched; ascending or decumbent; one to three feet long. *Leaves.*—Mostly alternate; sessile; narrowly lanceolate to ovate; six to eighteen lines long. *Flowers.*—Bright scarlet; in a loose spike; funnel-form; twenty lines long. *Calyx.*—Scarlet; four-cleft. *Petals.*—Four; obcordate; borne on the calyx-tube. *Stamens.*—Eight. Filaments and style more or less exserted. *Ovary.*—Four-celled; inferior. Stigma four-lobed. *Hab.*— From Plumas County to Mexico; and the Rocky Mountains east of the Great Basin.

In late summer and through the autumn, the brilliant blossoms of the California fuchsia brighten the somber tones of our dry, open hill-slopes. Its aspect is one of gay insouciance, which would drive away melancholy despite oneself, and though other plants have been put to rout, one by one, by the sun's fierce glare, nothing daunted, it puts on its brightest hues, like a true apostle of cheerfulness. It has been cultivated for some time, and is highly prized in Eastern gardens, where it has earned for itself the pretty title of "humming-bird's trumpet." It is not confined to our limits, but extends southward into Mexico, and eastward to Wyoming. We have seen it flourishing in the Sierras, where it is particularly beautiful.

It is called "balsamea" by the Spanish-Californians, who use a wash of it as a remedy for cuts and bruises.

It varies greatly in the size and hairiness of its leaves, in the form of its flowers, which are broadly or narrowly funnel-form, and in the exsertion of the stamens and style. The var. *microphylla* has a woolly pubescence, linear leaves often very small, three or four lines long, and other small leaves crowded in their axils. This is found in the south.

CALIFORNIA FUCHSIA—*Zauschneria Californica.*

There is no glory in star or blossom
  Till looked upon by a loving eye;
There is no fragrance in April breezes
  Till breathed with joy as they wander by.
              —*William Cullen Bryant.*

VI. MISCELLANEOUS

MUILLA.

Muilla maritima, Benth. Lily Family.

Root.—A small membranous-coated corm. *Leaves.*—Radical; linear; equaling the slender scape. *Scapes.*—Three to twelve inches high, bearing an umbel of small greenish-white flowers, subtended by several small lanceolate to linear bracts. *Pedicels.*—Five to fifteen; two to twelve lines long. *Perianth.*—Almost rotate; of six segments; two or three lines long. *Stamens.*—Six. *Ovary.*—Globose; three-celled. *Hab.* —The Coast, from Marin County to Monterey; also inland.

The generic name of this little plant is *Allium* reversed.

Though it has a coated bulb like the onion, it has none of its garlic flavor. It differs from the other umbellate-flowered genera of the Lily family in not having its flowers jointed upon their pedicels. It thus seems to be a link between the onion, on the one hand, and the beautiful brodiæas and bloomerias, on the other. It is not at all an attractive plant, though its blossoms are pleasantly fragrant.

It is found on the borders of salt marshes and in subsaline soils in the interior, as well as upon high hills in stony soils.

Another species,—*M. serotina,* Greene,—common upon inland hills in the south, is quite a delicate, pretty flower. Its greenish-white blossoms, with dainty Nile-green anthers, are nearly an inch across, and each segment has a pale-green midnerve. The plant has a number of very long, slender leaves, and its flower-stems are sometimes two feet tall and very slender.

SILK-TASSEL TREE.   QUININE-BUSH.

Garrya elliptica, Dougl.   Dogwood Family.

Shrubs five to eight feet high.   *Leaves.*—Leathery; white-woolly beneath; wavy-margined.   *Flowers.*—Of two kinds on separate shrubs; in solitary or clustered catkins; and without petals.   *Staminate catkins.*—Two to ten inches long, consisting of a flexile chain of funnel-form bracts, depending one from another; each having six flowers like clappers.   These flowers with four hairy sepals and four stamens with distinct filaments.   *Pistillate catkins.*—Of similar structure but stouter, more rigid.   Their flowers without floral envelopes; pistils two; fleshy and hairy; stigmas filiform; dark.   *Hab.*—Near the Coast from Monterey County to Washington.

This shrub might easily be mistaken for one of our young live-oaks, with its leathery leaves and gray bark; but the leaves are opposite, and not alternate, as with the oaks.   The bark and leaves have an intensely bitter principle, similar to quinine and equally efficacious.

Early in February, after the first spell of balmy weather, the bushes put forth their flowers, and then they are exceedingly beautiful.   The long pale-green chains at the ends of all the branches hang limp and flexile, shaken with every breath of wind, or, falling over other branches, drape and festoon the whole shrub exquisitely.   The catkins of the female shrub are stouter and more rigid than those of the male; but when the fruit is mature, they lengthen out into beautifully tinted clusters of little papery-coated grapes, which are quite attractive in themselves.   This is cultivated as an ornamental shrub in England.

G. Fremonti, Torr., another species, is distinguished by having its leaves pointed at both ends, not wavy-margined, and not permanently woolly; and also by its solitary catkins.   This is the shrub usually spoken of as "quinine-bush," "fever-bush," etc., and whose leaves were used as a substitute for quinine in the early days among the miners.   It is said that its roots, left in the ground after the cutting of the shrub, become marbled with green, and are then very beautiful for inlaying in ornamental woodwork.

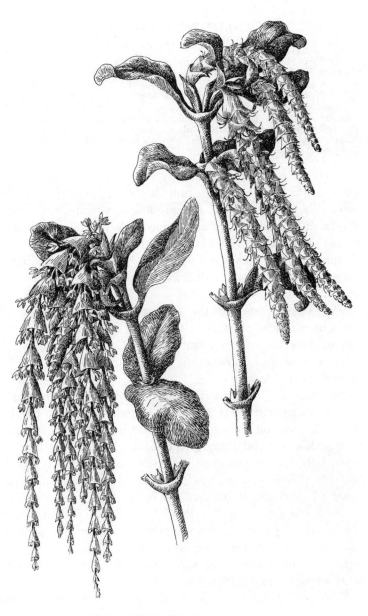

SILK-TASSEL TREE—*Garrya elliptica*.

CALIFORNIA LAUREL.

Umbellularia Californica, Nutt. Laurel Family.

Shrubs or trees, ten to one hundred feet high. *Leaves.*—Alternate; short-petioled; lanceolate-oblong; two to four inches long; smooth, shining green; very aromatic. *Flowers.*—In clusters. *Sepals.*—Six; greenish-white; two and a half lines long. *Petals.*—None. *Stamens.* —Nine; in three rows; the filaments of the inner row having on either side, at base, a stalked orange-colored gland. *Anthers.*—Four-celled; the cells opening by uplifting lids. *Ovary.*—One-celled. Style stout. Stigma lobed. *Fruit.*—Olive-like; an inch long; becoming purple. *Hab.* —From Oregon to San Diego.

Early in February we usually have some of our loveliest days. Life is then pulsing and throbbing everywhere at full tide. The clear sunshine, the murmur of streams, the odor of the freshly turned sod, the caroling of larks—all are eloquent of the springtime. The whole air is filled with a strange, spicy fragrance which makes it a delight to breathe. The California laurel is shaking out a delicious penetrating odor from its countless blossoms.

Mr. Sargent refers to this tree as one of the stateliest and most beautiful inhabitants of the North American forests, and one of the most striking features of the California landscape.

In France it is now much appreciated and cultivated in parks and gardens.

In southern California it is only a shrub; but in the central and northern counties it becomes a magnificent tree, a hundred feet in height and from four to six feet in diameter. It thrives best in the rich soil along stream-banks, though it grows also upon hillsides. It would be impossible to mistake this tree for any other; for its leaves, when crushed, give out a peculiar pungent odor which, if inhaled too much, will cause headache. The odor is something like that of bay-rum. The Indians, as well as our own people, acting upon the homeopathic principle, use them as a remedy for headache. The oil is also used effectively in toothache, earache, etc., and enters into the composition of certain patent medicines.

The wood of the laurel is one of the most beautiful employed by the cabinet-maker, and it is largely used in the manufacture of choice furniture. The olive-like fruit is ripe by July, and would remain upon the tree until the next year were not the squirrels so fond of it.

This tree is known in different localities by a variety of names, such as "spice-bush," "balm of heaven," "sassafras laurel," "cajeput," "California bay-tree," "California olive," "mountain laurel," and "California laurel." But the last of these is the one prevalent where its finest forms are found.

MOUNTAIN MAHOGANY.

Cercocarpus parvifolius, Nutt. Rose Family.

Shrubs two to twenty feet high; branching from a thick base. *Leaves.* —Alternate; short-petioled; cuneate; serrate across the summit; more or less silky above; densely hoary-tomentose beneath; six to eighteen lines long. *Flowers.* — Mostly solitary; axillary. *Calyx.* — Narrowly tubular, with a deciduous campanulate five-lobed limb. *Petals.*—None. *Stamens.*—Fifteen to twenty-five; on the calyx. *Ovary.*—One- (rarely two-) celled. Style simple. *Fruit.*—An akene with a silky tail, at length becoming three or four inches long. *Hab.*—The Coast Ranges from Lake County to southern California.

The mountain mahogany is a common shrub upon the interior hills of the Coast Ranges; and when one has once made its acquaintance, it is always easily recognized by its wedge-shaped, dark-green leaves, prominently veined and notched at the summit. Its flowers, having no petals, are green and inconspicuous; but the long, solitary plumes of its little fruit are very noticeable and pretty. Its wood is the heaviest and hardest we have.

Mr. Greene says that its leafy twigs have a sweet, birchy flavor, rendering them excellent food for cattle in late summer.

379

DUTCHMAN'S PIPE. PIPE-VINE.
Aristolochia Californica, Torr. Birthwort Family.

Stem.—Woody; climbing. *Leaves.*—Alternate; short-petioled; large; ovate-cordate; two to four inches long. *Flowers.*—Greenish, veined with purple. *Perianth.*—Pipe-shaped; the lobes of the lip leather-colored within. *Anthers.*—Six; sessile; adnate in pairs to the thick style under the broad lobes of the stigma; vertical. *Stigma.*—Three-lobed. *Ovary.* — Inferior; six-angled; six-celled. *Fruit.* — A large, leathery pod two inches long. *Hab.*—The Coast Ranges, from Monterey to Marin County; also in the Sierras. .

This odd flower is found rather sparingly in our middle Coast Ranges from February to April, and in some parts of the Sierra foothills, reaching even to the Yosemite. As it flowers before the large leaves come out, and the blossoms are much like dead leaves in color, it requires keen eyes to find it. It usually grows on low ground, in a tangle of shrubs under the trees, often festooning gracefully from branch to branch. Before the flowers are fully open, the buds resemble ugly little brown ducks hanging from the vine.

The common blue-black butterfly is often seen hovering over this vine, and it is said that its caterpillar is so fond of the fruit that it rarely permits one to ripen.

Later in the season, the large cordate leaves are quite conspicuous, and cause people to wonder what may have been the flower of so fine a vine.

TURK'S-HEAD CACTUS. TURBAN CACTUS.
Echinocactus viridescens, Nutt. Cactus Family.

Depressed, hemispherical, fleshy, leafless plants, with from thirteen to twenty-one prominent vertical ribs, bearing groups of rigid spines; usually less than a foot in diameter. *Spines.*—Straight or recurved; stout; reddish; transversely ribbed or ringed. *Flowers.*—Sessile; borne about the depressed woolly center; yellowish-green; about eighteen lines long. *Sepals.*—Many; closely imbricated; merging into the numerous, oblong, scarious petals; sometimes nerved with red. *Stamens.*—Very many. *Ovary.*—One-celled. Stigmas twelve to fifteen; linear. *Berry.*—Pulpy; green; scaly. *Hab.*—From San Diego inland.

The Turk's-head cactus looks very much like the end of a watermelon protruding from the ground, if one could imagine

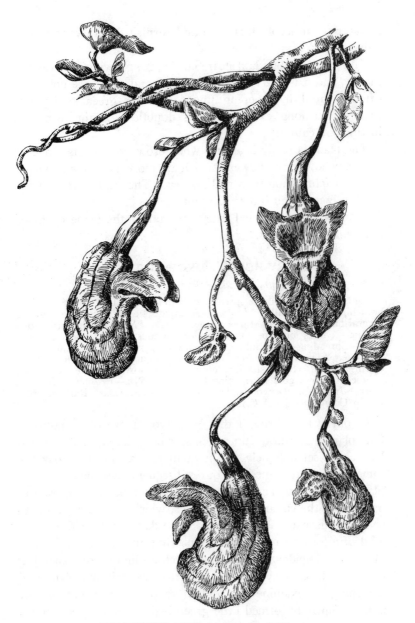

DUTCHMAN'S PIPE—*Aristolochia Californica.*

a watermelon deeply furrowed and furnished with very formidable spines.

This plant is abundant near San Diego, growing all over the mesas; and it is marvelous that horses and cattle are not more often injured by stepping upon these disagreeable, horrent globes; but long experience has doubtless taught them the instinct of caution.

The plant is really beautiful when crowned with its circle of gauzy, yellow-green flowers, which are more like some exquisite artificial fabrication than real flowers. The fruit of this cactus is slightly acid and rather pleasant.

The plant is cultivated in Europe under the name of *Echinocactus Californicus*.

FAIRY-BELLS. DROPS OF GOLD.
Disporum Hookeri, Britton. Lily Family.

Rootstock. — Creeping; spreading. *Stem.* — A foot or two high, branching horizontally. *Leaves.*—Alternate; ovate; cordate; acute; several-nerved; two or three inches long. *Flowers.*—Greenish; one to six; six lines long; pendulous under the ends of the branches. *Perianth.*—Spreading-campanulate. *Segments.*—Six; lanceolate; arched at the base. *Stamens.*—Six; equaling or exceeding the perianth. *Ovary.* —Three-celled. Style slender; entire. *Fruit.*—An obovate, somewhat pubescent berry; golden, ripening to scarlet. *Syn.—Prosartes Hookeri*, Torr. *Hab.*—Shady woods, but not by water; Coast Ranges, from Marin County to Santa Cruz.

In our walks through the April woods, we often notice a fine plant with branching stems, whose handsomely veined leaves are set obliquely to the stem and all lie in nearly the same horizontal plane. In our subsequent meetings with the plant it seems to change but little, and we begin to grow impatient for the coming of the flower, which, however, seems to show no disposition to appear. Some day, when bending over a bit of moss or a fern-frond, or peering into the silk-lined hole of a ground-spider, we suddenly catch a glimmer of something under the broad leaves of our hitherto disappointing plant, and hastening to examine it, we find to our amazement one or more exquisitely formed little green bells hanging from the tip of each branch. Later these are often succeeded by small berries, at first golden, and afterward scarlet.

The old generic name, *Prosartes,* comes from a Greek word signifying *to hang from,* and is in allusion to the pendulous flowers. The common name, "drops of gold," applies to the berry.

Another species — *D. Menziesii,* Don. — is found growing along stream-banks in the Coast Ranges from Marin County northward. This differs from the above in its longer, more cylindrical, *milk-white* flowers, and its salmon-colored berries. It usually blossoms a little later than the other species, lasting till June, and is exceedingly pretty.

COMMON MUGWORT.

Artemisia vulgaris, var. *Californica,* Bess. Composite Family.

Stems.—Rather simple; a foot or two high. *Leaves.*—Ample; slashed downward into long acute lobes; green above; cottony-woolly beneath; bitter; strong-scented; the upper often entire, linear, or lanceolate. *Flower-heads.*—Minute; two lines high, one broad; composed of tubular disk-flowers only; greenish, in long, slender, crowded panicles. *Hab.*—Near the Coast, from San Francisco northward.

This is a common weed along our roadsides, and is easily known by its slashed leaves with silvery under surfaces. These leaves are very bitter. This is closely allied to the wormwood, and by many people is called "wormwood."

ARTEMISIA. SAGEBRUSH.

Artemisia Californica, Less. Composite Family.

Stems.—Shrubby; four or five feet high; with many slender branches. *Leaves.*—Alternate; pinnately parted into three- to seven-filiform divisions; or entire and filiform; an inch or so long; strong-scented. *Flower-heads.*—Very small; two lines or less across; numerous, in narrow panicles; greenish; composed of tubular disk-flowers only. *Hab.*—Marin County to San Bernardino.

The artemisia, or, as it is more commonly called, "sagebrush," is an old friend that we always expect to meet in our walks on rocky hill-slopes. Its leaves have a clean, bitter fragrance, similar to that of the mugwort, but sweeter, and when crushed in the hand they emit a strong odor of turpentine.

Dr. Behr tells me that in the early days the miners laid sprays of it in their beds to drive away the fleas.

The Spanish-Californians regard it as a panacea for all ills, and use it in the form of a strong wash to bathe wounds and swellings, with excellent results.

Another species — *A. tridentata,* Nutt. — is the shrubby form, growing so abundantly all over the alkali plains of the Great Basin, where it holds undisputed possession with the prairie-dog and the coyote. It has narrow, wedge-shaped leaves, which are three-toothed at the apex; and the whole plant has a strong odor of turpentine.

This is highly esteemed by the Indians as a medicinal plant.

WILD PIE-PLANT. CANAIGRE.

Rumex hymenosepalus, Torr. Buckwheat Family.

Root.—A cluster of dahlia-like tubers. *Stems.*—About two feet high. *Leaves.*—Narrowly oblong or lanceolate; a foot long or less; acute; undulate; narrowed into a short, very thick petiole. *Flowers.*— Light raisin-color; in a large panicle a foot or so long. *Perianth.*—Of six sepals; the outer minute; the inner about five lines long; appressed to the ovary. *Stamens.*—Six. *Ovary.*—Three-angled; one-celled. Styles three; short. Stigmas tufted. *Hab.*—Dry, sandy plains of southern California.

The wild pie-plant is closely related to the garden rhubarb, and also to the dock and the sorrel. In early days in both Utah and southern California housewives used its stems as a substitute for the cultivated pie-plant, finding them quite acceptable. The Indians have long used the root in the tanning of buckskins, and they have also found in it a bright mahogany-brown dye, with which to paint their bodies.

Of late this plant has been attracting much notice under the name "canaigre," and it is hoped that it will prove a valuable substitute for tanbark. If it does, we shall hail it with delight as the savior of our beautiful oak forests. Tannin exists in large quantities in the thick roots; but it is yet a question

CANAIGRE—*Rumex hymenosepalus.*

whether it will prove remunerative to the farmer as a crop. At Rialto a company has been formed, which employs many men to gather and prepare the roots, and there will soon be thousands of acres of it under cultivation. The tops of the plants, with the small upper portions of the roots, which have all the eyes upon them, are cut off and replanted for the next year's crop, while the remainder of the root is sliced, dried, pulverized, and leached to extract the tannin, which is then ready for use.

The plant is a very noticeable one, with its red leaf-stems and veins and its large, dense cluster of small raisin-colored flowers, and it is often seen upon our southern plains. But I am told that over the border in Lower California it grows in great abundance, covering the ground for miles. It would seem as though its cultivation might be carried on with best results where nature produces it so freely.

HORNLESS WOOLLY MILKWEED.

Gomphocarpus tomentosus, Gray. Milkweed Family.

Densely white-woolly plants, with milky juice. *Stems.*—One to three feet high. *Leaves.*—Two to four inches long. *Flowers.*—Several, in a pendulous cluster on yarnlike pedicels; lateral upon the stem between the leaves. *Calyx.*—Five-parted; inconspicuous. *Corolla.*—Deeply five-parted; greenish without, pinkish within. *Stamens.*—Five; sunk in the column and alternating with the five hoods. *Hoods.*—Two lines across; saccate; open down the outer face. *Ovaries.*—Two; pointed; capped by a flat stigma. *Fruit.*—A pair of follicles; with many silken-tufted seeds. *Hab.*—Dry hills from San Diego to Monte Diablo.

In the south by late spring the very woolly stems and foliage of this milkweed become quite noticeable before any hint of blossoms appears. The thick, gray leaves look as though they might have been cut out of heavy flannel. By May the flower-clusters begin to take definite form, and at last the buds open and reveal a most interesting flower, whose structure is quite complicated. The center of the blossom is occupied by a fleshy column, in which are sunk the anthers, and upon which are borne certain round, dark wine-colored bodies called the

HORNLESS WOOLLY MILKWEED—*Gomphocarpus tomentosus.*

"hoods," which are in reality nectaries, holding honey for insect visitors. All the pollen in each anther-cell consists of a waxy mass, and the adjacent masses of different anthers are bound together by a gummy, elastic band, suspended upon the rim of the stigma. The stigma occupies the top of the fleshy column, and forms a cap, hiding from view the two tubes, or styles, leading down into the ovaries.

The milkweeds of California are divided between two genera, —*Asclepias* and *Gomphocarpus,*—the difference between them lying in the presence of a horn or crest rising out of the hoods in *Asclepias.*

Bees visiting the blossoms of the milkweeds are said to be frequently disabled by the pollen-masses, which adhere to them in such numbers and weigh them down so heavily that they cannot climb upon their combs, but fall down and perish.

MOUNTAIN LADY'S SLIPPER.

Cypripedium montanum, Dougl. Orchis Family.

Stems.—Stout; a foot or two high; leafy. *Leaves.*—Four to six inches long; pointed. *Flowers.*—One to three; short-pediceled. *Sepals and petals.*—Brownish; eighteen to thirty lines long; the two lower sepals united nearly to the apex. *Sac.*—An inch long; dull white, veined with purple. *Anthers.*—Two fertile (one on either side of the column); one sterile, four or five lines long, yellow, with purple spots; longer than the stigma. *Hab.*—The mountains from central California to the Columbia River.

The mountain lady's slipper is a rare plant with us, which affects cool, secluded spots in our mountain forests. The plants, of which two or three usually grow from a creeping rootstock, generally stand where some moisture seeps out. The leaves are ample and shapely, and the quaint flowers quiet and elegant in coloring.

The long, twisted sepals and petals and the oval sac give these blossoms the aspect of some floral daddy-long-legs or some weird brownie of the wood. We feel that we have fallen upon a rare day when we are fortunate enough to find these flowers, and we are reminded of Mr. Burroughs's lines:—"How

MOUNTAIN LADY'S SLIPPER—*Cypripedium montanum.*

fastidious and exclusive is the *Cypripedium!* . . . It does not go in herds, like the commoner plants, but affects privacy and solitude. When I come upon it in my walks, I seem to be intruding upon some very private and exclusive company."

In our Coast Ranges we may look for these blossoms in May.

We have but two or three species of *Cypripedium*. *C. Californicum*, Gray, is similar to *C. montanum*, but its blossoms have comparatively short greenish-yellow sepals and petals, and the sac is from white to pale rose-color. They have a more compact look, and lack the careless grace of those of the mountain lady's slipper. Their haunts are swamps in open woodlands in the northern part of the State, where they bloom in August and September, and are often found in the company of the California pitcher-plant.

REIN-ORCHIS.

Habenaria elegans, Bolander. Orchis Family.

Root.—An oblong tuber. *Stem.*—Rather slender; a foot or two high. *Leaves.*—Two; radical; oblong; three to six inches long; eighteen lines to two inches wide. *Flowers.*—Small; light green; in a dense but slender spike. Sepals and petals about equal; two lines long; obtuse. *Lip.*—Similar, with a filiform spur three to five lines long. (Otherwise like *H. leucostachys.*) *Hab.*—Near the coast, from Monterey to Vancouver Island.

In early summer the fragrant spikes of the rein-orchis stand half-concealed under the trees and along the banks bordering wooded mountain roads. The little greenish flowers are inconspicuous, and reveal themselves only to those who have the habit of observation. Early in the spring the rather large lily-like leaves were far more noticeable and handsome; but they seemed to weary of waiting for the tardy arrival of the blossoms, and faded away long since. The little flowers are very deliberate about unfolding themselves; and I have sometimes watched them when they seemed for weeks at a standstill before yielding to the summer's invitation to come forth.

They are arranged in a three-sided spike, on two sides of

REIN–ORCHIS—*Habenaria elegans.*

which the long spurs interlace and cross one another in quite a warlike manner.

TEASEL. FULLER'S THISTLE.

Dipsacus fullonum, L. Teasel Family.

Stems.—Erect; prickly; five feet high. *Leaves.*—Opposite; entire or serrate; connate at base and cup-like. *Inflorescence.*—In a dense oval head surrounded by a many-leaved involucre. *Flowers.*—Small; subtended by bracts in form of hooked bristles. *Corolla.*—Tubular; four-cleft; somewhat irregular. *Stamens.*—Four. *Ovary.*—Inferior; one-celled. Style one; simple. Fruit dry.

The teasel is not an uncommon sight along our roadsides, having spread considerably since its introduction from Europe, some years ago. The strong stems are tall and slender, and bear at summit the large bristly cones, surrounded by rigid, erect bracts. These cones are the inflorescence of the plant, and each downward-pointing little hook is a bract beneath a flower. Before the flowers come out, the buds show their round, green heads, packed away down among the bristles. Then for a time the cones are ringed or covered by the delicate flesh-colored flowers, which stand out from the bristles, giving the cone a soft, fluffy look. After these have passed away, the cavities in which they were stored give the cone a pitted appearance. These burs are exquisitely symmetrical, and have long been in use by the fuller to "tease," or raise a nap upon cloth, whence the name, "teasel." They are cut in halves or quarters, and these are set in frames which are worked by machinery. Many vain attempts have been made to manufacture an instrument to take the place of the teasel; but it is difficult to find anything that is strong enough to do the work that at the same time will not injure the cloth.

This is enumerated among the plants which are supposed to foretell the weather. Mr. Dyer quotes the following:—
. . . . " 'tezils, or fuller's thistle, being gathered and hanged up in the house where the air may come freely to it, upon the alteration of cold and windy weather will grow smoother, and against rain will close up its prickles.' "

SAMPHIRE. GLASSWORT.

Salicornia ambigua, Michx. Goosefoot Family.

Hab.—The Coast, from San Francisco to Oregon.

Ye marshes, how candid and simple, and nothing withholding and free,
Ye publish yourselves to the sky, and offer yourselves to the sea;
Tolerant plains that suffer the sea and the rains and the sun,
Ye spread and span, like the catholic man who hath mightily won
God out of knowledge, and good out of infinite pain,
And sight out of blindness, and purity out of a stain. —*Sidney Lanier.*

Though a humble enough plant in itself, the samphire, or glasswort, is the source of a wonderful glory in our marshes in the autumn. Great stretches of tide-land not already pre-empted by the tule are covered by it, showing the most gorgeous blendings of crimson, purple, olives, and bronzes, which, seen with all the added charm of shifting and changing atmospheric effects, far outrival any Oriental rug that could be conceived of.

This plant is easily known by its succulent branching, leafless stems and from the fact that it does not grow outside of the salt marshes. Its flowering is obscure, and all that can be seen is a few small stamens just protruding from the surface of the fleshy spike, which appears much like any of the other branches, the flowers being sunk in it.

The generic name is derived from two Latin words—*sal,* salt, and *cornu,* a horn—and conveys the idea of saline plants with hornlike branches. The English name, "samphire," is of French derivation, and comes originally from the old "l'herbe de Saint Pierre," formerly having been written "sampêtra" and "sampire." In Great Britain this plant is usually designated as "*marsh* samphire," to distinguish it from the ordinary samphire, which is a plant of the genus *Crithmum.*

This plant is much relished by cattle, and in England it is made into a pickle, while on the continent it is used as a potherb. Formerly, in Europe, it was burned in large quantities for the soda contained in its ashes.

MOTTLED SWAMP-ORCHIS. FALSE LADY'S SLIPPER.

Epipactis gigantea, Dougl. Orchis Family.

Rootstock—Creeping. *Stems.*—Leafy; one to four feet high. *Leaves.*—Alternate; sessile; clasping; ovate below; lanceolate above; three to eight inches long. *Flowers.*—Three to ten; in terminal racemes; greenish, veined with purple. *Sepals.*—Three; petaloid; lanceolate; an inch or less long. *Petals.*—The two upper about equaling the sepals. The lip concave; saccate; eared at base; with a jointed, pendulous tip. *Anther.*—One; sessile upon the top of the column. *Ovary.*—One-celled. *Hab.*—Throughout California.

The casual observer usually alludes to this plant as a "lady's slipper," and he is not so very far wrong, for it is closely related to the *Cypripedium,* and resembles it much in habit, in the aspect of its leafy stems, and in the general form of its blossom. But instead of having its lip in the form of a sac, it is open and curiously jointed, the lower portion swinging freely, as upon a hinge. When this lid is raised, one can fancy some winged seraph or angel enshrined within, but when lowered the semblance is more to a monk bowed in meditation.

These beautiful plants will be found abundantly fringing our streams in June and July, and the disciples of dear old Isaak Walton who then pass down the stream with rod and line are usually attracted by their quietly elegant colors. Dull purples and greens predominate, though the lip is tinged with orange or yellow.

In northern California and Oregon is occasionally found a rare and curious plant—the "phantom orchis," *Cephalanthera Oregana,* Richenb.f. This plant is white and ghostlike throughout, has stems a foot or two high, but no leaves—only three to five scarious sheathing bracts. Its blossoms are very similar in size and shape to those of *Epipactis gigantea.*

I have never had the pleasure of finding this floral oddity myself; but one season a friend sent me the only plant which was found in a thicket near a pretty camp upon the Sacramento River, in the Shasta region.

FALSE LADY'S SLIPPER—*Epipactis gigantea.*

CALIFORNIA PITCHER-PLANT.   CALF'S-HEAD.

Darlingtonia Californica, Torr.   Pitcher-plant Family.

Bog plants, with long horizontal rootstocks.   *Leaves.* — Tubular; furnished with a wing the length of the tube; hooded and appendaged above; eighteen to thirty-four inches high.   *Scape.*—Eighteen inches or more high, with green bracts crowded near the solitary nodding flower. Flower parts in fives.   *Sepals.*—Green; twenty lines long.   *Petals.*— Purplish; shorter than the sepals; constricted above into a terminal lobe. *Stamens.*—Twelve to fifteen in a circle around the ovary.   *Ovary.*— Top-shaped; truncate; five-lobed; five-celled.   Style five-lobed.   Stigmas thickish.   *Hab.*—The Sierras, from Truckee Pass into Oregon.

Our pitcher-plant is one of the most wonderful and interesting of all the forms that grow, linking, as it were, the vegetable world with the animal, by its unnatural carnivorous habits.   If you would like to visit it, this warm July day, we will take a mountain trail, leading around under lofty yellow pines, Douglas spruces, and incense-cedars, making our way through the undergrowth until we come to a swamp lying upon a hillside yonder.   While still some distance away, we can discern the yellowish-green of the myriad hoods as they lift themselves in the sunlight like spotted snakes.

If you have never seen the plant before, you will be in a fever of excitement till you can reach the spot and actually take one of the strange pitchers in your hand to examine it. Nothing could be cleverer than the nicely arranged wiles of this uncanny plant for the capturing of the innocent—yes, and of the more knowing ones—of the insect world who come within its enchantment.   No ogre in his castle has ever gone to work more deliberately or fiendishly to entrap his victims while offering them hospitality, than does this plant-ogre. Attracted by the bizarre yellowish hoods or the tall nodding flowers, the foolish insect alights upon the tube and commences his exploration of the fascinating region.   He soon comes upon the wing, which often being smeared with a trail of sweets, acts as a guide to lure him on to the dangerous entrance to the hoodlike dome.   Once within this hall of pleasure, he roams about, enjoying the hospitality spread for him.

CALIFORNIA PITCHER–PLANT—*Darlingtonia Californica.*

But at last, when he has partaken to satiety and would fain depart, he turns to retrace his steps. In the dazzlement of the translucent windows of the dome above, he loses sight of the darkened door in the floor by which he entered and flies forcibly upward, bumping his head in his eagerness to escape. He is stunned by the blow and plunged downward into the tube below. Here he struggles to rise, but countless downward-pointing, bristly hairs urge him to his fate. He sinks lower and lower in this "well of death" until he reaches the fatal waters in the bottom, where he is at length ingulfed, adding one more to the already numerous victims of this diabolical plant.

The fluid at the bottom of the well is secreted by the plant, and seems to have somewhat the action of a gastric juice in disintegrating the insects submerged in it. Many species of ants, flies, bees, hornets, grasshoppers, butterflies, moths, dragon-flies, beetles, etc., are to be found in the tube, sometimes filling it to a depth of two or three inches.

The disagreeableness of the vicinity of these plants can be imagined upon a hot day when the sun is shining "upon this sad abode of death" and all the air is tainted with their sickening odor.

The mountaineers call the plant "calf's-head," because of the large yellowish domes of the pitchers.

TABLE OF CHANGES IN NOMENCLATURE

to conform to *A California Flora* by Philip A. Munz and David D. Keck (University of California, 1959) and certain changes from scientific papers since that publication.

NAME IN THIS WORK	PAGE	NAME CURRENTLY ACCEPTED
Amelanchier alnifolia, Nutt.	88	*Amelanchier florida* Lindley
Anemone quinquefolia, L.	20	*Anemone quinquefolia* var. *Grayi* (Behr & Kell.) Jepson
Antirrhinum glandulosum, Lindl.	326	*Antirrhinum multiflorum* Pennell
Antirrhinum vagans, Gray	326	*Antirrhinum vexillo-calyculatum* Kellogg
Aphyllon	xxxvi	Orobanche
Aphyllon fasciculatum, Gray	176	*Orobanche fasciculata* Nuttall
Aquilegia truncata, Fisch. and Mey.	354	*Aquilegia formosa* var. *truncata* (Fischer & Meyer) Baker
Argemone platyceras, Link and Otto	72	*Argemone munita* Durand & Hilgard
Artemisia vulgaris, var. *Californica*, Bess.	383	*Artemisia Douglasiana* Besser in Hooker
Asclepias Mexicana, Cav.	318	*Asclepias fascicularis* Decaisne in A. Decandolle
Aster Chamissonis, Gray	338	*Aster chilensis* Nees
Audibertia	xxxv, lxxx	Salvia
Audibertia grandiflora, Benth.	356	*Salvia spathacea* Greene
Audibertia nivea, Benth.	321	*Salvia leucophylla* Greene
Audibertia polystachya, Benth.	68	*Salvia apiana* Jepson
Audibertia stachyoides, Benth.	320	*Salvia mellifera* Greene
Bloomeria aurea, Kell.	158	*Bloomeria crocea* var. *aurea* (Kellogg) Ingram

399

TABLE OF CHANGES IN NOMENCLATURE

NAME IN THIS WORK	PAGE	NAME CURRENTLY ACCEPTED
Bolelia	l, liv	Downingia
Bolelia elegans, Torr.	321	*Downingia elegans* (Douglas) Torrey
Bolelia pulchella, Greene	321	*Downingia pulchella* (Lindley) Torrey
Boykinia occidentalis, Torr. and Gray	83	*Boykinia elata* (Nuttall) Greene
Brodiæa capitata, Benth.	268, 304	*Brodiaea pulchella* (Salisbury) Greene
Brodiæa coccinea, Gray	244	*Brodiaea Ida-maia* (Wood) Greene
Brodiæa grandiflora, Smith	324	*Brodiaea coronaria* (Salisbury) Engler
Brodiæa terrestris, Kell.	326	*Brodiaea coronaria* var. *macropoda* (Torrey) Hoover
Brunella	xxxviii, lxxx	Prunella
Brunella vulgaris, L.	328	*Prunella vulgaris* L.
Bryanthus	xlv, lxxiv	Phyllodoce
Bryanthus Breweri, Gray	252	*Phyllodoce Breweri* (Gray) Heller
Calandrinia caulescens, HBK.; var. *Menziesii*, Gray	218	*Calandrinia ciliata* var. *Menziesii* (Hooker) Macbride
Calochortus Benthami, Baker	134	*Calochortus monophyllus* (Lindley) Lemaire
Calochortus luteus, var. *oculatus*	83	*Calochortus vestae* Purdy
Calochortus Maweanus, Leicht.	284	*Calochortus Tolmiei* Hooker & Arnott
Calypso borealis, Salisb.	216	*Calypso bulbosa* (L.) Oakes
Ceanothus divaricatus, Nutt.	262	*Ceanothus leucodermis* Greene
Cercocarpus parvifolius, Nutt.	379	*Cercocarpus betuloides* Nuttall ex Torr. & Gray
Clarkia elegans, Dougl.	234	*Clarkia unguiculata* Lindley
Cleistoyucca	xliv, lxxxv	Yucca
Cleistoyucca arborescens, Trelease	48	*Yucca brevifolia* Engelmann in Watson

TABLE OF CHANGES IN NOMENCLATURE

NAME IN THIS WORK	PAGE	NAME CURRENTLY ACCEPTED
Collinsia bicolor, Benth.	298	*Collinsia heterophylla* Buist ex Graham
Convolvulus luteolus, Gray	44	*Convolvulus occidentalis* Gray
Corallorhiza Bigelovii, Wats.	278	*Corallorhiza striata* Lindley
Delphinium scopulorum, var. *glaucum*, Gray	334	*Delphinium glaucum* Watson
Diplacus	xxxvii	Mimulus
Diplacus glutinosus, Nutt.	144	*Mimulus aurantiacus* Curtis
Dudleya Sheldoni, Rose	146	*Dudleya cymosa* (Lemaire) Britt. & Rose
Echinocystis	xxxv, lxvii	Marah
Echinocystis fabacea, Naudin	28	*Marah fabaceus* (Naudin) Greene
Ellisia	xxxviii, lxxvii	Eucrypta
Ellisia chrysanthemifolia, Benth.	40	*Eucrypta chrysanthemifolia* (Bentham) Greene
Erigeron salsuginosus, Gray	338	*Erigeron peregrinus* (Pursh) Greene
Eriophyllum arachnoideum, F. and M.	liii, 188	*Eriophyllum lanatum* var. *arachnoideum* (Fischer & Avé-Lall.) Jepson
Erysimum grandiflorum, Nutt.	136	*Erysimum Menziesii* (Hooker) Wettstein
Erythræa	xxxix	Centaurium
Erythræa venusta, Gray	224	*Centaurium venustum* (Gray) Robinson
Erythronium giganteum, Lindl.	140	*Erythronium* (3 western California species)
Flœrkia	xlvi, lxii	Limnanthes
Flœrkia Douglasii, Ballion	130	*Limnanthes Douglasii* R. Brown
Fragaria Chilensis, Ehrhart	10	*Fragaria chiloensis* (L.) Duchesne
Geranium incisum, Nutt.	220	*Geranium Richardsonii* Fischer & Trautvetter
Gilia aggregeta, Spreng.	366	*Ipomopsis aggregata* (Pursh) V. Grant
Gilia androsacea, Steud.	228	*Linanthus androsaceus* (Bentham) Greene

401

TABLE OF CHANGES IN NOMENCLATURE

TABLE OF CHANGES IN NOMENCLATURE

NAME IN THIS WORK	PAGE	NAME CURRENTLY ACCEPTED
Micromeria Douglasii, Benth.	64	*Satureja Douglasii* (Bentham) Briquet
Mimulus luteus, L.	138	*Mimulus guttatus* Fischer ex Decandolle
Mirabilis Californica, Gray	214	*Mirabilis laevis* (Bentham) Curran
Nemophila atomeria, Fisch. and Mey.	43	*Nemophila menziesii* var. *atomeria* (Fischer & Meyer) Brand
Nemophila aurita, Lindl.	282	*Pholistoma auritum* (Lindley) Lilja
Nemophila insignis, Dougl.	296	*Nemophila Menziesii* Hooker & Arnott
Nemophila intermedia, Bioletti	290	*Nemophila Menziesii* Hooker & Arnott (small form)
Nuttallia	xlvii, lxv	Osmaronia
Nuttallia cerasiformis, Torr. and Gray	18	*Osmaronia cerasiformis* (Torr. & Gray) Greene
Œnothera bistorta, Nutt.	142	*Camissonia bistorta* (Nuttall ex Torr. & Gray) Raven
Œnothera cheiranthifolia, var. *suffruticosa*, Wats.	142	*Camissonia chieranthifolia* ssp. *suffruticosa* (Watson) Raven
Œnothera ovata, Nutt.	114	*Camissonia ovata* (Nuttall in Torr. & Gray) Raven
Opuntia Engelmannii, Salm	175	*Opuntia littoralis* (Engelmann) Cockerell
Orthocarpus versicolor, Greene	54	*Orthocarpus erianthus* var. *roseus* Gray
Pæonia Brownii, Dougl.	346	*Paeonia californica* Nuttall ex Torr. & Gray, in part
Penstemon Menziesii, var. *Newberryi*, Gray	254	*Penstemon Newberryi* Gray
Rhododendron Californicum, Hook.	240	*Rhododendron macrophyllum* D. Don
Rhus Canadensis, var. *trilobata*, Gray	160	*Rhus trilobata* Nuttall
Ribes glutinosum, Benth.	220	*Ribes sanguineum* var. *glutinosum* (Bentham) Loudon
Sambucus glauca, Nutt.	41	*Sambucus mexicana* Presl

TABLE OF CHANGES IN NOMENCLATURE

NAME IN THIS WORK	PAGE	NAME CURRENTLY ACCEPTED
Smilacina amplexicaulis, Nutt.	24	*Smilacina racemosa* var. *amplexicaulis* (Nuttall) Watson
Smilacina sessilifolia, Nutt.	23	*Smilacina stellata* var. *sessilifolia* (Baker) Henderson
Sphacele	xxxvii, lxxx	Lepechinia
Sphacele calycina, Benth.	46	*Lepechinia calycina* (Bentham) Epling in Munz
Spiræa lucida, Dougl.	87	*Spiraea densiflora* Nuttall ex Torr. & Gray (for California plants)
Spraguea	xxxv, lix	Calyptridium
Spraguea umbellata, Torr.	72	*Calyptridium umbellatum* (Torrey) Greene
Stylophyllum	lxvi, xlvii	Dudleya
Stylophyllum edule, Britt and Rose	154	*Dudleya edulis* (Nuttall) Moran
Symphoricarpos racemosus, Michx.	231	*Symphoricarpos rivularis* Suksdorff
Trientalis Europæa, var. *latifolia,* Torr.	208	*Trientalis latifolia* Hooker
Trillium sessile, var. *Californicum,* Wats.	266	*Trillium chloropetalum* (Torrey) Howell (and varieties)
Troximon	liii, lxxiii	Agoseris
Troximon grandiflorum, Gray	169	*Agoseris grandiflora* (Nuttall) Greene
Vancouveria parviflora, Greene	90	*Vancouveria hexandra* (Hooker) Morren & Decaisne
Viola canina, var. *adunca,* Gray	310	*Viola adunca* Smith
Xylothermia	xlvi, lxiv	Pickeringia
Xylothermia montana, (Nutt.) Greene	236	*Pickeringia montana* Nuttall
Yucca Mohavensis, Sargent	22	*Yucca schidigera* Roezl ex Ortgies

TABLE OF CHANGES IN NOMENCLATURE

NAME IN THIS WORK	PAGE	NAME CURRENTLY ACCEPTED
Zygadenus	xliii	Zigadenus
Zygadenus Fremontii, Torr.	6	*Zigadenus Fremontii* Torrey
Zygadenus venenosus, Wats.	6	*Zigadenus venenosus* Watson

INDEX TO LATIN NAMES

[To assist in the pronunciation of the Latin names, the accented syllable in each word is indicated by an accent mark. If this syllable ends in a vowel, the vowel has the long sound; but if it ends in a consonant, the vowel has a short sound. Either the English or the Continental sounds may be given the vowels, though the former are more generally authorized. Synonyms are printed in italics.]

INDEX TO ENGLISH NAMES

GLOSSARY

Abortive, defective or barren.

Acuminate, ending in a tapering point.

Adnate, growing to; or said of an anther whose cells are borne upon the sides of the apex of the filament.

Appendage, any superadded part.

Appressed, lying flat against or together for the whole length.

Arborescent, treelike; approaching the size of a tree.

Attenuate, slenderly tapering to a point.

Auricle, a small earlike lobe at the base of a leaf.

Awn, a bristle-shaped appendage.

Barb, a sharply reflexed point upon an awn, etc., like the barb of a fish-hook.

Basifixed, attached by the base or lower end.

Beak, a narrow or prolonged tip.

Bifid, two-cleft to the middle or thereabouts.

Bilabiate, two-lipped.

Blade, the expanded portion of a leaf, petal, etc.

Bract, one of the leaves of a flower-cluster.

Bracteate, furnished with bracts.

Bractlet, a bract of the ultimate grade; as one inserted *on* a pedicel or ultimate flower-stalk instead of *under* it.

Bracteolate, having bractlets.

Bulbiferous, bearing bulbs.

Caducous, dropping off very early.

Campanulate, bell-shaped.

Capitate, headlike, or collected in a head.

Carina, a salient longitudinal projection on the center of the lower face of an organ.

Carinate, furnished with a carina, or keel.

Carpel, a simple pistil, or one of the several parts of a compound one.

Ciliate, marginally fringed with hairs.

Clavate, club-shaped.

Claw, the narrowed base, or stalk, which some petals, etc., possess.

Cleft, cut half way down or thereabout.

Coalescing, cohering; used properly in respect to similar parts.

Column, a body formed by the union of filaments (stamineal); or (in orchids) of the stamens and pistil.

Complete, said of flowers having all four sets of floral organs, calyx, corolla, stamens, and pistils.

Confluent, blended, or running together.

Connate, growing together; united in one.

Connective, the portion of the filament which connects or separates the cells of an anther.

Connivent, coming into contact or converging.

Cordate, heart-shaped.

Coriaceous, leathery.

Corymb, a flat-topped inflorescence flowering from the margin inward.

Corymbose, in corymbs, or in the form of a corymb.

Cruciferous, of four somewhat similar petals, spreading in the form of a cross.

Cymose, in cymes. (See *cyme,* in Explanation of Terms, p. xxx.)

Deciduous, falling at the end of the season.

Declined, bent or curved downward or forward.

Decumbent, reclining, but with summit ascending.

Decurrent, running down the stem; applied to a leaf with blade prolonged below its insertion.

Deflexed, bent or turned abruptly downward.

Dehiscing; opening by valves, slits, or regular lines; as a capsule or an anther.

Deltoid, having the shape of the Greek letter *delta;* broadly triangular.

Denticulate, minutely toothed.

Depauperate, impoverished in size by unfavorable surroundings.

Dichotomous, forking regularly by pairs.

Diœcious, with stamens and pistils in different flowers on different plants.

Disk, the central part of a head of flowers as opposed to the border or ray.

Dissected, deeply cut, or divided into numerous segments.

Divaricate, extremely divergent.

Divided, lobed or cut clear to the base.

Emarginate, notched at the extremity.

Entire, with the margin uninterrupted; without teeth or divisions of any sort.

Equitant, astride; as of leaves folding over each other in two ranks; as in the iris.

Erose, gnawed.

Exserted, projecting beyond an envelop; as stamens from a corolla.

Extrorse, facing outward; said of the anther.

Falcate, scythe - shaped; sickle-shaped.

Fascicled, in a close cluster or bundle; said of flowers, stalks, roots, and leaves.

Fertile, capable of producing fruit; as a pistillate flower; applied also to a pollen-bearing stamen.

Fibrous, composed of or of the nature of fibers.

Filiform, threadlike.

Flexuous, zigzag; bent alternately in opposite directions.

Foliaceous, leaflike in structure or appearance; leafy.

Foliolate, having leaflets; the number indicated by the Latin prefixes, *bi-, tri-,* etc.

Follicle, a pod formed from a single pistil, dehiscing along the ventral suture only.

Free, not growing to other organs.

Fugacious, falling very early.

Funnel-form, tubular, but expanding gradually from the narrow base to the spreading border or limb; *e. g.* the morning-glory flower.

Galea, a helmet; applied to the helmet-shaped upper lip of the corolla in *Labiatæ,* etc.; also in some *Scrophularineæ,* though not so shaped.

Gibbous, swelling out on one side.

Glabrous, without any kind of hairiness.

Gland, any secreting structure, depression or prominence, on any part of a plant, or any structure having such an appearance.

Glandular, bearing glands, or glandlike.

Glaucous, covered or whitened with a bloom like that on a cabbage-leaf.

Habit, the general form or mode of growth of a plant.

Herbaceous, having the character of an herb; not woody or shrubby.

Hispid, beset with rigid or bristly hairs, or with bristles.

Imbricate, overlapping, like shingles on a roof.

Incised, cut irregularly and sharply.

Included, inclosed by the surrounding organs; not exserted.

Indigenous, native to the country.

Inferior, said of the ovary when the calyx, corolla, or stamens are borne upon its summit or sides.

Inflorescence, the flowering portion of a plant, and especially the mode of its arrangement.

Innate, said of an anther when it is a continuation of the filament.

Introrse, facing inward, or toward the axis, as an anther.

Involucel, an inner or secondary involucre.

Involucrate, having an involucre.

Involucre, a circle of bracts subtending a flower-cluster.

Involute, rolled inward.

Keel. (See *carina.*)

Keeled, furnished with a keel, or carina.

Lacerate, torn; irregularly and deeply cleft.

Laciniate, cut into narrow, slender teeth, or lobes.

Liliaceous, lily-like.

Limb, the dilated and usually spreading portion of a perianth or petal as distinct from the tubular part, or claw.

Line, the twelfth part of an inch.

Linear, narrow and elongated, with parallel margins.

Lip, either of the two divisions of a bilabiate corolla or calyx; in orchids the upper petal (often, apparently, the lower) usually very different from the others.

Lobe, any division of a leaf, corolla, etc., especially if rounded.

Lunate, crescent-shaped, or half-moon-shaped.

Lyrate, lyre-shaped; pinnatifid with the terminal lobe large and rounded, and one or more of the lower pairs small.

Membranaceous, thin; rather soft and translucent, like membrane.

Monœcious, with stamens and pistils in separate blossoms on the same plant.

Mucronate, with a short, abrupt, small tip.

Nectar, the sweetish secretion of the blossom from which bees make honey.

Nectary, the place or gland in which nectar is secreted.

Nerve, a simple, unbranched vein or slender rib.

Nerved, furnished with a nerve or nerves.

Ob-, used as a prefix meaning inversely.

Obtuse, blunt or rounded at the end.

Odd-pinnate, pinnate, with an odd leaflet at the end.

Palate, a protrusion at or near the throat of a two-lipped corolla.

Panicle, a loose, irregularly branching inflorescence.

Papilionaceous, butterfly-like; applied to the peculiar irregular flower common in *Leguminosæ.*

Papillæ, minute, thick, nipple-shaped, or somewhat elongated projections.

Parasitic, growing upon and deriving nourishment from another plant.

Parted, cleft nearly, but not quite, to the base.

Perfoliate, said of leaves connate about the stem.

Persistent, not falling off; said of leaves continuing through the winter.

Petaloid, petal-like.

Petiolate, having a petiole.

Petiole, the foot-stalk of a leaf.

Petiolulate, having a petiolule.

Petiolule, the foot-stalk of a leaflet.

Pinnate, having its parts arranged in pairs along a common rachis.

Pinnatifid, pinnately cleft.

Pistillate, having a pistil or pistils, and no stamens.

Placentæ, lines or ridges on the interior walls of the ovary along which the ovules are disposed, called parietal placentæ; or a central axis serving the same purpose, called a central placenta.

Plicate, folded into plaits like a fan.

Puberulent, minutely pubescent.

Pubescent, covered with hairs, usually soft and short.

Rachis, the axis (backbone) of a spike, or of a compound leaf.

Radiate, diverging from a common center, or bearing ray-flowers; said of flower-heads of composite plants.

Radical, belonging to or proceeding from the root, or from the base of the stem.

Ray, one of the radiating branches of an umbel; the marginal flowers, as distinct from those of the disk, in *Compositæ,* etc.

Receptacle, a more or less expanded surface, forming a support for a cluster of organs (in a flower) or a cluster of flowers (in a head), etc.

Recurved, curved backward or downward.

Reflexed, abruptly bent or turned backward or downward.

Regular, symmetrical in form; uniform in shape or structure.

Retrorse, directed backward or downward.

Revolute, rolled backward from the margins or apex.

Rhomboidal, quadrangular, with the lateral angles obtuse.

Rudiment, an imperfectly developed and functionally useless organ.

Rugose, wrinkled; ridged.

Saccate, sac-shaped; baggy.

Sagittate, shaped like an arrowhead; triangular, with basal lobes prolonged downward.

Salver-form, narrowly tubular, with limb abruptly or flatly expanded.

Scabrous, rough to the touch.

Scape, a naked peduncle rising from the ground.

Scarious, thin, dry, membranaceous, and not green.

Scorpioid, incurved like the tail of a scorpion; said of an inflorescence.

Segment, one of the parts of a leaf or other organ that is cut or divided.

Serrate, having teeth directed forward, like the teeth of a saw.

Serrulate, minutely serrate.

Sessile, stemless.

Sinus, a recess or re-entering angle.

Sheathing, infolding like a sheath.

Spathe, a large bract or pair of bracts (often colored) inclosing a flower-cluster.

Spinescent, ending in a spine or rigid point.

Spinulose, with diminutive spines.

Spur, a usually slender tubular process, from some part of a flower, often honey-bearing.

Staminate, having stamens, but no pistils.

Staminodium, a sterile stamen, or something taking the place of a stamen.

Stellate, star-shaped.

Sterile, barren; incapable of producing seed; a sterile stamen is one not producing pollen.

Striate, marked with fine longitudinal lines.

Subtended, supported or surrounded; as a pedicel by a bract, or a flower-cluster by an involucre.

Subulate, awl-shaped.

Succulent, fleshy and juicy.

Superior, growing above; a superior ovary is one wholly above and free from the calyx.

Symmetrical, having the same number of organs in each whorl (said of flowers).

Terete, cylindrical.

Ternate, in threes.

Thyrse, a contracted or ovate panicle.

Thyrsoid, thyrselike.

Tomentum, dense, matted, woolly pubescence.

Trifoliolate, having three leaflets.

Tubular, tube-shaped.

Undulate, wavy.

Unisexual, of one sex; said of flowers having stamens only, or pistils only.

Urceolate, cylindrical or ovoid, but contracted at or below the open orifice, like an urn or a pitcher.

Valve, the several parts of a dehiscent pericarp; the doorlike lid by which some anthers open.

Ventricose, swelling unequally, or inflated on one side.

Versatile, swinging; turning freely on its support.

Villous, bearing long and soft, straight or straightish hairs.

Virgate, wandlike.

Viscid, glutinous; sticky.

Whorl, an arrangement of leaves, flowers, etc., in a circle about the stem or axis.

A CATALOGUE OF SELECTED DOVER BOOKS
IN ALL FIELDS OF INTEREST

A CATALOGUE OF SELECTED DOVER BOOKS
IN ALL FIELDS OF INTEREST

THE DEVIL'S DICTIONARY, Ambrose Bierce. Barbed, bitter, brilliant witticisms in the form of a dictionary. Best, most ferocious satire America has produced. 145pp. 20487-1 Pa. $1.50

ABSOLUTELY MAD INVENTIONS, A.E. Brown, H.A. Jeffcott. Hilarious, useless, or merely absurd inventions all granted patents by the U.S. Patent Office. Edible tie pin, mechanical hat tipper, etc. 57 illustrations. 125pp. 22596-8 Pa. $1.50

AMERICAN WILD FLOWERS COLORING BOOK, Paul Kennedy. Planned coverage of 48 most important wildflowers, from Rickett's collection; instructive as well as entertaining. Color versions on covers. 48pp. 8¼ x 11. 20095-7 Pa. $1.35

BIRDS OF AMERICA COLORING BOOK, John James Audubon. Rendered for coloring by Paul Kennedy. 46 of Audubon's noted illustrations: red-winged blackbird, cardinal, purple finch, towhee, etc. Original plates reproduced in full color on the covers. 48pp. 8¼ x 11. 23049-X Pa. $1.35

NORTH AMERICAN INDIAN DESIGN COLORING BOOK, Paul Kennedy. The finest examples from Indian masks, beadwork, pottery, etc. — selected and redrawn for coloring (with identifications) by well-known illustrator Paul Kennedy. 48pp. 8¼ x 11. 21125-8 Pa. $1.35

UNIFORMS OF THE AMERICAN REVOLUTION COLORING BOOK, Peter Copeland. 31 lively drawings reproduce whole panorama of military attire; each uniform has complete instructions for accurate coloring. (Not in the Pictorial Archives Series). 64pp. 8¼ x 11. 21850-3 Pa. $1.50

THE WONDERFUL WIZARD OF OZ COLORING BOOK, L. Frank Baum. Color the Yellow Brick Road and much more in 61 drawings adapted from W.W. Denslow's originals, accompanied by abridged version of text. Dorothy, Toto, Oz and the Emerald City. 61 illustrations. 64pp. 8¼ x 11. 20452-9 Pa. $1.50

CUT AND COLOR PAPER MASKS, Michael Grater. Clowns, animals, funny faces... simply color them in, cut them out, and put them together, and you have 9 paper masks to play with and enjoy. Complete instructions. Assembled masks shown in full color on the covers. 32pp. 8¼ x 11. 23171-2 Pa. $1.50

STAINED GLASS CHRISTMAS ORNAMENT COLORING BOOK, Carol Belanger Grafton. Brighten your Christmas season with over 100 Christmas ornaments done in a stained glass effect on translucent paper. Color them in and then hang at windows, from lights, anywhere. 32pp. 8¼ x 11. 20707-2 Pa. $1.75

CONSTRUCTION OF AMERICAN FURNITURE TREASURES, Lester Margon. 344 detail drawings, complete text on constructing exact reproductions of 38 early American masterpieces: Hepplewhite sideboard, Duncan Phyfe drop-leaf table, mantel clock, gate-leg dining table, Pa. German cupboard, more. 38 plates. 54 photographs. 168pp. 8⅜ x 11¼. 23056-2 Pa. $4.00

JEWELRY MAKING AND DESIGN, Augustus F. Rose, Antonio Cirino. Professional secrets revealed in thorough, practical guide: tools, materials, processes; rings, brooches, chains, cast pieces, enamelling, setting stones, etc. Do not confuse with skimpy introductions: beginner can use, professional can learn from it. Over 200 illustrations. 306pp. 21750-7 Pa. $3.00

METALWORK AND ENAMELLING, Herbert Maryon. Generally conceded best all-around book. Countless trade secrets: materials, tools, soldering, filigree, setting, inlay, niello, repoussé, casting, polishing, etc. For beginner or expert. Author was foremost British expert. 330 illustrations. 335pp. 22702-2 Pa. $3.50

WEAVING WITH FOOT-POWER LOOMS, Edward F. Worst. Setting up a loom, beginning to weave, constructing equipment, using dyes, more, plus over 285 drafts of traditional patterns including Colonial and Swedish weaves. More than 200 other figures. For beginning and advanced. 275pp. 8¾ x 6⅜. 23064-3 Pa. $4.00

WEAVING A NAVAJO BLANKET, Gladys A. Reichard. Foremost anthropologist studied under Navajo women, reveals every step in process from wool, dyeing, spinning, setting up loom, designing, weaving. Much history, symbolism. With this book you could make one yourself. 97 illustrations. 222pp. 22992-0 Pa. $3.00

NATURAL DYES AND HOME DYEING, Rita J. Adrosko. Use natural ingredients: bark, flowers, leaves, lichens, insects etc. Over 135 specific recipes from historical sources for cotton, wool, other fabrics. Genuine premodern handicrafts. 12 illustrations. 160pp. 22688-3 Pa. $2.00

THE HAND DECORATION OF FABRICS, Francis J. Kafka. Outstanding, profusely illustrated guide to stenciling, batik, block printing, tie dyeing, freehand painting, silk screen printing, and novelty decoration. 356 illustrations. 198pp. 6 x 9.
21401-X Pa. $3.00

THOMAS NAST: CARTOONS AND ILLUSTRATIONS, with text by Thomas Nast St. Hill. Father of American political cartooning. Cartoons that destroyed Tweed Ring; inflation, free love, church and state; original Republican elephant and Democratic donkey; Santa Claus; more. 117 illustrations. 146pp. 9 x 12.
22983-1 Pa. $4.00
23067-8 Clothbd. $8.50

FREDERIC REMINGTON: 173 DRAWINGS AND ILLUSTRATIONS. Most famous of the Western artists, most responsible for our myths about the American West in its untamed days. Complete reprinting of *Drawings of Frederic Remington* (1897), plus other selections. 4 additional drawings in color on covers. 140pp. 9 x 12.
20714-5 Pa. $3.95

THE ART DECO STYLE, ed. by Theodore Menten. Furniture, jewelry, metalwork, ceramics, fabrics, lighting fixtures, interior decors, exteriors, graphics from pure French sources. Best sampling around. Over 400 photographs. 183pp. 8⅜ x 11¼.
22824-X Pa. $4.00

THE GENTLEMAN AND CABINET MAKER'S DIRECTOR, Thomas Chippendale. Full reprint, 1762 style book, most influential of all time; chairs, tables, sofas, mirrors, cabinets, etc. 200 plates, plus 24 photographs of surviving pieces. 249pp. 9⅞ x 12¾.
21601-2 Pa. $5.00

PINE FURNITURE OF EARLY NEW ENGLAND, Russell H. Kettell. Basic book. Thorough historical text, plus 200 illustrations of boxes, highboys, candlesticks, desks, etc. 477pp. 7⅞ x 10¾.
20145-7 Clothbd. $12.50

ORIENTAL RUGS, ANTIQUE AND MODERN, Walter A. Hawley. Persia, Turkey, Caucasus, Central Asia, China, other traditions. Best general survey of all aspects: styles and periods, manufacture, uses, symbols and their interpretation, and identification. 96 illustrations, 11 in color. 320pp. 6⅛ x 9¼.
22366-3 Pa. $5.00

DECORATIVE ANTIQUE IRONWORK, Henry R. d'Allemagne. Photographs of 4500 iron artifacts from world's finest collection, Rouen. Hinges, locks, candelabra, weapons, lighting devices, clocks, tools, from Roman times to mid-19th century. Nothing else comparable to it. 420pp. 9 x 12.
22082-6 Pa. $8.50

THE COMPLETE BOOK OF DOLL MAKING AND COLLECTING, Catherine Christopher. Instructions, patterns for dozens of dolls, from rag doll on up to elaborate, historically accurate figures. Mould faces, sew clothing, make doll houses, etc. Also collecting information. Many illustrations. 288pp. 6 x 9. 22066-4 Pa. $3.00

ANTIQUE PAPER DOLLS: 1915-1920, edited by Arnold Arnold. 7 antique cut-out dolls and 24 costumes from 1915-1920, selected by Arnold Arnold from his collection of rare children's books and entertainments, all in full color. 32pp. 9¼ x 12¼.
23176-3 Pa. $2.00

ANTIQUE PAPER DOLLS: THE EDWARDIAN ERA, Epinal. Full-color reproductions of two historic series of paper dolls that show clothing styles in 1908 and at the beginning of the First World War. 8 two-sided, stand-up dolls and 32 complete, two-sided costumes. Full instructions for assembling included. 32pp. 9¼ x 12¼.
23175-5 Pa. $2.00

A HISTORY OF COSTUME, Carl Köhler, Emma von Sichardt. Egypt, Babylon, Greece up through 19th century Europe; based on surviving pieces, art works, etc. Full text and 595 illustrations, including many clear, measured patterns for reproducing historic costume. Practical. 464pp.
21030-8 Pa. $4.00

EARLY AMERICAN LOCOMOTIVES, John H. White, Jr. Finest locomotive engravings from late 19th century: historical (1804-1874), main-line (after 1870), special, foreign, etc. 147 plates. 200pp. 11⅜ x 8¼.
22772-3 Pa. $3.50

VICTORIAN HOUSES: A TREASURY OF LESSER-KNOWN EXAMPLES, Edmund Gillon and Clay Lancaster. 116 photographs, excellent commentary illustrate distinct characteristics, many borrowings of local Victorian architecture. Octagonal houses, Americanized chalets, grand country estates, small cottages, etc. Rich heritage often overlooked. 116 plates. 11⅜ x 10.   22966-1 Pa. $4.00

STICKS AND STONES, Lewis Mumford. Great classic of American cultural history; architecture from medieval-inspired earliest forms to 20th century; evolution of structure and style, influence of environment. 21 illustrations. 113pp.
                                                20202-X Pa. $2.00

ON THE LAWS OF JAPANESE PAINTING, Henry P. Bowie. Best substitute for training with genius Oriental master, based on years of study in Kano school. Philosophy, brushes, inks, style, etc. 66 illustrations. 117pp. 6⅛ x 9¼.   20030-2 Pa. $4.00

A HANDBOOK OF ANATOMY FOR ART STUDENTS, Arthur Thomson. Virtually exhaustive. Skeletal structure, muscles, heads, special features. Full text, anatomical figures, undraped photos. Male and female. 337 illustrations. 459pp.
                                                21163-0 Pa. $5.00

AN ATLAS OF ANATOMY FOR ARTISTS, Fritz Schider. Finest text, working book. Full text, plus anatomical illustrations; plates by great artists showing anatomy. 593 illustrations. 192pp. 7⅞ x 10¾.   20241-0 Clothbd. $6.95

THE HUMAN FIGURE IN MOTION, Eadweard Muybridge. More than 4500 stopped-action photos, in action series, showing undraped men, women, children jumping, lying down, throwing, sitting, wrestling, carrying, etc. "Unparalleled dictionary for artists," American Artist. Taken by great 19th century photographer. 390pp. 7⅞ x 10⅝.   20204-6 Clothbd. $12.50

AN ATLAS OF ANIMAL ANATOMY FOR ARTISTS, W. Ellenberger et al. Horses, dogs, cats, lions, cattle, deer, etc. Muscles, skeleton, surface features. The basic work. Enlarged edition. 288 illustrations. 151pp. 9⅜ x 12¼.   20082-5 Pa. $4.00

LETTER FORMS: 110 COMPLETE ALPHABETS, Frederick Lambert. 110 sets of capital letters; 16 lower case alphabets; 70 sets of numbers and other symbols. Edited and expanded by Theodore Menten. 110pp. 8⅛ x 11.   22872-X Pa. $2.50

THE METHODS OF CONSTRUCTION OF CELTIC ART, George Bain. Simple geometric techniques for making wonderful Celtic interlacements, spirals, Kells-type initials, animals, humans, etc. Unique for artists, craftsmen. Over 500 illustrations. 160pp. 9 x 12.   USO 22923-8 Pa. $4.00

SCULPTURE, PRINCIPLES AND PRACTICE, Louis Slobodkin. Step by step approach to clay, plaster, metals, stone; classical and modern. 253 drawings, photos. 255pp. 8⅛ x 11.   22960-2 Pa. $4.50

THE ART OF ETCHING, E.S. Lumsden. Clear, detailed instructions for etching, drypoint, softground, aquatint; from 1st sketch to print. Very detailed, thorough. 200 illustrations. 376pp.   20049-3 Pa. $3.50

DRIED FLOWERS, Sarah Whitlock and Martha Rankin. Concise, clear, practical guide to dehydration, glycerinizing, pressing plant material, and more. Covers use of silica gel. 12 drawings. Originally titled "New Techniques with Dried Flowers." 32pp. 21802-3 Pa. $1.00

ABC OF POULTRY RAISING, J.H. Florea. Poultry expert, editor tells how to raise chickens on home or small business basis. Breeds, feeding, housing, laying, etc. Very concrete, practical. 50 illustrations. 256pp. 23201-8 Pa. $3.00

HOW INDIANS USE WILD PLANTS FOR FOOD, MEDICINE & CRAFTS, Frances Densmore. Smithsonian, Bureau of American Ethnology report presents wealth of material on nearly 200 plants used by Chippewas of Minnesota and Wisconsin. 33 plates plus 122pp. of text. 6⅛ x 9¼. 23019-8 Pa. $2.50

THE HERBAL OR GENERAL HISTORY OF PLANTS, John Gerard. The 1633 edition revised and enlarged by Thomas Johnson. Containing almost 2850 plant descriptions and 2705 superb illustrations, Gerard's Herbal is a monumental work, the book all modern English herbals are derived from, and the one herbal every serious enthusiast should have in its entirety. Original editions are worth perhaps $750. 1678pp. 8½ x 12¼. 23147-X Clothbd. $50.00

A MODERN HERBAL, Margaret Grieve. Much the fullest, most exact, most useful compilation of herbal material. Gigantic alphabetical encyclopedia, from aconite to zedoary, gives botanical information, medical properties, folklore, economic uses, and much else. Indispensable to serious reader. 161 illustrations. 888pp. 6½ x 9¼. USO 22798-7, 22799-5 Pa., Two vol. set $10.00

HOW TO KNOW THE FERNS, Frances T. Parsons. Delightful classic. Identification, fern lore, for Eastern and Central U.S.A. Has introduced thousands to interesting life form. 99 illustrations. 215pp. 20740-4 Pa. $2.50

THE MUSHROOM HANDBOOK, Louis C.C. Krieger. Still the best popular handbook. Full descriptions of 259 species, extremely thorough text, habitats, luminescence, poisons, folklore, etc. 32 color plates; 126 other illustrations. 560pp. 21861-9 Pa. $4.50

HOW TO KNOW THE WILD FRUITS, Maude G. Peterson. Classic guide covers nearly 200 trees, shrubs, smaller plants of the U.S. arranged by color of fruit and then by family. Full text provides names, descriptions, edibility, uses. 80 illustrations. 400pp. 22943-2 Pa. $3.00

COMMON WEEDS OF THE UNITED STATES, U.S. Department of Agriculture. Covers 220 important weeds with illustration, maps, botanical information, plant lore for each. Over 225 illustrations. 463pp. 6⅛ x 9¼. 20504-5 Pa. $4.50

HOW TO KNOW THE WILD FLOWERS, Mrs. William S. Dana. Still best popular book for East and Central USA. Over 500 plants easily identified, with plant lore; arranged according to color and flowering time. 174 plates. 459pp. 20332-8 Pa. $3.50

EGYPTIAN MAGIC, E.A. Wallis Budge. Foremost Egyptologist, curator at British Museum, on charms, curses, amulets, doll magic, transformations, control of demons, deific appearances, feats of great magicians. Many texts cited. 19 illustrations. 234pp.   USO 22681-6 Pa. $2.50

THE LEYDEN PAPYRUS: AN EGYPTIAN MAGICAL BOOK, edited by F. Ll. Griffith, Herbert Thompson. Egyptian sorcerer's manual contains scores of spells: sex magic of various sorts, occult information, evoking visions, removing evil magic, etc. Transliteration faces translation. 207pp.   22994-7 Pa. $2.50

THE MALLEUS MALEFICARUM OF KRAMER AND SPRENGER, translated, edited by Montague Summers. Full text of most important witchhunter's "Bible," used by both Catholics and Protestants. Theory of witches, manifestations, remedies, etc. Indispensable to serious student. 278pp. 6⅝ x 10.   USO 22802-9 Pa. $3.95

LOST CONTINENTS, L. Sprague de Camp. Great science-fiction author, finest, fullest study: Atlantis, Lemuria, Mu, Hyperborea, etc. Lost Tribes, Irish in pre-Columbian America, root races; in history, literature, art, occultism. Necessary to everyone concerned with theme. 17 illustrations. 348pp.   22668-9 Pa. $3.50

THE COMPLETE BOOKS OF CHARLES FORT, Charles Fort. Book of the Damned, Lo!, Wild Talents, New Lands. Greatest compilation of data: celestial appearances, flying saucers, falls of frogs, strange disappearances, inexplicable data not recognized by science. Inexhaustible, painstakingly documented. Do not confuse with modern charlatanry. Introduction by Damon Knight. Total of 1126pp.
                                                    23094-5 Clothbd. $15.00

FADS AND FALLACIES IN THE NAME OF SCIENCE, Martin Gardner. Fair, witty appraisal of cranks and quacks of science: Atlantis, Lemuria, flat earth, Velikovsky, orgone energy, Bridey Murphy, medical fads, etc. 373pp.   20394-8 Pa. $3.00

HOAXES, Curtis D. MacDougall. Unbelievably rich account of great hoaxes: Locke's moon hoax, Shakespearean forgeries, Loch Ness monster, Disumbrationist school of art, dozens more; also psychology of hoaxing. 54 illustrations. 338pp.   20465-0 Pa. $3.50

THE GENTLE ART OF MAKING ENEMIES, James A.M. Whistler. Greatest wit of his day deflates Wilde, Ruskin, Swinburne; strikes back at inane critics, exhibitions. Highly readable classic of impressionist revolution by great painter. Introduction by Alfred Werner. 334pp.   21875-9 Pa. $4.00

THE BOOK OF TEA, Kakuzo Okakura. Minor classic of the Orient: entertaining, charming explanation, interpretation of traditional Japanese culture in terms of tea ceremony. Edited by E.F. Bleiler. Total of 94pp.   20070-1 Pa. $1.25

Prices subject to change without notice.
Available at your book dealer or write for free catalogue to Dept. GI, Dover Publications, Inc., 180 Varick St., N.Y., N.Y. 10014. Dover publishes more than 150 books each year on science, elementary and advanced mathematics, biology, music, art, literary history, social sciences and other areas.